'McKinstry shows a phenome tireless pursuit of relevant witr

'An absorbing read'

'Magnificent . . . an eloquent and empathetic book. McKinstry cleverly shows, with acute social insight, how football had a powerful cultural significance . . . the final sections of the book acquire the elements of genuine tragedy'     *Glasgow Herald*

'Excellent'                                         *When Saturday Comes*

'McKinstry's powerful book may be the first step in Ramsey's rehabilitation'                                    *Daily Telegraph*

'Delivers the goods . . . McKinstry's great merit is his ability to debunk some of the myths surrounding Ramsey'     *Spectator*

'This masterful biography gets under the skin of Sir Alf'
*Birmingham Evening Mail*

'The first truly comprehensive biography of England's greatest manager'                                          *Irish News*

'This is no hagiography . . . McKinstry has more than done justice to Sir Alf'                                *FourFourTwo*

'A timely portrait of a unique figure'
*Manchester Evening News*

'A thrilling and tortured drama played out in increasingly exotic locations'                                      *Daily Mail*

'A splendid biography of England's greatest manager'
*Daily Telegraph*

# LEO MCKINSTRY
# SIR ALF

A Major Reappraisal of the Life and Times
of England's Greatest Football Manager

**HarperSport**
*An Imprint of HarperCollinsPublishers*

First published in hardback in 2006 by
HarperSport
an imprint of HarperCollins*Publishers*
London

First published in paperback in 2007

1

A CIP catalogue record for this book
is available from the British Library

ISBN-13   978-0-00-719379-0
ISBN-10   0-00-719379-3

Set in PostScript Linotype Sabon by
Rowland Phototypesetting Ltd, Bury St Edmunds, Suffolk

Printed and bound in Great Britain by
Clays Ltd, St Ives plc

The HarperCollins website address is
www.harpercollins.co.uk

PHOTOGRAPHIC ACKNOWLEDGEMENTS

Action Images 4(tl), 11(b), 12(br); Colorsport 2(t), 5(b), 15(t, m&bl);
Corbis 4(b), 9(t), 11(t), 13(b), 15(br); Empics 4(tr), 9(b), 10(t),
11(m), 12(t), 14(mr&ml), 16(b); Getty 5(tl), 13(t); Mirrorpix 6(m&bl),
7(m&b), 8, 10(b), 12(m), 16(m); Popperfoto 1, 2(b), 3, 6(br), 7(t),
10(m), 13(m), 14(t&b); Rex 9(m); UPPA 5(tr), 6(tl), 12(bl), 16(t).

*This book is dedicated to the memory of
Dermot Gogarty, 1958–2005
Another man of dignity, courage and leadership*

# Contents

# *Preface*

Wembley, 30 July 1966. Amid scenes of jubilation, Geoff Hurst slams the ball into the top left-hand corner of the West German net. After a pulsating match, England are only seconds away from winning the World Cup. But as wave upon wave of ecstatic cheering echoes throughout the Wembley stadium, the England manager remains seated on the bench, showing not a flicker of emotion.

Sir Alf Ramsey's almost superhuman calmness at the moment of victory has become one of the iconic images of the glorious summer of 1966. For all his outward imperturbability, no one had greater cause to rejoice than him. He was the true architect of England's triumph, the man who had moulded his players into a world-beating unit. The experts and press had mocked when he had declared, soon after his appointment to the national job, that England would win the World Cup. After 1966, he was never laughed at again. Yet Ramsey was acting entirely in character on that July afternoon at Wembley. In his behaviour, he demonstrated the very qualities that helped to make him such a superb manager: his majestic coolness under pressure; his natural modesty which meant that he always put his players' achievements before his own; his innate dignity and authority.

Since the World Cup victory, Sir Alf Ramsey has rightly been regarded as the greatest of all British football managers, winning at every level of the game. Through his tactical awareness, motivational powers and judgment of ability, he not only turned England into World Champions, but also, perhaps even more incredibly, he took unfashionable Ipswich Town from the lower reaches of the old Third Division South to the First Division title in the space of just six years. No other manager has been able to equal this record. Sir Alex Ferguson may have won a boardroom-full of trophies at Old Trafford, but he has been almost untested on the highest international stage. Similarly Sir Matt Busby, Brian Clough and Bob Paisley all gained the English championship and the European Cup, but none of them managed any national side, in Clough's case to his bitter regret, having been turned down for the England job in 1977. Bill Shankly, the legendary boss at Anfield, and Stan Cullis, the iron manager at Molineux, each won three league titles and two FA Cups, but, again, their excellence was confined to the domestic arena. Of international British managers, Jack Charlton may have worked a near miracle with the Republic of Ireland but he could not do the same with any of his clubs, nor could Billy Bingham, who took modest Northern Ireland to successive World Cups in the eighties. Perhaps the man who comes closest to Ramsey was one of his successors at Portman Road, Sir Bobby Robson, who in his long and honourable career won the FA Cup and UEFA Cup with Ipswich Town, the Cup Winners' Cup with Barcelona and two domestic championships with both PSV Eindhoven and Porto, as well as taking England to the semi-finals of the World Cup in 1990. But the greatest prize eluded him.

For all his extraordinary breadth of achievement, however, Sir Alf Ramsey has always been an elusive figure, an enigma whose life story has remained shrouded in mystery. A private, shy man, he was never at ease with the limelight and throughout his career had an awkward relationship with the media. Even those who worked with him for years, such as his secretary at Ipswich, Pat Godbold, or his longest-serving England player, Bobby Charlton, say that they never got to know him. Partly because of his insecurities about his humble upbringing, he built a protective shield around himself. In contrast to the expansive Sir Bobby Robson, who has written at least four versions of his autobiography, Alf never produced any memoirs, nor did he give many revealing interviews to the press.

There have been three previous books about Sir Alf, of varying quality. In 1970, the journalist Max Marquis wrote a thin, viciously skewed account, *Anatomy of a Manager*, which was based on recycling negative press stories about Sir Alf. It was hysterical in its vituperation, limited in its scope. Another book, *England: The Alf Ramsey Years*, by Graham McColl, published in 1988, dwelt entirely on his record as manager of the national team, though it did have the seal of Ramsey's approval. A more comprehensive biography, *Winning Isn't Everything*, was written in 1998 by Dave Bowler, who has also produced a superb life of Alf's nemesis at Tottenham Hotspur, Danny Blanchflower. Bowler's portrait was balanced and used much original testimony, and was particularly good on Alf's tactical innovations. Yet it still left many aspects of Sir Alf's life and career uncovered.

By dint of extensive research and interviews, I have sought to provide a fuller, more rounded portrait of this remarkable figure. I have been able to unearth new information about his upbringing, his marriage, his early social life, particularly when he was a player at Spurs, his relationship with his England team and the circumstances surrounding his sacking. During my research, I was intrigued to learn of the real reasons why

England were knocked out of the World Cup in Mexico in 1970, when Sir Alf displayed a rare but disastrous neglect of certain logistical arrangements.

I have aimed to write more than just a conventional biography. By placing Ramsey in his historical context, I have also sought to analyse professional football and the fabric of British society over the span of his life. One of the many appealing features of Sir Alf's story is the way it covered a revolution not only in soccer but also in social attitudes. The labourer's son from Dagenham witnessed the end of the age of deference, the abolition of the maximum wage, the rise of the superstar player, the demise of amateur administrators, the collapse of rigid class structures, the first majority Labour government, the arrival of the permissive society and the disappearance of Empire. Ramsey himself, as a traditionalist in his personal outlook but a revolutionary on the soccer field, appeared to embody that fluid climate of resistance and change.

In helping me to cover this material, I owe a large debt to many people. A great number of ex-England and Ipswich footballers, who were managed by Alf, agreed to give interviews for this book, so I would like to record my thanks to: Jimmy Armfield, Alan Ball, Gordon Banks, Barry Bridges, Sir Trevor Brooking, Allan Clarke, Ray Clemence, George Cohen, John Compton, Ray Crawford, Martin Dobson, Bryan Douglas, John Elsworthy, the late Johnny Haynes, Ron Henry, Norman Hunter, Brian Labone, Jimmy Leadbetter, Francis Lee, Roy McFarland, Ken Malcolm, Gordon Milne, Alan Mullery, Andy Nelson, Maurice Norman, Mike O'Grady, Terry Paine, Alan Peacock, Mike Pejic, Ted Phillips, Fred Pickering, Paul Reaney, Joe Royle, Dave Sadler, Peter Shilton, Nobby Stiles, Ian Storey-Moore, Mike Summerbee, Derek Temple, Peter Thompson, Colin Todd, Tony Waiters and Ray Wilson. I must also express my gratitude to the many

Southampton, Spurs and England footballers who gave me the benefit of their views about playing alongside Alf: Eddie Baily, Ted Ballard, Ian Black, Eric Day, the late Ted Ditchburn, Terry Dyson, Stan Clements, Bill Ellerington, Sir Tom Finney, Alf Freeman, Mel Hopkins, Tony Marchi, Arthur Milton, Derek Ufton and Denis Uphill. Ed Speight, a Dagenham-bred youth player at Spurs during Alf's last days at White Hart Lane, generously showed me some of his correspondence with Alf.

I am, in addition, grateful to those journalists who gave me their views of Alf: Tony Garnett, Brian James, Ken Jones, David Lacey, Hugh McIlvanney, Colin Malam, Jeff Powell, Brian Scovell and Martin Tyler. I am especially indebted to Nigel Clarke, who knew Alf for more than 30 years and co-wrote his column for the *Daily Mirror* in the eighties. Key figures at the FA during Alf's reign, David Barber, Margaret Fuljames, Wilf McGuinness and Alan Odell, gave me many fascinating insights into Alf's style of management, while I further benefited from speaking to Hubert Doggart, son of Graham Doggart, who chaired the FA committee that appointed Alf as England manager in 1962. Dr Neil Phillips, the national team doctor in the second half of Alf's England career, could not have been more helpful with his advice and frank testimony.

Information about Alf's early days in Dagenham was given by Cliff Anderson, George Baker, Jean Bixby, Phil Cairns, Charles Emery, Father Gerald Gosling, Pauline Gosling, Beattie Robbins, Joyce Rushbrook, Gladys Skinner and Tommy Sloan. Invaluable assistance about other aspects of Sir Alf's life was provided by Terry Baker, Mary Bates, John Booth, Tommy Docherty, Anne Elsworthy, Peter Little, Margaret Lorenzo, Matthew Lorenzo, Bill Martin, Pat Millward, Tina Moore (widow of Bobby) and Bernard Sharpe.

Several experts were extremely generous in providing me

with contact numbers and historical details: David Bull, author of an excellent life of Southampton stalwart Ted Bates; Rob Hadcraft, who wrote a fine study of Ipswich's Championship-winning season in 1961–62; Kevin Palmer, amongst whose many works is a history of Spurs' two titles in 1950–51 and 1960–61; and Andy Porter, who has an encyclopaedic knowledge of ex-professionals' careers. Pat Godbold, still working at Ipswich after more than half a century, not only gave me an interview about her time as secretary to Alf but also helped with Ipswich contacts. Roy Prince, archivist with the Duke of Cornwall's Light Infantry Association, shed some light on Sir Alf's army career.

For all their help with other research material, I am grateful to staff at the BBC archives, the ITN archives, the British Newspaper Library, Southampton Central Reference Library, the Register of Births, Marriages and Deaths, the Probate Division, the Press Association, the library of the *Daily Mail*, Tottenham Hotspur FC, the Barking and Dagenham Record office at Valence House Museum, the *Barking and Dagenham Recorder* and the Football Association.

Lady Victoria Ramsey, Sir Alf's widow, felt she could not co-operate with this book, though she did write to me expressing how devoted she was to her late husband.

I would like to thank Tom Whiting and Michael Doggart at HarperCollins for overseeing this project and giving me endless encouragement and support.

Finally, I owe a huge debt to my dear wife Elizabeth, who put up with the many, isolated months I spent in research and writing without complaint. I can never thank her enough for putting me on the path to becoming an author.

*Leo McKinstry*
*Coggeshall, Essex, April 2006*

# *Introduction*

15 May 1999. The ancient Suffolk church of St Mary-le-Tower in Ipswich had never previously held such a large or distinguished congregation. Three hundred mourners were crowded tightly on its polished wooden pews, while hundreds more lined the streets outside. England's greatest living footballer, Sir Bobby Charlton, sat near the front, looking more sombre than ever. Alongside him were colleagues from the World Cup-winning team of 1966, including the bald, bespectacled Nobby Stiles, the flame-haired Alan Ball and Bobby's own gangly brother Jack, who had left his Northumberland home at first light to attend the event.

They had gathered on a bright afternoon to pay their last respects at the memorial service of Sir Alfred Ernest Ramsey, the former England and Ipswich manager who had died at the end of April after a long illness. The venerable provincial setting was appropriate to the man whose life was being honoured, since modesty was one of the hallmarks of his personality. For all his success as both player and manager, for all his brilliance as a leader, he continually shunned the limelight and was uneasy with public adulation. The august Gothic expanse of Westminster Abbey or the classical grandeur of St Paul's would not have suited a farewell for this least bombastic of men.

The personal qualities of Sir Alf were referred to throughout the service. Afterwards, outside the church, former players spoke of his loyalty, his essential decency and his strength of character. 'He was an incredibly special manager. I just loved being with him, because I knew everything was straight down the line,' said Alan Ball. 'He was responsible for the greatest moment I had as a footballer and I will never forget or be able to thank him enough for that,' said Jack Charlton.

In a moving eulogy, George Cohen, another of the 1966 Cup winners, described Ramsey as 'not only a great football manager but a great Englishman'. Highlighting the way Sir Alf would stick by his players, Cohen gave the example of the occasion when Sir Alf refused to give in to pressure from FA officials to drop Nobby Stiles from the 1966 side after a disastrous challenge on the French player Jacques Simon. Though the tackle, according to Cohen, had been 'so late Connex South East would have been embarrassed by it,' Sir Alf supported Stiles to the hilt and even threatened to resign if the FA ordered him to change the team. In a voice cracking with emotion, Cohen continued: 'Sir Alf established a strong bond with his players who stood before every other consideration. We all loved him very much indeed. What Alf created was a family that is still as strong today in feeling and belief as it was thirty-three years ago when we won the World Cup.' Cohen then speculated as to how Alf might have reacted to such words of praise. 'If he is looking down at this particular moment, he is probably thinking, "Yes, George, I think we have had quite enough of that." Finally, Cohen turned in the direction of Sir Alf's grieving widow, Lady Victoria. 'Alf changed our lives, not just because of what we achieved with him but because our lives were richer for having known and played for him. He was an extraordinary man. Thank you for sharing him.'

Though the memorial service had been billed as 'a celebration' of Sir Alf's life, it was inevitable that the day should also be wreathed in sadness at his loss. 'I could not be more upset if he was family,' said Sir Bobby Charlton. Big Ted Phillips, one of Ipswich's strikers during Ramsey's years at the Suffolk club, told me: 'At Alf's memorial service, I could not speak. There were tears rolling down my cheeks. They wanted me to say a few words, but I told them I couldn't do it. Alf meant so much to me. He was a superb guy. He was unique. Under him at Ipswich, we were like a big family.'

Yet the sense of sorrow went much deeper than merely regret at the passing of one of England's modern heroes. There was also a mixture of guilt, disappointment and anger that, during his lifetime, Sir Alf had never been accorded the recognition he deserved. He might have been the man who, in the words of Tony Blair, 'gave this nation the greatest moment in our sporting history,' but he was hardly treated as such by the football establishment. Throughout his career as England manager, many in the FA regarded him with suspicion or contempt. He was never given a winner's medal for the 1966 World Cup victory, something that rankled with him right up to the moment of his death. His pay was always pitifully low, far worse than most First Division managers of his time, and when he was sacked in 1974, he was given only a meagre pension.

The last 25 years of his life were spent in a sad, twilight existence. The lack of money was compounded by the refusal of the football authorities to make any use of his unparalleled knowledge of the game. While football enjoyed an embarrassment of riches from the early nineties onwards, Sir Alf was left in uncomfortable exile, isolated and ignored. As late as 1996, the FA denied him any participatory role in the ceremonies to mark the opening of the European Championship in England.

'I sometimes look back and become bitter about it. I achieved something perhaps no manager will ever do again, yet the wealth of the game passed me by. I would have liked to have retired in comfort, and have no worries about money, but that has not been the case. And I couldn't understand why, after I left the FA, nobody there was prepared to let me work for my country,' he said in 1996.

This neglect of Sir Alf was symbolized by the absence from his memorial service of a host of key figures from the football world, despite the attendance of most of the 1966 side. Invitations were sent to all 92 Football League clubs, but only five of them were represented. Neither the then England manager Kevin Keegan nor any Premiership manager were present, though there were no fixtures that Saturday. Not one current England player showed up. As Gordon Taylor, Chairman of the Professional Footballers' Association, put it afterwards: 'It is amazing. If we cannot honour our heroes, what is the point of it all – and was there ever a greater hero for our game than Sir Alf? Everyone in the English game who could have been here should have been. It is a matter of simple respect.'

But in truth, outside the confines of his England squad, respect was something that Sir Alf had rarely been shown. The reluctance to honour him was not confined to the FA. Ever since the triumph of 1966, he had been the subject of a stream of criticism for his approach to football. His manner was condemned as aloof and forbidding, his methods as over-cautious and ultra-defensive. He was widely seen as the leader who hated flair and distrusted genius, a dull man in charge of a dull team. 'Ramsey's Robots' were said to have taken all grace and romance out of football. 'Alf Ramsey pulls the strings and the players dance for him. He has theorized them out of the game. They mustn't think for themselves. They have been so brainwashed by tactics and talks that individual talent has been thrust into the background,' claimed Bob Kelly, the President of the Scottish FA. The 1966 triumph was belittled as the fruit of nothing more than perspiration, dubious refereeing and home advantage.

Indeed, many critics went even further, claiming that winning the World Cup had been disastrous for British football in the long-term, because it encouraged a negative style of play. Particularly regrettable, it was said, was his abandonment of wingers in favour of a mundane 4–3–3 formation, which relied more on packing the midfield than in building attacks from the flanks. Sir Alf's enthusiasm for the aggressive Nobby Stiles was seen as typical of his dour outlook, as was his preference for the hard-working Geoff Hurst over the more creative, less diligent Jimmy Greaves in the final itself against West Germany. In Alf's England, it seemed, the workhorse was more valued than the thoroughbred. The doyen of Irish football writers, Eamon Dunphy, who played with Manchester United and Millwall, put it thus: 'Alf came to the conclusion that his players weren't good enough to compete, in any positive sense, with their betters. His response was a formula which stopped good players.' Similarly, the imaginative Manchester City coach Malcolm Allison argued that 'to Alf's way of thinking, skill meant lazy'.

This chorus of criticism reached full volume in the early seventies, when Sir Alf became more vulnerable because of poor results. He was the Roundhead who kept losing battles. As England were knocked out of the European Championship by West Germany in 1972, Hugh McIlvanney summed up the mood against Alf:

Cautious, joyless football was scarcely bearable even while it was bringing victories. What is happening now we always felt to be inevitable, because anyone who sets out to prove that football is about sweat rather than inspiration, about winning rather than glory, is sure to be found out in the end. Ramsey's method was, to be fair, justifiable in 1966, when it was important that England should make a powerful show in the World Cup, but since then it has become an embarrassment.

Some of the attacks grew vindictive, with Alf painted as a relic of a vanishing past, clinging on stubbornly to players and systems no longer fit for the modern age. His old-fashioned, stilted voice and demeanour were mocked, his lack of flamboyance ridiculed. In early 1973, soon after England had beaten Scotland 5–0 at Hampden, with Mick Channon performing well up front, the satirical magazine *Foul!* carried a cruel but rather leaden article entitled 'Lady Ramsey's Diary', parodying the *Private Eye* series of the time about Downing Street, 'Mrs Wilson's Diary'. One extract ran:

He's terribly worried about this Mr Shannon (*sic*). 'You see, my dear,' he told me (it's amazing how different he sounds after those elocution lessons), 'we just can't afford to have individuals playing so well. It undermines the whole team effort. Besides, people will start expecting us to score five goals in every game, and we can't have that.'

The critics had their way in April 1974, when Sir Alf was sacked as manager after eleven years in the post. The FA's decision was hardly a surprise, given England's failure to qualify for the World Cup the previous autumn. But it still fell as a painful blow to Sir Alf, one from which he never really recovered. He once explained that only three things mattered to him – 'football, my country and my wife'. Football had turned out to be a fickle mistress, and for the remainder of his years he carried a feeling of betrayal. 'Football has passed me by,' he said towards the end of his life.

Since his sacking, no other England manager has come near to the pinnacle he climbed. When he departed in 1974, it seemed likely that England might one day reach that peak again. In the subsequent 30 years and more, however, the national side has endured one failure after another, with just two semi-finals in major championships during those three decades. Yet it should also be remembered that before Sir Alf's arrival as manager in 1963, England's record was equally dismal, having never gone further than a World Cup quarter-final; indeed in 1950, the national side suffered what is still the greatest upset in the history of global soccer, losing 1–0 to the unknown amateurs of the USA. Set in the context of England's sorry history, therefore, the extent of Sir Alf's achievement becomes all the more remarkable, putting into perspective much of the carping about his management.

He might not have inspired electrifying football, but for most of his reign he achieved results that would have been the envy of every manager since. Nobby Stiles told me: 'I cannot say enough in favour of Alf Ramsey. His insights were unbelievable. I would have died for him.' It is a telling fact that the 1970 World Cup in Mexico is the only occasion when England have ever gone into a major tournament as one of the favourites to win it – in 1966, England, still living with the burdens of their past record, were regarded as outsiders. The status that England had earned by 1970 in itself is a tribute to the supreme effectiveness of Ramsey's leadership. Moreover, his success in 1962 in bringing the League Championship to Ipswich Town, an unheralded Third Division club before he took over, is one of the most astonishing feats in the annals of British football management, unlikely ever to be surpassed.

Yet even now, as nostalgia for the golden summer of 1966

becomes more potent, the memory of Sir Alf Ramsey is not one treasured by the public. He is nothing like as famous as David Beckham, or George Best or Paul Gascoigne, three footballers who achieved far less than him on the international stage. In his birthplace of Dagenham, he seems to have been airbrushed from history. There is no statue to him, no blue plaque in the street where he was born or the ground where he first played. No road or club or school bears his name. The same indifference is demonstrated beyond east London. When the BBC recently organized a competition to decide what the main bridge at the new Wembley stadium should be called, Sir Alf Ramsey's name was on the shortlist. Yet the British public voted for the title of the 'White Horse Bridge', after the celebrated police animal who restored order at the first Wembley FA Cup Final of 1923 when unprecedented crowds of around 200,000 were spilling onto the pitch. With all due respect to this creature, it is something of an absurdity that the winning manager of the World Cup should have to trail in behind a horse. As one of Ramsey's players, Mike Summerbee, puts it: 'Alf Ramsey's contribution to international football was phenomenal. Yet the way he was treated was a disgrace. We never look after our heroes and in time we try to pull them down. I tell you something, they should have a bronze statue of Alf at the new Wembley. And they should call it the Alf Ramsey stadium.'

Part of the failure to appreciate the greatness of Alf Ramsey has been the result of his severe public image. He was a man who elevated reticence to an art form. With his players he could be amiable, sometimes even humorous, but he presented a much stonier face to the press and wider world. The personification of the traditional English stiff upper lip, he never courted popularity, never showed any emotion in public. His epic self-restraint was beautifully captured at the end of the

World Cup Final of 1966, when he sat impassively staring ahead, while all around him were scenes of joyous mayhem at England's victory. The only words he uttered after Geoff Hurst's third goal were a headmasterly rebuke to his trainer, Harold Shepherdson, who had leapt to his feet in ecstasy. 'Sit down, Harold,' he growled. Again, as the players gathered for their lap of honour, they tried to push Alf to the front to greet the cheers of the crowd. But, with typical modesty, he refused. This outward calm, he later explained, was not due to any lack of inner passion but to his shyness. 'I'm a very emotional person but my feelings are always tied up inside. Maybe it is a mistake to be like this but I cannot govern it. I don't think there is anything wrong with showing emotion in public, but it is something I can never do.'

Nowhere was Ramsey's awkwardness more apparent than in his notoriously difficult relationship with the media. Believing all that mattered were performances on the field, he made little effort to cultivate journalists. 'I can live without them because I am judged by the results that the England team gets. I doubt very much whether they can live without me,' he once said. Hiding behind a mask of inscrutability, he usually would provide only the blandest of answers at press conferences or indeed none at all. He trusted a select few, like Ken Jones and Brian James, because he respected their knowledge of football, but most of the rest of the press were given the cold shoulder. He also had a gift for humiliating reporters with little more than a withering look. As Peter Batt, once of the *Sun*, recalls: 'There was a general, utter contempt from him. I don't think anyone could make you feel more like a turd under his boot than Ramsey. It is amazing how he did it.' This hostile attitude led to a string of incidents throughout his career. Shortly after England had won the World Cup, for instance, Ramsey was standing in the reception of Hendon Hall, the team's hotel in north-west London. A representative of the Press Association came up to him and said:

'Mr Ramsey, on behalf of the press, may I thank you for your co-operation throughout the tournament?'

'Are you taking the piss?' was Alf's reply.

On another occasion in 1967, he was with an FA team in Canada for a tournament at the World Expo show. As he stood by the bus which would take his team from Montreal airport to its hotel, he was suddenly accosted by a leading TV correspondent from one of Canada's news channels. The clean-cut broadcaster put his arm around England's manager, and then launched into his spiel.

'Sir Ramsey, it's just a thrill to have you and the world soccer champions here in Canada. Now I'm from one of our biggest national stations, going out live coast to coast, from the Atlantic to the Pacific. And, Coach Ramsey, you're not going to believe this but I'm going to give you seven whole minutes all to yourself on the show. So if you're ready, Sir Ramsey, I am going to start the interview now.'

'Oh no you fuckin' ain't.' And with that, a fuming Coach Ramsey climbed onto the bus.

Such dismissiveness might provoke smiles from those present, but it ultimately led to the creation of a host of enemies in the press. When times grew rough in the seventies, Alf was left with few allies to put his case. The same was true of his relations with football's administrators, whom he regarded as no more than irritants; to him they were like most journalists: tiresome amateurs who knew nothing about the tough realities of professional football. 'Those people' was his disdainful term for the councillors of the FA. He despised them so much that he would deliberately avoid sitting next to them on trips or at matches, while he described the autocratic Professor Harold Thompson, one of the FA's bosses, as 'that bloody man Thompson'. But again, when results went against Sir Alf, the knives came out and the FA were able to exact their revenge.

The roots of Sir Alf's antagonism towards the media and the FA lay in his deep sense of social insecurity. He was a strange mixture of tremendous self-confidence within the narrow world of football, and tortured, tongue-tied diffidence outside it. He had been a classy footballer himself in the immediate post-war era, one of the most intelligent full-backs England has ever produced, and was never afraid to set out his opinions in the dressing-rooms of Southampton and Spurs, his two League clubs. Performing his role as England or Ipswich manager, he was the master of his domain. No one could match him for his understanding of the technicalities of football, where he allied a brilliant judgement of talent to a shrewd tactical awareness and a photographic memory of any passage of play. 'Without doubt, he was the greatest manager I ever knew, a fantastic guy,' says Ray Crawford of Ipswich and England. 'He had a natural authority about him. You never argued with him. He was always brilliant in his talks because he read the game so well. He would come into the dressing-room at half-time and explain what we should be doing, and most of the time it came off. He was inspirational that way.' Peter Shilton, England's most capped player, is just as fulsome: 'From the moment I met Sir Alf I knew he was someone special. He was that sort of person. He was a man who inspired total respect. Any decision he made, you knew he made it for the right reason. He had real strength of character. I have been with other managers who were not as strong in the big, big games. But Alf could rise above the pressure and dismiss irrelevancies.'

Yet Sir Alf never felt comfortable when taken out of the reassuring environment of running his teams. All his ease and self-assurance evaporated when he was not dealing with professional players and trusted football correspondents. He could cope with a World Cup Final but not with a cocktail reception. 'Dinners, speeches,' he used to say of the FA committee men, 'that's their job.' Amongst the Oxbridge degrees of the sporting, political or diplomatic establishments, he felt all too aware of his humble origins and lack of education. Born into a poor, rural Essex family, he left school at fourteen and took his first job as a delivery boy for the Dagenham Co-op. To cope with this insecurity, Sir Alf devised a number of strategies. One was to erect a social barrier against the world, avoiding all forms of intimacy. That is why he could so often appear aloof, even downright rude. From his earliest days as a professional, he was reluctant to open up to anyone. This distance might have been invaluable in retaining his authority as a manager, but it also prohibited the formation of close friendships.

Pat Godbold, his secretary throughout his spell as Ipswich manager from 1955 to 1963, says: 'I was twenty when Alf came here. My first impression was that he was a shy man. I think that right up to his death he was a very shy man. You could not get to know him. He was a good man to work for, but I can honestly say that I never got to know him.' Sir Alf guarded the privacy of his domestic life with the same determination that he put into management. The mock-Tudor house on a leafy Ipswich road he shared with Lady Victoria – or Vic, as he always called her – was his sanctuary, not a social venue. Anne Elsworthy, the wife of one of the Championship-winning Ipswich players of 1962, recalls Sir Alf and Lady Ramsey as a 'a very private couple. After he retired, I would occasionally see them in Marks and Spencer's in Ipswich, but all they would say would be 'Good morning'. They were not the sort to stand around chatting in a supermarket. When Alf went to play golf, he would just go, complete his round. He would not hang around the bar.'

Another strategy was to reinvent himself as the archetypal suburban English gentleman. The impoverished Dagenham lad, who could not even afford to go to the cinema until he was fourteen, was gradually transformed in adulthood into someone who could have easily been mistaken for a stock-broker or a bank-manager. The pinstripe, made of the finest mohair, was a suit of armour to protect from his detractors. When he went to Buckingham Palace to collect his knighthood in 1967, he went to extraordinary lengths to ensure that he was dressed in the exactly the correct attire. But by far the most obvious change was in his voice, allegedly the result of elocution lessons, as he dropped his Essex accent in favour of a form of pronunciation memorably described by the journalist Brian Glanville as 'sergeant-major posh'. Like Eliza Doolittle in *Pygmalion*, Sir Alf occasionally betrayed his origins when he slipped into the vernacular of his childhood, as on the embarrassing occasion in a restaurant car travelling to Ipswich when, in the presence of the club's directors, he told a waitress during dinner, 'No thank you, I don't want no peas.'

Tony Garnett, the Suffolk-based journalist who covered Ipswich's great years under Sir Alf, told me: 'He did drop some real clangers when he was trying to talk proper, as they say. One of the best was when Ipswich went abroad after they had won the championship and Alf began to talk about going through 'Customs and Exercise.' Nobody dared to correct him. He could not do his 'H's properly, nor his 'ings' at the end of a word.' With his attempts at precision, his lengthy pauses, his twisted syntax and his frequent repetition of the same phrase – 'most certainly' and 'in as much as' were two particular favourites – it seemed at times that he was almost trying to master a foreign tongue.

The Blackpool and England goalkeeper in the 1960s, Tony Waiters, who led Canada to the 1986 World Cup finals and has wide experience of working in America, says: 'It was always worth listening to Alf. But occasionally he would fall down on his pronunciation or would drop an "H" every so often. As a coach myself, I am aware that if you say the wrong thing, it could come back to haunt you. And sometimes Alf would give an indication that this was not his natural way of speaking. He was very deliberate in what he said. I work with a lot of people who are coaching in their second language. Generally speaking they slow down because they are thinking ahead and almost rehearsing in their own mind what they are going to say. With Alf, it was always good stuff but maybe he had to do a bit of mental gymnastics as he prepared to speak.'

For all his anxiety about his accent and his appearance, Sir Alf could never have been described as a snob. Just the opposite was true. He loathed pretension and social climbing, one of the reasons why he so disliked the fatuities of the FA's councillors. David Barber, who has worked at the FA since 1970, beginning as a teenage clerk, recalls Alf's lack of self-importance: 'Right from the moment I first took a job there, I was not in the slightest bit overawed by him. Though he was the most famous man in football at the time, he was down to earth. He was very nice, treated me like a colleague, not an office boy. He was uncomfortable with the press and FA Council members and in public could be a shy man, but with people like me, whom he worked with on a daily basis, he could not have been more friendly.'

Utterly lacking in personal vanity, Alf deliberately avoided the social whirl of London and was unmoved by fashionable restaurants and hotels. His knighthood did not change him in the slightest, while he always retained a fondness for the activities of his Dagenham youth, such as a visit to the greyhound track accompanied by a pint of bitter and some jellied eels. As reflected by his penurious retirement, he refused to exploit his position for personal gain, unlike most of his successors; in fact, it was partly his repugnance at commercialism that led to his downfall.

Alf's favourite self-preservation strategy, though, was to ignore the world outside and retreat into football, the one subject he really understood. Since his childhood, he had been utterly obsessed with the game. He was kicking a ball before he was learning his alphabet. It was the great abiding passion of his life. When he was truly engaged with the sport, his introversion would disappear, the barriers would fall. Apart from his wife, nothing else had the same importance to him. As his captain at Ipswich, Andy Nelson, remembers: 'He was a very private, quiet man, very unhappy to have any conversation that was unrelated to football. When we went on the train, we used to have a little card school. Roy Bailey, our goalkeeper, was a big figure in that. Alf would come into our compartment and start talking about football. And then Roy would say, "Anyone seen that new film at the pictures?" You would literally be rid of Alf in two minutes. He'd be off, gone.' Hugh McIlvanney told me that he could see the change in Alf's personality as soon as he shifted the ground onto football. 'Alf liked a drink and he could get quite bitter when he was arguing about football. That front of restraint, which was his normal face for the public, was pretty superficial; he quite liked to go to war. All the insecurity he so obviously had socially did not apply for a moment to football. He was utterly convinced of his case – and with good reason. He was a great manager in any sense.'

It is impossible to deny that, in his obsession with football, Sir Alf was a one-dimensional figure. He had a child-like affection for movies, especially westerns and thrillers, enjoyed pottering about his Ipswich garden and was genuinely devoted to Vickie. But he was uneasy with any discussions about politics, current affairs or art beyond privately mouthing the conventional platitudes of suburban conservatism. An unabashed philistine, he turned down an offer to take the England team to a gala evening with the Bolshoi Ballet during a trip to Moscow in 1973; instead, he arranged a showing of an Alf Garnett film at the British Embassy. He had an ingrained xenophobic streak, and had little time for any foreigners, in whose number he included the Scots. In fact, his dislike of the 'strange little men' north of the border was so ingrained that one Christmas, when he was given a pair of Paisley pyjamas as a present, he soon changed them at the shop for a pair of blue and white striped ones.

Nigel Clarke, the experienced journalist who worked more closely with Sir Alf than anyone else in Fleet Street and wrote his column for the *Daily Mirror* in the 1980s, provides this memory: 'Alf was certainly conservative with a small 'c'. But he was not a worldly man and we never really talked about current affairs or wider political issues. He was just happy talking about football. I think that was partly because he knew the subject so well. He could talk about football until the cows came home. He never wanted to discuss governments or religion or anything like that. His life revolved around football. He had little conversation about anything else. His face would lighten up when you mentioned something about the game. We would be sitting in the compartment of a train, going to cover a match for the paper, and Alf would be dozing. Then I might refer to some player and his eyes would open, he would sit up instantly, and say, 'Oh really, yes, I know him. I saw him play recently.' He just loved football, loved anyone who shared his passion for it.'

When it came to football itself, Sir Alf Ramsey was anything but a one-dimensional figure. Beneath his placid exterior, the flame of his devotion to the game burned with a fierce intensity. It was a strength of commitment that made him one of the most contradictory and controversial managers of all time. He was a tough, demanding character, who could be strangely sensitive to criticism, a reserved English gentleman who was loathed by the establishment, an unashamed traditionalist who turned out to be a tactical revolutionary, a stern disciplinarian who was not above telling his players to 'get rat-arsed'. His ruthlessness divided the football world; his stubbornness left him the target of abuse and condemnation. But it was his zeal that put England at the top of the world.

# ONE

# *Dagenham*

The Right Honourable Stanley Baldwin, the avuncular leader of the Conservative Party in the inter-war years, was not usually a man given to overstatement. But in 1934 he was so impressed by the new municipal housing development at Becontree in Dagenham that he was moved to write in an official report:

> If the Becontree estate were situated in the United States, articles and newsreels would have been circulated containing references to the speed at which a new town of 120,000 people had been built. If it had happened in Vienna, the Labour and left Liberal press would have boosted it as an example of what municipal socialism could accomplish. If it had been built in Russia, Soviet propaganda would have emphasized the planning aspect. A Pudovkin film might have been made of it – a close up of the morning seen on cabbages in the market gardens; the building of the railway lines to carry bricks and wood, the spread of the houses and roads with the thousands of busy workers, gradually engulfing the fields and hedges and trees. But Becontree was planned and built in England where the most revolutionary social changes can take place and people in general do not realize they have occurred.

1

The Becontree estate was certainly dramatic in conception and scale. It was first planned in 1920, when the London County Council saw that a radical expansion in the number of homes would be needed to the east of the city, in order both to provide accommodation for the men returning from the Great War and to alleviate the terrible slum conditions of the East End. This was to be Britain's first new town, a place providing 'homes fit for heroes'. The scheme to convert 3000 acres of land into a vast urban community was, as the LCC's architect boasted, 'unparalleled in the history of housing'. The establishment of the Ford motor works in Dagenham in 1929 was a further spur to the urbanization of the area. By 1933, with the building programme reaching its peak, the LCC proclaimed that, 'Becontree is the largest municipal housing estate in the world.'

Right in the midst of this gargantuan sprawl, untouched by bulldozer or bricklayer, there stood a set of rustic wooden cottages. These low, single-storey dwellings had been built in 1851, when Dagenham was entirely countryside. For all their quaintness, they were extremely primitive, devoid of any electricity or hot running water. And it was in one of them, Number Six Parrish Cottages, Halbutt Street, that Alfred Ernest Ramsey was born on 22 January 1920, the very year that saw the first proposals for the Becontree Estate. The row of Parrish Cottages remained throughout the development of the estate, an architectural and social anachronism holding out against the tide of modernity. They did not even have electricity installed until the 1950s and they were not finally pulled down until the early 1970s. In one sense, the cottage of his birth is a metaphor for the life of Alf Ramsey: the arch traditionalist, modest in spirit and conservative in outlook, who refused to be swept along by the social revolution which engulfed Britain during his career.

For much of his early life, Ramsey was not completely

honest about his date of birth. In his ghost-written autobiography, published in 1952, he stated baldly that he was born 'in 1922', without giving any details of the month or the day. Now the reason for this was not personal vanity but sporting professionalism. When Ramsey was trying to force his way into League football at the end of the Second World War, a difference of two years could make a big difference to the prospects of a young hopeful, since a club would be more likely to take on someone aged 23 than 25. In such a competitive world, Ramsey felt he had to use any ruse which might work to his advantage. His dishonesty was harmless, and it passed largely unnoticed until after he received his knighthood in 1967. Having been asked to check his entry for *Debrett's Peerage, Baronetage, Knightage and Companionage*, Sir Alf decided not to mislead that most elevated of reference works. As Arthur Hopcraft put it in the *Observer*, 'Alf Ramsey the dignified, the aspirer after presence, could not, I am convinced, give false information to the book of the Peerage.' But by then the issue of his age had ceased to matter; in any case, because of the stiffness of his character, he had always seemed much older than his stated years.

Parrish Cottages may have become outdated with the arrival of the Becontree Estate, but when Alf Ramsey was an infant they were typical of rural Dagenham, where farming was still the main source of subsistence. 'Dagenham was like a little hamlet. It was much more countrified until they built the big estate. There was a helluva lot of open space here in the twenties,' says one of Alf's contemporaries Charles Emery. 'Most people think of Dagenham as an industrial area. But until I was six there was nothing but little country lanes. I saw Dagenham grow and grow,' Alf wrote in 1970. A reflection of that environment could be seen at the Robin Hood pub in the north-west of the borough, where customers drank by the light of paraffin or oil lamps, and the landlord had to double as a ploughman. As one account from 1920 ran: 'A customer would enter the bar and finding it empty, would shout across the fields for the landlord. After a time he would arrive, and wiping his hands free from the soil, would draw a pint of beer, have a talk about the weather, and then depart again to the fields.'

A striking picture of life in Dagenham in the early twenties was left by Fred Tibble, who died in 2003 after serving as a borough councillor for 35 years. He grew up with Alf, often playing football and cricket with him, and remembered him as 'a very quiet boy who really loved sport'. The late Councillor Tibble had other memories:

> We were very much Essex, we were country people. Many people came to the village selling things. There was a muffin man, who would come to the area once a week, ringing a bell with a tray of muffins on his head. The voluntary fire brigade was based in Station Road in the early 1920s, and when the maroon sounded, men would have to leave their jobs and homes to man the appliances. It could be difficult in the daytime, as they would have to try to get the horse which was being used for the milk round. At the weekends and summer evenings, the police used a wheel-barrow to take drunks from the pub to the police station. The drunks would be strapped into the barrow. We always found that amusing. Sometimes we would climb up the slaughterhouse wall to take a look at cattle being pole-axed. We often hoped to get hold of a pig's bladder, which we could stuff with paper and play football with.

It was a country life that young Alf relished, especially because it provided such scope for football. He wrote in *Talking Football*:

Along with my three brothers, I lived for the open air from the moment I could toddle. The meadow at the back of our cottage was our playground. For hours every day, with my brothers, I learnt how to kick, head and control a ball, starting first of all with a tennis ball and it is true to say that we found all our pleasure this way. We were happy in the country, the town and cinemas offering no attractions to us.

But it was also a deprived existence, one that left him permanently defensive about his background. 'We were not exactly wealthy,' he admitted euphemistically. His later fastidious concern for his appearance stemmed from the fact that his family was poorer than most in the district, so he was not always dressed as smartly as he would have liked. If anyone commented on this difference, he retreated further into his shell, 'We grew up together in Halbutt Street. Alf was very introverted, not very forthcoming. I sometimes went to his house, a very old cottage, little more than a wooden hut. His family were just ordinary people. He was not especially well-turned out as a child. That only came later, when he bettered himself,' says his contemporary Phil Cairns.

Alf's father, Herbert Ramsey, made a precarious living from various manual activities. He owned an agricultural smallholding, while on Saturdays he drove a horse-drawn dustcart for the local council. He also grew vegetables and reared a few pigs in the garden at the front of Parrish Cottages. He has sometimes been described as 'a hay and straw dealer', though it is interesting that when Alf married in 1951, he referred to his father's occupation as a 'general labourer'. Others, less generously, have said he was little more than a 'rag-and-bone man'. Alf's mother, Florence, was from a well-known Dagenham family called the Bixbys.

Pauline Gosling, who was a neighbour of the Ramseys in Parrish Cottages, recalls:

The cottages had outside toilets and no hot water. If you wanted a bath, you had to heat up the water in a copper pan and then fill a tin tub by the fire. Friday was usually bath night. There was no electricity, so you had to use oil lamps. If you wanted to go out to the toilet at night, you had to take one of those. Alf's mother was a lovely lady. She and my mother were very close. They were a quiet family, very private, like Alf. They had worked the land for years around Dagenham. My own great-grandfather used to work on the land with Alf's great grand-dad.

Gladys Skinner, another former neighbour, says:

There was an outside loo in a little shed in their back garden. You could see their tin bath hanging up on the wall outside. They were never a family to tell other people their business. Alf's mother was a dear old thing. When they were installing electricity round here, she wouldn't have it, said it frightened her. Alf's father was also a very nice man. He sometimes kept pigs and we would go round have a look at the little piglets in the garden.

Alf always maintained that his was a close family. 'My mother is in many ways very like me. Like me she doesn't show much emotion. She didn't, for instance, seem very excited when I received my knighthood. But she is very human and I like to think I was like her in that respect,' he wrote in a 1970 *Daily Mirror* article about his life. He also felt that, despite the lack of money, his parents had taught him how to conduct himself properly. 'He told me that he was brought up very strictly and that is why he was such a stickler for punctuality and courtesy. He said that it was part of his upbringing to be courteous and polite to people,' says Nigel Clarke.

Alf was one of five children. He had two older brothers, Len and Albert, a younger brother Cyril, and a sister, Joyce, though he was the only one to go on to achieve public distinction. Cyril worked for Ford; Len, nicknamed 'Ginger', became a butcher; and Joyce married and moved to Chelmsford. Albert, known in Dagenham as 'Bruno', was the least inspiring of the siblings, utterly lacking in Alf's ambition or focus. A heavy drinker, he earned his keep from gambling and keeping greyhounds. Alf himself was always interested in the dog track, liked a bet and was a shrewd gambler. But he never allowed it to dominate his life in the way that Albert did. 'Bruno was a big chap. I can picture him now, with a trilby turned up at the front. He had a great friend called Charlie Waggles and the two of them never went out to work. At the time I thought that was terrible. They just gambled on the dogs,' says Jean Bixby, who grew up in Dagenham at this time. In later life, Bruno's disreputable life would cause Alf some embarrassment.

From the age of five, Alf attended Becontree Heath School. Now demolished, Becontree Heath had a roll of about 200, covering the ages of four to fourteen. Alf was neither especially diligent about his lessons nor popular with his fellow pupils. 'I was never particularly clever at school. I seem to have spent more time pumping at footballs and carrying goalposts,' Alf once said. 'He was a year above me but I remember him all right. Know why? 'Cos he looked like a kid you wouldn't get to like in a hurry,' said one of them in a *Sun* profile of Sir Alf in 1971. For all his introspection, Alf was not a cowardly child, as he proved in the boxing ring at school. 'I weighed only about five stones, but I was a tough little fighter. I won a few fights,' he later recalled. But when he was ten years old, he was pulverized in a school tournament by a much larger opponent. 'He was about a foot bigger than I was and I was as wide as I was tall. I was punched all over the ring.' That put a halt to his school boxing career, though for the rest of his life he retained a visible scar above his mouth, a legacy of that bout. Alf was also good at athletics, representing the school in the high jump, long jump, and the one hundred and two hundred yards. And he was a solid cricketer, with a sound, classical batting technique.

But, as in adulthood, football was what really motivated Alf Ramsey. 'He did not have much knowledge of the world. The only thing that ever seemed to interest him was football,' says Phil Cairns. 'He was very withdrawn, almost surly, but he became animated on the football field.' From his earliest years, Alf demonstrated a natural ability for the game, his talent enhanced not only by games in the fields behind Parrish Cottages, but also by the long walk to and from school with his brothers. To break the monotony of the journey, which took altogether about four hours a day, the boys brought a small ball with them to kick about on the country lane. On one occasion, Alf accidentally kicked the ball into a ditch, which had filled with about three feet of water after heavy rainfall. He was instructed by his brothers to fish it out. So, having removed his shoes and socks, he waded in, soon found himself out of his depth, and was soaked to the skin. On his return home, he developed a severe cold and was confined to bed for a week. He wrote later: 'That heavy cold taught me a lesson. I am certain that those daily kick-abouts with my brothers played a much more important part than I then appreciated in helping me secure accuracy in the pass and any ball control I now possess.'

Alf's ability was soon obvious to his schoolmasters. One of his teachers, Alfred Snow, recalled in the *Essex and East*

*London Recorder* in 1971: 'I was teaching at Becontree Heath Primary and I taught Alf Ramsey for two years. I remember him particularly well because he was so good on the football field. It didn't really surprise me to see him get where he has.' At the age of just seven, Alf was placed in the Becontree Heath junior side, in the position of inside-left. His brother Len was the team's inside-right. Alf's promotion to represent his school meant that, for the first time, he had to have proper boots. His mother went out and bought him a pair, costing four shillings and eleven pence – with Alf contributing the eleven pence from the meagre savings in his own piggy bank. 'If those boots had been made of gold and studded with diamonds I could not have felt prouder than when I put them on and strutted around the dining room, only to be pulled up by father. "Go careful on the lino, Alf," he said, "those studs will mark it,"' Alf's ghost-writer recorded in *Talking Football*.

By the age of just nine, Alf, despite being 'a little tubby', to use his own phrase, had proved himself so outstanding that he was made the school's captain, commanding boys who were several years older than himself. He had also been switched to centre-half, the key position in any side of the pre-sixties era. Under the old W–M formation which was then the iron tradition in British soccer, based around two full-backs, three half-backs, two wingers and three forwards, the centre-half was both the fulcrum of the defence and instigator of attacks. It was a role ideally suited to Alf's precocious footballing intelligence and the quality of his passing.

His performances brought him higher honours. He was selected to play for Dagenham Schools against a West Ham Youth XI, then for Essex Schoolboys, and then in a trial match for London schools. But in this match, Alf's diminutive stature told against him. He wrote:

I stood just five feet tall, weighed six stone three pounds and looked more like a jockey than a centre-half. In that trial, the opposing centre forward stood five feet, ten and half inches and tipped the scale at 10 stone. After that game I gave up all hopes of playing for London. That centre-forward hit me with everything but the crossbar, scored three goals and in general gave me an uncomfortable time.

Compounding this failure, a rare outburst of youthful impetuosity led to a sending-off for questioning a decision of the referee during a match for Becontree Heath School. The Dagenham Schools FA ordered him to apologize in writing to both the referee and themselves. He did so promptly, but it was not to be his last clash with the authorities.

For all such problems, Alf had shown enormous potential. 'He was easily the best for his age in the area,' says Phil Cairns. 'He was brilliant, absolutely focused on his game. He was taking on seniors when he was still a junior. Everyone in Dagenham who was interested in football knew of Alf because he was virtually an institution as a schoolboy. He was famous as a kid because of his football.' Jean Bixby's late husband Tom played with Alf at Becontree Heath: 'Alf was a very good footballer as a boy. Tom said that he had great control and confidence. He always wanted the ball. He would say to Tom, "Put it over here."'

Yet Alf's schoolboy reputation did not lead to any approaches from a League club. He therefore never contemplated trying to become a professional footballer when he left Becontree Heath School in 1934. 'I was very keen on football but one really didn't it give much thought. There was no television then, and football was just fun to do,' he told the *Dagenham Post* in 1971. Instead, he had to go out and earn a living in Dagenham to help support his family; this was, after all, the depth of the Great Depression in Britain, which spawned mass unemployment, social dislocation and political extremism. Alf first applied for a job at the Ford factory, where wages were much higher than elsewhere. But with dole queues at record levels, competition for work there was intense and he was rejected. Following a family conference about his future, he then decided to enter the retail trade, beginning at the bottom as a delivery boy for the Five Elms Co-operative store in Dagenham. The occupation of a grocer might not be a glamorous one, but at least it was relatively secure. People always needed food, and the phenomenal growth in the population of Dagenham in the 1930s provided a lucrative market for local businesses. In addition, there was a high demand for grocery deliveries in the area, because public transport was poor.

Alf immediately demonstrated his conscientious, frugal nature by giving the great majority of his earnings to the family household. 'Every day I'd cycle my way around the Dagenham district taking to customers their various needs. My wages were twelve shillings a week. Of this sum, I handed over ten shillings to my mother, put a shilling in the box as savings and kept a shilling for pocket-money,' he wrote. After several years carrying out these errands, Alf graduated to serving behind the counter at the Co-op shop in Oxlow Lane, only a short distance from his home in Halbutt Street.

He later claimed to be happy in his job, but what he missed was football. For two whole years, he could not play the game at all, since he had to work throughout Saturday and there was no organized soccer in Dagenham on Thursdays, when he had his only free afternoon. But then, in 1936, a kindly shopkeeper by the unfortunate name of Edward Grimme intervened. Grimme had noticed that a large number of talented Dagenham schoolboy footballers were being lost to the game because of their jobs. So he decided to set up a youth team called Five Elms United. Because of his excellent local reputation, Alf was soon asked to join. He had no hesitation in doing so, despite the weekly sixpence subscription, which left him hardly any pocket money. But he did not care. He was once more involved with the game he loved.

Grimme's Five Elms United held their meetings on Wednesday evenings and played on Sunday mornings in a field at the back of the Merry Fiddlers pub. Playing on the Sabbath was officially banned by the FA in the 1930s. Strictly speaking, after breaking this rule, Alf Ramsey should have been obliged to apply for reinstatement with the Association, once he became a League player, by paying a fee of seven shillings six pence. 'I was most certainly conscious that Sunday football was illegal then but it presented me with the only opportunity to play competitive football. Technically, I suppose, never having paid the reinstatement fee, I should never have been allowed to play for England or Spurs or Southampton,' Alf wrote later. So, in effect, the World Cup was won by an ineligible manager.

Playing again at centre-half, Alf showed that none of his ability had disappeared, despite his two-year absence from the game. In fact, he was physically all the more capable because of his growth in height and his regular exercise on the Co-op bicycle. Tommy Sloan, now one of the trustees of the Dagenham Football club, saw Alf play regularly before the war on the Merry Fiddlers ground: 'It was quite a good pitch there. All the lads played in the usual kit of the time, big shin guards and steel toe caps in their boots. Alf was a very impressive player. He used to tackle strongly, but fairly. He had a very powerful kick, especially at free kicks. He was subdued, never threw his weight about and was a model for any other youngster.' Alf himself felt he benefited from the demanding nature of those teenage games with Five Elms, 'I have often looked back upon those matches. Most of them were against older and better teams but we all learnt a good deal from opposing older and more experienced players. They were among the most valuable lessons of my life.'

It is interesting that many of the traits that later defined Alf Ramsey, including his relentless focus on football, his taciturnity and his attempt at social polish, were apparent in his teenage years. For all the poverty of his upbringing in Parrish Cottages, he had nothing like the usual working-class boisterousness of his contemporaries. George Baker, who grew up near Halbutt Street and later became head of the borough's recreation department, told me: 'I was born within two years of Alf and I knew him and his brothers. As a lad, he was not like the locals. He somehow seemed a bit intellectual, a bit distant. He spoke a little bit better than the rest of us. He was pleasant, but he was different.' Beattie Robbins came to know him in the thirties, because one of her relatives worked with him in the Co-op: 'I remember him as well spoken, just as he was in later life. He was very nice, but seemed quite shy. I knew him best when he was about 17. He was polite, dignified, a very reserved person. We once went on a coach trip to Clacton with the Five Elms team and he sat quietly on the bus at the front. He did not play around much like some of the others. His life seemed to be just football.'

As he grew older, Alf appeared only too keen to distance himself from his Dagenham roots. The journalist Max Marquis wrote sarcastically in his 1970 biography of Ramsey, 'There are no indications that Alf is overburdened with nostalgia for his birthplace . . . in fact the impression is inescapable that he would like to forget all connections with it.' His Dagenham contemporary Jean Bixby, who worked with Alf's brother Cyril at Ford, argues: 'The trouble with Alf Ramsey was that he tried to make himself something that he wasn't. He went on to mix in different circles and he tried to change himself to fit in with those circles. Yes, even as a child he was slightly different, but he was still ordinary Dagenham. Then he went away and changed. He was not one of the boys anymore. He became conservative, not like the others who all stuck together. He was one apart from them.'

At the heart of this unease, it has often been claimed, was a feeling of embarrassment not just over the poverty of his upbringing, but, more importantly, over the ethnic identity of his family. For Sir Alf Ramsey, knight of the realm and great English patriot, was long said to come from a family of gypsies. This supposed Romany background was reflected in the family's fondness for the dog track, in the obscure way his father earned his living and in Alf's own swarthy, dark features. 'I was always told that he was a gypsy. And when you looked at him, he did look a bit Middle Eastern,' says his former Tottenham Hotspur colleague Eddie Baily. Alf's childhood nickname in Dagenham, 'Darkie Ramsey', was reportedly another indicator of his gypsy blood. 'Everyone round here referred to him as "Darkie" and it was to be years later that I found out his name was actually Alf,' recalled Councillor Fred Tibble. Even today, in multi-racial Britain, there is less tolerance towards gypsies than towards most other ethnic minority groups. And the problems of prejudice would have loomed even larger in the much more homogenous Britain of the pre-war era. In a *Channel Four* documentary on Sir Alf broadcast in 2002, it was stated authoritatively that 'Alf had to put up with casual racism. Dagenham locals believed that he came from a gypsy background and so inherited his father's nickname, Darkie Ramsey.'

There is no doubt that Alf was acutely sensitive about these claims and this may have accounted for some of his habitual reserve. The journalist Nigel Clarke, who knew him better than anyone else did in the press, recalls this incident on tour:

> The only time I ever saw Alf really angry was when we were going through Czechoslovakia in 1973 with the England team – in those good old days the press would travel with the team. We were all sitting on the coach as it drove past some Romany caravans. And Bobby Moore piped up, 'Hey, Alf, there's some of your relatives over there.' Alf went absolutely crimson with fury. He would never admit to his Romany background and hated to discuss the subject. He used to say to me, 'I am just an East End boy from humble means.' But it was always accepted in the football world that he was a gypsy.

The rumours might have been widely accepted but that did not make them true. Without putting Sir Alf's DNA through some Hitlerian biological racial profile, it is of course impossible to be certain about his ethnic origins. Indeed, the whole question could be dismissed as a distasteful irrelevance were it not for the fact that the charge of being a gypsy seems to have played some part both in Alf's desire to escape his background and in the whispers against him within the football establishment. Again, Nigel Clarke believes that the issue may have influenced some snobbish elements in the FA against him: 'Alf had a terrible relationship with Professor Sir Harold Thompson. An Oxford don like that could not stand being lectured by an old Romany like Alf. That's when he began to move to get his power back and remove Alf's influence.'

Yet it is likely that much of the talk about Alf's gypsy connections has been wildly exaggerated, even invented, while the eagerness to turn a childhood nickname into a badge of racial identity seems to have been based on a fundamental error. According to those who actually lived near him, Alf was called 'Darkie' simply because of the colour of his thick, glossy black hair. In the 1920s in the south of England, 'Darkie' was a common moniker for boys with that hair type. 'The Ramseys were definitely not of gypsy stock,' says Alf's former neighbour Pauline Gosling. 'That is where that TV documentary got it wrong. I used to call him 'Uncle Darkie'. Alf got his nickname at school, only because he had very dark hair as a young child. It was nothing at all to do with being a gypsy. I know that for a fact.' Jean Bixby is of the same view: 'His brother Cyril and I worked in the office at Fords and he was a quiet, decent chap. I have heard it said that Alf was a gipsy, but to know Cyril, I could not believe it. Cyril did not seem to be from gypsy stock at all.' Nor did the family's ownership and farming of the same plot of land in Dagenham for several generations match the usual pattern for travelling people moving from one area to another. In fact, some of the land used for the building of the Becontree Estate around Halbutt Street had originally been owned by Alf's grandfather and was sold to the council. As Stan Clements, who played with Alf at Southampton in the 1940s, argues. 'I never thought Alf was a gypsy. I cannot see that at all. When I first met him, his entire appearance was immaculate. And gypsies don't own land for generations.' Alf's widow denied that he was gypsy. 'That wasn't true. I don't know where that came from,' Lady Victoria has told friends. And Alf himself, when asked about his origins in a BBC interview, snapped, 'I come from good stock. I have nothing to be ashamed of.'

Yet, despite this protestation, there always lurked within Alf a sense of distaste about his Dagenham upbringing. He went out of his way to avoid the subject and seemed to resent any mention of it. Terry Venables, who also grew up in Dagenham and later was one of Alf's successors as England manager, experienced this when he was selected for the national side in 1964, as he recalled in his book *Football Heroes*:

> When Alf called me into the England set-up, my dad said to me, 'Tell him I used to work with Sid down the docks. He was Alf's neighbour and he'll remember him.' It sounded reasonable at the time. Now picture the scene when I turned up for my first senior England squad get-together. For a start, I was in genuine awe of Alf, who came over and shook my hand. 'How are you?' he asked. 'Fine, thank you very much,' I replied. 'By the way, my dad says do you remember Sid? He was your next-door neighbour in Dagenham.' Had I cracked Alf over the head with a baseball bat he could not have looked more gob-smacked. He stared at me for what seemed like a long, long time. He didn't utter a single word of reply; he simply came out with a sound which if translated into words would have probably read something like, 'you must be joking'. He must have seen I was embarrassed by this but he certainly did not make it easy for me.

Ted Phillips, the Ipswich striker of Alf's era, recalls a similar incident when travelling with Alf through London:

> We were on the underground, going to catch a train to an away game. And this bloke came up to Alf:
> 'Allo boysie, how you getting on?' He was a real ole cockney. Alf completely ignored him, and the bloke looked a bit offended.
> 'I went to bloody school with you. Still on the greyhounds, are ya?' Alf still said nothing.
> When we arrived at Paddington, we got off the tube and were walking through the station when I said to Alf:
> 'So who was that then?'

And he replied in that voice of his, 'I have never seen him before in my life.'

It was the change in Alf's voice that most graphically reflected his journey away from Dagenham. Terry Venables, like several other footballers from the same area, including Jimmy Greaves and Bobby Moore, always retained the accent of his youth. But Alf dropped his, developing in its place a kind of strangulated parody of a minor public-school housemaster. The new intonation was never convincing, partly because Alf was a shy man, who was without natural articulacy and could be painfully self-conscious in public, and partly because his limited education meant that he lacked a wide vocabulary and a mastery of syntax. Hugh McIlvanney says:

Alf made it hard for some of us to like him because of the shame he seemed to feel about his background. We all understand there can be pressures in those areas but the voice was nothing short of ludicrous. There were some words he could not pronounce and the grammar kept going for a walk. That could be a problem for any human being but, for Alf, it almost became a caricature.

In his gauche attempts to sound authoritative, particularly in front of the cameras or the microphone, Alf would become stilted and awkward, littering statements with platitudes and empty qualifying sub-clauses. One extreme example of this occurred when he was being interviewed on BBC Radio in the early sixties:

'Are you parents still alive, Mr Ramsey?'

'Oh, yes.'

'Where do they live?'

'In Dagenham, I believe.'

In his 1970 biography, when Ramsey was still England manager, Max Marquis gave a vivid description of Alf's style. Describing his language as 'obscure and tautological', Marquis said that Ramsey

> is unable to communicate with any precision what he means because he will never use a single-syllable word when an inappropriate two-syllable word will do and he dots his phrases with some strange, meaningless interjections . . . His tangled prose, allied with his capacity for self-persuasion, has made for some of his quite baffling pronouncements. In public he lets words go reluctantly through a tightly controlled mouth: his eyes move uneasily.

Because Ramsey never felt in command of his language, he could vary wildly between triteness and controversy. He could be absurdly unemotional, as when Ipswich won the League title in 1962, perhaps the most astonishing and romantic feat in the history of English club football.

'How do you feel, Mr Ramsey?' said a breathless BBC reporter, having described him as 'the architect of this miracle'.

'I feel fine,' replied Ramsey, as if he had done nothing more than pour himself a cup of tea.

Yet this was also the man who created a rod for his own back through a series of inflammatory statements, like his notorious description of the 1966 Argentinian team as 'animals' or his claim in 1970 that English football had 'nothing to learn' from the Brazilians. As Max Marquis put it, 'Ramsey is like a bad gunner who shoots over or short of the target.'

A serious-minded youth, always striving for some kind of respectability, Alf did not have as strong a working-class accent as some of his contemporaries. Nevertheless, his speech could not help but be influenced by his surroundings.

'Dagenham had its own special brogue, and Alf spoke with that,' says Phil Cairns, 'It was a sort of bastardized cockney. He certainly had that accent as a child. I did notice how his voice changed when he got on in life. It was so obvious. When he had a long conversation, you would hear that he made faux pas.' Eddie Baily, who was Alf's closest friend at Spurs, told me of the difference he saw in Alf once he had gone into management with Ipswich Town:

> He was cockney to me but I noticed his voice changed after he left Tottenham. When I saw him after that, his voice was refined. I would say to him, 'What are you doing? Where did all this come from? You're speaking very well, my old soldier.' He would just laugh at that. I could always have a go at him. But I think the position that he took made him want to be a little bit better when he had to do negotiations and all that.

It has always been alleged that this distinct change in Alf Ramsey's voice was as a result of his taking elocution lessons in the mid-fifties. Indeed, the idea of Alf's elocution lessons has become more than just part of football folklore: it is now treated as a fact. Both Ramsey's previous biographers, Max Marquis and Dave Bowler, state without any reservation that he underwent such instruction. The late John Eastwood, who wrote a massively authoritative history of Ipswich football, reported that 'it was well known that Alf took himself off for the two-hour elocution lessons to a woman at the ballroom dancing school near Barrack Corner in Ipswich'. Another, far less believable, version has been put forward by Rodney Marsh, the charismatic striker of the seventies and later Sky TV presenter, who has claimed that Ramsey took 'elocution lessons, paid for by the FA, around the time of the World Cup in 1966'. Anyone who knew about either the parsimony of the FA or Alf's contempt for the Association's councillors would know that this assertion was nonsense.

Yet the absurdity of Marsh's statement only exposes the weakness of the conventional wisdom that Alf underwent elocution training. The fact is that ever since his youth, Alf was on a mission to improve himself – and a key element of that was to change his speaking voice, adopting the received pronunciation he heard from BBC broadcasters on the wireless, from officers in the army and from directors at League clubs. There was nothing reprehensible about this. Before the mid-sixties, working-class boys of ambition were encouraged to believe that retaining their accents could be a barrier to progress in their careers. Edward Heath, the son of a Broadstairs carpenter, adopted the elevated tones of Oxford before embarking on his rise to the top of the Conservative party.

With Alf there was no sudden dramatic switch in his voice from 'Cor Blimey' Dagenham to his imitation of the plummy vowels of the establishment; rather it was a gradual process, beginning in his teenage years and climaxing when he became manager of Ipswich. Over a long period his accent, never the strongest, grew milder until it was subsumed within his precise, artificial style of speech. From his earliest years as a professional footballer in the 1940s, Alf was seeking to improve himself in manner and appearance.

Stan Clements, who was training to become a civil engineer when he knew Alf at Southampton and was therefore more socially perceptive than most footballers of the time, says:

I always thought all those stories about his having elocution lessons were a load of old codswallop. His voice had a slight accent but it was controlled. It was not cockney but Essex. I would have said that when he was in the army and became a sergeant – and in those days there was a big difference in class between non-commissioned staff and the officers – he would have got to know the officers and there is no doubt that this influenced his speech.

Other Southampton contemporaries of the 1940s back up Clements. Pat Millward, whose husband Doug played for the Saints and then under Alf at Ipswich, recalls: 'Alf always spoke very nicely, even at Southampton. He did not use slang much, unlike the others. I'm sure he never had elocution lessons.' Eric Day, who played up front for the Saints, agrees: 'He was so taciturn, self-effacing. He always spoke in that very clipped sort of way. He thought his words out before he spoke them.' Mary Bates, who worked at the Southampton FC office during Alf's time, makes this interesting point: 'Even during his time at Southampton, his voice changed, not noticeably at first but certainly there was a difference. If I look back from 1949 to 1945, there was a marked change.'

The same story can be told when he went to Tottenham Hotspur, where again he was no loud-mouth shouting the odds in a broad vernacular. 'He sounded as if he came from the country. He spoke very slowly with a rural twinge in his accent, a sort of country brogue. It was the same as you would find in people from Norwich, a burr,' remembers Denis Uphill. Equally revealing is the memory of Ed Speight, who himself was born in Dagenham and joined Tottenham in 1954: 'He was a gentleman. He always spoke very quietly; rarely did I hear him swear. When he spoke, the top lip did not move. It was all from the lower mouth. Very clipped, staccato stuff.' Tony Marchi, who was another young player at Spurs in the early fifties, goes so far as to say that, in his memory, 'Alf had much the same voice when he was at Spurs as when he became England manager. It never really altered.'

The reality was that, by the early fifties, Ramsey was already beginning to demonstrate those concise, somewhat convoluted tones which were to become so much a part of his public character. Through listening to the radio and reading improving texts, he sought to acquire a more refined voice. In 1952, when he was still at Spurs, he had written about his lifestyle in *Talking Football*:

> In the evening I usually have a long read for, like Billy Wright, I have found that serious reading has helped me develop a command of words so essential when you suddenly find yourself called upon to make a speech. People, remember, are inclined to forget that speechmaking may not be your strong point. With this in mind, I always try hard to put up some sort of show when asked to say a few words.

Even the keenest advocate of the Victorian philosophy of self-help could not have put it better. And by the time he reached Ipswich in 1955, his voice only required a more few coats of varnish, not an entire rebuild. It seems likely that the varnish was provided, not by elocution lessons, but by more self-improvement allied to his connection to the most aristocratic boardroom in the country, whose number included a baronet and a nephew of the Tory Prime Minister.

Though some did not believe him, Alf was always adamant that he had not undergone any course in elocution. He stated in that *Mirror* article of 1970:

> I must emphasize that I am not a cockney. I make the point because I have been accused of taking elocution lessons. And told that it is to my credit that I had taken them. The truth is that I have not had elocution lessons. I wish I had. They might have been a help to me. All this business,

however, is not important to me. I've nothing to be ashamed of. I'm proud of my family, my parents and of all that has happened to me in my life.

As Alf indirectly admitted there, if he had really taken such lessons, it is improbable that he would have found communication so difficult. Nigel Clarke says:

I once pulled his leg about the rumour of his so-called elocution lessons, and he bristled and said, 'That is absolutely not true.' He then explained that he used to listen to the BBC radio announcers and modulated his tones to match theirs. I am sure that is true. I mean Alf would not even have known what the word elocution meant.

# TWO

## *The Dell*

A local government study of Dagenham in 1938 described the local population thus:

> Many are rough diamonds, but still diamonds. There is a general readiness to help each other when in trouble, a readiness to support various causes (but only after protracted and heated argument), an appreciation of good music, the usual fondness for Picture Palaces and an undue attachment to the Dance hall.

Eighteen-year-old Alf Ramsey could not easily have been described as a Dagenham 'rough diamond'. He showed no interest in dancing, was shy with women despite his dark good looks, had few musical tastes and avoided arguments except when they involved football. He had, however, developed an enthusiasm for the movies, one that was to stay with him all his life and would cause much amusement to the players under his management. He saw his first film when he was fourteen, a jungle adventure with Amercian B-movie star Jack Holt in the leading role. Alf soon had acquired a particular fondness for westerns, which so often revolved around the theme of a tight-lipped heroic outsider triumphing over the natives, the bad guys or the corrupt authorities.

But his first love remained football. During the 1937–38 season, he was playing better than ever at centre-half with Five Elms United, as he recorded himself: 'Since leaving school I had developed into quite a hefty lad, and in my heart I knew I had improved my football.' His exploits in the Five Elms defence brought him to the attention of Portsmouth, one of the country's senior League clubs. He and two other Five Elms players were approached by experienced scout Ned Liddell, who was for a time manager of Brentford, and asked if they might be interested in signing for Portsmouth as amateurs. Before this, claimed Alf, the thought of becoming a League player 'had never entered my mind. After all, I was too modest to think I was anything much as a footballer. I just played the game for fun and the exercise that went with it.'

For a young man obsessed with the game, the chance to play at the highest level was a glittering prospect. But he hesitated for a moment. Apart from some natural uncertainty about his ability, Alf was also worried about the financial insecurity of life in League football. After all, hundreds of youths were taken on every year by the 88 League clubs but very few of them made a decent living. Alf already had a secure job in the Co-op store in Oxlow Lane near his home; by 1938 he had graduated from delivery boy to counter hand and bill collector, the latter a role which required a certain amount of toughness. 'Going out to collect the bills occupied Monday morning as far as I was concerned. There were no embarrassing moments when collecting money. People either paid or they didn't, but in the main they paid.'

But when Alf met Ned Liddell again, he was assured that there would be no problem about keeping his Co-op job if he signed as an amateur. Moreover, Alf's family were not opposed to the idea. 'Well, son, it's up to you,' said his mother. So Alf, now relishing the thought of joining a top club, filled in the forms and sent them off to Fratton Park, Portsmouth's ground. He waited eagerly for a reply. None came: not a letter, a card, a telegram, a word from Ned Liddell. The weeks passed in silence until Alf gave up hope. 'No one, it seemed, was interested in young Ramsey of Dagenham,' he wrote later.

Portsmouth's gross discourtesy was a seminal experience for Alf. It left him with a profound distrust of the men running football, the club directors and officials who treated players with such haughty contempt and undermined careers with barely a thought. He came to share the view of Harry Storer, the hard-nosed Derby County manager who once questioned the right of a certain director to be an FA selector. Having been told that this director had been watching the game for 50 years, Storer replied: 'We've got a corner flag at the Baseball Ground. It's been there for 50 years and still knows nothing about the game.' As Stanley Matthews, who suffered from the administrators' arrogance as much as anyone, ruefully commented: 'Players were treated as second-class citizens. Football was a skill of the working class but those who ran our game were anything but.' Portsmouth's rudeness ensured that Alf, when he became a manager, never acted in such a cavalier manner; his concern for the well-being of professionals was one of the reasons he always inspired such loyalty.

Ignored by Portsmouth, Alf carried on working at the Oxlow Lane Co-op for the next two years, playing football in the winter, cricket in the summer. Nigel Clarke recalls:

I happened to mention to him one day that my son loved cricket. The next time we met at Liverpool Street station he turned up with a bat. It was a 1938 Gunn and Moore triple-spring, marked with the initials of his club, The

General Co-operative Sports and Social Club. Alf said to me, 'Make sure he uses it well. This one made plenty of runs for me.'

He also occasionally went with his brothers to League matches at Upton Park; the first ever match he saw was West Ham against Arsenal, during which he was particularly impressed with the Gunners' deep-lying centre-forward and play-maker Alex James, 'a chunky little fellow in long shorts'.

As with millions of other Britons, the quiet routine of Alf's provincial life was shattered with the arrival of the Second World War. In June 1940, ten months after the outbreak of hostilities, Alf was called up for service in the Duke of Cornwall's Light Infantry and was despatched to a training unit in Truro. It is a reflection of the narrowness of Alf's upbringing that he looked on his first journey to Cornwall with excitement rather than trepidation. Taking 'so famous a train as the Cornish Riviera was in itself a memorable experience for me. As a matter of interest, until I travelled to Cornwall, the longest journey I had undertaken was a trip to Brighton by train,' he wrote. The thrill continued when he arrived in Truro and was billeted in a top-class hotel, which had been commandeered by the army. 'This proved another memorable moment for me. It was the first time I had ever been into a hotel! Even with us sleeping twelve to a room on straw mattresses could not end for me the awe of living in a swagger hotel.'

Throughout his life Alf frequently appeared to be a naïve, other-worldly character, oblivious to political considerations, and that was certainly true of his delight at his surroundings in Cornwall. At the very time Britain was engaged in a life-and-death struggle for its survival as a nation, Alf was writing to his parents about the joy of 'living in a luxury hotel'. Yet that set the tone for Alf's war. He was luckier than most soldiers, spending all his years of active service up to VE Day on home soil. Never did he have to endure any of the brutal theatres of conflict like North Africa, Italy or Normandy. Attached to the 6th battalion of his regiment, his duties were in home defence, 'guarding facilities, manning road blocks, and preparing against German paratroop drops,' says Roy Prince, the archivist of the Duke of Cornwall's Regimental Association. In retrospect, it was not dangerous work, though it was demanding, as Alf recalled: 'The physical training we were so frequently given added inches to my height, broadened my chest and in general I became a fitter young fellow than when I reported for duty as a grocery apprentice from Dagenham.'

Unlike so many whose lives were ruined by the genocidal conflict of the Second World War, Alf found military service almost wholly beneficial. It brought him out of his shell, and helped demonstrate his innate qualities of leadership. In 1952 he wrote:

I have since reflected that to join the Army was one of the greatest things which ever happened to me. From my, to some extent, sheltered life, I was pitchforked into the company of many older and more experienced men. I learnt, in a few weeks, more about life in general than I had picked up in years at home. The Army, in short, proved a wonderful education.

The aura of authority that Alf always possessed – which had seen him become captain of his school's team at the age of just nine – led to his promotion to the rank of Quarter-Master Sergeant in an anti-aircraft unit. Nigel Clarke has this memory of talking to Alf about his army service:

He told me that he absolutely loved it and that his greatest times of all were down on the Helford River in Cornwall. It was in the army, he said to me, that he first really learned about discipline and about being in charge of people, taking command and giving orders. He used to say, 'I have never been very good at mixing with people but you have to in the army or else you are in trouble.'

The greatest benefit of all was that it enabled Alf to play more football than he had ever done previously – and at a higher class. Within a few months of arriving in Cornwall, he had been transferred to help man the beach defences at St Austell; there he became part of the local battalion team, captaining the side and playing at either centre-half or centre-forward. He was then moved to various other camps along the south coast before reaching Barton Stacey in Hampshire in 1943, where he was fortunate to come under the benign influence of Colonel Fletcher, a football obsessive who had played for the Army. Because of the war, several League professionals were in Alf's battalion side, including Len Townsend of Brentford and Cyril Hodges of Arsenal. Impressed by such strength, Southampton invited the battalion to visit the Dell for a pre-season game on the 21 August 1943. The result was a disaster for Ramsey's men, as they were thrashed 10–3. 'The soldiers are a very useful battalion team but they had not the experience to withstand the more forceful play of the Saints,' reported the *Southern Daily Echo*. It was Alf's first experience of playing against top-flight players and he found it something of a shock. 'At centre-half I was often bewildered by the speed of thought and movement shown by the professionals we opposed.' Despite the depressing scoreline, Ramsey's men had shown some promise, for a week later they were invited back to the Dell to play against Southampton Reserves. This time

Sergeant Ramsey's side provided much more effective opposition, winning 4–1.

Ramsey's performances in these two games had aroused the interest of Southampton. More than a month later he was summoned to Colonel Fletcher's office. Initially believing that he had committed some military office, Ramsey feared he was about to be reprimanded.

'Sit down, Sergeant,' said Colonel Fletcher when Ramsey arrived in his office. Alf was at once relieved, knowing that the Colonel would hardly have been so friendly if he was about to punish him. 'I have just had a telephone call from Southampton Football Club,' continued the Colonel. 'Apparently they are short of a centre-half for their first team tomorrow and would like you to play for them. Well, Sergeant, how do you feel about the idea?'

Ever cautious and modest, Alf then muttered something about his 'lack of experience'. Colonel Fletcher had little truck with such diffidence. 'This is a big opportunity, Ramsey,' he said, looking hard at the raven-haired sergeant. 'I suppose you have at some time or another considered becoming a professional footballer.' Alf, ignoring his abortive connection with Portsmouth, claimed untruthfully that he had 'never given it a thought'. But he assured the Colonel that he was 'prepared to give it a try'. Without another word, Fletcher was back on the phone to Southampton, reporting that Sergeant Ramsey was available for the match against Luton Town at Kenilworth Road. Alf admitted that, once he left the Colonel's office, he 'did a little tap-dance with delight. Even the orderly sitting behind a small desk forgot that I was a sergeant and joined in the laughter'.

Alf was instructed to report at Southampton Central railway station the following morning before the train journey to Bedfordshire. When he turned up that Saturday morning,

9 October 1943, he was met by the elderly, bespectacled secretary-manager of Southampton, Jack Sarjantson, a figure rare in the annals of League history for both the longevity and the range of service to his club. He had been appointed a Southampton director as early as 1914, had become club chairman in 1936, then resigned during the war to act as secretary-manager, before returning to the boardroom to serve as chairman and later vice-president in the 1950s. For all his advanced years, he was also something of a ladies' man, who, in the words of the Southampton historian David Bull, 'had a way of flirting with the young wives and girlfriends at the club's social functions'.

After introducing Alf to the other Southampton players, Sarjantson then asked Alf about his expenses. According to his 1952 autobiography, Alf told his manager that his only claim was for his 'twopenny halfpenny tram fare from my billet'. In response, Sarjantson 'dived into pocket' and pulled out the exact amount. But later, in 1970, Alf gave a much more convincing version, one that reflects the flexible attitude of clubs towards expenses in the days of the maximum wage:

> I told Mr Sarjantson that since we were stationed in Southampton I did not have any expenses. He said, 'Well, if I give you thirty bob is that enough to pay for your taxi fare?' I said it was more than enough. It was the first time anyone had given me any money for playing.

Alf was equally flexible about his age. In his 1952 book he claimed that when he played against Luton, 'I had just reached the age of twenty-two'. In fact, he was only three months away from his 24th birthday.

Having sorted out Alf's expenses so generously, Sarjantson then produced a set of forms for him to sign as an amateur.

After his last experience with Portsmouth, this time Alf was only too glad to know that his signature would definitely be followed by a match. 'As the London-bound train swished through Eastleigh station, I signed for Southampton Football club,' recorded Alf. On the train up to Luton, he sat beside the Saints inside-forward Ted Bates, later to be manager at the Dell, and who, like Alf, had been a grocery delivery boy in his teens and whose wife Mary was soon to become the first female assistant secretary in League football. 'Throughout the journey, he told me what I could expect from football: the kind of teams we would be meeting and other little facts which meant a great deal to a new recruit,' wrote Alf. His first appearance for the Saints was a tight match, one that left him disappointed with his own performance, which he felt was far below the standard of the rest of the side. Ten minutes from the end, Southampton were winning 2–1, when Alf gave away a penalty. 'I remember tackling someone rather hard,' he said in 1970. Luton scored from the spot and Alf sensed that 'several of my colleagues were giving me black looks'. Fortunately Don Roper restored the lead for Southampton soon afterwards, so Alf's first outing resulted in victory. And he had perhaps been too hard on himself: the view of the *Southern Daily Echo* was that 'the defence as a whole functioned satisfactorily'.

They did far worse in their next game, when Southampton were beaten 7–1 by Queen's Park Rangers in the League South, the makeshift wartime replacement for the Football League. 'Ramsey at centre-half rarely countered the combined skill of the opposing centre-forwards,' said the local press. But Sarjantson, with stretched wartime resources, did not drop the faltering defender immediately. Alf played three more League South games in that 1943–44 season before being posted with his battalion to County Durham. Despite his mixed fortunes, he had enjoyed his brief spell with the club. 'What fascinated me was meeting the players, sitting with them, having lunch on the train, talking football. All very interesting. It left a great impression on me, and probably started my ambition to become a professional footballer,' he wrote in 1970.

Yet Alf, with such limited experience, was still plagued by lack of belief in his own ability and worries about finance. It is striking that when he was stationed in Durham, he played little senior competitive football. He turned out for his battalion in one match at Roker Park against Sunderland, but failed to do enough to persuade Sunderland's manager, Bill Murray, to invite him to play in any wartime games, even though the relaxed registration rules of the period allowed a soldier to guest for almost any club he wanted – one reason why the garrison town of Aldershot was packed with star servicemen like Tommy Lawton. And when Alf was posted back to Southampton at the beginning of the 1944–45 season and performed well in a trial match, he once more hesitated about becoming a professional after Sarjantson had offered him a contract with Southampton, earning £2 per match. Alf was never one to make swift decisions. He told Sarjantson, with a touch of boldness that masked his inner doubts: 'Although I've played in professional football as an amateur, I know practically nothing about it. And what if I don't like the club?' Sarjantson replied that if Alf wanted to leave the club at the end of the season, Southampton would not stand in his way. Having received that assurance, Alf agreed to sign. He was finally a professional footballer

Just before the start of the 1944–45 season, Alf picked up an injury, playing for his battalion against – ironically – Southampton. It was therefore not until Christmas that he had his first game as a professional. And it could have hardly been a bigger fixture, as Arsenal took on Southampton at White

Hart Lane, Highbury having been badly bombed. Facing the legendary centre-forward Ted Drake, Alf had the best game of his career to date. He admitted he was a 'little overawed' at the start, but, according to the *Southern Daily Echo*, 'Ramsey, stocky and perhaps an inch shorter than Drake, did much that pleased, although the Arsenal leader scored two goals.' Ramsey, for the first time, had proved that he could make it at the highest level; his confidence soared as a result. And it went up even further when, as a result of injuries to other players, he was switched from centre-half to inside-left. When Southampton beat Luton 12–3 in March 1945, the second highest score in the club's history, Alf scored four times, with the *Echo* commenting that 'he can certainly hammer a ball'.

Altogether Alf made 11 League South appearances that season. At its close, Sarjantson asked him to sign again for the club. Alf agreed to do so, but 1945–46 turned out to be a frustrating season, as he made little real advance on the previous year. He played just 13 of the 42 League South matches, and was frequently asked to play up front as centre-forward, not his favourite position because of his lack of speed. 'I was nothing else than a stop-gap and was happier playing at centre-half.' But his natural football ability shone through wherever he played, in the front line or in defence. He scored a hat-trick in a 6–2 win over Newport and was lethal in two successive games against Plymouth. The writer and Southampton fan Bob Holley has left this account of Ramsey as a dashing striker, scoring twice in a 5–5 draw at the Dell in August 1945, delighting Saints fans in the painful aftermath of the war:

It is difficult now to picture how drab everything was in the summer of 1945, the bombsites, the shortages, clothes 'on points' and food rationing still in force, and how deprived we all felt of professional sport. Small wonder that, in the first post-war season, so many fans crammed through the turnstiles each Saturday despite the fact that there were only two makeshift Leagues – the pre-war First and Second Division clubs divided geographically, north and south.

Turning to the game against Plymouth, he wrote that it

left us breathless and excited and not particularly bothered that we had dropped a point. Their centre-forward scored a hat-trick. Our centre-forward, however, had bagged two. He was a tearaway sort of player, shirt sleeves flapping, hair all over the place, not particularly skilful as I remember but able to 'put himself about' as centre-forwards were expected to do in those days. His name? Ramsey, Alf Ramsey – or 'Ramsay' as the programme for this game, and indeed many thereafter incorrectly put it.

The biggest cause of frustration, however, was not programme misspellings or positional changes, but the fact that in December 1945, when most of Britain was trying to return to peacetime normality, Sergeant Ramsey was shipped off to Palestine by the War Office. He was there for six months, and once again his gift for football leadership quickly emerged, as he was asked to captain a Palestine Services XI, a team which contained such distinguished players as Arthur Rowley, who scored more goals in League football than any other player, and Jimmy Mason, the brilliant Scottish inside-right. On his return home in June 1946, Alf found a letter from the new Southampton manager, Bill Dodgin, the former Saints captain who had taken over from Sarjantson at the end of the war. Dodgin told Ramsey that he wanted to meet to discuss the terms of a new contact. At the same time, the Dagenham Co-op were offering Alf a return to his old job behind the counter. It may now seem absurd that Alf could have even been tempted by this latter offer, yet, as he admitted himself, a sense of vulnerability ran through his blood. 'What folk forget to mention,' he told his mother, 'are the failures. Football is not as easy as some would have you think. Anyway, I'm not convinced that I am good enough to earn my living at the game.'

Alf agreed to meet Dodgin in a sandwich bar at Waterloo, just the sort of mundane venue with which he was most comfortable throughout his life. Dodgin told Ramsey that they were prepared to pay him the weekly sum of £4 in the summer, £6 in the season, and £7 if he got into the League. With his characteristic mix of self-confidence and wariness, Alf told the Southampton manager that the offer was not good enough. 'I wanted to start a career in football – but not on £4 a week,' he explained later. It is a measure of Alf's importance to the club that his strategy worked. He was invited down to the Dell and offered enhanced terms: £6 in the summer, £7 in winter and £8 if he got into the League side. This time he accepted.

But immediately after he signed, his concerns about money again came to the surface. Because in the summer of 1946 he was still officially in the armed forces, awaiting demobilization, Alf did not receive the £10 signing-on fee to which professionals would normally be entitled in peacetime. In his 1952 book, *Talking Football*, Alf claimed, 'That did not matter.' The reality was very different. Alf was actually furious at missing out on his £10. Mary Bates, who had taken up her position as Southampton's Assistant Secretary in August 1945 after working for the Labour Party in Clement Attlee's landslide general election victory, has this recollection:

£10 was quite a lot at that time. And this day he came to sign as a professional. When he arrived in the office he was in his infantry gear.

'What are you doing in your uniform?'

'I haven't quite left the army yet.'

'Well, until you do, I can't pay your signing on fee. You'll have to wait until you're demobbed before I can officially sign you on. Those are my instructions.'

He nearly went beserk at those words. He was so upset. He had obviously been expecting the money. It was very unlike Alf, who was normally so calm. He was usually very nice, gentlemanly. But he did almost lose his temper on this occasion. He was usually very pleasant, but he was not very pleasant about losing his £10.

After seven years of disruption, the Football League officially resumed in August 1946. But, after all the drawn-out negotiations over Alf's contract, it was hardly a glorious return to professional football for him. Still unclear about his correct position, he began the season in the reserves. In the autumn, however, coach Bill Dodgin and trainer Syd Cann made a crucial move, one that was to completely change Alf's playing career. Sensing that Alf was uncomfortable at both centre-forward and centre-half, they suggested that he moved to right-back. It was exactly the right place for Alf, one that exploited his ability to read the game, to judge the correct moment for intervention and to make the telling pass.

Though he had been a fine footballer in his youth, he had never been blessed with the sort of exceptional natural talent which defines true greatness. After all, he had never fulfilled his ambition to play for London Schoolboys; nor had any League club shown any serious interest in him before the war; and his performances with Southampton since 1943 had been inconsistent. His prowess on the field had lain more in his mental strengths: his coolness under pressure, the respect from other players and his gift of anticipation. Now, with a characteristic spirit of determination, Alf set about moulding himself for his new role at full-back. He sought to improve his technique with long hours of practice on the training ground, working particularly on the accuracy and power of his kicks. He raised his fitness levels, not just by training in the gym, but also by taking long walks through the Southampton countryside. Above all, he strove to develop a new tactical awareness. Fortunately for Alf, the trainer at Southampton, Syd Cann, had been a full-back with Torquay United, Manchester City and Charlton, and was therefore able to pass on the lessons of his experience through practice sessions and numerous talks over a replica-scale pitch – measuring one inch to the yard – in the dressing-room at the Dell. The master and pupil developed a close relationship, as Cann later recalled in a BBC interview:

My first memories of Alf were as a centre-forward. He played several times there in the reserves, not too successfully, and I felt that perhaps he had better qualities to play as a full-back. And after discussions with the manager Bill Dodgin, we decided to try him in this position. We spent a lot of time in discussions, Alf and I. He was a very keen student. He wanted to learn about the game from top to bottom. We had a football field painted on the floor of the dressing-room at Southampton and Alf came back regularly in the afternoons, spending hours discussing techniques and tactics. I have never known anyone with the same sort of application, with the same quickness of learning as Alf Ramsey. He would never accept anything on its face value. He had to argue about it and make up his own mind. And once he had made up his mind that this was right, it was put into his game immediately. I spent hours on the weaknesses and strengths of his play. He accepted, for instance, that he was inclined to be weak on the turn on and in recovery. So we worked on that so he became quicker in recovery. Very rarely was he caught out. He was the type of player who was a manager's dream because you could talk about a decision and he would accept it and there it was, in his game.

Ramsey's diligence soon had its reward. On 26 October 1946 Alf was selected for Southampton's Division Two game at home to Plymouth, after the regular right-back Bill Ellerington had picked up an injury. Eight years after that fruitless approach from Portsmouth, Ramsey was finally about to play League football, and he was understandably nervous. When Saturday afternoon arrived, however, he was helped by the reassuring words of his fellow full-back and Saints captain Bill Rochford: 'You're not to worry out there. That's my job. It's another of my jobs to put you right, so always look to me for any guidance.' That encouragement was very different to the ridicule often accorded to debutants. But then Rochford was very different to the cynical old pro more worried about his own place than the fortunes of the side. Uncompromising, passionate, selfless, he was hugely admired by his fellow Southampton players. 'He was the Rock of Gibraltar,' says· Eric Day. Bill Ellerington, Alf's rival for the right-back position, reflects:

Bill Rochford was my mentor. We called him Rocky. He was a good captain. It's easy to be a good captain when you're winning. But when the chips were down, Bill was great at keeping us going. He could tear you off a few strips. Once against Bradford we were winning 3–0 with only about ten minutes to go and I flicked the ball nonchalantly back to the keeper and it went out for a corner. 3–1. Then they had a free kick. 3–2. We managed to win with that score but afterwards Bill tore me to shreds for being casual. He was right.

Rochford's guidance helped Alf through his first game, as Southampton won easily. 'Steady Alf, I'm just behind you,' the captain would shout during the game. But Alf quickly recognized how deep was the gulf between the League and the type of soccer he had previously experienced. Alf wrote in *Talking Football*:

It dawned on me how little about football I know. Everybody on the field moved – and above all else thought – considerably quicker than did I. Their reactions to moves were so speedy they had completed a pass, for instance, while I was still thinking things over.

After one more game in the first team, Alf was sent back to the reserves once Bill Ellerington had recovered.

It was inevitable that Alf should find it a struggle at first to cope. The only answer was yet more practice, learning to develop a new mastery of the ball and a more sophisticated approach. Again, he was indebted to the influence of his captain Bill Rochford:

Playing alongside him made me realize that there was considerably more to defending than just punting the ball clear, as had become my custom. During a match I made a mental note of how Rocky used the ball; the manner in which he tried to find a colleague with his clearances; the confidence he always displayed when kicking the ball at varied heights and angles.

The great difficulty for Alf was that, no matter how much he improved his game, his path back to the first team was blocked by Bill Ellerington, who was one of the best full-backs in the country and would, like Alf, win England honours in that position. 'Bill was a great tackler and a terrific kicker of the ball. He could kick from one corner flag to the opposite corner, diagonally, a good one hundred yards – and that was with one of those big heavy old balls,' says Ted Ballard, another Southampton defender of the era.

Alf managed to play a few more first-team games that year but his big break game in January 1947, in rather unfortunate circumstances for Bill Ellerington. That winter was the bitterest of the 20th century. Week upon week of heavy snow hampered industry, disrupted public transport and so seriously threatened coal supplies that the Attlee government was plunged into crisis. More than two million men were put out of work because of the freeze, while severe restrictions were placed on the use of newsprint. Football, too, was in crisis. In the Arctic conditions, 140 matches had to be postponed. In the games that went ahead, the lines on the icy pitches often had to be marked in red to make them clear. Such was the public frustration at the lack of football that when Portsmouth managed to melt the snow at Fratton Park using a revolutionary steam jet, the club was rewarded with a crowd of 11,500 for a reserve fixture.

The freeze also had a direct effect on Alf's career. Towards the end of January, Southampton went to the north-east resort of Whitley Bay, in preparation for a third-round FA Cup tie against Newcastle. Alf, as so often at this time, was a travelling reserve. One afternoon, the senior players went out golfing. In the cold weather, most of them wore thick polo-neck jerseys – except Bill Ellerington, who braved the course in an open-neck pullover. That night 'Big Ellie' felt terrible; he woke up the next morning wringing wet. He was rushed to hospital, where he was quickly diagnosed to be suffering from pneumonia. 'I completely collapsed and ended up in hospital for three months. I did not come out until April,' says Ellerington. One man's tragedy is another's opportunity. Alf was drafted into the side against Newcastle, and he showed more confidence than he had previously displayed, though he was troubled by Newcastle's left-winger, Tommy Pearson, as the Saints lost 3–1 in front of a crowd of 55,800, by far the largest Alf had ever experienced.

With Ellerington incapacitated, Alf was guaranteed a good run in the side, and he kept his place for the rest of the season, growing ever more assured with each game. In February 1947 the *Daily Mirror* predicted that 'only a few weeks after entering the big time, Alfred Ramsey is being talked of as one of the coming men of football'. The paper went on to quote coach Bill Dodgin, who paid tribute to Alf's dedication: 'You can't better that type of player. The player who thinks football, talks football and lives football is the man who makes good.'

One particularly important match for Alf took place at the Dell in April against Manchester City, when he had the chance to witness at first hand City's veteran international full-back Sam Barkas, who, at the age of 38, was playing his last season. Ramsey was immediately captivated by the skills of Barkas and decided to make him his role model. 'It was the most skilful display by any full-back I had seen,' he told the *Evening News* in 1953. 'The brilliance of Barkas' positional play, his habit of making the other fellow play how he wanted him to play, all caught my eye. What impressed me most of all was Sam Barkas' astute use of the ball. Every time he cleared his lines he found an unmarked colleague,' he wrote later.

Exactly the same attributes were to feature in Ramsey's play over the next eight years; one of Alf's greatest virtues was his ability to absorb the lessons of any experience. In his quest for perfection, he was constantly watching and learning, experimenting and practising. As Ted Bates put it in an interview in 1970:

Alf was very single-minded. He would come to the ground for training and he wanted to get on with it – no messing about. I believe he was a bit immature then but you could not dispute his single-mindedness. He sole interest was in developing his own game. He was the original self-educated player – all credit to him for that. But he always had this polish – it is the only word – and it made him stand out in any team.

Alf's soccer intelligence, allied to a phenomenal dedication to his craft and an unruffled temperament, made him a far more effective player than his innate talent warranted. Eric Day says:

He had a very, very good football brain. If he hadn't, he would not have played where he did, because he was not the most nimble of players. Not particularly brilliant in the air, because he did not have the stature to jump up. But he was a decent tackler and a great passer. He could read the game so well, that was his big asset. That was why he became such a great manager.

Ted Ballard has the same assessment:

He was a great player, a super player. He was a quiet man, very strict on himself, very sober and trained hard. The only thing he lacked was pace; he could be a bit slow on the turn because he was built so heavily round the hip. But he made up for it with the way he read the game so well.

Stan Clements, who played at centre-half and was himself a shrewd judge of the game, told me:

He was two-footed. You would not have known the difference between one foot and the other. He was a tremendously accurate passer. When he kicked the ball, it went right to the other player's foot. All the forwards in front of him always said that when Alf gave them the ball, it was easy to collect. They liked that because they could pick it up in their stride. His judgement of distance, his sense of timing was just right. The point about Alf was that he was so cool. One of the remarkable things about him was that at free-kicks and corners, when the goalmouth was crowded, he seemed to have the ability almost to be a second keeper on the goal-line. He seemed always to be able to read exactly what was going on. His anticipation was superb. He was always in the right position to chest the ball down and clear it. He must have saved us at least a goal every other game. He understood football better than most people. I always knew he would make a good manager, because of his ability to size up the game. Bill Dodgin and Syd Cann, the trainer, used to have this layout on the floor of our dressing-room, with counters for the players. And they would use this to analyse our tactics, especially in set-pieces. Alf was always very good at understanding all that; he would take it all on board quickly.

Alf was so dedicated that, even at the end of the 1946–47 season, when he returned to Dagenham, he carried on practising in the meadows behind his parents' cottage: 'I used to take a football every morning during those months of 1947 and spend an hour or two trying hard to "place it" at a chosen spot.' Alf knew that only by developing his accuracy would he be successful in adopting the Sam Barkas style of constructive defence. The hard work paid off, and Alf did not miss a single game during the 1947–48 season; indeed, he was the only Southampton player to appear in all 42 League fixtures. Such was the strength of Ramsey's performances that Bill Ellerington, who had gradually recovered from his illness, could not force his way back into the side, though, as he told me, that did not lead to any personal resentment:

I was working hard to get back. I am not being heroic but it was either that or packing the game in. But Alf was playing really well. He was a good reader of the game, a good player of the ball in front of him. A bit slow on the turn but he was made that way. On tackling, he knew when to go in and not to go in. And he made more good passes than most players. He was always cool. There was no personal rivalry between us. I never even dreamed about animosity or anything like that. We were just footballers. Mind you, looking back, Alf was ambitious. He was a hard lad to get to know. He was not stand-offish, but you could never get at him. He was not one of the boys. We travelled everywhere by train in those days, and I was part of a card school, but Alf did not join in. He never got in trouble, because he was not interested.

As Bill Ellerington indicates, Alf's personality did not change much once he became a successful professional. He remained undemonstrative, reserved, unwilling to mix easily. 'He would not go out of his way to talk to anybody,' recalled Ted Bates, 'but if you wanted his advice, he'd give it. When we played, early on, I roomed with him, and he was always the same, very quiet, getting on with his job.' Eric Day, the Southampton right-winger, used frequently to catch the train from South-ampton to London because his parents lived in Ilford:

> I saw him a lot but there was never much conversation. I
> am not a great talker and Alf certainly wasn't one. When-ever we chatted, it was only ever about football. He could
> be a bit short with people, though he was never rude. Alf
> didn't suffer fools gladly, I'll tell you that. He was a bit
> secretive; he just didn't chat. Maybe that's because he was
> a gypsy. Gypsies are extremely close-knit; they keep it in the
> family. You never heard him shouting, not on the field or
> in the dressing-room or on the train. If he had any strong
> feelings about anyone, he just kept them to himself. He was
> a very honest bloke. He did not like talking about people
> behind their backs. You never heard him tear anyone to
> shreds. He was very modest. There was nothing of the star
> about him.

The Southampton goalkeeper of the time, Ian Black, highlights
similar traits:

> Once he had finished training, you seldom saw him. That is
> fair enough. People are made in different ways. But it did
> not make him any the less likeable. I think he had quite
> a shy nature; he was friendly enough but he did not like
> much involvement with others. Though he would talk plenty
> about the game, he was not much of a conversationalist
> otherwise.

Throughout his time at Southampton, Ramsey lived in digs
owned by the club, which he shared with Alf Freeman, one
of the Saints' forwards. The two Alfs had served together in
the Duke of Cornwall's Regiment, though Freeman had seen

action in France and Germany in 1944–45. Now in his mid-eighties and with his powers of communication in decline, Freeman still retains fond memories of living with Alf:

We had good times together in the army. We were pretty close then. In our Southampton digs, we were looked after well by our landlady. Alf was a lovely man but he was very, very quiet. He was shy and never talked much. Unlike most of us players, he did not smoke or drink much. He always dressed smartly. He liked the cinema, and also did a lot of reading, mainly detective stories.

The late Joe Mallet, who was one of Southampton's forwards, told Alf's previous biographer in a powerfully worded statement that Ramsey and Freeman had fallen out:

They were close but they had a disagreement and though they lived together Alf would never speak to Freeman. If you got on the wrong side of Alf, that was it, you were out! You couldn't talk him around; he would be very adamant. If he didn't like somebody or something, he didn't like them. There were no half measures! He was a man you could get so far with, so close to, and then there was a gap, he'd draw the curtain and you had to stop. I don't think he liked any intrusion into his private life. Alf wouldn't tolerate anything like that. He'd be abusive rather than put up with it.

But today Freeman has no recollection of any such dispute: 'There was never any trouble between us. I don't know where Joe Mallet got that stuff about a disagreement. That just wasn't true. I always got on well with Alf. He was a good man to me. I liked him very much.'

Pat Millward came to know Ramsey better than most

through Alf's friendship with her husband Doug, who played for both the Saints and Ipswich. Though she recognizes that Alf's diffidence could come across as offensive, she personally was a great admirer:

People used to think that Alf was difficult because he did not have a lot to say. He would just answer a question and then walk away. A lot of people did not like him. They thought he was too quiet, too pleased with himself. 'He fancies himself, doesn't he? Who does he think he is?' they would say, without really knowing him. But I loved him. He was just the opposite of what some people thought. He was down-to-earth, never bragged, never put on airs, never went for the cheers. And he was such a gentleman, always polite and well-mannered. I remember I was working in the restaurant of a department store in Southampton, and the store had laid on an event for the players, where they were all to receive wallets, and their wives handbags. The gifts were set out on two stands and the players could take their choice. Alf was among the first to arrive. But he held back until all the rest of them had taken what they wanted.

'Shouldn't you get your wallet?' I asked.

'No, Pat, it's fine. Let the others get theirs.'

He was a special man. Doug thought the world of him. He was never a joker, but if he liked you, he showed it. On the other hand, if he didn't like you, he had a way of ignoring you.

Revelling in professional success, Alf was more fixated with soccer than ever. But he still enjoyed some of the other pursuits of his youth, like greyhound racing and cricket. Bill Ellerington recalls:

We would often go to the dog track near the Dell on Wednesday evenings and Alf would come with us. Looking back, he was a very good gambler. There would be six races, six dogs each, and Alf would just go for one dog. Whatever the result, win or lose, he finished. He was not like most of the boys, chasing their money. He was very shrewd. At the time, I just accepted it, but looking back, it showed how clever he was. I always felt there was a bit of the gambler about him, even when he was England manager in the 1966 World Cup. He had this tremendous, quiet self-confidence about him.

Stan Clements also remembers Alf's enthusiasm for the dogs, but feels that Alf's lack of social skills has been exaggerated:

Alf was a nice fella once you knew him, easy to get on with. He had worked for the Co-op and was good with figures. His family were involved in racing greyhounds, in fact some of them used to live on that, so he knew about gambling. At that time in the late 1940s, dog-racing was extremely popular; it was a cheap form of entertainment for the working-class. Alf would usually go to the dogs on a Wednesday with Alf Freeman. He was also good on the horses. He was very quick at working out the odds. He was not tight with his money, or anything like that. He was quite prepared to open his wallet. He was a cool gambler; you never saw him get excited. He would put his bets on in a controlled manner. He would assess the situation. He could lose without it affecting him. In everything he did, he was never over-the-top. He always had control of himself. He enjoyed a drink, but he was not a six pints man.

Speedway racing was another interest of Alf's and he would regularly visit the local track at Bannister Court near the Dell.

He became good friends with the local racer Alf Kaines, and he persuaded Southampton FC to allow Kaines to join the players sometimes for physical training during the week. Stan Clements also remembers that Alf displayed an innate sense of co-ordination in every sport:

He was the sort of individual who was always good with the round ball. Some of us began to play golf. We had a little competition and the one who made the lowest score got a set of clubs. And who won? Alf, of course. When we were playing snooker, he was very controlled, so he did not miss many shots. The same was true of his cricket. We were once playing a match in Portsmouth and the opposition had a couple of good bowlers who were attached to Sussex. Our team was put together at the last minute, just from those who wanted to play – and Alf was not one of them. But all of us went down to the match, some of us, like Alf, just as spectators. Soon the opposition were running through us like anything. Then Alf Freeman told us that Alf had been a good cricketer in the army, so he suggested that Alf go in. Alf was a bit reluctant, as he was wearing a navy blue suit at the time. But we persuaded him to don his pads over his dark trousers. So he went out to bat like that. And immediately he stopped the rot, scoring a half century. It was not wild stuff, but controlled, sensible hitting. Nothing silly but he played all the shots.

A couple of beers, a day at the cricket, a night at the dog track, these were the main forms of entertainment for the footballers of the late 1940s, just as they were for most of the working class. In contrast to the multi-millionaires of today's Premiership, most professionals then remained close to the ordinary public in terms of earnings and lifestyle. None of the Southampton players, including Alf, owned a car, while most of them lived in rented accommodation. Almost all their travel was undertaken by rail and if they had to change trains in London, they took the tube, with their kit following in a taxi. Their official wages were not that far divorced from those of clerical staff. The average pay in the League in 1948 was just £8 a week and the maximum wage was set at £12, despite the fact that the clubs and the FA were enjoying record-breaking attendances. That year, 99,500 people paid £391,000 to see England play Scotland at Wembley, yet the 22 players involved received just £20 each, their payments amounting to little more than 1 per cent of the total gate. Even worse, they were punitively taxed on their earnings by the Labour government, so they actually received only £11 in their pockets. Looking back, former Saints winger Eric Day comments:

It was not a very glamorous life. I was paid £6 a week in the winter, £4 in the summer, £2 for a win and £1 for a draw. Plus the club charged me 30 bob a week for rent. So I did not have much left over. Certainly I could not have dreamt of having a car. But I felt I was lucky. I had been in the forces for six years, and to come out as a free man, and then to be paid for playing football was something beyond my imagination.

Goalkeeper Ian Black shares the same view about the effect of the war:

The wages were decent compared to manual work. I think footballers of my generation were more concerned about conducting themselves properly. Most of us had been in the forces, not the best times of our lives, and I suppose coming from that environment created a deep impression. Many of us just felt lucky to be playing football and did not want to spoil it.

Apart from the dismal financial rewards, the other drawback that the players of Alf's generation had to contend with was the poor equipment and facilities. The bleak, down-at-heel atmosphere of post-war Britain extended all too depressingly to football. Training kit was poor, pitches were a mud-heap – when they were not frozen – and the cumbersome boots were more fit for a spell in the trenches. The classic English soccer footwear remained the 'Mansfield Hotspur', which had first been designed in the 1920s and made a virtue of its solidity, with its reinforced toe and protection for two inches above the ankle. The two main types of ball, the Tugite and the Tomlinson T, were equally robust. Both tended to absorb mud and moisture, becoming steadily heavier and larger as a match progressed. As goalkeeper Ian Black recalls: 'There was not much smacking in the ball from a distance then. When it was wet, if you managed to reach the half-way line, it was an exceptional kick.' Bill Ellerington says:

The ball was so heavy in those days. Beckham could not have bent it on a cold, damp February night. The ball used to swell right up during a game. If you did not hit it right, you'd have thought you'd broken your ankle. If you headed the ball where the lace was, you felt you'd been scalped. You had to catch it right. Our shin pads were made of cane and the socks of wool so they got heavy in the damp. The facilities were terrible at the Dell. We had a great big plunge bath and just one or two showers. In February, when the pitches were thick with mud, the first in got the clean water. At the end, the water was like brown soup. On a cold winter's day, the steam from the bath would make the walls drip with condensation. You did not know where to put your clothes. If you had a raincoat, you would place it first on the hook so your clothes did not get wet. But you just accepted it.

But this was the environment in which Alf was now proving himself. By early 1948 he was in the middle of a run of 91 consecutive League games for Southampton, and was winning increasing acclaim from the press. After a match against West Bromwich Albion, in which he twice saved on the goal-line, he was described in the *Southern Daily Echo* as 'strong, incisive, resourceful'. The team were pushing for promotion and also enjoyed a strong FA Cup run which carried them through to the quarter-finals before they were beaten 1–0 at home by Spurs on 28 February. The *Echo* wrote of Alf's performance in this defeat:

Alf Ramsey is playing so well that he is consistently building up a reputation which should bring some soccer honour to him. He certainly impressed highly in this game and is steadily and intelligently profiting under the experienced guidance of partner and captain Bill Rochford.

Of Alf's burgeoning influence, Ian Black says:

The spirit of our side was first class and my relationship on the field with Alf was very good. He was such a great reader of the game. He always seemed to know what was going to happen next. He lacked a bit of pace but he made up for it with his wonderful positional sense. He was a first-class tackler because he had such a good sense of timing. He never went diving in recklessly. He was never a dirty player. He hated anything like that. Nothing ever seemed to ruffle him. He was always very smart, conducted himself impeccably. Unlike some players, he was never superstitious. He never caused upsets or became aggressive. He was very confident of his own ability, which is half the battle in football. Alf had a natural authority about him. His approach, his knowledge of the game would influence players. So it was no surprise to me that players responded to him when he was a manager. He was the boss; they would understand that. There was no messing about with him, even when he was a player. I don't mean that he was difficult, but he was able to impose his views and because they were often so right, he was all the more respected.

At the end of the 1947–48 season, the *Football Echo* described Alf as Southampton's 'most improved player'. Though Southampton had failed to win promotion, as they finished behind Birmingham City and Newcastle, the sterling qualities of Alf attracted the interest of the national selectors. In May, Alf received a letter from Lancaster Gate informing him that the FA were 'considering' him for the forthcoming close-season tour of Italy and Switzerland. Then a few days later, as he sat in his digs listening to the six o'clock news on the BBC Home Service, he heard to his joy that his place in the sixteen-strong party had been confirmed. Alf was rightly thrilled at this elevation; 'I could not believe my good fortune,' he wrote later, and for the first time in his life he was the focus of intense national media interest, with photographers and reporters turning up at the Dell to cover the story of the delivery boy made good. 'While his choice as the sixteenth member of the party will occasionally surprise in many quarters, Ramsey nevertheless deserves the honour. He has had only one full season in League soccer and has made such rapid progress that the selectors have watched him several times,' reported the *News Chronicle*.

He came down to earth when he reported for duty at the Great Western Hotel in Paddington, prior to England's departure for the continent. To his surprise, on his arrival at the hotel, he was completely ignored, not just by a succession of England players like Billy Wright, Tommy Lawton and Frank Swift, but also by the England management. 'For a very long time, in fact, I sat in that lounge waiting for something to happen.' Eventually he went up to the trainer, Jimmy Trotter, to introduce himself. Even then, Trotter did not recognize Ramsey and it took him a few moments before he grasped who Alf was. The humiliating experience, reflective of the shambolic way England was run before the 1960s, taught Ramsey an invaluable lesson. When he became national manager, he made sure that he personally greeted every new entrant to his team, as Alan Mullery recalls:

My first meeting was with Alf in 1964 when I turned up at the England hotel in London. It was a very nice introduction. He came straight up to me, shook my hand and said, 'Welcome to the England squad. Make yourself at home.' He did it extremely well. From the first moment, I found his man-management superb.

The next day, Alf travelled with the England party to Heathrow Airport, which had opened less than two years earlier and was still using a tent for one of its terminal buildings. It was the first time Alf had been near an airfield, never mind an aeroplane, and he was initially an anxious passenger as the 44-seat DC-4 Skymaster took off. But as the plane flew over the Alps on its way to Geneva, Alf forgot his nerves and admired the breathtaking views of the snow-capped mountains. At Geneva, the England party was transferred to a pair of DC-3 Dakotas, before flying on to Milan, whose airport was too small to accommodate the Skymaster. From Milan, the squad was then taken to the lakeside resort of Stresa, prior to their game against Italy at Turin. It was a world away from the austerity of post-war Dagenham and Southampton, and Alf found it a shock to see 'the apparently well-fed and beautifully clothed people' of northern Italy. The Italian football manager, Vittorio Pozzo, appeared to understand the severity of food-rationing in Britain, for when he greeted the England team to the Grand Hotel in Stresa, he gave every member a small sack of rice. What today might seem an offensive present was only too eagerly accepted by each player, for, as Alf put it, 'in those days rice was almost as valuable as gold'. Later in the trip, he was given a trilby hat, an alarm clock and two bottles of Vermouth as gifts, which he handed to his mother on his return to Dagenham.

Given his limited experience, Alf never expected to be in the full England team for the game at Turin. It was, thought Tom Finney, 'the best England side I played with'. And this was to be one of England's finest post-war victories, winning 4–0 thanks largely to some superb goal-keeping by Frank Swift and two goals from Finney. What interested Alf most, watching on the sidelines, was that because of the England team's fitness, their players lasted the pace much better than the Italians. It was something he would remember when it came to 1966.

The England team then travelled to Locarno, where they stayed in another luxurious hotel and enjoyed a full banquet on the evening of their arrival. Again, Alf could not help but be struck by the contrast with the drabness of life in Britain. Amidst all this splendour, Alf had another cause for celebration: he was picked to play his first representative game for his country, turning out for the B side against Switzerland. The result was an easy 5–1 win. Alf himself felt that he had 'played fairly well', while the *Southern Daily Echo* announced that he had 'pleased all the critics'. When the England squad arrived back in London, most of the players returned to their homes. But Alf Ramsey had another, far more arduous journey ahead of him. For Southampton FC had agreed to undertake a tour of Brazil at the end of the 1947–48 season, the trip having been promoted by the strong links between the City Council and the Brazilian consulate in Southampton.

The rest of the squad travelled out to Rio aboard the cruise liner *The Andes*, on which they were treated like princes. All the petty restrictions of rationing were abandoned, like the weekly allowances of just 13 ounces of meat, one and half ounces of cheese, two pints of milk and one egg. 'We had food like you never saw on the mainland. We had five- or six-course meals laid in front of us. And the training on board was pathetic, just running around the deck, so by the time we arrived we were hardly in peak condition,' says Eric Day. 'We could eat all we wanted. A lot of us put on half a stone in ten days,' remembers Ted Ballard.

Alf did not have it nearly so easy. With the Southampton tour well under way in Brazil by the time he returned from England duty, he had to fly out on a circuitous route to Rio via Lisbon, Dakar and Natal in South Africa. When he arrived at Rio, no one had arranged to meet him and, without any local currency or a word of Portuguese, he spent two hours wandering around the airport looking for assistance, before an official from the local Botafogo club – which had helped to arrange the tour – finally arranged to have him flown on to Sao Paulo, where the Southampton team was currently based. It was hardly the smoothest of introductions to Latin America, and subsequently Alf was never to feel at ease in the culture. His presence, however, was badly needed by Southampton, who had been overwhelmed by the Brazilians and had lost all four of their opening games on the tour. 'The skill of the

Brazilian players really opened our eyes. We had never seen anything like that. The way some of them played shook us,' says Ian Black. The Brazilians' equipment also appeared to be light years ahead: 'They laughed at our big boots because they had such lightweight ones, almost like slippers,' remembers Bill Ellerington.

It is a tribute to Alf's influence on the team that, almost as soon as he arrived, both the morale and the results began to pick up. 'When Alf came out there, he made a big difference. We were all down, because getting beaten on tour is no fun. Alf was great on encouragement, at getting us going. He was a terrific motivator, an amazing bloke,' argues Ted Ballard. Alf's influence lay not just on the motivational side; he also helped to devise a tactical plan to cope with the marauding Brazilian defenders, who, in contrast to the more rigid English formation, played almost like wingers. Alf felt that the spaces that they left behind, as they advanced up the field, could be exploited by playing long diagonal balls from the deep into the path of Eric Day, the outside-right. It was a version of a system he would use with dramatic effect a decade later with Ipswich.

Assisted by Alf's cool presence, Southampton won their next game 2–1 against the crack side Corinthians in Sao Paulo. But, in the face of victory, the behaviour of the crowd – and one of the Corinthian players – fed Alf's nascent xenophobia. At one stage, after a black Corinthian player had been sent off for a brutal assault on Eric Day, the crowd erupted. Fireworks were let off. Angry chanting filled the stadium. Then, as Alf later recorded, 'just when I thought things had quietened down, some wild-eyed negroes climbed over the wire fencing surrounding the pitch and things again looked dangerous'. A minor riot was only avoided by the intervention of the military police. The banquet with the Corinthians was just as awkward for Alf, as he had to sit beside the player who had been sent off. The event, said Alf in 1952, was

> among the most embarrassing I have ever attended. I tried to speak to him and in return received only a fixed glare. Even when my colleagues tried to be pleasant with him all they received for their trouble was the same glare. There was something hypnotic in the way this negro stared at us. He certainly ranks as the most unpleasant man I've ever met on or off the football field.

The Southampton team then went on to Rio, where again they won, with Alf captaining the side for the first time when Bill Rochford was rested. They were installed in the Luxor hotel overlooking Copacabana beach, but their stringent training regime prevented them enjoying too much of the local life. 'Brazil had the most beautiful women I have ever seen in my life,' says Bill Ellerington. 'They used to parade up and down the beach, though they always had one or two elderly women with them. And by the time we finished playing and training, we were too tired to think about anything like that.' The last two games of the tour ended in a draw and a defeat, before the players took the plane, rather than the boat, back to Southampton.

The tour had been a revelation for Alf. On one hand it had enhanced his footballing vision, encouraging him to think in a far more original way about tactics and his own role. He now saw, he wrote, that 'a defender's job was also to make goals as well as stopping them'. But on the other it had given him a negative opinion of Latin American crowds, administration and the press. He was astounded, for instance, when walking on to the pitch for the match at Sao Paulo that 'radio commentators, dragging microphones on to the field, rushed up to us and demanded – yes, demanded! – our views'. It was the start of a not very beautiful relationship with the world's media.

# THREE

# *White Hart Lane*

At the start of the 1948–49 season, Alf Ramsey's progress seemed assured. He was a key member of the Southampton side, sometime captain, and an England B international. His growing confidence was reflected when he was called up for another representative game, on this occasion playing for English Football League XI against an Irish League XI at Anfield in September. His room-mate in that game was another debutant, the Newcastle striker Jackie Milburn – cousin of the Charlton brothers who were to play such a central role in Alf's managerial career. Milburn was struck by the intensity of his colleague, who wanted to sit up late into the night talking tactics. 'Alf was never a great one for small talk when he was with England parties,' said Milburn later. 'Football was his one subject of conversation. He was always a pepper-and-salt man, working out moves and analysing formations with the cruet table.'

The English League XI, which won 5–1, was captained by none other than Stanley Matthews, the ascetic, dazzling Blackpool winger, who, since 1932, had been captivating spectators with his formidable powers of dribbling, swerving and acceleration. A cold, emotionally taut man, whose rigorous training regime included a weekly fast on Mondays, he was not universally loved by his professionals; many of them felt that his trickery on the wing did more to please the crowds than win games for his side. In an amazingly harsh passage about his team-mate, England captain Billy Wright wrote in 1953 that Matthews 'made most of us foam at the mouth because he held up the line and allowed opposing defenders to cover up'. He went on to attack Matthews' brand of 'slow-motion football', adding that Matthews, 'although giving joy to thousands of fans, was sometimes nothing but a pain in the neck to colleagues who waited in vain for the pass that never came.' Coming from someone who failed dismally as a soccer manager because he was 'too nice', those words of Wright's could hardly be more brutal.

Alf, however, developed a good understanding with Matthews during the English League game. And he soon had the chance to play alongside Matthews again, when in December 1948 he was called up to the full England side, after the long-serving Arsenal right-back Laurie Scott suffered a knee injury. The match took place at Highbury on 2 December and resulted in an easy 6–0 win for England over Switzerland. Alf refused to be overawed on his debut. During the match Alf made a pass to Matthews and then, to the astonishment and amusement of the rest of the English League team, shouted 'Hold it, Stanley!' at the great man, who had never been used to taking orders from anyone, least of all a young defender with only one full season behind him. The words from Alf were instinctive, lacking in any self-consciousness and were born of years of practice with the Saints' right-winger Eric Day. Yet they smacked of youthful arrogance, something compounded when Alf wrote in *Talking Football*: 'To my surprise, Stanley Matthews played football as I believed it should be played between winger and full-back. Stanley took up position perfectly to take my clearances.' To his detractors, that remark was a symbol of Ramsey's arrogance. 'It was rather like a new racing driver out for a spin with Jackie Stewart telling him to change gear at the next bend,' claimed Max Marquis, always on the lookout for anything to drag down Alf. But to Ramsey himself, he was just being realistic; he had found another player who preferred thoughtful, constructive defence rather than the meaty hump into the crowd. 'I was in a better position than Stanley to see the situation so naturally I advised him,' Alf explained to England's captain Billy Wright. Indeed, Matthews soon became an admirer of Ramsey. In an article in 1950, he praised the way Alf relied 'on positional play, interception and brainwork to beat his winger. I know which type I would rather face. The man who rushes the tackles is easier to slip than the calculating opponent who forces you to make mistakes.'

What was so impressive about Alf on his debut was his calmness, even under severe pressure. 'Ramsey looked as suave and cool as a city businessman – particularly when he headed from under the bar in the second minute,' thought the *Daily Mail*. It was a view shared by Alf's captain Billy Wright:

> I must admit I found it a little disconcerting at first to have a full-back behind me who was always as cool as an ice-soda. Ramsey's expressed aim was to play constructive football: I soon learned that nothing could disturb this footballer with the perfect balance and poise, no situation, however desperate, could force him into abandoning his immaculate style.

But then, just as Ramsey's fortunes appeared to be taking off, disaster struck. On 15 January 1949, Southampton visited Home Park to play a friendly against Plymouth, both teams having been knocked out of the FA Cup. 'One minute before half-time, I slipped on the damp turf when going into a tackle with Paddy Blatchford, the Plymouth Argyle outside left. A terrible searing pain went through my left-knee . . . the most agonizing I have ever experienced,' wrote Alf. In fact, as he was carried from the field, Ramsey feared that his professional career was over. Fortunately, an X-ray showed that he only had badly strained ligaments and should be able to play again before the end of the season.

Whether he would return to the Southampton side was another matter. For Alf's position was immediately filled to great effect by Bill Ellerington, who had waited patiently in the reserves after recovering from his bout of pneumonia, playing just 12 League games in the previous two years. Just as Alf had done in January 1947, so Bill now seized his chance, producing such solid performances at the back that he was to win two England caps before the end of the season. But Ellerington's success spelt problems for Ramsey, particularly because Southampton were pressing hard for promotion. In March 1949, while Alf was still limping badly, manager Bill Dodgin came up to him at the Dell and warned him that he was 'going to find it very hard' to regain his place in the first team. Alf was appalled at this comment, regarding it as a calculated insult. The sensitive side of his nature led him to brood obsessively about it, as he sunk into a period of mental anguish. 'The world did indeed appear a dark and unfriendly place. For one fleeting moment I seriously contemplated quitting football,' said Ramsey later.

He certainly wanted to quit Southampton, now that Bill Ellerington appeared to be the favoured son. More ambitious than ever, Alf – unlike Bill – was not content to wait months in the reserves. Despairing of his future at the Dell, Alf wrote to the club's chairman J.R. Jukes requesting a transfer. Initially Jukes tried to dissuade Alf, but to no avail. As Jukes reported to a special board meeting on 8 March, 'Ramsey was adamant in his desire to be transferred to some other club, his stated reason being that he felt he was lowering his chances of becoming an international player by being played in the reserve side'. The entire board then called Ramsey into the meeting and told him that 'it would be far more to his advantage and future reputation if he remained at the club and went up with them, as we all hoped would be the case, into the First Division'. But Ramsey would not budge and told the directors that he was 'willing to go anywhere'.

Ramsey's opinion of Bill Dodgin had plummeted during the row. He felt that the Southampton boss should have shown 'more understanding of my personal feelings'. Even if Ramsey appeared excessively touchy, his criticism of Dodgin was mirrored by a few of his colleagues at the Dell. Known to some as 'Daddy', Dodgin was a former lumbering centre-half who spent four years at the Dell as coach and manager, but, despite a strong team, failed to win promotion. He was generally liked by the players, especially for his decency and sense of humour, but some felt he lacked sufficient authority, especially on the tactical side. 'Technically, he was not a good manager,' says Eric Day. 'We did not have much in the way of team talks. I never found him good on motivating. I doubt if Alf ever learnt much from Bill. If anything, it would have been the other way round.' Ted Ballard largely agrees:

> Bill Dodgin was a decent bloke, but he wasn't perfect. His weak point was his knowledge of the game. He could not really put his views across in those vital moments, like the ten minutes before half-time. I think he suffered a bit from lack of confidence. Players like Bill Rochford were stronger than he was.

But Alf's view that Dodgin had done him a cruel injustice was not shared in the Southampton dressing-room, where there was strong admiration for Bill Ellerington. Another of the Saints' full-backs Albie Roles, who appeared briefly in the 1948–49 season, was inclined to think that Bill was the better player in comparison to Alf: 'He tackled harder. He was more direct, more decisive with his tackling. And he could hit the ball right up along the ground. He didn't have to lob it. Alf Ramsey may have been the better positional player, but Bill was a good footballer.' Joe Mallet had this analysis:

> Bill Ellerington had things that Alf didn't have and vice-versa. Bill used to clear his lines whereas Alf used to try and play the ball out of danger – which sometimes wasn't the right thing to do. Bill's all-round defensive game was better than Alf's. Alf Ramsey was always beaten by speed and by players who took the ball up to him – tricky players, quick players. But he was a brilliant user of the ball. That's how he got his name, on the usage of the ball: good passing, very good passing; but sometimes he used to take chances with short ones, in the danger area around the goal.

In fact, Mallet believed that Alf's incautious approach, allied to his lack of pace, which was a central reason why Dodgin did not fight to keep him. Just a week before Ramsey had incurred his knee injury at Plymouth, Southampton had travelled to Hillsborough for an FA Cup tie against Sheffield Wednesday. As the Saints came under fire in the first half, they reverted to using the offside trap. But according to Mallet, Ramsey wrecked this tactic through his over-reliance on captain Bill Rochford. Over the years, said Mallett, Ramsey had grown so used to the effectiveness of Rochford's sense of timing, moving forward on the left flank at just the right moment to catch any attack offside, that Alf was inclined to 'take liberties'. Even when Alf was beaten on his own right flank, he had got into the habit of shouting 'offside', because he presumed Rochford would have moved into an advanced position to thwart the opposition. In this particular match at Hillsborough, according to Mallet:

Sheffield Wednesday had an outside left who was a quick small player. Alf went up, 'Offside!' They broke away. They scored. And at half-time in the dressing-room there was a row – between Alf and Bill Rochford, who said, 'You've to keep playing the man. You've got to run. Even if you think it's offside, you've still got to go with him.' So this was the reason that Alf Ramsey took umbrage and left the club.

Alf always took offence easily, as his later tetchy relationship with the press testifies, and there can be little doubt that the row at Hillsborough contributed to his desire to go. Several clubs, amongst them Burnley, Luton and Liverpool, expressed an initial interest in buying him but there was now the additional pressure of the looming transfer deadline for the season, which fell on 16 March, just eight days after the board had accepted Ramsey's demand for a move. By the morning of the 16th, however, only Sheffield Wednesday had come up with a definite offer. Ramsey, as a southerner, did not want to move north, fearing that he 'might never settle down in the provinces'. Moreover, Wednesday, despite a richer pedigree, were less successful in the 1948–49 season than Southampton, finishing five places lower in the second division table. What Alf did not know was that, by the late afternoon, Tottenham Hotspur had suddenly also come forward with an offer. At half past four, he was sitting in his digs, contemplating his failure to get away from the Dell, when the trainer Sam Warhurst turned up in his car and immediately rushed Alf back to the ground, where he was brought into Bill Dodgin's office and asked if he wanted to become a Spurs player. Alf instantly wanted to accept.

Sadly for him, it was now too late to beat the transfer deadline. The potential deal fell through. Alf was stuck at the Dell for the remainder of the season, a disastrous period in which the Saints gained only four out of a possible fourteen points and missed out on promotion behind Fulham and West Brom. But once the season was over, the Spurs offer was revived, partly as a result of personnel changes at White Hart Lane. At the beginning of May, Joe Hume, the Spurs manager who had presided over the abortive deal, was sacked by the board on the rather unconvincing grounds of ill-health. His replacement was not some big managerial star from another top-rank club. Instead, the Spurs board chose Arthur Rowe, a former Tottenham player who was then manager of lowly, non-League Chelmsford City. But the Spurs directors had shown more perspicacity than most of their breed. For Arthur Rowe possessed one of the most innovative football minds of his generation. He was about to embark on a footballing revolution at Tottenham, one that would send shockwaves through the First Division. What Rowe immediately needed were thinking players who would be able to help implement his vision. And it was soon obvious to him, after talking to Spurs officials who had tried to sign Ramsey in March, that Alf fitted his ideal type.

So on 15 May 1949, Spurs made another bid for Ramsey. This time there were no difficulties. Alf was only too happy to move to Tottenham, not just because it was an ambitious and famous institution, twice winners of the FA Cup, but, more prosaically, because the club agreed that he could live at home with his parents in nearby Dagenham. For a hard-pressed family and a frugal son, this was a real financial benefit.

At the very moment Alf left Southampton, so too did the manager he had come to so dislike, Bill Dodgin, who, much to the surprise of the Saints players, had agreed to take up the manager's job at newly promoted Fulham. It has often been claimed that Dodgin's departure was prompted by his annoyance at Alf's transfer. Nothing could be further from the truth. When Rowe was about to sign Alf, Dodgin was on another tour of Brazil, this time as the guest of Arsenal. As David Bull recorded in his excellent book *Dell Diamond*, the biography of Ted Bates, Bill Dodgin was in the reception of his hotel in Rio when he was handed a telegram from the Southampton directors informing him of Arthur Rowe's offer for Ramsey. He immediately cabled back, 'go ahead – dodgin.' In truth, Dodgin had fallen out badly with Ramsey and had no wish to keep him at the Dell. It was other issues that led to Dodgin's decision, such as his urge to return to his native London and manage a First Division side.

Two other myths were circulated about Ramsey at the time of his move. The first was that the transfer cost Spurs £21,000, making Alf by far the most expensive full-back in soccer history; the *Southern Daily Echo* was moved to describe it as a 'spectacular deal'. The reality was less exciting. The actual cash sum Spurs paid was only £4,500, the £16,500 balance made up by swapping Ernie Jones, their Welsh international winger, for Ramsey. The second was that Ramsey, as widely reported in the press, was only 27 at the time of the move. In fact he was 29, an age when many footballers are starting to contemplate retirement. For Alf, the best was still to come.

In addition to moving to Tottenham, Alf's private life was about to undergo an enormous change. The request to live with parents may have implied that he was planning to live a life of strict celibacy, in keeping with his reserved character, but that was far from the case. During his time at Southampton, he had met and fallen in love with a slim elegant brunette, Rita Norris, who worked as a hairdresser in the city. With a degree of embarrassment, Alf later described how their romance began:

> We were introduced by a friend at a club, nothing whatever to do with football. Immediately we had what one must call a special relationship. I don't know why I had this particular feeling only for her. I don't think anyone can describe such a thing. It is impossible to put into words.

Alf emerges as touchingly human in his awkward confession as to how love was awakened within his reticent soul.

It was Alf's first serious affair, as his fellow Southampton lodger Alf Freeman recalls. 'Alf was very shy, and I don't think he had any girlfriends before her.' During the late forties Alf and Rita started courting regularly, going to the cinema, the theatre, even the speedway and dog tracks. These venues in Southampton were owned by Charlie Knott, a big local fishmonger and a friend of Rita's. 'I lived in Portsmouth then,' says Stan Clements, 'and I used to get them tickets for the Theatre Royal. He would take her there once a week, usually on a Thursday. They did not have a car, so they came down by train. They were a very nice couple. She was like him, quiet and polite'. Here Clements highlights one of the reasons why Alf was so immediately drawn to Rita Norris. As well as being darkly attractive, she had the same serious temperament as Alf. Like him, she was determined to better herself, having been born in humble circumstances: her father, William Welch, was a ship's steward who later became a lift attendant. Rita had higher ambitions. She was keen on the ballet, had good taste in clothes and was well-spoken. 'She was a very good ballet dancer. Just as Alf was a gentleman, she was a lady, with nice manners, though some of the Southampton players thought she was a bit strait-laced,' says Pat Millward.

Given the depth of their romance, it was inevitable that the subject of marriage arose. 'We were engaged for some time before we were married. I don't recall how long. It is not important,' said Alf in 1966. Alf, as occasionally before, was being somewhat economical with the truth, for the tenure of his engagement turned out to be extremely important. The fact is that Alf was unable to marry Rita Norris when he wanted in the late forties – because she was already married to another man. Alf, the most loyal and upright of football figures, was – in the eyes of the law at least – helping his girlfriend to commit adultery for years. On Christmas Day 1941, Rita Phyllis Welch, aged 21, had married Arthur Norris in a Church of England ceremony at the Nelson chapel in Southampton, the more impressive nearby St Mary's Church, the usual venue for such occasions, having been bombed by the Luftwaffe. By trade, Arthur Norris was a fitter, like his father, and he was soon employed working as an aircraft engineer in the Fleet Air Arm. Within less than two years of their marriage, in February 1943, Arthur and Rita had produced a daughter, to which they gave the rather unusual artistic name of Tanaya, though she was generally called Tanya.

But as with a huge number of wartime marriages, the union between Arthur and Rita broke down and in 1947 they separated. Under the more strict law of the period, Rita could not officially gain a divorce until a period of at least three years had elapsed. And even after her divorce, she would not be able to re-marry for another year. So she and Alf, even though they were deeply in love, were trapped. Pat Millward recalls:

Alf told me privately he was waiting, waiting all the time for her to get her divorce. He was a little nervous that people in Southampton might throw it at him that he was involved with a married woman. But I never heard anyone say anything about it. Mind you, Alf was always very secretive about her. He never talked much about the relationship. The first moment I think I was aware of it was that time when my department store was giving out the wallets and handbags to the Southampton players. Alf was very uptight about getting the right handbag for her, so I chose it for him.

Rita's divorce finally game through on 30 November 1950, the official grounds given that Arthur Norris had 'deserted the Petitioner without cause for a period of at least three years immediately preceding the presentation of the petition'. Little more than a year later, on 10 December 1951, Alf Ramsey, aged 31 years – he always gave his true birth date where officialdom was concerned – was married at the Register Office in Southampton, before going on to a brief honeymoon in Bournemouth. The wedding was sandwiched between an away fixture at Blackpool and a home game against Middlesbrough. In line with the reclusive nature of the affair, Alf kept quiet about his marriage and it therefore came as a surprise at Spurs. 'Secret wedding honeymoon ended today for Alf Ramsey, Spurs right back and first choice for England and his bride who was formerly Rita Welch of Southampton,' announced the *Daily Mirror* on 12 December 1951. 'He kept the wedding so secret that even Spurs' manager Arthur Rowe did not know of the ceremony at the Southampton Register Office. On the train returning from Blackpool Ramsey asked for "two or three days off" to be married.'

It would be wrong to exaggerate the impropriety of the circumstances surrounding Alf's marriage. Divorce, though still far less common than it is today, was becoming increasingly prevalent, partly because of the high rate of failure in wartime marriages. In 1920, when Alf and Rita were both born, there were just 3,090 divorces in England. By 1939, the figure had risen to 8,254. By 1950, however, the divorce rate had soared to 30,870 a year. So it is hardly as if Alf and Rita were causing a public scandal. Though the true nature of Alf's marriage has never before been revealed, there have occasionally been wild rumours in the football world about his relationship with Rita. It was whispered breathlessly, for example, that she was 'the daughter of an admiral'. Others said that Alf had 'stolen his bride from his best mate'. Neither is remotely true. Rita was, like Alf, born in the working class and had merely contracted an unfortunate first marriage. 'There was no sense of Alf stealing her,' says Pat Millward. 'When they met, she was already waiting for a divorce.' Nevertheless, Rita Norris' past undoubtedly heightened Alf's sense of wariness about discussing his private life. It was another uncomfortable subject that he would prefer to avoid, like his father's job or his alleged elocution lessons or his supposed gypsy background. After his marriage, the barriers were put up even higher, as Margaret Fuljames, his secretary at the FA for many years, recalls:

He hated any intrusion into his private life. Like the *Daily Mail* would ring almost every year on his birthday, looking for a diary piece, a light little comment from him or his wife, and Alf would never have anything to do with that. He felt it was nothing to do with who he was or his job as England manager.

For all its inauspicious beginnings, Ramsey's marriage proved a successful one. Rita changed her name to Victoria, though

Alf always knew her as Vic, and she was happy to concentrate on building their home and supporting Alf. In typically practical terms, Alf once set out the proper role of a player's spouse:

> A footballer's wife needs to run the home completely so that he has no worries; give him the sort of food he likes and should have; and to work only for his good and the good of his career. She must know that she will rarely see him at weekends – and the better player he is, the less she will see of him. A footballer could be ruined by a wife who let him have all the household responsibilities, fed him the wrong diet and gave him no peace of mind. My wife has been splendid. I have been very lucky.

In her turn, Vickie returned the compliment. 'I was privileged to have met and married Alfred and I enjoyed a very wonderfully happy life with a kind and generous man,' she wrote to me.

Alf proved a loyal, honourable husband, giving her not the slightest moment's suspicion that he might stray. Unlike a lot of successful sportsmen, who revel in the flash of a knowing smile or a whiff of perfume, Alf was too innocent to be at ease with sophisticated femininity. 'I don't know much about women and the only women I know are footballers' wives,' he said, at a time when the phrase 'footballers' wives' had yet to become the embodiment of predatory lust. His love for Vickie was certainly genuine. 'He's the nicest man in the world. Never quarrels or loses his temper. He even listens to *my* views on football,' Vickie told the *Daily Mail* in 1962. They never had any children of their own, but Alf proved a good stepfather to Vickie's daughter Tanaya, who went on to marry an American and settle in the USA.

Pat Millward says: 'They were a very close couple. Alf was

devoted to her.' Despite his comments about a wife's duties, Alf was not the stereotyped husband of his generation, treating all housework as the preserve of women. Ken Jones has this recollection of the domesticated Alf:

In 1974 I was doing some magazine pieces with him and Brian James, the *Daily Mail*'s football writer. So I picked him up at Liverpool Street and took him over to my house. We did some work in the morning, and then sat down to lunch cooked by my wife. All went well and we had a few drinks – Alf liked a drink. Then after lunch, I said, 'Right, back to work.'

To which Alf immediately said, 'Hold on, what about the washing up?'

'The washing up?' I said in astonishment.

'Yes, the washing up.' And he went off into the kitchen to help with my wife. There he was, with his elbows in the sink. From that day on, he was always a hero to my wife.

John Booth, who became a close friend of Alf after his retirement, says: 'Everything always had to be spotless with Alf. He liked everything clean and tidy. He once came into my kitchen and started cleaning the sink and kettle.'

Whatever his virtues of fidelity and domesticity, it could not be claimed that Alf was the most romantic of men. Even Victoria, in one of her rare comments to the press, expressed her desire for her husband to show more emotion. 'I wish he would let his hair down occasionally and throw his cap over the moon. It would do him a power of good. There is nothing spectacular ever in his reactions,' she said in 1965. Early in his marriage, his relentless tunnel vision about football could be hurtful. On one occasion, when she was waiting outside the Spurs dressing-room after a game, he came out, completely ignored her because he was so wrapped up in his own thoughts, and proceeded to walk down the corridor until he was reminded that he had forgotten his wife. Ron Reynolds, the Spurs deputy goalkeeper of the early fifties, recalled meeting Alf and Vickie at a social event:

We had a meal and afterwards there was a dance. Alf came over to me and said, 'I want you to meet somebody.' He took me along and introduced me to Vickie. Within a matter of thirty seconds, he said, 'You won't mind having a dance with her, will you?' Alf didn't want to dance, he wanted to talk about football to the people there and so he lumbered me! She was very nice, but I was just a country lad, twenty-two years old, a bit out of my depth. I was practically speechless:

His innate lack of demonstrativeness stretched into his marriage. He famously explained that if he and his wife ever had a row, he liked to 'shake hands and make up'. Nigel Clarke says that he 'never, ever saw he and Vickie touch each other, embrace or be tactile. They would shake hands when they saw each other. I always had the feeling that Alf was not very worldly wise in sexual matters.' And though he was a loving step-father, he could not always get excited about his daughter's youthful activities. Tony Garnett, who covered all of Alf's Ipswich career, told me of this incident:

Alf was a shrewd man but he was very limited in anything bar football. I remember I ran into Tanya on the train at Liverpool Street. She had just been to the ballet. She was keen on that, like her mother. And I said to her, 'You know your dad is just two compartments ahead.'

'Oh, I don't want to go and sit with him. He won't be interested in what I have been doing.'

For all his carefully cultivated refinement, Alf could occasionally be crudely masculine. Roy McFarland, the Derby and England defender, remembers an incident in December 1971, when England were on tour in Greece. There was the usual banquet after the game, which the players imagined would be followed by the usual boring speeches. Instead, a ravishing, scantily clad belly-dancer appeared before them. McFarland recalls:

All the lads started coming back from the bar for a closer look. Once she had finished her act, some of us went out to get some fresh air, and then we got on the bus. Alf came out of the reception, sat down in his usual seat, then turned to us and said: 'Lads, what about that belly dancer! Fucking great pair she had, didn't she?' It was so unexpected. We could not stop laughing. He said things like that, which made him all the more endearing. It was a warm feeling to be part of that humour.

George Cohen, the Fulham full-back who knew and understood Alf better than any of the 1966 winners, gave this thoughtful analysis of their marriage:

Alf was, no doubt, a product of his times and when they had passed few men would ever have had more difficulty in adapting to a new style – and new values. His marriage to Vickie was a perfect reflection of this. He worshipped her but he also expected everything of her. She served him, as so many women did their husbands in those days and in return he adored her. If ever anyone walked in a man's shadow it was her. She had that Victorian attitude that he would live his life, do what he had to do and she would make sure that he had his meals and that his shirts were washed and ironed immaculately. It is not easy to imagine him as a particularly romantic lover. His passion, you had to suspect, was reserved for his country.

Alf was still a bachelor when he reported for duty in August 1949, with his marriage more than a year away. Despite almost a decade's experience with the Army and Southampton, he confessed that he felt a few nerves as he entered White Hart Lane for the first time. He was given the Number 12 locker in the dressing-room beside Bill Nicholson, the tough York-shireman with whom Alf was to have an awkward relation-ship. But he was immediately put at ease by the friendliness of the new Tottenham manager, Arthur Rowe. Like Alf, Rowe was a quiet but determined personality. 'Here was a man, I felt, who knew what he wanted and how he hoped to achieve his ambition,' wrote Alf in *Talking Football*. Alf was even more impressed when Rowe gave his first team talk, in which he told the players that he wanted them to 'play football all the time'. The best way to do this, he argued, was by a swift, short passing game, pushing the ball to a colleague and then running into position to accept the return. 'Make it simple, make it quick,' he told them. And those six words soon became the slogan for Spurs' approach. It was one that immediately appealed to Alf. Contrary to the antediluvian *FA Coaching Manual*, whose 1949 version – unchanged for 16 years – stated that 'a back's first duty is to clear his lines', Alf had long believed in a more progressive brand of soccer. And that first afternoon, Rowe gave a practical demonstration of his philos-ophy. According to the account by journalist and former Arsenal footballer Bernard Joy, Rowe took them out to the pitch, where he stationed himself ten yards from the touchline. On his instructions, the trainer Cecil Poyton stood nearby with a stopwatch ready. He then asked the Spurs captain, Ron Burgess to take a throw-in, which Rowe immediately hit first time to winger Les Medley.

'How long did that take?' he asked the trainer.

'Two seconds,' said Poyton.

Burgess was then asked to repeat the throw-in. This time Rowe trapped the ball, then pushed it on to Medley.

'Four seconds,' shouted Poyton.

Finally, Burgess took a third throw. This time Rowe reacted as so many players would have done in a match, trapping the ball with the right foot, tapping it onto the left, and then onto the right again before hitting a pass to Medley.

'Eight seconds,' called Poyton.

Back in the dressing-room, Rowe reinforced his point. 'If you hold the ball instead of moving it straightaway, you give the defenders all the time they need to mark your colleagues who have moved into the open spaces. Worse still, a team-mate will have time to run into position and then out again before the pass is made.'

As a player with Spurs in the 1930s, Rowe had been heavily influenced by the Tottenham manager of the time, Peter McWilliam, who taught him the importance of positional play. 'The movement of men without the ball is as vital as that of the man in possession,' was one of McWilliam's sayings. Rowe absorbed these lessons, building his game around keeping possession and hitting accurate passes. In the process he made himself into a far more constructive centre-half than most of the type who predominated in the pre-war era. After he retired as a professional, he went to coach in Hungary, where he witnessed the development of new tactical methods which were in such contrast to the muddy, hard-hitting physicality of the English game. Such was Rowe's standing that Hungary actually offered him the post of national coach in 1939, but the war intervened. He returned to Britain, where he first coached an Army XI and then, after 1945, Chelmsford City, which was used as a laboratory for his radical ideas and soon became one of the most successful non-League sides in the country.

Silver-haired and respectful, Rowe was not the sort of man to impose any dogma on his players. He preferred to talk about his plans with them, encouraging suggestions and discussion. As Eddie Baily, the Spurs inside-left, remembers:

> Arthur had arrived at a club of natural footballers. He did not come in with some great system and tell us exactly what to do. He encouraged us in certain directions, got us thinking, trying things and then, when it all came together, he would say, 'That's it, that's the way to play.'

Rowe was no dry lecturing theorist. A fine professional himself, he knew how to talk in the dressing-room. One of the fashionable coaching slogans of the time was 'peripheral vision', a term which attracted Rowe's derision. 'You know what that means? It means seeing out of your arse.'

In encouraging his players to think and play more enterprisingly, Rowe knew that Alf would be crucial to the team's success. In a BBC interview in 1970, he paid Alf this tribute:

> When I went back to join Tottenham as their new manager in 1949, it was my pleasure to meet Alf Ramsey for the first time. He was another new boy, like myself, and I was delighted to realize that in him I had a player that I could talk to, who would help me in the desires I had to build Tottenham into the great club I had always hoped it would

be. If you can like people on sight, I think we both liked each other. I asked the boys to accept my thoughts about the game, that it was a simple game if you kept possession and passed accurately to the same shirts that you wore. The more accurately you did it, the quicker and better would be your attack. There was no diabolical change in the team for tactical purposes. I always used to speak to Alf and Ron Burgess, telling them what I was thinking of doing. I would ask them their thoughts and the response usually came within 20 seconds and it was usually the same from Ron Burgess, 'If you say so Art, that'll go.' Then there would be another time lag and then Alf would say, 'Yes, I think you are probably right.' It was a tremendous reassurance to myself. There was never any problem between myself and Alf.

Rowe's ideas owed something to watching boys playing football in the street, flicking a tennis ball against a wall and then collecting the instant rebound in full stride. He had also been a fan of Clem Stephenson of the Huddersfield Town side of the 1920s, which had won a hat-trick of championships:

I was enthralled when I played against him; he best illustrated the style I wanted my teams to play. He played everything off quickly. He was never caught in possession. I saw how much trouble he caused and I thought, 'What if you could get them all playing like that?'

It was an early away victory that gave Rowe the chance to ram home his message. The Spurs team were sitting on the train with Rowe, talking over the last-minute goal which had brought victory:

I spread the sugar around, trying to map about the moves leading up to our goal. It was one to savour because there were about seven passes starting out from our own penalty area. I argued that if we could plan moves like that, instead of just hoping for it to happen, we would score more often.

What evolved was the renowned Spurs fast-moving style of 'push-and-run', which soon exposed the stereotyped inadequacies of English football. And much of the phenomenal success for this method could be credited to Alf Ramsey, whose primary gifts were his footballing brain and his usage of the ball. Under Rowe, Alf became far more than a defender. With his superbly accurate passing, he was a constant instigator of attacks, taking the ball from keeper Ted Ditchburn and then interplaying with inside-forward Les Bennett or outside-right Sonny Walters, who was encouraged by Rowe to come deep into his own half, something that wingers did not usually do in this period. As Rowe explained:

I put it to Alf Ramsey that while I knew he was brought up on using long, measured passes, these tended to leave him out of action once he had played them. But had he ever thought how much more accuracy was guaranteed, how much more progress could be made, if he pumped 15 or 20 yard passes to a withdrawn Walters? . . . We had one more option; with Ramsey's precision, once advanced he could drive the ball down the right for Les Bennett coming to the near post, to turn the ball inside with his head. Ramsey's advances would throw a heavier load in defence on Bill Nicholson but he was the ideal cover at half-back – sound, solid and a rattling tackler.

As Denis Uphill, who played intermittently as an inside-forward with Spurs at this time, puts it:

> Alf was different to the usual defender. He was a great passer, with good ball control. The game to him was like a game of chess. With Arthur Rowe there as well, you had enough brains for half the team. He and Arthur always got on well. I always sensed Alf was someone special. I used to notice this quality most when we were at team meetings. He would stand out then. Even Arthur would listen to him whereas if most of us spoke, he would not pay too much attention.

Rowe himself once said that Ramsey 'thirsted for tactical knowledge. He wanted to know the why's and where's of every movement. He was an out and out perfectionist.'

Rowe's dynamism ensured that Spurs made a dramatic start to the 1949–50 season and were soon at the top of the table. From the end of August until January 1950, the team had an unbeaten run of 22 matches. Apart from Ramsey at right-back, Rowe's side had enormous strength in depth. Ted Ditchburn was one of the bravest, most consistent goalkeepers in England, missing just five matches in seven seasons; Ron Burgess, the commanding left-half, was captain of both Spurs and Wales; Harry Clarke was a solid, dependable centre-half; Bill Nicholson, later the double-winning manager of Spurs in 1960–61, brought a granite Yorkshire determination to the right flank. Up front there was the big-chested, black-haired Channel Islander Len Duquemin, and the crowd's favourite Eddie Baily, a cheeky cockney who possessed a brilliant first-touch and instinct for finding goal. The side of diverse talents swept through the Second Division with their daring tactics and breathtaking pace. The excitement they generated drew huge crowds to White Hart Lane. Even though they were in the Second Division, Spurs had the highest average attendance in the League, at 54,405 per game. Some of the gates were staggering: 70,305 turned out to see Spurs against Alf's former side Southampton, while 66,880 gathered for the game against Hull City. One of those spectators, Ed Speight, who joined Tottenham in 1954 as a youth player, remembers his thrill as a teenage fan watching Alf in action at White Hart Lane:

I stood on the terraces and I only had eyes for Alf, partly because full-back was my position at school. Alf was my man. He was God. He couldn't run. Anyone fast would just go past him. What Alf could do brilliantly was read the game. He got by through thinking. He was a great passer. I felt that he knew where he was going to pass even before he got the ball.

With his sharp intelligence, Ramsey was at the centre of many of Spurs' innovations. At a time when most keepers would just hoof the ball up the field, he developed a creative partnership with Ted Ditchburn, who had a long, uncannily accurate throw. The understanding between Alf and Ted enabled Spurs to keep possession, as well as deceive their opponents. In Dave Bowler's fine book, *The Life of a 1950s Footballer*, Ron Reynolds, Ted's deputy, provided this description of one of their bold moves:

The push-and-run style suited Alf perfectly. You would see Alf running back, towards his own goal, with the ball in front of him. He then used to delay a ball back to Ted Ditchburn. Alf did that to give the winger, who was chasing, the thought that he could get it. And then of course Alf used to peel off towards the touchline and Ted just threw it to him. This was fascinating for me to watch.

In his interview with me, Ted Ditchburn was modest about his role:

I wasn't a good kicker of the ball. That is probably why I threw it out so much. But I was pretty accurate. It was not a problem for me to reach the half-way line. It was interesting that Alf always wanted the ball thrown straight to him, not in front to run on to. That was because he was a bit on the slow side.

Ditchburn also revealed that the relationship on the pitch was not always harmonious: 'Alf had this habit, when we were under pressure, of being on the goal-line and calling out, "I've got this side covered." I felt like saying to him, "For Christ's sake, I've got to cover the whole bloody lot."'

Alf was delighted at the licence that Rowe gave him to go forward. In contrast to his later defensive image as England manager, he believed there should be 'no limit to where a defender will go to attack,' he wrote in 1952. 'Maybe you have noticed how often I go upfield to cross a ball or even have a shot at goal. That a defender should not attempt to score a goal is something to which I can never subscribe.'

Ramsey put those words into spectacular reality during a game against Grimsby Town in November 1949. Playing at Blundell Park, Spurs went into the interval 2–1 down, their unbeaten record under threat. Then eight minutes into the second half, Alf was near the half-way line when he cut out a long cross-field pass. He moved forward, split open the defence with a brilliant feint as if he were about to pass, then dribbled past three Grimsby players until he was in the penalty box. As the keeper advanced, Alf, with perfect timing, smashed it wide of him and into the net. He had run more than forty yards from his first interception to his final strike. It was his first League goal in open play – he had taken the occasional penalty for Southampton – and was to remain the best of his career. As the reporter on one of the local Tottenham papers, *The Enfield Gazette*, recorded:

> The goal of a lifetime is an expression used somewhat loosely by soccer scribes in praise of a particularly fine effort. Yet, for all that, I am prepared to guarantee that the goal scored by Tottenham Hotspur right-back Alf Ramsey, in the 53rd minute of the match at Blundell Park, will never be forgotten by those privileged to be present. Rather it will serve to provide them with a talking point in the years ahead. This does not qualify as the greatest goal I have ever seen, but for sheer cheekiness it takes pride of place. To describe it as merely unorthodox would be the understatement of the century.

Inspired by Alf's astonishing effort, Spurs went on to win 3–2.

Tottenham were magnificent that 1949–50 season, cruising to the Second Division title with seven games to spare. And in his speech to the Tottenham AGM in August 1950, Arthur Rowe stated that Alf's role in promotion had been vital: 'As much as anything else, I would rate our good time last year to the acquisition of Alf Ramsey – one of the best full-backs I have ever watched. A nicer fellow never walked; a grand influence on and off the field.' Spurs scored more goals (85) and conceded fewer (35) than any of their rivals, their push-and-run style continually perplexing opponents. Even First Division sides found it just as hard to cope when they played Arthur Rowe's team. Spurs beat Stoke in the third round of the FA Cup, then hammered Sunderland 5–1, before going out to Everton, though only by a single, disputed goal. 'It was a style that was lovely to play in, the movement off the ball – really enjoyable,' said keeper Ted Ditchburn.

Eddie Baily, the comedian of the side, remembers the happy atmosphere in the Spurs dressing-room:

> Arthur loved good football and we all talked about the game in the club. But there would be a lot of banter around.
>
> Like Ted Ditchburn might win a game for us on his own and he would come in and throw his gloves on the floor and say, 'What was bleedin' going on in front of me?'
>
> 'Well played, Ted.'
>
> 'Bleedin' well played! I've earned you lot your two quid bonus for that.'
>
> To me that's good banter.

On Alf as a player, Eddie says:

> He was lucky coming to Tottenham because we had some very good players, none more so than Bill Nicholson in front of him. Alf was never quick, but he had very good control, read the game well, and could get in good positions thinking wise. He was always a reader, always a dissector of what went on.

But, recalls Eddie, this trait could lead to problems in the dressing-room, especially as Alf's self-confidence grew:

> Most people got annoyed with Alf. When I say that, I mean that he came into a team with people like Ted Ditchburn and Bill Nicholson, seasoned players, and he liked to tell them what to do. People would be saying, 'Who does he think he

is?' They got annoyed because he gave the impression that he read the game and everyone else had to follow. They appreciated his ability, but they could not put up with him. So when he started to tell them what to do, they would just say, 'Oh no, here he goes again.'

And I would reply, 'Leave it alone. He's all right. What difference does it make?'

'Cos he gets on my bleedin' nerves.'

Alf used to try it a bit with me but I would just tell him to mind his own business because I was never frightened of him. In fact, I used to like him. A lot of others thought he was stand-offish but I could get through to him, maybe because I was cockney and so we were both basically from the East End.

When we used to travel away, we would pair up in rooms in the hotels and bed and breakfasts. Wherever we went, Alf was always with me. On our trips, when we were talking football, I used to tease him, 'You're the only one who's perfect. You're so perfect. Nobody else is right.' Alf would laugh at that. And I would go on. 'I'm fed up with you telling me what I should do or what Les should do. I'll tell you, you should be lucky you've got me and Les.' That was the way we would talk to each other. There was an understanding between us.

We would travel by train, good old Pullman, first class. Every club would have its own card school and Alf was in ours. He loved a game of solo, I do believe. But even then, he would tell people that they had put the wrong card down. That was his make-up. He was actually a nice bloke, but those around him got tired of his criticism.

Welshman Mel Hopkins is another former Spurs player who remembers that side of Alf. Much younger, less experienced than Eddie Baily, he was never in a position to challenge Alf:

He would tell you what was expected of you. I always sensed this iron will within him. If he said to you, do it this way, then that's the way it had to be done. He had great faith in his own ability. He could be a little bit cantankerous as well. Every Friday morning, we would have a team meeting. Arthur would say something, someone else would chip in and the meeting would go on. And after a while most of us would be thinking, 'Oh God, when is this going to finish?' Then finally, Arthur would say, 'Right lads, anything else?' We all knew that, whenever he said those words, Alf, right on cue, would come in, 'Yes, just one point I would like to bring up.' That used to really get on the players' wick.

Ted Ditchburn also remembered a voluble Alf:

He had a lot to say in the dressing-room. In team talks, he certainly wasn't shy. He was very forward in fact. He was a clever footballer, tactically, and good on the ball. He got on well with Arthur Rowe. I think Arthur appreciated his technical ability. But Alf was no friend of mine. We did not fall out but I never got on with him like the other Spurs players. It was as simple as that. I was not the only one who felt like that. He was that type of bloke. He had his own little world.

In his book *Talking Football,* Alf painted a picture of his lifestyle as a Spurs footballer and newly married husband. Given that he was on the maximum wage in 1952 of just £14 a week and was living in rented accommodation in Barking, it was hardly lavish, but then Alf was never a man of extravagance. And the spirit of modesty and conservatism shone through his description of his tastes. 'My favourite clothes are a sports jacket – or club blazer – and flannel trousers. I do not like 'arty' shirts. Give me a quiet one with a collar attached every time and a good plain tie. I never wear a hat of any kind.' Eddie Baily remembers that Alf 'was always immaculately dressed. He never had a hair out of place. He never, ever, looked dishevelled or scruffy. Somehow, even when he played football, he always looked smart. He was never piled up with mud – and they were very muddy pitches in those days. In fact, we never played a game unless there was at least six foot of mud.' He was one of the few Spurs players to have a car, owning a green Ford Anglia though in his early days he generally used public transport when on football business. In his autobiography, Alf went on to explain that his favourite dish was his mother's meat pie, that he drank little and rarely smoked, that he enjoyed watching and playing cricket, and listening to the radio. He also claimed, in rather over-blown, unconvincing language, that he adored comic acts in variety shows: 'I get my biggest kick out of the comedians when I can literally roll down the aisles with laughter.' In an interview with the *Evening Standard* in this period, he further revealed that he and his wife had become enthusiasts of record collecting. 'Our library is rather small at the moment. We like all popular music, ranging from jazz to opera.' Asked by the *Standard* about his other interests, he replied, showing an unwonted irony, 'I am a "housewife" now. There is the gardening to do, the car to be kept clean and a host of domestic duties too.'

On his weekly routine, he explained that he generally rose at 7.30 am and caught a 9.25 train from Barking to Tottenham for training – often with Syd McClellan, who also lived in Dagenham. In the evening, he tried to be in bed by ten o'clock. The hardest day was on Tuesday: eight laps of the track, followed by a vigorous work-out in the gym and then a practice match. Wednesdays were generally reserved for five-a-side games, Thursday for more lapping and sprint practice, and Friday for a few light exercises followed by the team talk. Contrary to a lot of professionals, Alf always loved watching football and on his free afternoons would go to anything from top League matches to junior games in the local park, though Thursday was kept for his weekly visit to the cinema with Vickie. In his book, he did not mention one of his other favourite afternoon activities. 'Alf liked to bet,' says Eddie Baily. 'I was from a family of bookmakers and one of my relatives would often say to me, "Alf was over here today, having a few quid on."' On Saturdays, if he were playing at home, he would rise a little later, at nine o'clock, read the papers or a book until eleven, and then have a large breakfast with steak and eggs before taking the train to North London. It was a world away from the diet and habits of the modern soccer star but that was the practice followed by most of his team-mates. Eddie Baily, for instance, used to leave his house at eleven after a breakfast of three eggs, rashers of bacon, tomato and bread, then take two trolleybuses to White Hart Lane, bantering with supporters the whole way to the ground.

Throughout his life, sociability never came easy to Alf. As Nigel Clarke puts it, 'Alf did not really need people. He needed situations and football gave him all the situations he cared for.' Even at the peak of his playing career at Tottenham, Alf was the same. Mel Hopkins says:

He was hard to get close to. The team of that era were like a family, doing everything together. But out of that team, Alf was the loner. He would not mix much when we were having a few drinks. He seemed a bit more sophisticated than the rest. He went his own way. He was a serious type who measured everything in life, not just his passes.

Ron Reynolds, the deputy keeper, had this recollection:

> I don't think anyone at Spurs really got to know him, not even Syd McClellan. Both came from Dagenham and they'd travel in daily. Syd would say that on some days Alf would chat away, but on others you wouldn't hear a thing from him. He used to say that Alf was hard to pin down. 'Of all the players I had dealings with, he's the one I could never figure out. Even later on, when I got in the team and in fact in training, I normally stripped next to Alf, and he rarely had much to say. Once training was finished, he was gone.'

Ted Ditchburn felt that this was partly due to Alf's wife:

> She had a big influence on him. She was a strong person. She was nice, elegant, but again, like Alf, very solitary. She didn't really want to know the other wives. I hardly socialized with Alf at all. We used to play the odd game of darts, no great boozing, but were invited along by various supporters' clubs. And Alf never joined us.

Bill Nicholson, himself not a great socializer, later described Alf as

> not an outgoing-type. He had a history in the East End, we were led to believe, and no one asked him about it. He was eager to acquire knowledge and gave you the impression that he was storing it up for when he became a manager. He wasn't the type to share it.

But this is not the whole picture. It should be remembered that Alf was still only 29 when he joined Tottenham. He was not so elevated as to avoid all social participation. 'When he did come out with us, he could be quite good company. He was not aloof in that respect. Oh no, when he let himself go, he could be one of the lads, but he nearly always held back,' says Mel Hopkins. Eddie Baily, who was closer to Alf than anyone, has happy memories of Alf's friendliness:

A lot of people couldn't get on with him, but I could. He was my mate. When we went away, we would sit on the train and have a beer together – Alf liked a beer. When we arrived somewhere, we'd go together to the cinema or a show or a boxing match. He was not really a loner when you got to know him. Vickie was a nice person. She was like Alf, smart, polite. She wasn't a tart. She never got lively. But Alf was different when he was with me. He was relaxed, not trying to be someone else. He could let his hair down, use a bit of language. He couldn't tell a joke but he liked one. But only in certain company would he let go.

Eddie Baily recalls that Alf, before he was married, would sometimes let his guard right down:

If my family was having a party or something on a Saturday night when we go back from a game, I would say to Alf, 'Do you want to come along?' So he would end up in someone's house having a few beers. And then, he would drop a bit, he lost the image of the top-class international footballer. He was just muckin' with the rest of us. Sometimes, I don't know how he got home. On two occasions, I had to walk him around Millfields in Clapton to try to sober him up.

But another family party that Alf attended had even more disastrous physical consequences, as Baily remembers:

One time, he ended up in the flat of my mum-in-law and was so out of it that he had to sleep there. Very funny thing about my mother-in-law, bless her heart: when Alf got his knighthood in 1967 she said to me, 'Do you know what? He's been in my bathroom. And he was sick all over the floor.'

Ted Ditchburn was at that Baily family gathering too: 'I can see Alf now, bent over the toilet. Still we have all done it.'

Alf had more professional reasons to celebrate in the 1950–51 season, Spurs' first in the top flight since they had been relegated in 1934–35. After a stuttering start, including a 1–4 home defeat to Blackpool in the opening game, they quickly found their top gear. Playing Rowe's free-flowing system to devastating effect, they won eight straight victories between the end of September and mid-November, scoring 28 goals in the process. Stoke were crushed 6–1, Portsmouth 5–1 and, most remarkably of all, Newcastle United 7–0, witnessed by a crowd of over 70,000 at White Hart Lane. The *Daily Telegraph* gave a graphic description of how Tottenham operated:

The Spurs principle is to hold the ball a minimum amount of time, keep it on the ground and put it into an open space where a colleague will be a second or two later. The result is their attacks are carried on right through the side with each man taking the ball in his stride at top pace, for all the world like a wave gathering momentum as it races to the far distant shore. It is all worked out in triangles and squares and when the mechanism of it clicks at speed, as it did Saturday, with every pass placed to the last refined inch on a drenched surface, there is simply no defence against it.

Ron Burgess described it as 'the finest exhibition of football I have ever seen.' Eddie Baily, who scored a hat-trick in that Newcastle game, later recalled: 'Our style commanded a lot of respect from others because of its freshness, because of the way it was played and the men who played it. You felt that you were helping to lift the tone of the game and so you got that respect from the crowds as well.' By December 1950, Spurs were at the top of the First Division table and held on to the lead through January and February, though Manchester United were close behind. Then in March they tore away again with another burst of fine victories, including a 5–0 destruction of West Bromwich Albion.

Throughout these months, Alf was playing the best football of his life. His captain Ron Burgess wrote that Alf was 'in grand form that season. He not only scored four goals himself, but his perfectly placed free-kicks led to a number of goals.' He went on to describe Alf as 'a brilliant defender under any condition and circumstance' who was 'a player for the big occasion'. The quality of Alf's vision was central to the success of push-and-run in the First Division. Such was his authority on the field that he became known to his colleagues as 'The General'. He was the master of strategy, the lynchpin of a side that built its attacks from the back, the scheming practitioner who put Rowe's plans into action. George Robb, who joined Spurs in 1951, told author Dave Bowler:

Tottenham became a great side through push-and-run, which was tailor-made for Alf. There was no long ball from him, and he was one of the crucial members of the side, along with the likes of Burgess. Alf played a tremendous part in setting the pass pattern, which wasn't typical of the British game. It was a revolutionary side, very well-knit.

Robb recalled The General's influence off the field as well:

> In team talks Alf certainly played an important part – he was full of deep thinking about the game but very quietly spoken. He was appreciated by the rest of us as being a cut above, tactically calm and unruffled. You'd go in the dressing-room for training and you'd have Eddie Baily, a tremendous clown, making a terrific row and Alf would just sit there, taking it all in, occasionally coming in with a shrewd observation, a cooling statement; he was ice-cool, just as his game was. Alf was looked upon as classy, constructive, so he set a new pattern.

Spurs were still top of the table by mid-April 1951 and when they met Sheffield Wednesday on Saturday the 28th they needed only two points to clinch the title. The match kicked off at 3.15 pm, as was traditional in this period, and for most of the first half, Spurs were unable to break down the Wednesday defence. Then, as the clock was about to reach 4 pm, Eddie Baily went past three defenders, then fed Len Duquemin, who hit a rasping shot into the net. 'I have heard the Hampden Park roar and the Ninian Park roar, and they were mere whispers to the roar that greeted that goal, and that pulsating din of excitement did not diminish from then until the end of the game,' wrote Spurs captain Ron Burgess. Despite many frantic goalmouth moments at both ends in the second half, the score-line remained the same at the final whistle. Spurs were the champions, the first time they had won the title in their long history. 'The crowd went crazy, and I don't think many of the players were too sane at that particular moment,' said Burgess.

There was one more game left in the season, and Tottenham celebrated in style, beating Liverpool 3–1. After the game,

Burgess was presented with the League trophy by Arthur Drewry, the President of the Football League, who said of the champions, 'I not only congratulate them on having won it but also on the manner in which they did so.' A couple of days later, all the Spurs players and staff were invited to a 'Grand Celebration Dance' at the Royal on the Tottenham Court Road. Supporters had to pay 10 shillings 6 pence for a ticket to the event, where they were promised four hours of Ivor Kirchin and his Ballroom Orchestra.

It was a happy end to Alf's second season in Spurs colours. But on other fronts, the prospects were darker.

# FOUR

## *Belo Horizonte*

Within months of transferring from Southampton to Spurs in the summer of 1949, Alf had justified the move by regaining his place in the England team after he had lost it to his Saints full-back rival Bill Ellerington. Languishing in the Saints reserves, his cause would have been hopeless. But his superb form for Tottenham soon attracted the England selectors, and he was picked for the match against Italy at White Hart Lane. England managed to win 2–0, but the result was harsh on the Italians, who had dominated much of the game and had only been prevented from scoring through a memorable display of goalkeeping by Bert Williams. Alf himself had a difficult match, not just in coping with the Italian winger Carapellese, but also in working with right-half Billy Wright. The *Daily Sketch* commented: 'Wright could not be satisfied with his performance. There were times in the game when he went too far upfield, leaving Alf Ramsey exposed to the thrusting counter-attacks of the quick and clever Italian forwards.' But, as always, Alf was learning, and the key lesson he took from the game was the importance of positional play. 'That November afternoon I realized more than ever before that it is sometimes more important to watch the man rather than the ball, to watch where the man you are marking runs when he has parted with the ball,' he wrote.

Alf had performed creditably enough, however, and soon became a fixture in the England team, winning 31 caps in succession. One of his fellow players in that Italian game was the revered Preston winger Sir Tom Finney, who was immediately impressed by Alf:

> I felt he was a really outstanding full-back, with a good idea of how the game should be played. He was very good at using the ball; unlike some others, he never seemed just to punt it up the field and hope that it got to one of his own side. He always felt that the game should be played on the floor. But he was not particularly fast, and I don't think he liked playing against people who were clever on the ball and quick.

Like most of the Tottenham players, Sir Tom never found it easy to mix with Alf;

> To be honest, he was a bit of a loner. He was not easy-going. He did not suffer fools gladly. He was a theorist who had his own ideas on how the game should be played, but he kept those ideas to himself. He had a very quiet personality, never swore much. I always got on all right with him but I never found that he was a fella who wanted to talk a lot. I would not say that he had many great friends in the England set-up. Unlike some less experienced players who have just broken through into the international team, Alf never felt the need to link up with anyone.

According to Sir Tom, though Alf was generally 'very serious' he could display an odd, dry sense of humour. On one occasion, when Spurs had drawn with Preston at Deepdale in the FA Cup, Sir Tom popped his head round the corner of the

Spurs dressing-room to say hello to Alf, who was, after all, an England colleague. In his account in his autobiography, Finney wrote:

> Alf, who was standing close to the door, seemed quite animated.
>
> 'Not much point you lot coming all the way to London for the reply,' he barked. 'There will be nothing for you at Spurs.'
>
> I was taken aback, not so much by what had been said but more by who had said it. I looked Alf in the eyes for a moment but it was impossible to tell whether he was being aggressive, jocular or simply mischievous. He was dead right though – four days later we lost by a single goal at White Hart Lane.

It was always an absurdity that Sir Tom Finney, one of the finest footballers in history, should have to run a business as a plumber in Preston because his earnings from the game throughout the forties and fifties were so meagre. When he and Alf played against Italy in 1949, the maximum wage stood at just £12 a week, while England players received a match fee of just £30, plus £1-a-day expenses if the team were playing abroad. It was a semi-feudal system, one where players were tied to their clubs even against their will, since the clubs held their registration and no move was possible without the directors' permission.

Yet this oppressive relationship was only a reflection of the deeper malaise in football at the time. England was the nation that gave football to the world in the 19th century, but it had failed to progress much since then. Complacently living in the past, the game's administrators and journalists still told themselves that English football was the finest in the world.

The evidence for this global supremacy, it was claimed, lay in the fact that England had never been beaten by a foreign side at home. It was not strictly true even in 1949, when the Republic of Ireland won 2–0 at Goodison Park, but, despite all the years of bitter enmity across the Irish Sea and Ireland having competed in two World Cups as a sovereign state, Eire was transformed into a home nation for the purposes of maintaining the undefeated record. Alf's trip with Southampton to Brazil in 1948 had shown him the rapid developments that were happening elsewhere in the world, especially in terms of tactics and equipment. But England clung to the reassuring, outdated certainties of W–M formations and ankle-wrapping boots. Training was hopelessly unsuited to a modern, fast-moving game. Indeed, many coaches still clung to the grotesque notion that professionals should be deprived of the ball during the week, so that they would be more hungry for it on Saturday. In place of perfecting their ball skills, they had to carry out endless laps of the track. 'The dislike of the ball was pretty universal in training. I thought it was crazy,' says Sir Tom Finney. The physical treatment of players was equally primitive. It was usually carried out by a former club stalwart who knew nothing of dealing with injuries.

The paralysis within English football was perhaps most graphically highlighted in the antique way the FA and the Football League were run. Both were managed more like a somnolent Oxford college than a professional sports body. The Football Association, which was composed largely of representatives from the counties and old universities, had a certain contempt for men who earned their living from the game. Snobbery, poor record keeping and amateurism were rife throughout the organization. When Stanley Rous first became secretary in 1934, there were complaints about his inappropriate dress for matches. 'I would remind you,' said one old councillor, 'that your predecessor would go to matches in a top hat and frock coat.' This kind of nonsense was still carrying on after the war, with FA members more worried about protocol than performance. The Football League was just as bad. The Yorkshireman Alan Hardaker, who was later to be compared to a cross between Caligula and Jimmy Cagney because of his autocratic methods, arrived at the League's headquarters in Preston in 1951, as deputy to the secretary Frederick Howarth. Hardaker was shocked at what he found. Housed in an old vicarage, the League kept no proper records and stored files in the attics. Like some Victorian colonialist, Howarth relied on telegrams rather than the telephone. His loathing for the press equalled that for modern technology. 'Howarth was against change of any sort, particularly if it meant more work for him,' wrote Hardaker. As a result, 'The League was like a machine that had been lying in a corner for three quarters of a century.'

The antiquated approach extended to the selection of the national team. What should have been the job of the England manager was instead in the hands of a group of opinionated, often elderly, figures who had absolutely no experience of international football. The eight FA selectors were inordinately proud of their role and enjoyed their trips abroad, but they disastrously lacked judgement or any long-term vision. Riddled with prejudices, often displaying blatant bias towards players from their own clubs, they showed no consistency, no understanding of the needs of modern football. 'There was always this chopping and changing. Someone would have a tremendous game for England and then be dropped, for no reason,' says Sir Tom Finney. At their meetings, the selectors would go through each position in turn, seeking nominations and then holding a vote to decide the choice if there were a dispute. On occasions, they could be breathtakingly ignorant.

In his first games for England, Bobby Moore was frequently mistaken by one selector for the Wolves midfielder Ron Flowers, purely because they both had blond hair. Similarly, John Connelly, the Burnley winger, recalled talking to a selector during the 1962 World Cup in Chile: 'All the time it was Alan this, Alan that. He thought I was our reserve goalkeeper, Alan Hodgkinson.'

The man trying to grapple with this system was Walter Winterbottom, who had been appointed England manager and FA Director of Coaching in 1946. The very fact that these two enormous jobs were combined in one individual only demonstrates the indifference that the FA showed towards the management of the national team. In the face of his burden, Winterbottom fought hard to bring some rationality to the chaos. Before the war, he had been an undistinguished player with Manchester United before a back injury ended his career. Having paid his way through Carnegie College of Physical Education, he served as a PT instructor in the Air Ministry during the war, rising to the rank of wing-commander. His military credentials, earnest, academic manner and plummy voice appealed to the socially conscious chiefs of the FA. But Winterbottom was no cypher. As passionate and obsessive about football as Alf Ramsey, he had analysed the game in depth and, through his position as Director of Coaching, he aimed to start a technical revolution in English football by raising skills and tactical awareness. Many of the future generations of top managers were inspired by Winterbottom's coaching. 'Walter was a leader, a messiah, he set everyone's eyes alight,' said Ron Greenwood. Sir Bobby Robson was moved to call him 'a prophet. He was my motivator in terms of my staying in football.' Alf himself wrote of one of Winterbottom's team talks during his first England tour in 1948: 'His tactical knowledge of Continental teams, and his outlook on the Italian methods and temperament left a lasting impression on me.'

But, as well as the vicissitudes of the selection process, Winterbottom was faced with two other major problems. The first was the reluctance of some major stars to accept any degree of instruction, especially from someone who had never played international football. With a narrowness typical of the period, certain players believed that fitness and ability were all that mattered, with coaching regarded as alien and demeaning. In an interview with the BBC, the centre-forward Tommy Lawton recalled an early pre-match session with Winterbottom:

He said to us, 'The first thing we'll do, chaps, is that we'll meet in half an hour. I've arranged a blackboard and we will discuss tactics.'

I looked at him and said, 'We'll discuss WHAT?'

'Well, how we're going to play it and do it.'

So I said, 'Are you telling me that you've got a blackboard downstairs, and, God forbid, you're going to tell Stan Matthews how to play at outside right and me, you're going to tell me, how to score goals? You've got another think coming.'

For all its arrogance, Lawton's contempt illustrated the deeper, long-term problem with Winterbottom: his failure to command automatic respect from players. Winterbottom was too remote, too theoretical to motivate his teams. His lack of top-class experience told against him. Once, on a coaching course, he asked a group of professionals:

'Can you give me a reason why British players lack environmental awareness?'

'Because we didn't get enough meat during the war,' came the cynical reply.

Unlike Alf, he did not have that natural, intangible aura which incites devotion. 'Walter was a likeable fellow,' says Roger Hunt, one of the 1966 winners, 'but he didn't instill the same degree of discipline as Alf did later. Somehow, he came across more like an old-fashioned amateur.' Alan Peacock, the Middlesbrough and Leeds striker, is even more scathing:

Alf was very different to Walter Winterbottom. I was not impressed with Walter at all. He was like a schoolmaster. That's how he came across. It was so much better under Alf; he knew how to set teams up. But Walter was more like a cricket coach from the Gentlemen. He had little under-standing of the way professionals operate. Walter was too scared to upset anyone. Some players need a kick up the arse, others can be talked to.

Bobby Charlton, who played for four years under Winter-bottom, felt that

there was no sense of belonging in the team. Walter had this impeccable accent, whereas football's a poor man's game, players expect to be sworn at, a bit of industrial language. Through no fault of his own, Walter used to make it seem an academic language. He used to go through things in discussion that I felt were obvious to people who were supposed to be good players. It was theory all the time.

Jimmy Greaves, who like Charlton began his England career in the late fifties, has this analysis of the difference between Winterbottom and Ramsey:

Walter was a joy, although I never understood a word he said. I used to think, what on earth is he talking about, but I loved him all the same. I had the same respect for Alf, but the fun did go out of it. The thing about Walter was he could smile quite easily in defeat. If I wanted a manager who'd make friends, it would be Walter. If I wanted a winning team, I'd take Alf. He brought atmosphere and spirit. This was something Walter failed to do. Too often during Walter's era, teams were like strangers, on and off the pitch.

The consequences of Winterbottom's inadequate leadership, inconsistent selection policies and poor administration were made clear in the most dramatic fashion in 1950, when England entered the World Cup for the first time. Until then, the FA had refused to enter the competition, deeming it too inferior for England. Indeed, between 1927 and 1946, the British associations were not even members of FIFA, having withdrawn after a series of disputes over issues such as separate membership for the Irish Free State. In a signal of FIFA's welcome for Britain's return from isolation, it was generously decided that the 1949–50 Home International series could be used as a qualifier for the tournament in Brazil, with the top two teams going forward to the finals. England topped the table easily, having beaten all three of the other nations. But the Scottish FA had previously announced that they would not be going to Brazil unless they won the Home International championship. Travelling as runners-up would not be good enough. Despite pleading from England and FIFA, Scotland stuck with this self-denying, pig-headed decision, and remained at home. It was a move that only fuelled Alf's growing dislike of what he came to call 'the strange little men' north of the border.

Despite never having competed before, England were one of the favourites for the World Cup, largely because of the lustre of their name. But it was obvious, almost as soon as the party had gathered, that the preparations were inadequate. Instead of heading to South America a few weeks early to acclimatize, the England team held some practice sessions on the ground of Dulwich Hamlet FC at Dog Kennel Hill. 'I would have preferred to have gone to Brazil, got accustomed to the conditions and, of course, had a series of trial matches under the conditions we should have had to face,' said Alf, adding ruefully that the FA's finances did not stretch to this. In fact, England flew out barely a week before their first game. The Lockheed Constellation took off from Heathrow early on 19 June at the start of a journey lasting 31 hours, with stops on the way at Paris, Lisbon, Dakar and Recife, before landing in Rio on the 21st. 'The whole thing was a farce really, a shambles. We had a week's training in Dulwich, then the journey to Brazil seemed to take for ever. By the time we stepped off the plane, everyone was knackered,' recalls Alf's Spurs team-mate Eddie Baily, who was making his first England trip. Baily was also disturbed by the absence of any proper medical support. 'Can you believe it? All that way across the world and no bleedin' doctor.' Exhausted, the players made their way to the Luxor Hotel by the Copacabana beach, where they were shocked by the conditions they found, as Winterbottom later recalled:

Probably it was my fault because we should have gone into things more thoroughly but the Luxor was hopeless for our needs. As soon as we arrived, I knew there would be problems. When I inspected the kitchens, I was almost sick; the smell went up into the bedrooms, the food was swimming in oil and it was practically impossible to arrange suitable meals. Nearly all the players went down with tummy upsets at one time or another.

As Stanley Mortensen, one of the team's wits, put it, 'Even the dustbins have ulcers.'

The players encountered further difficulties as they practised in the South American heat, as Alf, who prided himself on his fitness, wrote:

During our training spells two things quickly impressed themselves upon me. The first was that during practice matches, I found it very hard to breathe. Secondly, at the conclusion of even an easy kick-around, I felt infinitely more tired than after a hectic League match at home.

But for all their problems, England did not seem to face a difficult passage to the next round, having been drawn against Chile, the USA and Spain. And progress seemed assured when England defeated Chile 2–0 in their opening game. Next came the apparent formality of beating the unknowns of the United States, a country that had no more interest in soccer than England had in baseball. For this game, the team had to fly 300 miles inland from Rio to Belo Horizonte, a modern city whose layout impressed Alf from the air: 'such a beautifully planned city with "baby skyscrapers", much loftier than any buildings we have in this country.' Alf was not so enamoured by the coach-ride from the airport to the team's base at the British-owned Morro Velho gold mine 16 miles from Belo Horizonte. According to Alf, this involved 'the nightmare experience of being driven around the 167 hairpin bends on a road which seemed to cling to the side of the mountain'. Nor was the accommodation, a series of chalets on a miners' camp, a great improvement on the Luxor Hotel. 'They stuck us in wooden huts. It was really primitive. We couldn't sleep at night,' recalled the goalkeeper Bert Williams. Even so, on the eve of the match, the players were in high spirits, enjoying a sing-along led, inevitably, by Eddie Baily, whom Alf often compared to the cockney comic Max Miller. No one doubted what the outcome would be the following day. One old miner at the camp asked Alf, 'Tell me, how many do you think you'll win by?' Back home, the *Daily Express* argued that the American team was so hopeless that England should give them a three-goal start. Double figures were possible, thought John Thompson of the *Daily Mirror*. Arthur Drewry, the Grimsby fishmonger who added to his duties as President of the Football League by serving as the chief selector for the England XI in the World Cup, was so confident that he decided the US game should be treated as little more than a practice match before the real contest against Spain. With barely a word of explanation, he overruled Winterbottom, who had wanted Stanley Matthews picked.

But the mood of optimism was dampened when the players reached the Belo Horizonte stadium, where they found a narrow pitch with coarse grass and a sprinkling of stones; 'I'd known better playing as a kid on the marshes,' says Eddie Baily. The dressing-rooms, which had only just been completed and reeked of building materials, were so dingy that Winterbottom took the players off to change at a local athletic club, ten minutes' bus ride away. On their return, the England team were greeted by a large hostile crowd of 20,000 gathered behind the 12-foot high concrete wall that surrounded the pitch. The atmosphere was intimidating, claustrophic. 'This is the first time I've ever played in a prison,' said Bert Williams to Alf.

Still, they were only playing the USA. And within minutes of the kick-off, England – wearing blue shirts to avoid a clash with the white of the Americans – were already on the attack, scything through the inexperienced American defence. It seemed only a matter of time before there would be a goal from England's front line, which included such legends as Tom Finney, Stan Mortensen of Blackpool and Wilf Mannion of Middlesbrough. But, after half an hour of missed opportunities, the scores remained level. Then, in the 37th minute, came the truly unexpected. A long, speculative shot was hit towards England's penalty box. There seemed little danger, for Bert Williams had it covered. But just as he was moving for it, the American centre-forward Joe Gaetjens – who later died in a prison in Haiti after taking part in the attempted coup against the corrupt regime of Papa Doc Duvalier – burst forward instinctively. As he dived, the ball appeared to hit the back of his head, took a wicked deflection and flew past Williams into the net. The English thought it was a freakish goal; the Americans praised Gaetjens' heroism.

England went into half-time still 1–0 down. Winterbottom reassured them that the goals were bound to come, but as one of the forwards, Roy Bentley, commented, 'It had begun to feel as though we could play for a week and not score.' It was the same sorry story in the second half. England squandered a wealth of easy chances, frequently hitting the woodwork or blasting over the bar. 'I was sitting alongside Stan Matthews, and he kept saying, "Bless my soul, bless my soul," remembers Eddie Baily. England captain Billy Wright later recalled how frustrated Alf became: 'Even Alf Ramsey, who used to be expressionless throughout a game, threw up his arms and looked to the sky when a perfect free-kick was somehow saved by their unorthodox keeper.' The England players even felt the referee was conspiring against them, especially when, in the dying minutes, another of Ramsey's free-kicks was met firmly by Stan Mortensen's header and appeared to cross the line, only for the referee to disallow the goal. There was to be no reprieve. After 90 minutes, England had lost by that single Gaetjens' strike. 'I have never felt worse on a football pitch than at that final whistle,' said Billy Wright. The crowd erupted in disbelief and ecstasy, setting fire to newspapers on the terraces and letting off a barrage of fireworks into the blue sky. When the result was flashed to newsrooms in England across the wires from Reuters, there was incredulity. It was widely thought that a typing error had been made, with the real score being England 10, USA 1.

But the players were all too aware of the catastrophe. 'The dressing-room was like a morgue. It felt like a disgrace to lose to a team of no-hopers. I think it was the darkest moment of my career,' says Sir Tom Finney. In attempts to lessen the shame, a number of legends grew up. One was that England had been desperately unlucky, since nothing more than fate had prevented a deserved victory. 'I think a fair result would have been 12–1,' says Bert Williams. Alf Ramsey himself summed up this attitude: 'So far as we were concerned there was a gremlin upon that football and it was not our day, the United States running out winners by that "streaky" goal.' Another complaint was that the USA had fielded a team of ineligible players from overseas; the florid, faintly ridiculous Desmond Hackett of the *Daily Express* wrote that the American eleven 'seemed to have come straight from Ellis Island because there was not an American-born player in the side'. This is nonsense. Eight of them were born in the US, while the other three, whose number included the former Wrexham midfielder Eddie McIlvanney, were cleared by FIFA under the residency rule. It was, in any case, a pitiful charge. Why should England have had anything to fear from a group of journeymen, no matter where they came from?

From an American viewpoint, however, England were far

less dominant than was later suggested. An interesting article in the magazine *Soccer America* highlighted how poorly England played – and not just the forwards. The US full-back Harry Keough, for instance, felt that 'England took us too lightly and tried to come in too close early in the game before shooting'. Keough went on, in reference to Bert Williams' argument that England should have won 12–1: 'He isn't telling it all. He had to tip over one from our left-winger, Ed Souza, with 15 minutes to go. And with three minutes left our right-winger Frank Wallace took off on a breakaway and only had Williams to beat, which he did, but Alf Ramsey followed the play and saved it.' But Ramsey, claimed Keough, 'had otherwise a bad day, with Ed Souza beating him frequently'. And even the *Daily Mail* admitted that Souza 'played a victory march against Wright and Ramsey'. In *Talking Football*, Ramsey described Ed Souza, with a hint of mournful euphemism, as 'a truly great player who possessed a pair of educated feet in addition to a pair of broad shoulders which he used fairly and often.'

To this day, England's defeat by the USA remains the greatest upset in the nation's sporting history. It haunted the players for years, a stain on their reputations. The supposed champions of the world had been turned into an international laughing stock. 'I hate thinking about it even now,' Bert Williams said recently. For Alf Ramsey, the defeat rankled deeply. One journalist, who mentioned the match years later, recorded that 'his face creased and he looked like a man who had been jabbed in an unhealed wound'. Educated in the days when there was still an Empire, Alf was a ferocious English patriot, one who always described his nationality on official forms as 'English' rather than 'British'. His almost visceral attachment to his country was one of the cornerstones of his existence. And when the chance came more than a decade later, he was determined to avenge this humiliation.

Broken and bewildered, England played their last group game against Spain, needing a win to gain a play-off place. Brought into the side alongside Stan Matthews, Eddie Baily did his best to raise morale:

Walter said to me before the kick-off, 'Just settle in and give Stan the ball.'

'Is he going to give it back?' I said.

There was nothing funny about the result. England were beaten 1–0 and crashed out of the World Cup. Again, there were complaints about the refereeing and the conditions. 'I have never played in a game so hot. The temperature must have been 105 degrees. At half-time, we went down into the dressing-room and had to put on oxygen masks,' says Eddie Baily. 'The referee allowed an unbelievable amount of obstruction and shirt-pulling. I remember Alf, who had this thing about fair play, being furious.' Alf even claimed that the Spaniards must have thought they were playing basketball, such was their propensity to use their hands. With the kind of patronizing insularity that was to become his hallmark, Alf said in 1952 of the referee's interpretation of the rules, 'It is going to take a considerable time for the whole world to see football as we do.'

In truth, it was going to take England a long time to catch up with the rest of the world. Convinced that their team had been the victims of nothing more than bad luck, the self-satisfied football establishment learnt little from the Brazilian fiasco. The illusion was maintained that England were still the best in the world. There were to be no changes in policy or structure or playing style. The attitude was captured by the statement of Bob Jackson, manager of Portsmouth, the club which won successive championship titles in the late forties:

'What suits Continentals and South Americans doesn't necessarily suit us. We have a way of playing that has stood the test of time. Given more favourable conditions and a fair crack of the whip, we can beat anybody.'

England may have been failing, but for Alf personally the years immediately after the American debacle were the best of his international playing career. Now in his thirties, he was at the peak of his confidence, his understanding of the game enhanced by experience. It is a tribute to his effectiveness that in an era of fluctuating selection policy, Alf was not to lose his place for three seasons. His own captain, Billy Wright, was glowing in his praise of his right-back. He once described Alf as 'the coolest player I have ever seen in an international match' and 'one of the greatest of modern defenders. He brought with him into the game tremendous thought and initiative.' Playing in front of Ramsey, said Wright, 'I have come to appreciate the tremendous accuracy of his passes. He strokes the ball along the grass with radar-like accuracy.' He went on to refer to Alf's unique understanding of the game:

> I could sit for hours and talk football with Alf Ramsey. He has the priceless ability of being able to put over new ideas in a splendid fashion, encourages his colleagues to reveal their own theories and in every way is a remarkable character whose contribution to the game has definitely helped to improve the standard of defensive play.

As an example of Alf's thinking, Wright cited his tactics playing for Spurs against the Newcastle and Scottish winger Bobby Mitchell, one of those quick players who always worried him. Before the match, Alf examined the pitch at White Hart Lane, looking closely at the two ends where he would operate. He said little, but proceeded to have one of the best League games of his life, continually forcing Mitchell into the dampest areas. 'Even the world's greatest ball-players cannot play in mud,' said Alf afterwards.

Ramsey had become such a central figure in the English team that when Wright was dropped in the autumn of 1950 because of poor form, Alf was chosen as the England captain for the Home International against Wales, a game which England won easily 4–2. Alf, in the words of Tom Finney, was 'an ideal captain, very methodical. He studied the game a lot and knew so much about it.' With Wright still absent, Alf retained the captaincy for the next match, against Yugoslavia. England's vulnerability was becoming more apparent than ever, as Ramsey's team were held to a 2–2 draw, the first time that a continental side had achieved a draw on English soil. Making his debut in that game was the brave-hearted Bolton centre-forward and former coalminer Nat Lofthouse. 'From the start, Alf did all he could to make me, the only new international in the side, feel at home,' said Lofthouse. 'His great knowledge of soccer and his ability to discuss the game in an interesting way, made a profound impression on me.' Talking of his wider qualities, Lofthouse called Alf 'the greatest driver of an accurate ball I have ever seen. When he makes up his mind to send a clearance to you, the ball invariably finds its target. The tremendous accuracy and faith that Alf has in himself also gives confidence to others.'

After a solid game against Yugoslavia, Alf had a far more painful ordeal: his first major after-dinner speech. To the end of his life, Alf found such appearances difficult. An awkward, stilted speaker, he was unable to enliven his performances with either humorous anecdotes or powerful delivery. 'I don't think he took kindly to public speaking. He was not very good at it; he was very clipped,' says the journalist Ken Jones. Alf confessed that, at that 1950 banquet, 'I was extremely nervous.

I would rather take a penalty at Wembley than again go through such an experience.' He managed to get through it, however, with 'a few words of thanks'. Fortunately for Alf, he would give up this ambassadorial role, when Billy Wright returned to the captaincy in early 1951, having recovered his form.

Ramsey showed no signs of any decline in his. He had become so cool that even with England he would retain the Spurs approach, often trapping clearances deep in his own half, inviting a challenge from his opponent before pushing the ball to a colleague. One of his increasingly important gifts was his deadliness at set pieces, as Nat Lofthouse recalled in 1954:

Another of Ramsey's intelligent moves, developed because of his beautifully controlled kicking, has brought many goals from free kicks. Ramsey and I have practised this move for hours before international matches. He possesses an uncanny knack of being able to place a football almost on a pinhead. Such accuracy is, of course, the outcome of years of hard work, a factor people are inclined to forget when they see the master soccer-man in action. It is, however, only when you have been out on the pitch with Alf Ramsey that you appreciate his greatness.

In 1953, Billy Wright wrote of Alf's quest for perfection:

For hours Alf Ramsey and Nat Lofthouse practised this move. I have rarely known Ramsey to be completely satisfied with his efforts and although early on he was placing the ball on Lofthouse's napper eight times out of ten, Alf, we all knew, would never be content until he could do it ten times out of ten.

Alf's manager, Walter Winterbottom, in a BBC interview in 1970, emphasized his importance as an England player, praising him for being 'so consistent'. Winterbottom went on:

> We always felt confident in him. He was a thinking full-back, one who believed in precision passing. He was good with his drives; he could hit the ball very true. He was also precise in those long, floating lobs, about forty yards up the field. He could put an absolutely precise centre which would allow someone like Nat Lofthouse – who was a bit like Geoff Hurst – to run in at an angle and meet the ball at the right moment to outwit the keeper. Alf was already then forming opinions around this idea of concentrated defensive work, of never losing the ball when you had possession and of this all-round playing and hard working of the team. The things coming through now I could see when he was playing.

A profile in the *Daily Mirror* in February 1951 called Alf 'the soccer intellectual'. It stated that

> to Ramsey, football appears as a succession of chess problems, an exercise of the intellect. For all that, he can produce a lustiness and strength in the tackle when needed. He passes the ball with supreme accuracy and precise pace. He spends as much time in practice as any inside-forward might. These are the qualities of Ramsey's game reflected in himself. He dresses quietly, immaculately. In conversation, he is reflective. He said one very significant thing to me: 'I don't care too much to be told that I have had a wonderful game. I prefer it when someone points out a fault. Then I can do something about it.'

Alf was particularly impressive in the match against Argentina, when England looked incapable of breaking down the South Americans until his calm assurance pulled them through to win 2–1. Bernard Joy of *The Star* described Alf's performance as

> the finest full-back display I have seen in many years. Ramsey played as though there were no Argentinos within miles. He refused to be stampeded into helter-skelter methods and particularly in the second half sent forward a stream of precision passes. Ramsey it was who realized that the only way to draw the Argentine defence from goalmouth was to start short passing bouts in midfield. And his brainy free kick with the ball to the far post instead of into the centre of the crowded penalty area won the match.

Alf's authority was even more crucial in the match against Austria in November 1951, when England's unbeaten record against continental sides came under its most severe threat yet. Led by their brilliant attacking centre-half Ernst Ocwirk, Austria were one of the most powerful teams in Europe at the time, and with only 25 minutes to go, as they led 1–0, they seemed to be on the verge of a famous victory. But then Eddie Baily won the ball, weaved his way through the Austrian defence and was about to shoot when he was brought down. The referee instantly gave a penalty.

The eyes of the huge Wembley crowd instantly turned to Alf, whose unflappable temperament had made him the chief penalty taker for Spurs and England. As he walked up to the spot, Eddie Baily said to him, 'I've done all the fuckin' hard work for you, Alf, now make sure you score.' A silence descended around the stadium, everyone knowing that England's long cherished record depended on the 'The General'.

Preparing to take the kick, Alf exuded his usual steadiness, behaving as casually 'as if he were taking a stroll along Bournemouth Front,' said Billy Wright. But Alf was always good at covering up his feelings. Inwardly, recorded Alf, 'my heart was beating madly and the goal appeared to have shrunk to about half its normal size'. The tension grew while Alf placed the ball slowly and deliberately on the spot. As in everything else in football, he was a master of detail when it came to penalties. 'In the course of practice I have noticed that if you kick a football with the lace facing the sky it invariably rises high and, after making some experiments, I discovered that the best way to place the ball for a spot kick is to make the lace face the keeper.' Finally satisfied with his placement, he took a few steps back and then, on the referee's signal, moved towards the ball. Just as his right foot was about to make contact, he saw the Austrian keeper move slightly to his right. 'At once, like a boxer going in for the kill, I side-footed the ball into the other side of the net.' A vast, echoing roar went round the terraces as the ball sped across the lush Wembley turf into the corner.

Three minutes later England took the lead, again thanks to Alf. All the hours of practice with Nat Lofthouse paid off, as one of his perfectly flighted free-kicks sailed over the Austria defence and straight onto the head of Nat Lofthouse, who knocked it down into the net. But Austria refused to give up and late in the game scored the equalizer through a penalty. To England's relief, the score-line finished 2–2. The unbeaten home record against Europe remained intact. With little sense of perspective, the *Daily Mail* praised England for 'a glorious fighting display that completely rehabilitated the reputation of English international football, threadbare since our World Cup defeat'. This may have been an exaggeration, but Alf certainly deserved the plaudits. He was, according to the *Mail*,

England's 'ice-cool hero'. Alf himself described the game as 'my greatest international'.

One England player making his debut in that historic game was the young Arsenal winger Arthur Milton, who also played cricket for Gloucestershire and England; indeed, he was to be the last ever double international. Today, Milton has interesting memories of playing alongside Alf:

Alf was very quiet in the dressing-room, very quiet. But I was the new boy, so he came and had a chat, telling me to go out and play my game and enjoy it. I found him reassuring, comforting. Walter Winterbottom, the manager, was not all that forthcoming. Billy Wright was the captain, but I found Alf the most reassuring of those three. I could see that he was very in control of himself. He did not make a fuss. To be honest, I got lost a bit in the game, not having had much experience, but I got no ball from Billy Wright. I always felt that Bill Nicholson was a much better wing-half than Billy Wright. Now Alf, he was a real class act. He stood out. Not perhaps such a good defender as a distributor of the ball. He was good in defence but nothing exceptional. But his use of the ball was always fantastic. Lovely mover he was.

Throughout 1952, Alf remained a fixture in the England team, playing in all seven internationals, including the famous 3–2 win against Austria in Vienna, when Nat Lofthouse ran half the length of the field to score the winner. In the crowd at the Prater stadium, there was a large contingent of British soldiers, members of the multi-national Forces of Occupation, and at the final whistle they poured onto the field in celebration. A surprised Alf was hoisted on the shoulders of one khaki-clad Tommy, who told him, 'We ain't half pleased mate. The local lads have been telling us for months what they were going to do to you. Well, you well and truly done 'em, mate.' For all his obvious class, Alf allowed occasional errors to creep into his play. Against Portugal at Goodison in 1951, for instance, he mis-hit a backpass which allowed the Portugese to equalize 2–2, though England eventually ran out winners 5–2. Even worse was his howler against Northern Ireland in Belfast in November 1952. The Celtic forward Charlie Tully, one of the quick mercurial wingers who always troubled Alf, took an inswinging corner. On the near post Alf seemed to have it covered and was preparing to head the ball away, when suddenly he swerved outside its path. The ball sailed into the net, 'as if pulled by some magnetic force', to use the phrase of England goalkeeper Gil Merrick. Afterwards, with typical conviction and no word of apology, Alf told Merrick, 'I let it go because I thought it was going to hit the side netting.'

Alf kept his England place in the first half of 1953, though during a tour of South America in the summer, he succumbed to dysentery, another reason why he came to distrust the continent. Moreover, he was not taken with what he felt was the poor behaviour of both the fruit-throwing crowds and the ankle-tapping, shirt-pulling players. By the autumn, there were signs that his age was beginning to catch up with him. Due to a series of minor injuries, he had to miss games against Wales and Northern Ireland, thereby ending his long-unbroken run of England appearances which stretched back to 1949, a heroic achievement considering that the likes of Stanley Matthews, Jackie Milburn and Nat Lofthouse were regularly left out because of selectoral whims, while Arsenal defender Leslie Compton, brother of Denis, was picked for his first cap in 1950 at the age of 38. Alf had recovered sufficiently to return for the match against the Rest of Europe in October 1953, held to celebrate the 90th anniversary of the founding of the FA. Just as against Austria two years earlier, England's unbeaten record at home was under the most stringent challenge – and, once again, it was Alf who prevented defeat. In the dying minutes of an exciting, open game, England were losing 3–4. But then, with just 60 seconds left, Stan Mortensen was brought down in the penalty area. As collected as ever, Alf picked up the ball, showing no sign of the intense pressure he was under. Nat Lofthouse continues the story:

> Alf took his time in arranging the ball with the lace facing the goalkeeper in order to keep it low. Then he stepped up to the ball, sold a perfect dummy to Beara and as the Yugoslav goalkeeper threw himself to the right plonked the ball past his left hand. I have never heard the crowd go quite so mad at Wembley as they did that afternoon. As he turned away, Alf gave me a wry smile.

That was about the height of public emotion he ever showed.

Derek Ufton of Charlton played his only game for England against the Rest of Europe, and says that he can

> remember the game like yesterday. The Europeans all had great skill, great pace; they kept the ball, left us chasing shadows and we were lucky to get out of it 4–4. Alf was superb to me. Billy Wright was the captain. He was lovely off the field, but on the field he played his own game, ran about and led by example. I got no help from him. Walter Winterbottom was a terrific guy, but we did not really have proper team talks, tactical discussions. As regards Alf, I cannot speak highly enough of him. He may have been quiet, but it's a funny thing on a football pitch. You might have 100,000 in the crowd but they are at a distance. So you get this constant hum but you can actually talk to each other in whispers. During the match, Alf spoke to me as

quietly as he always did. So we just talked through the game. He was a tremendous help to me. Everyone regarded him highly in the England team. He was always what they called a cultured defender. He took his time with everything, and always had time on the ball, a great touch and great delivery. He was incredibly cool about his penalty.

Despite winning Derek Ufton's approval, the day of reckoning was rapidly approaching for both Ramsey and England. At 33, Alf did not have long left at the highest level. And it was inevitable, given England's worrying recent form, that the unbeaten record would soon be broken. After all, they had performed dismally in the World Cup and had drawn four of their last seven games at home. Nevertheless, a depressing complacency still hung over the game. 'I remain convinced that we still lead the world in the matter of technical knowledge and in our approach to the game,' wrote Billy Wright in 1953. That mood was about to be shattered by the visit of the Hungarians on 25 November 1953. The Marvellous Magyars had set the world of football alight with their fluid, attacking formation, their captivating ball skills, their intuitive understanding and their daring unorthodoxy. Ostensibly amateurs with other employment in the communist state of Hungary, they actually trained with more purpose and rigour than most English club professionals. The Olympic champions of 1952, they had been unbeaten for two years. Unlike the England team, the Hungarians continually practised as a unit. As Winterbottom, the principal victim of England's erratic approach to selection, said later with a justifiable note of regret, 'They all played in Budapest, training week in week out as a national team, playing against club sides at home and abroad, so they were constantly together, knitting to perfection.'

The clash was billed by the British press as 'The Match

of the Century'. It turned into a walkover, as England were thrashed 6–3. The gap in class was evident even before the kick-off. In contrast to the English tradition of coming out from the dressing-room just five minutes before the start, the Hungarians were on the Wembley turf warming up for twenty minutes. Malcolm Allison, later a revolutionary coach himself, was a youthful spectator in the crowd. He later recalled watching in admiration as two players 'volleyed the ball to each other eight times over 25 yards without it touching the ground'. The Hungarian dominance immediately manifested itself once the match started. A few short passes down the field, and Hungary had scored within the first minute. England never recovered from that crippling start. Utterly perplexed by the pace and tactics of the Hungarians, they were swept aside and conceded a three-goal lead before they scored their second. England's bewilderment was symbolized by the unfortunate experience of Blackpool centre-half Harry Johnstone, who had not a clue how to deal with the deep-lying centre-forward Hidegkuti. If he tried to go with Hidegkuti, then he left space for other Hungarians to exploit. But if he stayed in defence, Hidegkuti was free to act as play-maker. Nor did England's captain Billy Wright know how to cope. In one memorable moment, he ended up on his backside after trying to tackle his opposite number Ferenc Puskas, just as Puskas, in the England penalty area, pulled the ball back with his right foot before slamming it into the goal with his left.

As Puskas later explained, the Hungarian system was not dissimilar to Spurs' push-and-run:

We didn't nurse the ball, but kept passing it so quickly that an onlooker might have thought the ball was burning our feet. But however quickly we got rid of it, we saw that it usually went to one of our own side. This quick game, combined with the fact that we had freed ourselves from the burden of the old-fashioned rule of staying in one's original position, did much to tire the England defence.

Puskas also stressed the importance of positional play, one of Alf's guiding principles: 'Throughout the game we demonstrated the golden rule of modern football and that is: the good player keeps playing even without the ball.' Alf believed in this so strongly that, early in his England career, he had the nerve to lecture Billy Wright: 'I suggested to him that perhaps he was watching the ball too much rather than the man.'

With the kind of blinkered partisanship that later became a feature of his management, Alf refused to concede that England had been outclassed: 'Four of those goals came from outside the penalty area. We should never have lost.' And Alf had some support in that analysis from Walter Winterbottom, who agreed that Gil Merrick, the moustachioed Birmingham keeper, had a poor game: 'Merrick was my disaster; nice fellow, strong, good at club level, but for England he sometimes lost his nerve. Against Hungary I felt they were stoppable shots, but he got nowhere near them.' Merrick himself, who six months later suffered an even greater mauling when England were beaten 7–1 in Budapest, thought that the explanation lay with 'deadly football to which we had no answer because we simply couldn't match them for speed'. In his 1954 book *I See It All* he gave this insight into the Hungarian approach. His views are fascinating for the way they predicate the England team of 1966, which famously eschewed traditional wing play. From the kick-off, wrote Merrick,

any man in the line can and does appear in any position . . . The wingers, like the rest of the team, do not hold the ball and dribble with it; they don't have to because they are always given the ball either in the clear or when they are racing past a defender ... In complete contrast to the Englishman, the Hungarian wingers hardly ever cross the ball ... The overall picture is one of a side moving at speed, individually working the ball almost as quickly and with great accuracy and with every man knowing what his partner is doing.

Alf suffered even more than Merrick from the fall-out over the 6–3 defeat at Wembley. He was finished as an England player. One of the finest of post-war international careers had come to an end. And the curtain would soon start to fall on his days at Tottenham.

# FIVE

# *Villa Park*

'In due course the day comes – there's no dodging it – when some of the regular players pass their peak and start on the downhill journey,' wrote Alf in 1951. That moment arrived for him around 1953, when the physical weaknesses in his game were no longer outweighed by his intelligence.

Throughout his career, he had suffered from a lack of pace and an inability to turn quickly because he was heavily built around the hips. The journalist and broadcaster Michael Parkinson always stuck to the theory that Alf disliked wingers because of his own experience of playing against them. He cited the example of watching Alf, when he was a Southampton full-back, being tormented by Barnsley's 'galloping magician' Johnny Kelly. According to Parkinson, Alf

never recovered from the trauma of trying to stop Kelly that wet and windy afternoon at Oakwell when Southampton were the visitors. Kelly was inspired that day. There was something about Ramsey that put him in a devilish frame of mind. He turned the full-back inside out to the point where Ramsey was humiliated.

Parkinson then claimed that 'Kelly so unhinged Ramsey, making him hate wingers so much, that when he became coach he embarked on a mission to ban them from the game'.

Parkinson's amusing thesis bears little relationship to the reality of how Alf set about building his England teams. Yet there is no doubt that a fast player could brutally expose him. 'If someone really came at him, that was the thing he hated,' said Ted Ditchburn. Billy Liddell of Liverpool and Bobby Mitchell of Newcastle were two wingers he found especially difficult. And it was the Hungarian captain Ferenc Puskas who wrote that Alf had 'the fault of turning too slowly'. These deficiencies were becoming more glaring as the great Spurs Championship-winning side began to go into decline. They finished second to Manchester United in 1951–52, but fell to tenth place the following season and 16th, close to the relegation zone, in 1953–54. Push-and-run was a style that could only be operated by players of supreme fitness, and, along with Alf, Ron Burgess, Bill Nicholson, Les Bennett and Ted Ditchburn were all in their early and mid-thirties. During this time, Alf was also hampered by an abdominal injury, which further slowed him down and occasionally caused him intense pain. The advice of the Tottenham physiotherapist was that he should continue to play as much as possible, since movement on the field could provide the equivalent of an internal massage. In effect, Alf was told to 'get on with it', even if he was more restricted than ever.

Spurs fans started to complain about Alf's preference for ball play rather than clearing his lines. Certain players felt that a staleness was creeping into some of his moves, like the delayed back pass to the keeper, followed by a run up the touchline to receive the throw. As Ron Reynolds, who was playing more regularly in the Spurs goal by 1953, put it, 'Alf could not see that it was the same thing all the time, it was stereotyped and that, as the goalkeeper, you had a view of everything in front of you, which might give you better options'. The problems with Alf's approach were highlighted in the FA Cup semi-final against Blackpool at Villa Park on 21 March 1953, which turned into one of the darkest days of Alf's career. Until the last minute, he had enjoyed a superb game, completely neutralizing the Blackpool left-winger Bill Perry. Then Blackpool won a free-kick near the half-way line. The ball was sent over to the left flank, where Alf seemed to have easily won the chase against Bill Perry. Goalkeeper Ted Ditchburn told me what happened next:

> He tried to be a bit clever. As the kick came across, he ended up facing his own goal. He was trying to judge the ball as it fell over his shoulder, then play it when it bounced. But it struck his knee and then ran away from him. Jimmy Mudie, the Blackpool inside-forward, latched on to it immediately and put it in the back of the net. We were out of the Cup. I was not too pleased with that, though I did not have much of a go at Alf.

Even in the last minute of a vital Cup tie, when most other defenders would have just tried to belt the ball into the crowd, Alf wanted to play elegant football. But his mistake had cost Spurs a place at Wembley. 'We just sat and stared into space. There is nothing worse than to lose in a semi-final, and to go out to a goal like that was just unbearable,' said Bill Nicholson.

Alf had to endure a barrage of criticism from fans and press alike for weeks. One Spurs director said bitterly: 'Ramsey stupidly gave the goal away. He could have easily kicked the ball out of play.' In public at least, Alf was contrite but dignified. In an interview with the *Daily Express* the day after the defeat, he said: 'I don't think any man must lose himself in self-pity. Football is my craft and as a craftsman I am paid not to make mistakes. I miskicked it. There it is. I can only say I am terribly sorry.' Alf then told the paper of his movements in the immediate aftermath of the game:

> I travelled home with my wife and a friend by car. Perhaps it was just as well I was not with the team – it would have been hard to know what to say. Usually Sunday is a happy day for my wife and me. I like to do a bit of gardening and in the afternoon we usually go for a drive. But today my wife and I have just stayed at home.

In the privacy of the Spurs dressing-room, however, Alf demonstrated that obstinate, hard headed streak which would later, as England manager, win him matches but make him enemies. Rather than wallowing in remorse, he insisted on analysing the move that led to the Blackpool goal, handing out criticism to other players. In particular, he attacked Eddie Baily for disputing the referee's decision over the free-kick. Baily recalled:

> Alf reckoned I was gesticulating at the time. The kick was taken quickly and then the next thing Jimmy Mudie was in front of goal and had scored. So when we got into the dressing-room, he said, 'What were you bloody arguing about out there?'
> 'What are you on about? What were you doing?' I replied. That's the way we talked.

Alf felt that if Eddie had not stopped to argue with the referee, then he could have provided more cover in defence at the free-kick. 'Alf could patronize you. He would not really say sorry. He wanted to look like he was not in the wrong. He hit a poor ball and he somehow ended up blaming me. That was his way, claiming it was my fault.' Ted Ditchburn also recalled,

'It was one of those things. But I don't recall Alf ever saying he was sorry.'

For all his reluctance to accept the blame in front of his colleagues, Alf knew he had made a terrible error. It was one that haunted him for the rest of his life, 'an awful moment in my career,' he once said. The East Anglian journalist Tony Garnett gained an insight into how much Alf was pained by the memory of that day:

Alf had a certain sentimentality about him. Once Ipswich were playing Aston Villa and about an hour before the kick-off he said, 'Come with me, I want to show you something.' So we walked out onto the pitch and then he pointed to a little area of turf. He said, 'You know, that's where I lost the ball in the FA Cup semi-final and gave away the goal which led us to lose.' He was pointing to the very spot of ground where it happened. The incident must have haunted him.

For someone as coldly rational as Alf, it was no consolation that, without his mistake, there would have been no Matthews Final in 1953, that most romantic of club games when the 38-year-old winger inspired Blackpool to a 4–3 victory over Bolton.

In the following season, 1953–54, when Alf was dropped from the England team, there was widespread speculation that his days at Spurs were numbered. One rumour was that he would return to Southampton, then in the Third Division, to take up a player-coach role. 'Ramsey himself has not yet made any statement but I know that he and his wife Rita, a South-ampton girl, would be happy with the appointment,' wrote Frank Butler in the *News of the World* in April 1954. By then Alf was 34, yet the ageing process appeared to be slowing down, for Butler unknowingly knocked off three years: 'At 31, Ramsey, one of soccer's most intelligent players – he is known as The General – is naturally looking to the future.' Later that year, Wolves were said to have expressed an interest in acquiring Ramsey as a coach to assist their manager, the explosive, controversial, devout Christian Stan Cullis. 'My news will be greeted with mixed feelings by Tottenham followers,' wrote Roy Peskett in the *Daily Mail*. 'Since Spurs hit a bad patch this season, much criticism has been levelled at Ramsey's slowness.' And Peskett believed that Alf could have a great future in this new role: 'Ramsey, a fine type on and off the field, is the ideal coach. I have seen him demonstrate to schoolboys, putting them at their ease and showing them the basic principles in simple, convincing fashion.' All this talk was unfounded. Ramsey did become a coach in 1954, but only in a small part-time role at the minor non-League club Eton Manor.

He was not yet finished as a Spurs player, even as the title-winning side began to break up. Indeed, when Ron Burgess left in the 1954 season to join Swansea, Arthur Rowe appointed him as the new club captain, a job in which his single-mindedness soon made itself felt, as George Robb recalled:

Alf wouldn't stand any nonsense, so that was a good thing for a potential manager. If he thought someone wasn't pulling their weight during a game, he'd let them know! He wasn't disinclined to reproach somebody. In team talks, he would be more forthcoming, putting his own ideas forward.

Alf's asperity could lead to fierce arguments within the club. One such occasion was later recalled by Arthur Rowe for the BBC:

We were in a team meeting. It had gone quite peacefully and I said, 'We should do the things we agreed to do, and we shouldn't do the things we agreed not to do.' And then I asked quite calmly, 'So why do we do it?' And at that, Alf suddenly exploded, 'Yes, WHY do we do it?' I quickly realized that beneath his peaceful, bland exterior was a volcano of passion and ambition and loyalty and fierce enthusiasm. This is how it was.'

Though Arthur and Alf never descended to rows, the same was not true of Alf's relationship with Bill Nicholson, who played right-half in front of Alf. 'Bill was a typical Yorkshireman and his attitude did not always go down too well with Alf. I don't mean in a nasty way but they would not see eye to eye,' says former inside-forward Denis Uphill. In the same vein, Ron Reynolds told his biographer, Dave Bowler, that he could remember

some absolutely enormous blazing rows between Alf Ramsey and Bill Nicholson, which was odd really because both didn't have much to say most of the time – unless it was to have an argument. Alf was terrible like that – he didn't suffer what he saw to be fools gladly and he would quickly chew you out if he disagreed with you – but Bill could give as good as he got. Typically dour Yorkshireman, very blunt. He got fed up that Alf would cut him out of the game, he'd bypass him and go straight on to the forwards, he'd race upfield and just expect Bill to slot in behind him. Bill only got one England cap where Alf got dozens and I think Bill sometimes thought that he was winning them for Alf and not getting himself noticed.

One journalist who came to know Alf in the early fifties was the writer Ralph T. Finn, who covered games at White

Hart Lane and wrote two books about Spurs. A man of monumental self-importance, he was inclined to exaggerate his closeness to Alf. Nevertheless, having watched Alf in action and talked to him at Spurs, Finn left this compelling portrait in 1966, based on his own experiences of more than a decade earlier:

Our Alf was a student of the game. He didn't just play it: he lived it. He had playing principles and was prepared to abide by them. There was his own superb confidence in his own ability, his own judgement, his own decisions. He seldom believed, even then, that he could misread a playing situation. He had superb positional sense fostered, I would suppose, by the fact that his superior mind could read the ones of most of the players who opposed him. I'm not saying he was or is brainy. Or intellectual. Or even cultured. But there was a certain shrewdness, a certain air of assurance, a certain quiet faith in his own words that lifted him out of the rut of people who say things without conviction or say them expecting to be contradicted. Alf never looked for or expected contradiction. His own team-mates called him The General. He skippered them off the field as well as on. He was with them but never really of them. Aloof is the word for it. He was, and still is, aloof. It is not, as I remember, a quality he has affected, though he might well have developed it. But he was always apart from the herd as if he'd been born on a better side of the bed than they. Let me not give you the impression he was disdainful or class-conscious or arrogant. Proud, yes; but arrogant, no.

In another passage Finn recalled that he often gave lifts to Alf and other players from Tottenham:

I remember having Alf and his wife and about half a dozen others in my car one evening. So full was it that she sat on his lap. I used to have three-cornered chats with Arthur Rowe and Alf Ramsey when I travelled to away matches with them. Alf was always intelligent. A deep thinker. A man with ideas of his own.

Despite this image of aloofness, many of the younger players at Spurs have affectionate memories of a kinder side of Alf. Ron Henry, who later played for England under Alf's management, told me:

I joined Spurs in 1954. I can remember going into the dressing-room on my first morning and old Cecil Poyton, the trainer, said to me, 'Use that peg there, Ron, will you?'

'Well who's next to me?'

'Alf Ramsey.'

I could have fallen through the floor, because I'd been supporting Tottenham since I was nine years old. But once I'd met him, I got on well with him. He used to take me aside and give me little pieces of information on what to do. Some pros can be very hard on young players but it was not like that at Spurs. He was a quiet man but when we were going to away games, he would come up to me on the bus and give me advice. 'Son, if you behave yourself, and keep going as you are, you'll be a good player. But you've got to get experience first.'

He was a good bloke. I always thought he would make a good manager. He had something special about him. He loved football. That's all he wanted to talk about. He seemed to have no interest in anything else. But he never showed off. He would come into the dressing-room, have his shower, get dressed, get in his car. He was a gentleman through and through. But, away from football, he was very shy. He did not like speaking in front of strangers. He would almost seem to start blushing then. He had his own little circle and that was it. A conversation with him would be, 'Yes, yes, now off you go.'

Like Ron Henry, Terry Dyson has a similar recollection of Alf's decency, this time manifested by concern over playing gear:

I joined Spurs just as Alf was coming to the end. I remember he was injured one time and I was changing for the game, trying to get my socks on. In those days, the white of the Spurs sock was almost as long as the blue. 'Bloody hell, these are a bit long,' I thought to myself, because I couldn't get the white bit turned down properly. Then Alf came over with a pair of tie-ups, and did it for me, so the socks looked at lot neater. His reputation was very big in the club – and I could see why.

Ed Speight was another who joined Spurs in 1954:

We were going to Cheshunt for training on my first day and Arthur Rowe tells me, 'Go and sit over there,' gesturing half-way down the coach. So I go down and this guy gets up, 'How do you do, my name is Alf Ramsey.'

I am a quivering mass. I am meeting God. I sit down beside him.

'And where do you come from?'

'Dagenham."

'Oh, that's good.'

I thought afterwards, Arthur Rowe must have deliberately put me beside him. But Alf did not say anything about

Dagenham, even at that first meeting. He lived in Barking then. Syd McClellan, another Dagenham lad, and myself would take the trolleybus from Dagenham Heathway to Barking and then Alf would give us a lift to Tottenham in his Ford Anglia. He was always well-dressed and had this presence about him. He looked a little Mediterranean in appearance but he never talked about his background, not in the car or the coach or at the training ground. I would not say Alf did not speak, for that would be wrong. But he was always more likely to react to a conversation than instigate it. He was always on guard, always. He had this mask and would never reveal much. If Alf made a comment, everyone listened because he had something to say.

I remember one of the few times I ever saw Alf lead the conversation. We were at lunch after training and Alf had been at some reception the night before.

'Yesterday I met the most beautiful woman in the world.'

Everyone stopped. If that had come from one of the younger players, we would not have thought much of it. But from Alf, it was different. He was talking about the actress Ava Gardner.

Denis Uphill shared a cabin with Alf on a Spurs trip to Canada in 1954:

Alf was officially my minder, that's what Arthur Rowe said. Unlike a lot of the rest of passengers, Alf and I did not get seasick on the crossing of the Atlantic. I remember one time we were training on deck when Alf and I got a call to go back to our cabin, because water was coming into it. What had happened was that Les Medley, who was in the cabin next to ours, had left the porthole window open during a rough patch and the sea came straight in, flooding out the place. There was some cursin' then. Alf was all right to share with, but he was ever so inward. Not nasty. You never heard him say a bad word about anyone but if the conversation wasn't about football he would just switch off. He did read the papers a bit; he liked the *Express*, especially the cross-word puzzles. Canada was terrific, very different to post-war Britain, much more open. We travelled across the country by train and usually stayed in these big log cabins. If we stopped off somewhere to have a drink, Alf would usually just have a quiet one, nothing serious.

Despite acquiring the captaincy in 1951 it was obvious that Alf's playing career was drawing to a close. Arthur Rowe was such a supporter of Alf that he wanted him to remain at the club in a coaching role, though Bill Nicholson also had eyes on such a post and had more direct experience, having served as the coach of the Cambridge University football team. This was another reason why Alf and Bill clashed so bitterly towards the mid-fifties, said Ron Reynolds: 'There was a very strong rivalry because I think they both had come to the conclusion that they were going to stay in the game after they'd finished playing and I think they both had designs on Tottenham.' The problem for Alf was that Arthur Rowe's influence at the club was on the wane. An emotional, intense man, he felt so keenly about the decline in the club's performances that he was plagued by ill-health throughout the 1954–55 season. The nadir was reached in February when Spurs, looking in danger of relegation, were knocked out of the FA Cup by York City from the Third Division North. The glory days of push-and-run were definitely over, and Rowe was on the verge of a nervous breakdown. Jimmy Anderson, Rowe's long-serving deputy, took over as manager on a temporary basis during Rowe's sick leave. Anderson, who had never been a top-class professional, had little of Rowe's tactical awareness – or his admiration for Alf. Anderson preferred a more robust, traditional approach to defence than Alf's sophistication. 'He was no great lover of Alf,' says Eddie Baily.

A further blow to Alf's hopes of staying at Tottenham occurred when Danny Blanchflower was signed from Aston Villa in December 1954 for £30,000, to replace the ageing Bill Nicholson. The move made Blanchflower, the Belfast-born midfielder, the most expensive wing-half in English soccer history. Ed Speight says:

I'll always remember being in the back of car, driven by Alf. Syd McClellan was in the passenger seat. We were driving to Tottenham. Alf was silent for a while then he said, 'I don't know what's going to happen because I think I'm finished.'

'What do you mean, Alf?'

'They're about to sign Blanchflower.'

On the face of it, Blanchflower and Ramsey should have made a richly creative duo, for both were strong personalities with fresh ideas about the way the game should be played. Like Alf, Blanchflower made up for his lack of speed with tremendous vision. Over the coming years he was to prove one of the most adventurous figures in British football as he captained Spurs to the first League and Cup Double of the twentieth century in 1961. But on the field, the partnership could never have worked, even if Alf had been at his peak. Unlike Bill Nicholson, who provided defensive cover when Alf advanced up the field, Blanchflower was an attacking player on the right himself. He would have refused to play the Nicholson role, falling back while Alf charged past him. Off the field, with all the insecurities and sensitivities bred of his background, Alf disliked yielding his position as Tottenham's primary strategist. Natural human pride left The General feeling jealous towards this loquacious Ulsterman. 'Alf and Danny were never going to get on,' said Ted Ditchburn. 'Danny was a great guy, you could not help but like him. And he used to talk a good game as well, rabbit, rabbit, rabbit. But Alf could not put up with another bloke talking tactics.' Eddie Baily remembers an occasion at a hotel in Manchester when Alf's dislike of Blanchflower became evident:

Danny was a type of player like Alf, he wanted to influence what was going on around him. Danny was talking to Alf and me for a while, and then went off. Immediately Alf said to me, 'Who does he think he is?'

'He's exactly the same as you. That's the way you used to carry on,' I replied.

Alf and Danny were never going to hit it off because their personalities were too much the same.

As a manager, Alf was no warmer towards Blanchflower, who went into journalism at the end his playing career. When Blanchflower, working for the *Sunday Express*, asked Alf for an interview just after he had taken over the England job in 1963, Alf told him, 'I don't give private interviews', which was untrue, as he spoke frequently to the likes of Ken Jones and Brian James. Writing about this rebuff, Blanchflower noted in his *Express* column, 'Alf Ramsey has always seemed a distant man to me, slightly withdrawn and easy to misunderstand.' Later, during the World Cup of 1966, Blanchflower was trenchant in his criticisms of Alf's England, even after victory. 'In intention England were as defensive as any team in the tournament. Persistence and stamina were the qualities that carried the team through. England endured.' His musings against Ramsey prompted outrage from the public. 'Traitor, go back to Germany or Northern Ireland,' one England supporter told him. Frank Magee of the *Mirror* called Blanch-flower 'a mouth on two legs'. Alf himself once rounded on Blanchflower at a Football Writers' Association dinner: 'You're a bloody liar. What gives you the right to say what you like?'

Rowe's illness and Blanchflower's arrival spelt the end for Ramsey. From the turn of the year, now aged 35, his hold in the Tottenham side was weaker than ever. In March 1955 he was injured at Preston and missed a couple of games. When he returned to the side in late April in the game against Leicester at Filbert Street, he suffered 'a terrible roasting at the hands of a winger named Derek Hogg,' to use his own words. He was dropped for the remainder of the 1954–55 season. At its close, with Spurs again finishing in 16th place, Rowe retired permanently from White Hart Lane on the grounds of ill-health, though he was later to enjoy managerial success at West Brom and Crystal Palace. Jimmy Anderson now took over full-time, and immediately made his feelings about Alf clear. His first act was to install Bill Nicholson as his coach. Then, when Spurs went on an end-of-season tour of Hungary, Alf, still nominally captain of the club, was left out of the party without any warning. Whatever the mixed feelings towards Alf, there was shock at the way the senior professional had been treated. 'It was a bitter blow for Alf, and all the players agreed it was a rough trick to play on him, turfing him out like that,' said Ron Reynolds.

Alf recognized that he was finished at Tottenham. If he wanted to continue in football, he would have to look else-where. 'I was 35-years-old and obviously concerned about my future. I really didn't know what was going to happen to me. I knew my days as a player were numbered, and there was only one way things could go for me in this respect – downhill,'

Alf wrote in 1970. During the summer of 1955, he undertook a coaching job in Southern Rhodesia, bringing Vickie and Tanaya with him to Africa. When he returned, still nominally on Tottenham's books, he was informed by Jimmy Anderson that Great Yarmouth wanted him as their player-manager. Alf wrote to the club to say he was 'flattered by the offer' but had to turn it down because 'I want to stay in League football'. Fortunately for Alf, another East Anglian club were also interested in him.

Ipswich Town FC were looking for a new manager to replace the present 67-year-old incumbent Scott Duncan, who had decided, after almost 18 years in the job, to concentrate on his duties as secretary. One of Ipswich's directors, Ned Shaw, the owner of a local greyhound stadium, knew the Ramsey family through his dog-track connections, so he was aware that Alf was seeking a new position. Ipswich were always a club for following correct procedures, so the Chairman Alastair Cobbold approached Spurs in July for permission to speak to Alf. Only too keen to offload Ramsey, Jimmy Anderson agreed immediately. 'Ramsey has always impressed me as a fine type and just the man for us,' announced Cobbold, explaining why he wanted Ramsey. On his return from Africa, Alf met the chairman and his nephew John Cobbold at the Great Eastern Hotel in Liverpool Street. The meeting went well, with Alf impressed by the sense of purpose that the Cobbolds demonstrated. The only sticking point was over Alf's role. 'They wanted me as player-manager but I told them I would only concentrate on one job. As far as I was concerned, it would be impossible to play with the players I would be coaching,' said Alf later. This issue settled, it was announced to the press on 9 August 1955 that Alf would be the new manager of Ipswich Town.

John Cobbold, who soon succeeded his uncle as club

chairman, once said, 'Persuading Alf Ramsey to come to Ipswich was one of the more successful things I have done in my life.' It was a typical English upper-class understatement. But at the time of Alf's appointment, it might have seemed that the Suffolk club was taking a risk with a complete novice, for Alf had no managerial experience whatsoever nor any coaching qualifications. In fact, according to Walter Winterbottom, Alf had deliberately avoided trying to acquire an FA badge, despite some impressive work coaching schoolboys. 'Alf didn't want to go through the coaching scheme. There were a lot of players who didn't want to be embarrassed by taking examinations and tests, which was natural – they felt they were First Division players, why should they be examined? It was an idea that filled them with horror. Alf wasn't too keen on that, but he was a student of the game.' The Board had based their decision purely on Alf's reputation as a high-class, intelligent player, yet football is littered with examples of such stars failing disastrously in management. Not one of Alf's England colleagues during the 1950 World Cup became successful bosses; Billy Wright, for instance, sunk into alcoholism after a woeful spell in charge of Arsenal, while Stanley Matthews was sacked from Port Vale over making irregular payments to young players. On the other hand, Ipswich hardly had a glittering pedigree or status. They had only been in the League since 1938, having gone professional just two years earlier. Most of these years had been spent in the Third Division South. In 1954, they had been promoted to the second, but after just one season were immediately relegated again, a few months before Alf joined. 'I was surprised when he went to Ipswich because at the time they were nothing really and they didn't seem to have much potential,' said his Spurs team-mate George Robb.

Nor could the club claim any strong footballing tradition.

Ipswich in the mid-fifties was a rural town of 100,000 inhabitants, far more isolated than it is today. Its countrified nature was not unlike Dagenham in the 1920s. There was literally a cattle market on the way to Portman Road, and sometimes a cow would stray from the rest of herd, though Alf would never allow such an event to upset his equilibrium, as his Ipswich secretary Pat Godbold recalls: 'Occasionally on market day a cow would come into the ground. But if Alf saw one, he would merely go to the trainer, Charlie Cowie, and say, "Charlie, there's a cow on the pitch. Please deal with it." He never got cross or excited.'

The rusticity of the town was reflected in the primitive facilities of Portman Road. Though Ipswich had one of the finest, smoothest pitches in the country, tended by the devoted groundsman Freddie Blake, this horticultural excellence was not matched elsewhere. The stands and terracing were poor, the dressing-rooms were primitive, and the club offices, including the manager's, were little more than wooden sheds. Andy Nelson, who became captain during Alf's reign, recalls: 'Ipswich was a lovely old town then. It was almost like a village, with one big high street. I had never been there before and I must admit I was a bit shocked at the state of the club when I joined in 1959. Tiny little wooden stands, sleepers everywhere, including behind the goal. It was not the most attractive place in the world. The dressing-rooms were terrible. The wind came howling through.' Ray Crawford, the centre-forward of the Ramsey era, has this memory: 'The actual playing surface was perfect. There was a good stand on one side and the other was like a shack. The dressing-rooms were a total joke. They were like an old run-down cricket pavilion with bare boards on the floor. You had to be careful when you stepped out of the bath otherwise you were liable to get splinters in your feet. We often had to put our clothes over the windows, otherwise the spectators could look in. Because we stood on the benches to change, avoiding the floorboards, they could have seen our backsides.' Pat Godbold, who joined Ipswich as a secretary in 1954 and, more than half a century later still works there, says that the offices were just as bad. 'When I was here with Alf, there were just four of us on the office staff. Today there are about 140. Our office then had actually been a Nissan hut during the war. It was partitioned off into five sections, with coconut matting on the floor. The roof leaked so we had to put out saucepans to catch the drips.' Even the medical facilities were inadequate, recalls Ted Phillips. 'When I wrecked my knee in one practice match and had to go to hospital, the transport was Alf's car. His old Ford Anglia was the ambulance.'

Ipswich might have had run-down facilities, but it had one of the grandest boards in the League, dominated by the Cobbold family who had made their money in brewing. Lady Blanche Cobbold, widow of Lieutenant-Colonel Cobbold – who, as club chairman had used his influence to secure League status in 1938 and then was killed by a German flying bomb during the war – was the sister-in-law of Harold Macmillan, the senior Tory politician. In 1957, the year that Macmillan succeeded Anthony Eden as British Prime Minister, John Cobbold, one of the sons of Lady Blanche, took the place of his uncle Alastair as chairman of the board. Aged just 29, he was by far the youngest chairman in the League. He was also one of the most eccentric – and tragic. A failed Conservative politician who had twice been beaten in the contest for the Ipswich seat by Dingle Foot, brother of Michael, Cobbold cut a bizarre figure around Portman Road, dressed in tennis shoes and a shabby old fur coat, bound up with tape and full of miniatures. His high-spirited enthusiasm often descended into tiresome immaturity, his fondness for drink into chronic alcoholism, his sense of the absurd into foul-mouthed obscenities. Regularly banned from driving because of his drink problem, he often had to hire a chauffeur to ferry him round in his Rolls-Royce. He adored his role as Ipswich chairman but he knew almost nothing about football. One time at Leicester during the Bobby Robson era, Ipswich were losing 2–0 when Cobbold turned to Robson. 'Well done, what magic words have you been saying to the lads?' Robson was puzzled for a moment. Then the truth dawned. 'Mr John, Leicester are in blue. We're in our away strip.'

Stories of outlandish behaviour abounded. 'He was the one who would always start the bread roll fights in restaurant cars. He always had a glass of Scotch in his hand,' says the Ipswich midfielder John Compton. During a visit to Bloomfield Road, he hired a monkey from a local entertainer and introduced him to the Blackpool board as one of Ipswich's new directors. According to Robson, Cobbold was once due to make a speech at a football dinner in a London hotel. As usual, he had been imbibing heavily throughout the day: 'Eventually it was his turn but when he stood up, he swayed, closed his eyes and sank gracefully to the floor. He disappeared under the table and never said a word. He was carried out to a standing ovation.' The journalist Tony Garnett recalls a trip to Stoke, when the Ipswich team were installed in the North Stafford hotel:

> Johnny was in such a state that he was just being frivolous, throwing bread rolls at other diners. The Head Waiter comes in and says, 'Mr John, there's a call for you,' which of course there wasn't. So Johnny crawls out on all fours, right across the foyer and into the lounge on the other side, where he starts trying to climb up the curtains.

At times, John Cobbold could be downright vulgar. Bobby Robson was once in the Gents with him at the Great Eastern Hotel when he noticed that Cobbold did not wash his hands:

'Mr John, where I was brought up we were taught to wash our hands after using the toilet.'

'Bobby, where we were brought up, we were taught not to piss on our hands in the first place.'

In keeping with his aristocratic status, Cobbold had a large elegant home at Kirton near Felixstowe, and on the 2000 acres of land he kept a family of donkeys as pets. Once when Ipswich were anxious to sign a Portsmouth star, Cobbold had the player and his wife to tea at Kirton, thinking that the impressive surroundings would help to secure the deal. But as the couple sat down, Mr John's wicked eye noticed his pets on the lawn. 'You don't fuck donkeys, do you?' he said nonchalantly to the outraged player, who subsequently refused to sign for Ipswich.

When Ipswich won the title under Alf, a *Daily Mirror* reporter said to Cobbold, 'I suppose it's been one long season of wine, women and song for Ipswich?' to which the Chairman replied, 'I don't remember much singing.' But with Cobbold there would not have been many women either, for he was a lifelong bachelor and almost certainly a homosexual. At the time, homosexuality was not only a social taboo but a criminal offence; in November 1958, just a year after John Cobbold became Ipswich chairman, the Tory foreign minister Ian Harvey had to resign after being caught in the bushes with a guardsman. It was particularly forbidden in the masculine, traditionalist world of football, so Cobbold sought an outlet for his sexual interests elsewhere. 'John Cobbold was a strange character. There was no question that he was homosexual, but he used to go to America for his recreation,' says Tony Garnett. Ted Phillips told me that the players knew of his inclinations:

'We were all aware that he was a bit the other way.' Though he liked being with his team, he was too aware of his position to proposition any of them. But his troubled sexual nature must have contributed to his alcoholism and loneliness. 'When he was with his friends and drinking, everything was all right. But when it was time to go home, he was a very sad man,' believes Brian Scovell, the distinguished journalist who has written a book about the Cobbold family. His craving for company was reflected by an incident when he was having a drink in Portman Road with a reporter, who explained, after several large gins, that he had to leave.

'So soon. Where are you off to?' said Cobbold

'Well, to be honest, I have to get up to London because I'm flying to Paris tonight. Got to cover a European game tomorrow.'

'Really? I'll join you.'

Despite his sexual orientation, the Ipswich players of Ramsey's time adored Mr John for his openness, generosity and humour. Ray Crawford says:

He was a great chairman. He was about the same age as me. When we were away, he used to come round to our hotel for a drink. He loved company, loved sitting up late having a drink. He would just say to the landlord of wherever we were, 'Oh just send me the bill', and someone from the Cobbold firm would sort it out. But he didn't talk football much. 'Go and sit with Alf if you want to talk about football,' he would say.

John Cobbold had a powerful sense of respect for Alf, especially when Alf started to prove his qualities as a manager. 'He is a dedicated professional in everything he does,' Cobbold once told the BBC. Yet there is a suspicion that Cobbold, always looking for some puerile amusement, found the studious Alf something of a bore, as Andy Nelson, captain of Ipswich during the golden era, remembers;

John was a lovely man. He loved Alf to death, though he would sometimes take the mickey out of him behind his back. When we were away, John would come up to me with, say £20, and say, 'Don't let Alf see this but get the lads a drink.' Once we were on tour in Denmark and we were sitting around the dining room of our hotel. John came in and whispered to me, 'Where are you off to tonight? Please don't leave me with Alf.'

In his turn, Alf would grow weary of Cobbold's antics, especially when they detracted from the focus of the team. A restrained man himself, he disliked Cobbold's encouragement of heavy drinking. Tony Garnett recalls being in the boardroom at Derby County with Alf, John Cobbold and Harry Storer, the Derby manager:

Harry has a bottle of gin in one hand and a bottle of whisky in the other. He's pouring out Johnny's stuff which is going straight down his throat and Alf's stuff which is going straight into a nearby vase of flowers. Alf didn't want to go back and embarrass himself in front of his players.

One of Cobbold's tricks was to pass around the miniatures from his coat, something that infuriated Alf. Ted Phillips has this memory:

Alf didn't like Mr John's attitude. The only time I have heard Alf really swear was when we were on a train coming back from Plymouth. Mr John called us into his compartment and was dishing out the Scotch for the lads. Suddenly Alf burst in. His language was pretty ripe. He told us all to leave, then told Mr John to 'Fuck off.' That was about all Mr John would have understood in his state.

Tony Garnett recalls, 'The Chairman would sit next to Alf at matches and would sometimes be a bit silly. Alf used to bollock Johnny Cobbold for interrupting him. "Listen, I'm trying to concentrate, Mr John," he'd say.'

John Cobbold might not have known much about football or personal self-discipline. But he gave successive managers his unequivocal backing. Unlike most other clubs, the Ipswich board were not in the habit of threatening their manager with the sack, even when results were poor. As the saying went at the club, 'The manager's name is not chalked on a board with a wet sponge attached.' From Scott Duncan through to Bobby Robson, managers were allowed the crucial ingredient of time in which to build their teams. Because of this attachment to stability, it was joked that the only moment that the Ipswich directors ever recognized a crisis was when the boardroom was short of good sherry.

Stability was also one of Alf's greatest virtues. Unlike so many managers, who come into a club and want to sweep out every vestige of the previous regime, Alf remained loyal to those who had served under Scott Duncan, such as the two trainers Jimmy Forsyth and Charlie Cowie. His extreme modesty and dislike of intimacy meant that he never surrounded himself with a band of acolytes, following him from post to post. Essentially a conservative, he preferred improvement to revolution when it came to personnel, trying to work with the raw materials that he had been given. But he was not too impressed with the material he had to work with on his arrival. The board had organized for him a practice between two teams made up of members of the playing staff. Alf, who went to watch with Vickie, was shocked at the low standards:

> I had no plan for Ipswich when I went there. In fact the first thing I had to do was to forget my set ideas on how football ought to be played. My experience had been in the First Division. I soon found that what I faced at Ipswich was very different. In fact the club put on a trial match for me to see what talent I had available. At half-time my wife turned to me and said, 'Let's go home.' The trial, by comparison with what we had been used to, was as bad as that.

Matters hardly improved a fortnight later, when Ipswich had their first game of the 1955–56 season and lost 0–2 at home to Torquay, 'as poor a performance as one can recollect at Portman Road,' said the *East Anglian Daily Times*. But Alf still refused to panic. 'The team certainly cannot play any worse than they did on Saturday, but I simply must give them a fair crack of the whip,' he told the *EADT* reporter.

It was a tough baptism, as Ipswich only gained four points from their first three games. But soon the influence of Alf was felt. He was not only a superb judge of technique and of tactics, but he also knew how to bring the best out of any player with potential. Almost as soon as he stepped into Portman Road, the squad knew they were dealing with a naturally gifted manager. Wilf Grant, who had been at Southampton with Alf and was one of the Ipswich staff when Alf arrived, had been asked by Scott Duncan what Alf would be like when he took over his appointment. 'He'll be good, but he will be the boss.' Grant later said of Alf:

> We were not much of a side when he took over but he gave us a chance. One thing immediately impressed me: we

trained hard, tried hard and were still thrashed at home to Torquay. We expected wholesale changes in the team and a dressing down. But Alf merely analysed the faults and kept the same team for the next match. That started us on a run of success.

The big Welsh left-half John Elsworthy, who had been at Ipswich since 1949, recalled that:

Things immediately began to change under Alf. He introduced training drills for free-kicks and throw ins. We had done nothing like that before. It was great. Everything Alf worked on had a purpose. From the moment he arrived I knew he was someone special. Scott Duncan was a mean manager. He was really more of an administrator. From the first morning Alf was out in his tracksuit. He would join in the training. We got playing a lot of five-a-side, using three or even just two-touch rules, which was terribly difficult. If the ball came to you from a height, you had to chest it down and hit it immediately. Three-touch was better, because you could chest, trap and then play it. But it was all great practice. Alf laid tremendous emphasis on passing. We all realized immediately how good he was as an organizer. He taught us simple lessons, like he told us, 'Keep possession. Get them chasing you. Don't go chasing them.' All he asked you to do was the easy thing well. So he encouraged us to hit the ball with the inside of the foot; that way you can either slice it or pull it. He got us passing like that. Before him, we had just gone through our own routines. We were a struggling side when he came, but he quickly pulled us together. He was amazing. When I first saw what he was going to do, I really looked forward to training and playing.

By far Alf's most significant tactical move, which took place in January 1956, was his decision to convert the Scots-born Jimmy Leadbetter from an inside-forward to a left-winger. Leadbetter, who had previously been with Chelsea and Brighton, was languishing in the reserves when Alf arrived, but the new manager, with his instinctive recognition of talent, saw how Jimmy could be properly utilized. As with Alf, what Jimmy lacked in pace, he made up with the phenomenal accuracy of his passing – 'he could land a ball in a bucket from 60 yards,' says the journalist Brian James. And Alf felt that Leadbetter's usage of the ball from the deep could tear apart defences, just as Alf had done in the glory days of push-and-run. Today Jimmy recalls how Alf broached the change with him:

> I was out training and Alf came over and asked how I fancied playing outside-left. I told him that I hadn't played in that position since school. And then I said:
> 'You know I'm not fast Alf.'
> 'Yes, but you know what to do with the ball.'
> 'Oh aye, I love passing the ball.'
> Alf had sprung all this on me, but he was clever that way. He got me thinking. He put into my mind the idea of going to outside-left. And not being so fast, compared to other boys, did not bother me. It's what you do with the ball, not your pace, that's important. All the time, Alf was letting me do the talking.
> 'How would you go about it?' he asked. And so we discussed how I did not need to beat the full-back and get to the byline. Instead I could hit the ball into the space in front of the forwards. It was great man-management by Alf. One of the secrets of his success was that he never asked a player to do what the player didn't want. He understood

professionals completely. He was a deep thinker about football. He could recall incidents from matches weeks earlier and would say, 'You remember that, Jimmy?' And I could not even remember last week's game.

Alf's skilful leadership began to bear fruit as Ipswich stormed up the table. Surprisingly, in contrast to his later years with England, Alf's first managerial side was noted for its flair rather than its solidity, as John Eastwood and Tony Moyse remarked in their official history of Ipswich: 'They were without doubt the classiest side in the division, and their natural attacking tendencies were shown by the fact that they scored four or more goals on no less than nine occasions.' But Alf did shore up the defence with the purchase at Easter 1956 of the new goalkeeper, Roy Bailey, the father of Manchester United and England keeper Gary Bailey. At a time when the players cycled to the ground, the flamboyant Bailey raised some eyebrows when he arrived at Portman Road in a sleek Ford Prefect, complete with personalized number plates. Pat Godbold, Alf's secretary, explains: 'Roy was the first player to have his own car, as Scott Duncan had not allowed it. But this rule had nothing to do with Alf, so he didn't have a problem with Roy's car.'

Alf's first season was such a success that the club missed promotion from the Third Division South by just two points, having been cruelly hit by injuries; at one stage towards the end of the 1955–56 season, six players were in plaster. As a result of this achievement, Alf looked forward to strengthening his position. Never someone who relished interference, Alf had grown frustrated with Scott Duncan who was still the club secretary despite his advanced years. Described by one former Ipswich player Ken Malcolm as 'a miserable little Scot', Duncan could not relinquish the reins of his old job and was on the ground every day. But when Charlton Athletic tried to lure Alf to The Valley as their new manager, following the resignation of Jimmy Seed, the Ipswich board realized how valuable Alf was for the future of the club. Alf turned down the Charlton offer, saying characteristically that he had to honour his Ipswich contract. But the board at Portman Road also decided that Duncan would have to interpret his job description in a less expansive way. Two years later, in 1958, Duncan finally retired, going home to his native Scotland. Alf assumed the role of secretary–manager, giving him the total control he had always sought since he first arrived at Ipswich. 'He is a man who likes to have everything at his fingertips,' John Cobbold said when Alf took over the secretaryship in addition to management.

Apart from enhancing his authority, Alf also strengthened his squad in the close season of 1956. In the position of right-back he signed Larry Carberry, an ex-sheet-metal worker who had just completed two years National Service in the King's Regiment. And up front, he brought back Ted Phillips from loan with the Suffolk non-League club of Stowmarket. Phillips, a tearaway country youth who made his living as a forester, had been on Ipswich's books but, before Alf's arrival, had done nothing to persuade the club to retain him. Once more, Alf's judgement proved shrewder than others. Phillips turned out to be a devastating striker, one with an even more ferocious long-range shot than Bobby Charlton's, and he immediately justified Alf's decision by scoring a record-breaking 41 goals in his debut season at the club. Phillips was impressed by Alf from their very first meeting:

He was a bit shy but I remember, after the first speech I heard him make, I thought to myself, 'We've got a good bloke here.' He really sounded as if he knew what he was talking about. I felt he was someone special. He was brilliant at giving instructions. Like if we had been short of a player on a Saturday, Alf could just go out to a bloke in the street and have a chat with him, explaining exactly what he wanted. And that bloke could play well, just on the basis of what Alf said. He always wore a tracksuit and he used to play a lot in practice matches. He was still a good player, with two good feet. He used to order the first-team squad onto the pitch to practice manoeuvres. We would often be out there for two hours doing them. Remarkably, every time we practised one of Alf's tactics, we seemed to score on a Saturday.

Phillips' awesome striking was to be a crucial ingredient in Ipswich's improvement in the 1956–57 season. 'Big Ted, he could hit a ball – and that was with the big old heavy thing. I wonder what he'd have done with the balloon they play with today,' says Jimmy Leadbetter. 'He often had no idea where it was going, he just hit and hoped. But he scored some cracking goals, many of them from a distance.' Journalist Tony Garnett gives this indication of the power of Phillips:

Ted had his simple way of playing, which was to hit the ball bloody hard. I remember once being on the ground when Ted was training. I said to him, 'Bet you I can save some of your shots.' It was a stupid thing to say really. So Ted starts firing these bullets at me when suddenly a window opens in Alf's office and Alf pokes his head out, 'Stop that immediately, Ted, you'll kill him.'

Tony Garnett believes that Ted could also have been a first-class cricketer, for he was a good enough fast bowler to have led the attack for Suffolk. 'He was a very quick bowler, one of the quickest around at the time. His temperament might have let him down. He once opening the bowling for Suffolk, and for the first ball of the day he sent down an apple, a nice, red, shiny apple. He got reported to Lord's for that.

Furthermore, as Ted himself testifies, 'Alf disagreed with the idea of my becoming a professional cricketer. He said that I might get injured.'

Ipswich, playing in new continental-style V-necked shirts, made a poor start to the 1956–57 season and after seven games were bottom of the table. In fact, so dismal was their form that there was even speculation that Alf might be sacked. As he later admitted: 'Things were very bad indeed. I became unsettled and unhappy. But more important I became infuriated because one can only do one's best and I felt I was doing my best without the luck that is necessary to get results.' Beneath his passive exterior, Alf was a highly sensitive man and he was so worried about the rumours against him that he decided to have a confidential word with the chairman Alistair Cobbold. Cobbold proved more sagacious than his frivolous nephew might have been:

Alastair Cobbold's remarks I have never forgotten. He told me, 'Well, I thought you were a little braver than that, that you knew you had to grow an extra skin.' You must expect setbacks in life and you must grow these skins to protect yourself from criticism and rumours that are not true.

Alf tried to do just that – and the media were to feel the consequences for the next two decades. Some journalists might have said that Alf did not just grow an extra skin but created his own impenetrable suit of armour, such was his contempt for the press. In fact, the writer Ralph Finn said that he saw a dramatic change in Alf's attitude once he became manager of

Ipswich. In one anguished passage, Finn wrote that Alf had developed

> the self-satisfied preening of the introverted cat rather than the extroverted exhibitionism of the prancing dog . . . I am sorry to say that Alf has ceased to know me. When he was manager of Ipswich I first noticed that his normal aloofness had grown even more distant . . . Alf Ramsey and his aloofness make me feel inferior. Of course I hate being made to feel this way. Everybody does. I hate the thought that this man can make me feel like a grubby little boy. I resent it.

Alf, however, always remained sensitive, as Walter Winterbottom recalled: 'He found it difficult to take any kind of personal remark. I remember some official of the Sports Council made a fairly inoffensive point about the England team, when Alf was manager, as a conversation opener at a dinner and Alf was upset and taut for the rest of the evening.'

The day of Alf's meeting with the Chairman, Ipswich won 2–1 at Plymouth. It was to be the turning point in their season. Once the team found their stride in the autumn, they were unstoppable, racking up a series of heavy victories. Torquay were beaten 6–0, Newport 5–0 and Shrewsbury 5–1. Alf's guidance was crucial in inspiring the drive to the top of the table, as Ken Malcolm, one of the full-backs, remembers:

> Alf was a great man, with great tactical sense. If you played on Saturday and maybe made a couple of mistakes, then on Monday you might be running round the track and Alf would creep up to you and whisper, 'We'll soon get that out of you.' He was very quiet. He never shouted or swore at us. I remember once we were on the training ground and Alf said to me:

'You're timing your jumps wrongly for heading.'

'OK, Alf.'

'Listen, I'll pump some balls up to you. Take your time and knock them back to the keeper or into touch.'

So Alf's hitting all these balls to me, encouraging me all the time, getting me to clear them properly. It was hard work with the big old leather ball, but it was great practice, really improved my heading.

On the last day of the season, Ipswich had to win at Alf's old ground of The Dell in order to be sure of promotion and the Third Division South championship, provided that Torquay, their main rivals, did not win at Crystal Palace. Ipswich duly beat Southampton 2–0, but then had to wait for the result from Palace, where the game had kicked off 45 minutes later. 'It was terrible,' remembered Jimmy Leadbetter. 'We had all these rumours coming through that Torquay had won. Then we found out it was a draw. We went up on goal average. Coming home, getting near Ipswich, the train driver was pulling the whistle all the way, and we had a great reception.' 3,000 supporters had gathered at the station to welcome the team. Such was the density and enthusiasm of the crowd that Alf had to be escorted by the police from the train onto the team coach. There followed a party organized, inevitably, by John Cobbold, who had taken over from his uncle. For once, Alf dropped his guard and joined in the drink-fuelled event. With some relish, John Cobbold later told Bryon Butler of the BBC:

Alf is not the dour inaccessible man he sometimes likes to make out. He can be the greatest fun at a party. When we won the Third Division Championship at Southampton, we obviously thought we'd better have a little celebration. I

'Strong, incisive, resourceful.' Alf Ramsey as Southampton's right-back, demonstrating the powerful kick that made him such an accurate passer.

Alf with Saints winger Eric Day. 'Alf was very modest. There was nothing of the star about him,' is Day's verdict.

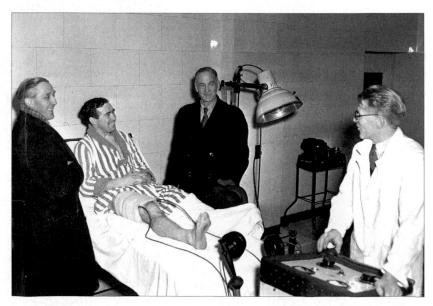

Alf having treatment for torn ligaments in January 1949. The injury led to his departure from the Dell.

LEFT: Belo
Horizonte 1950,
USA 1, England 0.
Alf watches in
horror as the
Americans score
on their way to
the biggest upset
in World Cup
history.

ABOVE: Alf with
the great
Tottenham 'push-
and-run' side,
which won
the League
Championship in
1950–51.

LEFT: Unflappable
as ever, Alf puts a
penalty away for
England against
Austria at
Wembley, 1951.

Playing against Scotland at Hampden, Alf watches as Bert Williams saves acrobatically.

Captain of England against Portugal, 1951. Alf loathed the public speaking side of his duties.

Alf makes a flailing reflex kick at thin air during England's 6–3 defeat by Hungary at Wembley in 1953. It was Alf's last appearance for his country.

Alf goes on the attack for Spurs against Arsenal in the London derby at White Hart Lane in 1953.

'He was an out and out perfectionist,' said Alf's Tottenham manager Arthur Rowe.

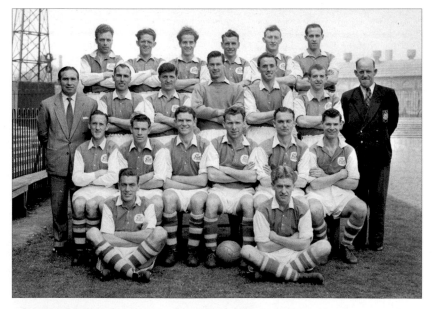

'The rescuer of wasted talent,' was John Arlott's description of Alf as manager of Ipswich. Others saw him as a miracle worker.

Alf toasting success with the eccentric, alcoholic Ipswich chairman John Cobbold.

With Cobbold and Mayor of Ipswich Charlotte Green, watching club captain Andy Nelson savouring the taste of victory as the League title goes to Portman Road, 1961–62.

RIGHT: Professor Sir Harold Thompson, who was Alf's nemesis at the FA.

FAR RIGHT: Alf's predecessor as England manager, the cerebral Sir Walter Winterbottom.

Discussing tactics with two of his loyal England lieutenants, trainer Harold Shepherdson, left, and doctor Neil Phillips.

Alf with Bobby Moore. Away from the playing arena, their relationship was often a difficult one.

The England boss in his bare, cramped office in the FA headquarters at Lancaster Gate.

Alf cracks into a rare smile as manager of Birmingham City, greeting young fans by the dug-out.

'There is nothing spectacular ever in his reactions,' said his loyal wife, Lady Ramsey.

know Alf does not like this story but I am going to tell it. At one moment he was under the table, singing, 'Maybe it's because I'm a Londoner'.

Ipswich's only previous foray into the Second Division had ended in immediate relegation. Alf Ramsey was determined that this would not happen on his watch. 'We are at the moment a small club, but we have big ideas,' he told the *Daily Mail* in August 1957. Just how big they were would soon become apparent.

# SIX

# *Portman Road*

Ramsey's first two seasons in management had ended in triumph. The next three were to be a time of consolidation rather than glory, as Ipswich hovered around the middle of the Second Division table. It was a solid but hardly dazzling achievement, and towards the end of the fifties attendances at Portman Road actually began to fall as the club failed to make the rapid progress that the fans had hoped for, with gates actually sinking by 4,000 to an average of 14,000 between 1957 and 1960, despite the building of a new stand.

One major problem for Alf was that his limited resources meant that there was little cover for injuries. Thus when Ted Phillips was forced to miss most of the 1957–58 season with a cartilage problem, Ipswich suffered a worrying shortage of goals. Moreover, several of his signings during this period, such as Len Garrett from Arsenal and Jimmy Belcher from Crystal Palace, turned out to be disappointing. Jimmy Leadbetter admits that Ipswich initially found it tough in the Second Division: 'You get some very good players but you also get hacked a bit more, kicked up in the air and no questions asked! It took us some time to adjust.' But, given Ipswich's previous record, it would be wrong to exaggerate the sense of failure. In none of the first three seasons after their promotion did they look like being relegated, and they often had significant results, such as defeating both Liverpool and West Ham in their first meetings with these renowned names. And they also enjoyed some memorable days in the FA Cup. At Old Trafford in January 1958, just a few short poignant weeks before the Munich air crash, they put up a heroic performance against the Busby Babes in front of 53,000; 1–0 down, they almost equalized in the last five minutes, when Jimmy Leadbetter hit the post, only for Bobby Charlton to score at the other end. It was Alf's first glimpse of the United forward who would later become the key figure of Ramsey's England.

Alf was not just consolidating Ipswich's tenure in the Second Division; he was also tightening his grip on the club, becoming secretary-manager on the retirement of Scott Duncan in the middle of 1958. Determined to wield absolute control at the club, Alf had fought hard for this post, overcoming the concern of directors about his lack of any administrative experience. And he soon made his authority felt, as he later explained:

> When I became secretary-manager, most certainly nothing was done on the ground without me knowing about it. If there was a screw needed in or a lock or a bolt to be put on a door, the maintenance staff would check with me to see if it was all right to go ahead. It was simply a question of me knowing everything that was going on.

The journalist and former footballer Tony Pawson wrote that Alf was 'a good administrator' with a 'Civil Service impeccability of manner'. That is also the memory of his secretary throughout this period, Pat Godbold:

> He was well-organized and went quietly about his work. He was usually into Portman Road about nine o'clock. He took

the training in the morning on the practice pitch, then in the afternoon he would do the paperwork, making arrangements for away games, booking hotels and so on. He was very fluent in dictating letters, mainly because the subject was usually football, where he had such confidence. He was a gentleman to work for, courteous in an old-fashioned way. If he gave me some letters to type at a quarter to five, knowing I usually left at five, he would be very apologetic for having kept me late. He did not do much in the way of public relations. He was very different in that respect to Bobby Robson, who always kept a hectic schedule. Alf did not like to accept any appointments for supporters' functions or openings or anything like that. I don't know that I should call him aloof, but he was certainly very shy. He did not like to join in conversations – except about football. He was not someone to talk to about football if you weren't prepared for it. I came into the office on a Monday morning after a good victory on Saturday and said happily, 'What a great goal Ted scored.' Alf looked up from his desk and then talked the whole movement through from start to finish in the greatest detail. After that I decided I could not talk about football to him any more because I just could not keep up with him. But he was never inclined to open up about anything except football. He was always immaculate, never without a collar and tie in the office, but he was never flashy.

Alf claimed in his 1952 book to be a non-smoker, but Pat tells a different story, one that indicates how the trials of management may have forced him into the habit:

I once went into his office and began talking to him over his roll-up desk. Suddenly all this smoke started to billow from behind it. I could not believe it. Another time his wife came down to the ground and asked me to get some cigarettes from his office. She said they were in the pocket of his jacket. I don't think Alf liked anyone to know that he smoked a bit.

Jimmy Leadbetter has a similar memory. 'I did not know Alf smoked but I caught him one day in his office with a cigarette – he was sort of hiding it, I didn't say anything.'

Even though he was not under the same media pressure at Ipswich that he was later as England manager, Alf still had an innate suspicion even of the local press. Tony Garnett joined the *East Anglian Daily Times* as a reporter in 1958:

My sports editor Alan Everitt had a fairly short fuse and Alf had a habit of keeping him waiting for interviews, for no particular reason. Alan Everitt always maintained that Alf would be in his office just reading *Charlie Buchan's Football Monthly*, keeping him waiting through sheer bloody-mindedness. One day Alan lost his rag about this and said to me, 'You do the football.' I was only 19 then. It was a huge break. I saw a lot of Alf, but he was a difficult man to get to know. I remember once when I volunteered that a certain player had a good game, he just said to me, 'You would think so.' He was implying I did not know anything about it. That was a big put-down. If I had been older I might have taken the hump.

Through his work on the *East Anglian Daily Times*, Tony ended up ghosting Alf's programme notes for Ipswich Town. 'He didn't even look at them. All I had to do was make sure that I said nothing that was quotable. Absolutely bland so there could be no comeback, that was the order; he didn't want to know about that at all.'

It was during these early years at Ipswich that Alf was supposed to have undertaken elocution lessons. It is an unlikely claim, given that Alf's drive for self-improvement stretched right back to his childhood. Jimmy Leadbetter, a huge admirer of Alf's, doubted the rumours but felt they were, in any case, an irrelevance:

One or two of the players used to take the mickey out of him because of his voice. They thought he was la-di-dah. I've always hated that, having a go at someone just because of the way they talk. The important thing was that you could always understand exactly what Alf was saying. Yes, he could be awkward with people. No one is perfect. But if Alf wanted to better himself, you have to respect him. He was a fine man.

It has been argued that Alf felt he had to change his voice in the fifties because he believed he would be hampered in his career in management by his Dagenham tones, especially now he was surrounded by the Old Etonians of the Cobbold family. Yet this is greatly to exaggerate the strength of Alf's working-class accent and the social rigidities of 1950s Britain. There is an historical tendency to imagine it was only in the sixties when class barriers began to come down, thanks to the arrival of Harold Wilson and the Beatles. In truth, Britain has always been a highly fluid and mobile society. After all, another famous man of Ipswich, Cardinal Wolsey, had achieved the summit of political power in the 16th century, despite being born the son of a butcher. In Alf's own life before his arrival at Ipswich, Britain had a Prime Minister, Ramsay MacDonald, who was the illegitimate son of Scottish crofter; a Foreign

Secretary, Ernie Bevin, who had been a Somerset labourer and never lost the aitch-spraying accent of his youth; and a Health Secretary, Aneurin Bevan, who was a former miner from Tredegar and always spoke with a high-pitched Welsh voice. Contrary to the myth that it was not until the sixties that there was a flowering of working-class culture, in Alf's formative teenage years in the 1930s a wide range of working-class life had been celebrated: through the entertainment of that pair of Lancastrians, George Formby and Gracie Fields, by far the biggest two British film stars of their generation; through the comedy of Max Miller; and through novels like Walter Greenwood's *Love on the Dole*. The Labour landslide of 1945 demonstrates that England was not a rigid society. In football, there was no BBC-voiced, well-bred archetype for managers. They came from all types of social and geographical backgrounds, whether it be working-class Merseyside – Stan Cullis at Wolves – or Scottish coalfields – Matt Busby at Manchester United. Alf's mentor, Arthur Rowe, never abandoned the north London accent of his upbringing, while Alf's predecessor at Portman Road had such a broad Scottish accent that he could be almost incomprehensible, as Ted Phillips recalls:

> Scott Duncan once spoke to me and I looked at him with a complete blank.
> 'Didn't you hear what I said?'
> 'I heard you but I didn't understand you.'

Yet Duncan could work happily with the Cobbolds for 20 years without modifying his voice. So Alf's long-term reincarnation as suburban gent was driven far more by his own personal insecurities than by any wider professional need to conform.

For Alf, football was always a refuge from the complexities

of the wider world. The training pitch and the stadium were his domain, the place where he did not need to justify himself to anyone. This was the environment he loved and knew best, where he was free to be himself. By the end of the decade, his innate excellence as a manager was starting to yield results. He not only introduced new training regimes, which helped to improve the standards of the players he had, but he also made a number of shrewd purchases in the transfer market. A vital element in building a more successful team was to acquire a centre-forward to partner Ted Phillips up front, and in the autumn of 1958 he found one at Portsmouth. For the bargain price of just £5,000, he purchased 22-year-old Ray Crawford, a dashing striker who had done his National Service in the Malay jungle but had fallen out with Pompey's manager Freddie Cox. Crawford had just got married and moved into a new flat in Portsmouth, so he was reluctant to switch to East Anglia, especially because it would mean dropping down one division, but Cox's intransigence meant he had little choice. When he and his wife Eileen arrived in Ipswich, they were immediately impressed by the decency of Alf:

He met my wife and I at the station and then drove us round the town, showing us the club houses we could rent. The one we chose was beautiful, almost new, with three bedrooms. I think we paid £1 and 10 shillings a week in rent for that. Alf could not have been more charming. He went out of his way to help us. I soon found that all the Ipswich wives loved Alf, because he appreciated them. I don't think you would find one of them that didn't like Alf. He had something of a film star about him – always immaculate. I wouldn't say he was a ladies' man, not at all, but he always stressed that a good marriage was a big part of being a happy player.

During this time, Alf himself lived in an Ipswich club house on the Crofton Road with Vickie and his step-daughter Tanaya, who went to a local Catholic school before taking a series of secretarial jobs in London.

Crawford was equally impressed with Alf as a manager, particularly in comparison to what he had previously experienced:

At Portsmouth, I was never told anything. But Alf would come out and talk to you. And if you wanted to be successful, you listened. Because of Alf, moving to Ipswich was the best thing I ever did. On Fridays he would give a talk to us about the previous Saturday's game. He would start with Roy Bailey and then go round everyone, talking us through the match. The man's memory was amazing. It was like he was replaying a film of the entire match in his head. Every incident he would recall, every mistake would be analysed. Then he'd move onto the game coming up. He'd tell us the mannerisms of the opposition; again, that was something I'd never heard at Portsmouth but Alf always made you aware of what your opponent would be up to. So, if we played Sheffield United, I'd be against Joe Short and Alf would say, 'Don't be misled by his size. He's good in the air. He might only be around five foot seven but his timing is perfect. He can pass the ball as well.' Details like that. When things went wrong, he did not slag us off. All he would say was, 'You didn't do very well today, boys, and you did not deserve anything.' Just the look on his face would cut right into you. If he came in and said, 'Well done lads,' it was like being given £100. The key point about the Ipswich team was that we always tried to carry out what Alf said. That's what he liked. If you gave it a try and did what he said, he would back you. But if you went your own way, he did not have much time for you. I had to work at my game. I was full of energy, ran my heart out and Alf told me what to do. 'Get the ball wide to Jimmy and get in the box,' he'd say. Alf never got into confrontations. You didn't argue with him, you just listened.

Ray Crawford scored 25 goals in 30 games in his first season of 1958–59, which helped to ensure safety for Ipswich. Alf saw that Crawford was rapidly developing an effective partnership with Ted Phillips, so when Liverpool made a bid for Ted, it was instantly rejected. But Alf also knew he needed to strengthen the defence, so in the summer of 1959 he bought from West Ham the big, self-assured centre-half Andy Nelson. It was another of Alf's clever buys, costing just £8,500, and Nelson soon proved his value by appearing in every match of the 1959–60 season. Within a year of his arrival, Alf had made him club captain, taking over the reins from Reg Pickett. Like Ray Crawford, Andy Nelson was astonished by the depth of Alf's grasp of football:

He had this photographic memory of every position, every move, right throughout any game. If he said to you, 'This fella is totally left-sided. Don't worry about his right-foot', he was speaking with real understanding. He knew everything about the assets and weaknesses of everyone you were playing against. I never once saw him lose his temper, which is unusual in football. But he could put his finger instantly on what had gone right and wrong. His concentration in the main was on passing. He could not stand it if someone just whacked the ball up the field. He wanted someone on the end of every pass.

Andy Nelson was also struck by the way Alf retained his own footballing gifts:

He would often join in our practices and five-a-sides. There was nothing he loved more than that. He was still a beautiful passer of the ball, out of the top drawer. Sometimes I'd watch him hitting a ball against the wall at the end of the training ground. He'd be there for ages, repeatedly hitting it first time, which is not always easy. He never lost his talent.

At the end of the 1959–60 season, Alf bought three more players to complete the construction of a team which could mount a realistic bid for promotion. In true Ramsey style, all three were languishing in obscurity before they were transformed by Alf's alchemy; not for nothing did John Arlott describe Alf as 'The Rescuer of Wasted Talent'. The Scottish defender Bill Baxter, who was in the middle of National Service at Aldershot, was bought for just £400 from the Scottish non-League club Broxburn Athletic. The winger Roy Stephenson came from Leicester for £3,000 and wing-half John Compton moved from Chelsea for just £1,000. Compton has these recollections of his arrival at Ipswich:

I had nine years at Chelsea but had not really made it when Alf bought me. I remember my first meeting with him to sign the forms. His office was just a little shed with a tin roof. It was June and there was a sudden thunderstorm. The rain was pounding so hard that we could not even hear each other talk. My first impression was that he seemed a nice man, down to earth, though he spoke rather well, not like a Londoner. He was a football man through and through. I had played under Ted Drake at Chelsea and there was a lot of cup-flying in those days. He was very fiery. If you did not play well, you really got it from him. With Alf there was nothing like that. He did not go in for big noisy speeches.

He preferred to tell individual players what he wanted. He taught me a lot, putting me in at left-back. He used to say to me, 'Show the winger the line, make him go down the line.' It is surprising the number of good wingers who never came inside. Because I was a bit quick, it was no problem for me to catch them.

Being a Londoner himself, born and bred in Poplar, John Compton has one special memory of Alf:

We both liked our jellied eels. So when we were coming back through Liverpool Street from an away game, he would say to me, 'Come on John, let's go round to Tubby Isaacs.' Tubby was big friendly man who had this stall near the station and had known Alf since his Tottenham days. He and Alf would have a little chat and then we'd get our two dishes of jellied eels. Alf always loved that.

With his team assembled, Alf now started to develop a revolutionary strategy. And it was here that he showed his real managerial genius. In 1960, English football was still largely wedded to the traditional W–M, 3–2–5 formation which had predominated since the introduction of the centre-half and the pivoting defence in the 1920s by Herbert Chapman, the far-sighted boss of Huddersfield and then Arsenal. There had been a few departures from this approach, such as Arthur Rowe's push-and-run style at Tottenham, based on smooth passing, or Stan Cullis' more bludgeoning system at Wolves, where opposition defences were put under constant pressure by long balls pumped into their area. But generally English managers gave little thought to innovations. The most famous manager of the fifties, Matt Busby, was typical; the blend of his teams was more important to him than their methods. 'Go out and enjoy yourselves' was often the sum of his instructions to his players. But Alf did not have players of the calibre of Manchester United. To succeed, he would have to utilize his material in a radical new way.

The central attacking feature of Alf's scheme was to play Jimmy Leadbetter and Roy Stephenson as deep-lying wingers, feeding the striking partnership of Phillips and Crawford. The great advantage of this plan was that it exploited the accuracy of Stephenson and, even more so, of Leadbetter, whom Alf had intuitively recognized as one of the most gifted distributors in English football. Leadbetter would not have to beat the full-back and get to the byline before crossing, the traditional way that wingers operated. Instead he could hold his position, sometimes even in his own half, before guiding another missile in front of the two rampaging forwards. The strategy minimized Leadbetter's defect, his slowness, and maximized the quality of his passing. It also gave a permanent dilemma for the defenders supposed to be marking Jimmy. If they were drawn into midfield to keep with him, they created space in their own area for Phillips to exploit. If they held back, then Jimmy was free to spray around the ball unhindered. Jimmy told me:

> It was a great system and it foxed so many teams. I was a great believer that if you were in control of the ball you were in command of the game. I loved passing, giving a ball for someone to run onto. I always felt that if I hit a ball past the full-back and there was someone to connect with it and put it in the net, then I had done my job. Yet the full-back, at the final whistle, might be quite happy because he thought I had not actually beaten him.

Jimmy Greaves once gave a good description of Leadbetter in appearance and action:

The comic actor Sid James looked old when he was in his early twenties, but in his sixties he didn't appear any older. That was the case with Jimmy. His gaunt features, receding hairline and thin, bony frame made him appear more like the man from the Pru collecting the weekly insurance money than a top-flight footballer ... Appearances can be deceptive. Jimmy was a highly gifted, mercurial player with a very sharp football brain ... He probed and prodded and used his astute vision and superb distribution to create numerous openings for his forwards.

Alf was never a man to indulge in excessive praise, but he did so when he talked about Jimmy's influence, 'He is 33 years of age,' said Alf in 1962, 'and does not look much like a footballer but as a person, there is no one better and as a player, there is no one greater. In my own mind, I don't think there will ever be another Jimmy Leadbetter.'

Alf's use of deep-lying wingers, allied to a striking duo, was a synthesis of various ideas he had absorbed during his playing career: the Hungarians' fluidity of 1953, the Brazilians' unorthodoxy during Southampton's tour of 1948 and the World Cup of 1950, and Tom Finney's penetration with England when he played deeper than he usually did for Preston. As the FA Secretary of the fifties, Stanley Rous, recalled: 'Tom Finney often told me how much he enjoyed playing for England, as he was allowed to lie deep with the full-back not daring to follow him. This gave him all the space he needed to confuse defenders.'

But all Leadbetter's brilliance with the ball would have achieved little without the firepower up front from Phillips and Crawford. They were a complementary pair: Crawford, the cool, clinical poacher who was deadly from a short distance; the explosive Phillips creating mayhem with his thundering blunderbuss. Andy Nelson, the captain, reflects on the attacking formation:

> Neither Jimmy Leadbetter nor Roy Stephenson were outstandingly quick but Alf was a thinker, more than any manager around then. At the time, wingers would just stand by the opposition full-back and usually do bugger all. But Alf had Jimmy and Roy withdrawn so they were in limbo land. They were both intelligent players and they would murder people because other teams could not work out who should pick them up. Then you had Phillips and Crawford. Ray was fantastic in the penalty box but could not really get a goal from outside. Ted could get them from anywhere within 35 yards of goal. He had unbelievable power. So they were a good partnership.

Ray Crawford says:

> Ted and I just clicked. I was an 18-yard player. I never shot from outside the box, but for Ted 30 yards was nothing. He just used to smash them in. Ted would have these long-range shots and I always expected the keeper to drop it. If he did so, it was in the net. I might get in five times in a row, and nothing would happen, then on the sixth the keeper would spill it and I would score. That's how I got so many of my goals.

John Elsworthy, a clever, mature midfielder with great positional sense, was another to benefit from the space created by Alf's system:

> The opposition just did not know what to do. I would be going through, causing trouble. I would play it to Ray, who

laid it off to Ted, who could be lethal from a distance. It was all down to Alf. He was a tremendous reader of the game. He would come in at half-time and pick up on something that was going wrong. Or during practice matches, if someone made a mistake, he would stop the game and explain what had gone wrong and what they should have done. He was so precise. You didn't make the same mistake again. Alf was unique. He just appeared on the horizon and transformed the club.

That transformation was driving Ipswich towards the First Division, something that would have been unthinkable when Alf joined in 1955. 1960–61 was Ipswich's silver-jubilee season as a professional club, and they celebrated in style. In September 1960 they climbed to the top of the table and were never out of contention for the rest of the season. Between 10 December 1960 and 18 March 1961 they went unbeaten, dropping only three points, and their run included some superb wins, especially the 3–1 defeat of Sheffield United at Bramall Lane. Promotion was secured with a 4–0 victory over Sunderland in April, and the following week the Second Division Championship with a 4–1 crushing of Derby County. Crucial to Ipswich's triumph had been the duo of Phillips and Crawford, who hit an astonishing 70 goals between them, with Crawford netting 40 and Phillips 30. Throughout the run-in to the title, Alf retained his usual composure, one of his many qualities as a manager. There was no over-hyped talk about promotion, no extra pressure put on the players. As John Compton remembers, 'He was always calm. There was none of that stuff you get from other managers, "Come on lads, you can do it."' That almost superhuman restraint was demonstrated on the afternoon that Ipswich won promotion against Sunderland. About an hour after the game finished,

John Cobbold wandered out of the boardroom, the inevitable bottle of champagne in hand, and found Alf still sitting in the stand, watching a schools cup match between Ipswich and Norwich.

'Fancy a glass?' said the gregarious chairman.

'No thank you, I'm working.'

This may, of course, have been an example of Alf's parch-dry sense of humour. In a football environment, he was not the stern, forbidding leader that the public usually saw. Yes, he kept a distance from his team – all successful managers have to do that and Alf's natural reticence, once a social problem at Spurs, became an advantage at Ipswich – but he could also be warm-hearted and relaxed at the appropriate moment. A cold autocrat could not have engendered the sort of spirit that Alf brought to his Ipswich and England teams, nor would he have inspired the near universal affection that players felt for Alf:

'He was a sincere man, not a hard one,' says John Elsworthy, who recalls how devoted Alf was to his players. 'I'd just come back from a cartilage operation and was playing in the reserves at Brighton when I clashed with a centre-half and fractured my skull. It was agony. But I came back by train, and Alf, who had been with the first team, met me at the station, and then went with me in an ambulance to hospital. He was brilliant that day. He said to my wife, "Don't worry Anne, I'll look after him."'

Because Alf treated professionals as adults, he did not feel he needed to be a ruthless disciplinarian. As Ray Crawford puts it:

It was a great club under Alf. He was a fantastic man. Everyone was treated the same and he made you feel at home. We all were very loyal to him. When we were travelling away, on a Friday or after a game, he would allow us to have a beer. We also had a darts team that would go round pubs in the local villages, meeting supporters. Roy Bailey would arrange the visits. Most of the lads would turn up, though we were bloody awful at darts. We would have a few drinks, sensible stuff. Alf knew we went out. It was never a problem with him, though he never came out with us. So we had a social club as well as a football club.

But all the players grew used to his myopia about football. 'He was not really interested in anything else,' says John Elsworthy. 'If we were on the train, Alf might be reading the paper. But the moment we started talking about football, down went the paper and he was with you. It was his life.' As John Compton recalls, 'If there was a group of you in a compartment, Alf would listen and talk as long as the subject was football. As soon it went onto something else, he would get up and go into another compartment.'

Tony Garnett has an interesting example of Alf's leniency:

He was a very good manager in that he could turn a blind eye to things. I remember once I was totally out of order. Ipswich were playing in Manchester and I had driven up there in my old Ford Special, fibreglass body, V8 engine. It was Alf's habit to take all the boys to the cinema on a Friday night. Andy Nelson said to Ted Phillips and me, 'Let's sit behind Alf in the cinema and as soon as the lights go down, let's get out and go for a game of darts and a drink.' The three of us drove out to a pub in the country. We got back to the hotel just before Alf, but he'd known what was going on all the time. 'So you didn't like the film then, Andy?' was all he said.

John Compton remembers Alf's warmth coming out in practice matches, when Alf would sometimes play against the first
team. 'He used to get some stick from the lads. There was a
lot of banter, especially from Ted. Ted would go up and barge
Alf over in the mud, and then we'd all jump on top of Alf. He
could take all this, even took it with a smile.' But at other
times, the players felt protective towards Alf, who could be a
physically courageous man if the occasion demanded it. Ted
Phillips remembers this incident:

Alf spoke his mind where the needs of the team were concerned. We were travelling to an away game by train and
someone else had got our compartments. We were standing
in the corridor when Alf came along. He went straight into
the compartment, used some pretty ripe language and soon
had the other passengers out. He nearly had a fight with
them but he soon kicked them out. When we got off the
other end, there was a bloke waiting for Alf. So we all
surrounded Alf and walked him safely through the station.
We felt very protective towards him. He was able to inspire
such loyalty.

In turn, Alf had a soft spot for Ted, his rollicking, rustic
forward. 'Ted was a comedian and a character. Alf knew what
he was like and just took it all in his stride,' says Ray Crawford.
He was often drawn to such types, whose open, playful
cheeriness was in such contrast to his own innate reserve. The
cheeky Eddie Baily had been his closest friend at Spurs; noisy,
blunt Jack Charlton was to become one of Alf's favourite
England players. Acting the clown or the comic, all three of
them felt free to poke fun at Alf. But the crucial point, Alf
knew, was that there was no maliciousness about any of their
antics. What Alf despised was the sly sarcasm with a cruel

179

edge that he occasionally experienced from the likes of Jimmy Greaves, Bobby Moore and Rodney Marsh. Such was Alf's fondness for Ted that he gave him a great deal of leeway. One of Ted's most bizarre tricks took place during a Boxing Day match against Leicester:

> I'd got hold of this ginger wig, so I put it on in the dressing-room and as I ran out onto the field, a big groan went round the ground. Everyone was saying, 'Who's that ginger bloke?' And I kept up the joke by not shooting at goal in the warm-up. The Churchman's end was moaning because they could not make out who I was. But when I took off the wig just before the start, the roof nearly came off the stands. Alf had a good laugh about it.

Another trick was played more directly on Alf:

> We were having lunch in a hotel in Southport. The soup was being passed along and I took note of which bowl was Alf's, and then I dropped a plastic cockroach in it. Alf called over the waitress, 'I'm afraid that there is an insect in my soup.' Of course we were all giggling down my end of the table. And Alf glowered in my direction, 'What is so funny then, Ted?'
> 'Oh nothing Alf, my soup was all right.'
> He knew immediately I was to blame.

Ted continues proudly:

> I think I am the only bloke ever to chuck cold water over Alf. One day after training he was lying in his bath, which was in the referee's room, and I got this big bucket of water,

crept in, slung it over him and ran out. He shot up immediately, wondering what had happened. He didn't know who it was – but he probably had an idea.

Another of Ted's ruses was to take footballs from the store and then hide them around the ground, in places like a floodlight gantry or the pile of coal behind the boiler or under Alf's bath:

One time Alf took us up to Chantry Park for a run. I tucked a ball under my tracksuit and started jogging. Then, as we went round, I quietly took it out and kicked it towards Alf, 'Where on earth did that come from?' he said in surprise. Then he looked over at me.

Training runs often brought the worst out in Ted. During a cross-country exercise, Ted and Andy Nelson, after a heavy darts session the night before, had fallen so far behind the rest of the pack that they decided to hitch their way back into Ipswich on the back of a sugar-beet lorry. Unfortunately, unbeknown to them, Alf happened to see the pair as they jumped off the vehicle outside Portman Road. They were summoned to his office on their return.

'I'm very disappointed in you Ted.'

'Why's that, Alf?'

'Because you're usually out in front, leading everything like you do on Saturday. And there you are today, riding on the back of a lorry.'

'Who told you that?'

'I saw you.'

The two were ordered to come back to the ground at two o'clock for extra training. Ted takes up the story:

We had lunch in town, then it started to belt down. We waited for the rain to clear so we did not get back until after half-two. Alf was standing there, with a bag of balls. 'You've got five minutes to get your kit on and get out here,' he said. We went out, did a few laps, then started crossing the ball, while Alf went in goal. Andy was chipping these balls to me and I was running in and really hitting them hard. After about five shots, Alf started to rub his hands in pain. 'Right, that's enough of that, let's go in.'

Alf would occasionally become exasperated with Ted, as when Ted walked straight into a lamp post just outside Vicarage Road before a game against Watford. 'I had bought a local paper and was reading it as I went along. I cut my head open and nearly knocked myself out. Alf went beserk because there were no substitutes allowed in those days. "Couldn't you watch where you're going?" he said.' But Alf could be humorous with Ted as well. 'We were playing Sheffield Wednesday at home and I got caught in terrible traffic on the A12. I nearly missed the kick-off but actually got a hat-trick in the game. "Come late next time," said Alf.' Alf also accepted that Ted, a totally instinctive player, did not need to pay too much attention in team talks. 'I must admit that I would sometimes nod off and Alf would have to wake me up. "Sorry Alf, I'd say."'

It was widely believed that the likes of Phillips, Nelson, Leadbetter, Crawford and Bailey would not last long in the First Division, given that hardly any of them had experience of the top flight. The view in Fleet Street was that Ipswich would be 'a one-season wonder'. The only question was which team would share the other relegation berth. It would have been absurd to argue that 'Ramsey's Rustics', as they were known, might challenge Manchester United, Burnley or Tottenham, who had just completed the double. In August

1961, the odds quoted for Ipswich winning the title were 100 to 1. And even Alf was privately a little apprehensive, as captain Andy Nelson recalls:

> One day in the summer of 1961, I went to see Alf in his office, still all pleased that we had won promotion. The fixture list had just come out and we had Bolton away, then Burnley away, then Burnley at home soon afterwards.
> 'It looks very good, doesn't it?' I said to Alf.
> He turned to me and smiled, 'It frightens me to death.'

Yet Alf retained faith in his squad. Contrary to expectations, he did not go out on a spending spree to prepare for the First Division. The one player he bought was inside-forward Dougie Moran for £12,000 from Falkirk. This parsimony was not just because of lack of resources – though that was certainly an issue, with gates still below 15,000 – but also because Alf believed he had the system and the men to enable Ipswich to hold their own. His experience of the Spurs push-and-run side of a decade earlier taught him that a strong unit and an unorthodox approach could defeat well-established opponents.

The year of 1961 was one of huge change in football. The maximum wage was finally abolished thanks to the campaigning of the Professional Footballers' Association under the energetic and eloquent leadership of Jimmy Hill. The threat of a strike by the PFA, allied to fears of an exodus of top players overseas, had forced the League to remove that oppressive, unjust relic of soccer's feudal past. Contrary to the scaremongering by the traditionalists, the end of the maximum wage actually led to clubs raising professional standards as they pruned their playing staffs to meet higher costs. 'It made clubs get rid of all the crap and the people who were not going to make it,' says Ray Wilson. 'We had five teams at

Huddersfield. We are talking about very ordinary sides at an ordinary club. It was ridiculous. There were people at the club who had more years than games. I don't think the people running football were very professional.' Individually, all players benefited. Some of the biggest stars saw an explosion in their earnings: Johnny Haynes' weekly pay at Fulham went up to £100 a week, while the gifted Irishman Jimmy McIlroy won a rise from Burnley to £70 a week. Ipswich's more modest squad saw their average pay increase from the old maximum of £20 to £25, with some of the top players, like Ray Crawford, earning £30. Alf himself, as secretary-manager, was responsible for collecting the club's entire £700 wage bill in cash from the bank and distributing it in small brown envelopes to staff.

Beyond football, the British public was enjoying a new era of consumer affluence after the hardship of the post-war years. The mood was perfectly captured by Harold Macmillan's 1957 speech in Bedford when he said that 'most of our people have never had it so good'. Commercial television arrived; home ownership hugely expanded; for the first time ordinary Britons could afford to own cars and refrigerators, and travel by air to the Continent. Alf was one of those who took advantage of the new freedom by going to Majorca for a two-week break with Vickie and Tanya in the summer of 1961.

Yet Ipswich were reluctant to submit to the 'winds of change', to use another phrase of Macmillan's. Like much of provincial Britain in the sixties, both town and football club remained anchored in the past. John Cobbold, for instance, refused to allow advertising hoardings around the perimeter of the pitch, on the grounds that they were vulgar. The quaint atmosphere was reflected by John Elsworthy's memory that even in 1960 the players used to have a weekly lunch at the department store of Footman and Pretty on Thursday, paid for by the club, and then many of them would disappear early to the cinema, because admission before 1.30 pm was just one shilling. Nor did the facilities come into line with the modern age. Ray Crawford. says:

> Our training kit was vile. The trainer Charlie Cowie used to come in with a big pile of kit and just drop it in the middle of the floor. I would not know whose shorts I was putting on. You'd have socks with holes in them, shirts with tears in them. I'm sure local clubs had better training kit. In the season we were promoted, we were allowed to buy our own boots – the new lightweight styles were coming in – but only up to a certain amount. My own boots cost about £7 but the club would only pay half of that. Our treatment room was comical. It just had one heat lamp. Ted once picked up an injured seagull on the training ground. Charlie put it under this lamp, though it probably had a broken wing.

Ted Phillips has this example of Charlie Cowie's rudimentary methods:

> In one practice, Alf and Jimmy smashed into each other. Both were flat out. We were shouting for Charlie, who ran on and went to Alf first. 'Get away, Charlie,' said Alf. He would not let him touch him. If Charlie gave you a massage, he'd rub the skin off your legs.

It was this sort of atmosphere that led cynics to question whether Ipswich would survive long in the First Division. But from the start of the season, Ramsey's team defied expectations. The opening game saw a draw at Bolton. Then, the following Saturday, Ipswich put up a heroic fight at Turf Moor against Burnley, League Champions of 1960 and regarded as Spurs' greatest rivals for the title. Three times Ipswich came from behind to equalize, before going down 4–3. Alf described it as 'the greatest performance I have ever seen from any Ipswich team since I have been connected with the club'. Tony Garnett, travelling with the team, gained an insight into Alf's inspirational qualities as a manager:

> I had imagined that it would be a struggle for Ipswich to stay up. But then Alf allowed me to sit in on his team talk before the Burnley game. It was bloody brilliant. I thought I could have gone out and beaten Burnley myself. He was able to impart this amazing confidence into his players. And he told people exactly what he wanted them to do, how the opposition would play, who they would be marking. It was extraordinary really. I thought to myself, 'Bloody hell, I fancy this game.' The talk was not long but it was absolutely to the point.

Ipswich really woke up the press and the British public when they slaughtered Burnley 6–2 at home in the return game a week later. By October, the team had reached fourth place in the table; by November, they had climbed to second. Among their notable victories was a 3–2 defeat of Spurs at home and a 4–1 triumph over Manchester United. Yet their superb form was regarded as nothing more than a bubble that was bound soon to burst. As Roy Bailey, the keeper, said, 'Our tactics might be simple but most sides come here and say, "You won't catch us out," and then get hammered.' According to ex-Liverpool and England footballer Gordon Milne, later a distinguished manager, even Bill Shankly had some of this disdain: 'Shanks used to say of them, "Jimmy Lead BEATER – he always called him Lead BEATER – can't walk. A good tackle will cut him in half. And they have two farmers playing up front." ' Chelsea, visiting at the beginning of December, also had a typically complacent attitude. Their striker Barry Bridges, later to play for England under Alf, recalls:

We had a young side at Chelsea then and we were doing quite well. We were in the dressing-room before kick off. We were really cocky, boasting how we would chase Ipswich off their legs. We had a guy called Harry Meadows, who used to play with Jimmy Leadbetter at Chelsea and was now our trainer. There was a knock on the door and this fella comes in and says in a Scots voice, 'Is Harry about?' So Harry goes out into the corridor to talk to Jimmy. And he comes back in, about ten minutes later. We said to him,

'Who was that, Harry?'

'That was Jimmy Leadbetter. He's playing today.'

'What? He's bloody fifty. He must be fifty if he's a day.'

We really gave Harry some stick. We had a laugh about it. Then we went out, got absolutely stuffed 5–2 and Jimmy was the best player. He sat in the middle of the park and pinged balls to the big strikers. Absolutely skinned us alive. That was Alf's team, he was a great reader and thinker.

Ray Wilson, one of the 1966 winners, warned Bobby Charlton about Ipswich just before Manchester United's first visit to Portman Road:

I'd been playing against them for years in the Second Division. We would have the ball most of the time, and then we would come off the field having lost. When United were about to play Ipswich, Bobby said to me, 'What's this Ipswich like?'

'I'll tell you this, Bobby. If you're not careful, you'll have the ball about sixty per cent of the time and you'll come off scratching your head because they'll have made a fuckin' arse of you.'

That's what happened. Ipswich beat United 4–1. And I could understand it. Man U went forward and got stuffed. I later ran into Bobby and he said, 'Well, Ray, you were wrong about one thing. We didn't have sixty per cent of the ball. We had seventy-five per cent of it.'

George Cohen of Fulham was another future England player who was perplexed by Alf's methods. 'We lost at Portman Road 2–1 in February and they were playing something I just didn't recognize and didn't know who I should be marking. Jimmy Leadbetter hardly went outside his own bloody half, yet he was lobbing balls behind me for Crawford and Phillips.' Ipswich enjoyed good fortune as they avoided any injuries to key players throughout the season; all of their first eleven played at least 37 games in the 1961–62, and nine of them played 40 or more. This leant an iron consistency and a deep understanding to the team as a playing unit. Ray Crawford, who went on to score 33 goals this season, was playing so well that he was called up to the full England team against Northern Ireland. But Crawford, who was only to win one other cap, was disappointed by Winterbottom in comparison to Ramsey:

Alf just inspired you. It was such a contrast to playing for England under Walter Winterbottom. I played twice but nothing was ever said to me. There was no team, no tactics, no talk about the opposition or what we would do. I came away so disillusioned by it. I'm playing for Ipswich and Alf Ramsey is sharing things with me. Then I go to England and nothing is happening. Alf is teaching me things yet then

I go to the man who is supposed to be the top coach in the country and I am left thinking to myself, 'Why did he not have the ability to stand up in front of senior players and tell us what he wanted?' I remember talking to Walter one Saturday afternoon at Ipswich. He was not saying one good word about Jimmy Greaves and yet he's the coach. He was saying to me, 'Jimmy is very lazy. Jimmy won't do this and Jimmy won't do that.' And I thought to myself, 'You should be telling Jimmy what to do.' I thought that was very poor by Walter.

As well as producing excellent football, Ipswich also gained a reputation under Alf for fair play. As a professional himself, he had disliked dirty tactics. Tommy Docherty, who came up against Alf while at Preston, told me: 'He was rare for that era, the early fifties. He would not foul the winger. He would take the ball off by clean and legal means. He was an absolute gentleman as a player. If there is such a thing, perhaps he was too nice.' Those were the standards he generally kept as manager at Ipswich. During the 1959–60 season, for example, Ipswich did not have a single player booked all season, a feat achieved by only one other League club. When Ipswich visited Eastwood that year, the Bristol Rovers programme recorded, 'Ipswich are now regarded as one of the most sporting and attractive teams in the Second Division, which is not surprising when one thinks of the members of the Cobbold family being on the board and Alf Ramsey being manager.' Again, during the 1961–62 season, the FA Disciplinary Committee noted that Ipswich were one of only two League clubs which received no unfavourable reports. But Alf should not be thought of as some saintly paragon of sportsmanship. Winning was more important to him than the pursuit of some Corinthian ideal, as he was to show as England manager by his loyalty to Nobby

Stiles and his words to the notorious Leeds hard man Norman Hunter: 'Norman, you do what you have to do.' And, with tough figures like Andy Nelson, Dougie Moran and Billy Baxter, Ipswich were no soft touch. 'Dougie and Billy, they were bloody hard nuts,' says Andy Nelson. Nor did Alf show any fastidious regard for FA rules about approaching players at other clubs, what today is known as 'tapping up'. Ron Reynolds, who had moved from Spurs to Southampton, recalled this incident after Ipswich had visited The Dell in February 1961:

> After the game I ended up having a chat with Alf. I'll never forget this, because Alf was not the type of player you could converse with, so this was out of the ordinary. He was a very odd one, a loner. As I came out of our dressing-room and approached the visitors' dressing-room, Alf came out and walked along with me, and it was as near to an invitation as any player could get to join them, which was, of course, completely illegal. He was tapping me up for a move to Ipswich without having talked to Ted Bates or anybody else at Southampton.

Reynolds believed that Alf feared Ipswich's keeper Roy Bailey might be returning to his native South Africa, so he would need a replacement:

> He was full of questions, very solicitous, asking me, 'How do you like it at Southampton? Are you enjoying your football down here? We would give you a lot more pleasure from the game. We could give you First Division football next season.' In the end I just told him, 'Sorry Alf, I'm happy where I am.'

Bailey stayed in England, however, and in 1961–62 was help-ing Ipswich to dominate the First Division. It was typical of Alf that he turned Bailey, who had been rejected by Palace, into a top-class keeper. By the spring, Ipswich were in second place, with the Championship developing into a two-horse race between themselves and Burnley. Spurs' hopes were effec-tively ended by defeats at home and away to Ipswich. Before the match at Portman Road in October, Bill Nicholson had wanted to change tactics to cope with the Ramsey method but, as he later recorded, he failed to convince his key player, Dave Mackay, at his team meeting:

> I suggested that our midfield players should mark Stephen-son and Leadbetter, leaving the full-backs to move inside to take care of Crawford and Phillips. Blanchflower agreed with me but Mackay didn't: he said we had just won three matches playing the way we wanted to play. 'Why change just to suit them?' he said. 'We're good enough to beat them playing our normal style.' It was one of the few times I bowed to the players' wishes. We lost 3–2 and when the return match was played at White Hart Lane later in the season we went down 3–1 playing the same way.

Brian James of the *Daily Mail* was in the press box that day:

> It was an astonishing game to watch because Ipswich were playing exactly the way they wanted and Tottenham were occupying spaces where the game was not being played. Spurs had players out there marking nothing but empty space, with no one picking up the two Ipswich front men who were thundering in at the far post.

For Alf, the victory at White Hart Lane was one of the sweetest of his career. It was a form of revenge for the way he had been treated by Spurs seven years earlier. He had outsmarted two of the men, Nicholson and Blanchflower, who had been behind his departure. For one of the few times in his life, he displayed some emotion, as his Ipswich skipper Andy Nelson recalls:

> We played superbly that night. It was a game I will never forget. Alf was so keen to go back there and for him it was an absolutely marvellous result. Afterwards, he went round the dressing-room shaking hands with everyone, and you could see his eyes glaze up. He was having a little cry.

At the end of March, soon after this victory at White Hart Lane, Ipswich went to the top of the First Division. But even then it seemed unlikely they could win the title, as Burnley, in second place, had three games in hand. But Burnley then suffered a dramatic collapse, allowing Ipswich to stay in the lead. Ipswich went into their last match of the season, against Aston Villa at Portman Road, knowing that if they won, Burnley would have to gain maximum points from their last two games. The Ipswich–Villa contest was a scrappy affair, with the Ipswich team displaying a rare bout of nerves. At half-time the score was 0–0. But then in the 72nd minute there was an opening. John Elsworthy has this memory:

> It was the most tense game I ever played in because we had to get a result. We were drawing for quite a long while and then we got a corner. I'll never forget it. As soon as it was hit, I went into the box and suddenly I found that I had a clear header. I was only six yards out and I was confident of scoring. But as I leapt I was level with the cross-bar and I headed it straight. I can see it now. The ball hit the under-

side of the bar and came out. I nearly died. I thought I'd blown it. But the next thing I knew was Ray Crawford getting hold of it. He was one of the biggest poachers I ever knew, anything loose was his. As the ball bounced, he dived and put it in the net. That was it. We were on our way. And Ray then got another goal in the final minutes.

Ipswich had won 2–0, and when the news came through that Burnley had been held at home by Chelsea, they knew they had won the Championship. A large section of the 28,000 crowd rushed onto the field, hoisting Crawford and Phillips on their shoulders, while in the directors' box John Cobbold was already hard at work on a crate of champagne. In the dressing-room afterwards, the little bald trainer Jimmy Forsyth was thrown fully clothed into the bath.

But amidst the scenes of jubilation, Alf remained an impassive figure. He pushed the players forward to accept the cheers of the crowd, remaining in the background himself. 'He did not want any praise. When people congratulated him, he gave all the credit to the players,' says Jimmy Leadbetter. But once the crowd had departed and Alf was left alone he did indulge in one expression of pure joy. Just as in the previous year, after Ipswich had gained promotion, he was sitting in the stand, gazing out on the pitch, when John Cobbold turned up. With barely a word, Alf took off his jacket, handed it to Cobbold, walked down onto the pitch and then, on his own, proceeded to do a lap of honour in front of the empty terraces, wearing collar, tie and highly polished shoes. It was a private, endearing, very human gesture from someone who was too embarrassed to show his feelings in public. In Alf's memory, Cobbold 'cheered every stride I took'. Cobbold, who was by his own admission wreathed 'in a fog of alcohol', described it as 'a bloody marvellous intimate moment'.

Ipswich were the first side in League history to win the Championship in their initial season in the First Division. They were also only the second club after Wolves to win Third, Second and First Division titles, though Wolves had taken thirty years over such an achievement, whereas Ipswich had taken just six. Alf was rightly showered with praise. The BBC, in an interview after the game, called him Ipswich's 'great manager' who had promoted 'the real virtues of simplicity and team spirit'. *The Times* described Alf as 'probably the one great genius the game has produced in recent years'. For the *East Anglian Daily Times*, he was 'the Miracle Man'. In its tribute, the paper said:

> The Town's triumph is his and his alone. He knew that his basic idea of football, directness and simplicity was the right one. He cares deeply for the footballers in his care and knows far more of their capabilities and limitations than they know themselves and we have seen them blossom and react to his coaching. Completely unemotional, never over-excited or deeply depressed, he has performed a modern miracle in football.

They were justified words, for Alf had shown a unique talent for squeezing the best out of players through motivation and technical advice. His Championship-winning side had cost only £30,000. As always, though, Alf downplayed his role, telling the BBC: 'I cannot make a player improve. That is really up to the player. I have been fortunate at Ipswich in that, though we did not have any great players here, we have men of very high character, and I think that shows in the way they play.'

But, warned the *East Anglian Daily Times*, there was 'just one small shadow' over this moment of glory: 'It is that Mr Alf Ramsey may feel that he has done enough with Ipswich Town and may cast his eyes around on other fields to conquer.'

# SEVEN

## *Lancaster Gate*

Soon after Ipswich had won the title, Alf was interviewed by the BBC and inevitably was asked about the possibility of managing the national side. 'The England job has never entered my mind. I have never considered the England team at all, not at all. I have a job at Ipswich and I still have a lot of work to do here.' Then, in a prescient comment about the role of the England selectors, he added, 'I could not imagine anyone taking on a job with such responsibilities without having a completely free hand.'

The question had been put because that summer Walter Winterbottom had finally resigned as England manager after 16 years in the job. For all his dedication and intelligence as a technical coach, he had never been an inspirational leader. 'He was not really equipped to be England's team manager,' said Alan Hardaker, Secretary of the League. 'He had no experience of football at international level or management at any level. His way of expressing things was not a way readily grasped or appreciated by many players.' The 1962 World Cup in Chile had been the last straw, as England gave another disappointing performance and limped out in the quarter-final. The organization for the trip was characteristically shambolic; because of the absence of any team doctor, the Sheffield Wednesday centre-half Peter Swan almost died of a throat infection, having been given the wrong treatment. Winterbottom had hoped to become Secretary of the FA, with Sir Stanley Rous having been elevated in 1961 to the Presidency of FIFA. But Winterbottom had his enemies within the FA, so instead the job went to an officious mediocrity, Denis Follows, who had previously been Secretary of the British Airline Pilots' Association. 'He was not an impressive man. He was what I would call a wishy-washy sort of a person,' says Dr Neil Phillips, who was team doctor under Alf.

The FA initially hoped that the Burnley captain, Jimmy Adamson, would take on the England job. A deep thinker and a recent Footballer of the Year, Adamson had been Winterbottom's coaching assistant during the 1962 World Cup. But during that tour, he grew disillusioned with the pessimistic, griping attitude of several of England's internationals. In addition, Burnley were not keen to let him go and he was reluctant to move from his northern home. The offer was rejected, so the FA then decided to advertise the post. It was vital that they hired the right man, for in 1960 FIFA had decided that the 1966 World Cup finals should be played in England. There could be no repeat of the humiliations of previous decades. While awaiting responses, the FA's International Committee approached several other leading figures in the game, including Alf's old Tottenham rival Bill Nicholson, who said that 'the England job wasn't for me'. Others, like Billy Wright and Stan Cullis publicly expressed their lack of interest. More disappointment followed when the FA saw that out of the 59 applications received in response to the advertisement, not one was remotely suitable. At a meeting of the International Committee on the 1 October 1962, it was agreed that FA Chairman Graham Doggart should ask permission from the Ipswich board to approach Alf Ramsey.

Surprisingly, given Ipswich's record, Alf's name had not been mentioned before, though Winterbottom had resigned as early as July. Winterbottom himself had never envisaged that Alf would be right for the post. 'There is no real link between the skills you need to run a successful club and those that you need to run a national side well,' he said, a comment that hardly reflects well on his judgement given the comparison between Ramsey's subsequent record and his own.

The languid, aristocratic flavour of Ipswich is captured by the way the club responded to the FA's request. Hubert Doggart, the son of Graham, told me:

> My father wrote to John Cobbold, the Chairman of Ipswich, seeking permission to approach Alf Ramsey. But he received no reply for a fortnight. By this time the press were becoming increasingly agitated about the appointment. So, not having heard anything, my father rang Kirton, the Cobbold home. The phone was answered by a butler who explained that the Chairman was unavailable because he was shooting for three weeks up at his lodge in Scotland. Well, the FA could not wait that long. My father impressed on the butler the importance of the matter and the butler then read out the FA's letter over the phone to John Cobbold in Scotland.

Cobbold returned to Ipswich immediately and convened a meeting of the board at which, according to Cobbold's account, 'we reluctantly agreed that it was entirely up to Alf and that we would certainly not stand in his way'. As authorized by his committee, Graham Doggart travelled to Ipswich on the 17 October, where he was met at the station by John Cobbold and was then taken to meet Alf at Portman Road. At this meeting, Doggart told the FA, 'we talked together for about two hours and I was most impressed by his attitude to the challenge which the post of England team manager presented'. Alf said he needed to think about the offer. On the afternoon of 24 October, after a lunch in London with Doggart and Winterbottom, he accepted the post.

It has often been claimed that Alf 'took a month' to make up his mind about the England offer, with some of his critics implying that his pride had been ruffled by the fact that he had been the FA's second choice. The slightest glance at the chronology will show that this is untrue. Alf actually accepted the offer in little more than a week of Doggart first making it. The gap between the FA Committee authorizing the approach to Ipswich on 1 October and the announcement to the press on the 25th was due entirely to John Cobbold's pheasant shooting. But Ramsey always was a methodical man, not one given to impulsive decisions. Claiming that the job offer was 'a tremendous surprise,' he explained that he took eight days to make up his mind because 'I wanted to discuss it with my wife, consider our position and complications for a moment'.

There were two chief concerns for him. The first was his association with Ipswich Town. Loyalty was one of his most powerful personal traits – indeed, it was to help cause his downfall in 1974 – and he felt a debt to the club that had given him his first job in management. Moreover, on the playing side, Ipswich were in serious trouble by October after all the euphoria of the previous season. Alf believed it would be wrong to walk out suddenly on his team at a moment of deepening crisis. He therefore stipulated that he would only take the England job at the end of the 1962–63 season. 'I have a responsibility to Ipswich, especially in view of their position in the First Division table. I must remain here for the rest of the season and see us safe,' he told the *East Anglian Daily Times*.

His second concern was the influence of the FA selectors. If Alf was to have charge of the England team, he needed total control over its affairs, just as he had at Ipswich. For all his faults, Winterbottom had never been allowed to do his job properly because of the interference from these prejudiced, often ignorant officials, as Alf had directly experienced in the 1950 World Cup when Arthur Drewry had personally insisted on the exclusion of Stanley Matthews from the game against the USA. Even the FA's own Secretary throughout the 1950s, Stanley Rous, admitted the selection committee was an absurdity. 'The committee would discuss each position in turn and vote on it if necessary. Invariably personal preferences intruded and positions were considered in isolation, rather than thought being given to the team as an entity.' Bobby Moore believed that Winterbottom was broken by the selectors. 'I could not understand how he allowed himself to be messed about by the amateurs of the committee. I felt he lost the will to fight the system.' Alf decided he would not put up with this nonsense, and the FA, becoming increasingly anxious about filling the post, were in no position to negotiate. Alf was given the control he sought, while the selectors were reduced to the role of scouts whose advice the new manager could happily ignore. The international committee would still meet, though only as a formal body, much like the constitutional monarchy in a democracy. The real power had passed to Alf. David Barber, an official at the FA during the later part of the Ramsey era, recalls how much members of the committee resented the loss of authority:

I took some of the minutes at the committee meetings and if there was a match coming up the Chairman would ask Sir Alf to read out the squad. And as Alf did so I could feel the members shuffling uneasily in their seats because they were denied any input. After all those decades of choosing the teams, they now had to bow to the manager. And I sensed some awkwardness there.

Alf was rarely motivated by money – as he once said to Ray Crawford, 'You can only eat three meals a day and you only need one bed to sleep in' – and he was still living in an Ipswich club house and driving a Hillman in 1962. His annual salary paid by the FA was only £4,500, more than double what Winterbottom had been earning but less than the £5,000 he received from Ipswich. For him it was an honour to be asked to take charge of the national team. He was effectively to be England's first professional manager after decades of ineffectual amateurism. And the press generally welcomed his appointment. 'Soccer has seen nothing like him since Herbert Chapman masterminded Arsenal in the thirties,' wrote Mike Langley in the *Daily Express*:

He is a man with a brain like a combination of camera and computer. A man intensely loyal to his players. A man able to persuade a camel that it is really a Derby winner. He is an adaptable man, a cockney kid now as well spoken as an Earl. And if England should win the World Cup in 1966, how about the story ending 'Arise Lord Alf of Wembley'.

*The Times* commented, 'Ramsey, as a man, a player and a manager, has already proved himself. Ramsey the man is not demonstrative. He is reserved, but a deep thinker. Like some scientific boffin, he can appear detached, immersed in figures and equations and not given to grandiose statements.' Perhaps the most personally revealing profile was written by Michael Williams in the *Daily Telegraph*:

Alf Ramsey does not smoke and he drinks with discretion. He wears smart, sober suits, black shoes, clean collars and ties with rather large knots. He speaks slowly, chooses his words with care and always has a half-smile on his face. He has an attractive wife and daughter, a nice car and lives in a pleasant house in a road just off the Ipswich by-pass. He is not a spontaneous man, indeed his self-control is almost something to be wondered at. He is the same in defeat as in victory, hiding his thoughts behind steady, dark eyes. Essentially he is a serious man. He forms his own opinions and sticks to them. He is not afraid to disagree with his club chairman and directors. Indeed, it is they who turn somersaults to agree with him. His dedication to the game is utter and complete. Once I recall, when Ipswich were returning from some northern match on a Saturday night, he bumped into Arthur Rowe, under whom he learned so much at White Hart Lane. Four or five hours lay ahead before we arrived in London. Throughout, Ramsey and Rowe talked and talked and talked football. Nobody else entered the conversation; there was no opportunity. And rarely, if at all, did they smile. They were lost in a world of their own.

Rowe himself commented of the appointment, 'If you looked the whole world over, you couldn't have found yourself a better man. He is a shining example of what you can make yourself from application and honest effort.' But Frank Magee of the *Daily Mirror* later reflected on the private circumspection that existed within journalistic circles. In an interview in 1970 Magee said:

I suppose the best way to sum up my own reaction and the reaction of most press men to Alf is to trace the whole affair right back to the beginning. To be quite honest, we viewed his appointment with dismay. This was essentially because Alf was not a communicator himself, quite unlike his predecessor Walter Winterbottom, who was always a marvellous subject no matter how his team had done or how he himself was criticised. And I think press relations are the one aspect of his job that Alf still does not completely understand. He is only really relaxed when he is with his players.

Within the town of Ipswich, the mood was one of sadness at his departure, but pride at the honour bestowed on the club. Alf's appointment was announced during the week of the Cuban missile crisis, when the world stood on the brink of nuclear annihilation. As the *East Anglian Daily Times* wryly commented:

> In this particular part of the world, the talk gets round to Cuba only after all the possibilities involved by Mr Ramsey's promotion have been exhausted. This is sometimes referred to as a sense of proportion or a sense of balance. And the fact that Mr Ramsey shares the same headline space as Messrs Khrushchev and Kennedy would be regarded as a considerable compliment – to Khrushchev and Kennedy.

On a more serious note, the *EADT* believed that Alf was sure to succeed in his new post, because one of the primary lessons of his career was 'his determination to see a thing through. Once he has set his mind on a task, he will not give up until his objective has been reached.' Alf's standing within the club was reflected when John Cobbold gathered all the staff in the dressing-room to break the news of his elevation. According to Cobbold:

> All of them wondered what the hell I was doing there. I had never addressed them as a group in my life. I said, 'Alf is going at the end of the season', and they were stunned, simply stunned. So I said, 'It's all right, we've not sacked

Alf. He has been appointed England manager', and everyone just cheered and clapped and cheered again. It was a marvellous tribute but Alf deserves it. He made Ipswich Town.

Later, Kenneth Wolstenholme, the respected commentator, revealed that Cobbold 'was in tears' when Alf was appointed.

For all the applause given to Alf, his Ipswich team suffered a disastrous loss of form for most of 1962–63. Even before the season had begun, Ipswich were experiencing problems. After winning the title, they had embarked on a summer tour of Germany, only to find themselves booked into a brothel in Hamburg. As Tony Garnett recalls: 'It was the only time I ever saw Alf genuinely lost for words. The Ipswich party had to stay in a hotel of ill repute just a stone's throw from the notorious red light district. There was nothing Alf could do about it but he was less than happy, while John Cobbold thought it highly amusing.' More seriously, back in England, the system which had won the Championship had finally been rumbled by the more astute First Division managers. In the traditional opening match of the season, the Charity Shield, Ipswich had been beaten 5–1 by Spurs. On Nicholson's instructions, the two deep-lying Ipswich wingers were marked by the midfielders Blanchflower and Mackay, while Crawford and Phillips were taken by the Spurs full-backs and the centre-half. Maurice Norman, one of the Spurs defenders, recalls, 'It could have hardly gone better. Very little came from the Ipswich flanks and there were three of us to deal with the two centre-forwards. It was almost a doddle.' This start set the pattern for the following months, as Ipswich slid to 21st place by November. Performances were not helped by a series of injuries and a bitterly cold winter, which meant that Ipswich did not play a single League game between 26 December 1962 and 23 February 1963. The stresses of First Division football were also beginning to tell on several ageing members of the squad. Because of lack of money and Alf's instinctive loyalty to his players, he was reluctant to freshen the squad. 'There's no doubt Alf was a mastermind, but we struggled because we were stuck with what we had,' says Ray Crawford.

As he was to show with England, Alf was brilliant at forging a winning unit, but where he was much weaker was in rebuilding. He could create, but he could not sustain. His stubbornness drove him to stick with the players and tactics that had first brought him success, even when they were no longer working. 'We will defend our League title in the same way we won it,' he announced, words that would find a painful echo with England in the seventies. In the summer of 1962, Alf bought just one new player, Bobby Blackwood from Hearts for £12,000, keeping all 28 of the previous season's squad, an act of almost reckless loyalty. Concentrating on the coaching of first-team players, he had never shown much interest in scouting or developing a youth team, which meant that there was little playing material in reserve.

The absence of any infrastructure came as a shock to the man appointed by Ipswich to succeed Alf Ramsey. Jackie Milburn, the legendary Newcastle striker who had recently finished a three-year stint as player-manager of the Belfast club Linfield, arrived at Portman Road in January 1963, believing that he and Alf would co-operate until April, when Alf officially took up his post with England. But Milburn did not find much of a welcome from Alf, who bore him a grudge from his playing days. During a practice match within days of his arrival, Milburn found himself being tackled brutally by Alf. 'I had been fouled at Spurs eight years earlier and had got up in a terrible rage and pushed over the man nearest to me – who happened to be Alf Ramsey. I'd forgotten all about it until then but the way Alf looked at me, I knew he hadn't forgotten it,' recalled Milburn. That incident set the tone for an icy relationship. Alf did not think much of Milburn's behaviour as a player or his ability as a manager. Milburn claimed that not only did Alf refuse to give him much influence at the club, but he even barred him from team talks. When Milburn sought advice from his old Newcastle team-mate Joe Harvey, he was told, 'Take no more bloody shit.' As a result, Milburn aired his grievances at a meeting with John Cobbold. According to the account left by Milburn's son, 'Dad was patted somewhat patronisingly on the shoulder and reassured that Mr Ramsey's shadow would only hang over him until the end of the season.' But matters did not improve, especially as results on the field remained poor and Ipswich hovered above the relegation zone. Inspired by the all-too spectacular example of the club chairman, Milburn sought comfort in drink. 'He would splash out on a bottle and sit alone at the club or in a hotel room when away scouting and sip until he'd blotted the parts of his mind he'd intended,' wrote his son.

Milburn was not the only one at Ipswich exasperated with Alf. In April 1963, Eric Steel, an Ipswich director and manager of a Suffolk firm of newspaper wholesalers, resigned from the board, complaining about Alf's excessive powers and unwillingness to invest in the club's future. Steel said he had continually urged the club to buy new players but had been told by the chairman, 'Let's leave that to Mr Ramsey, shall we?' Steel also felt that Ipswich's reserves were 'poor' but 'here again nothing was done. The management has been negligent.' Warming to his theme, Steel described the board as a 'bunch of Ramsey yes-men' and went on, 'Alf won't like me anymore and I'm sorry about that, but I'll not be a yes-man.'

Contrary to Steel's worst fears, Ipswich scraped to safety in 17th place thanks to a run of wins towards the end of the season. But even after Alf's departure, Milburn, now manager in his own right, found him as unhelpful as ever. On one of Alf's visits to Portman Road, Jackie asked him if, in his capacity as England manager, he knew of any players he could recommend to Ipswich. Alf replied with a monosyllabic 'No' and walked away. 'That really puzzled me, coming from a man who was purported to care so much about his former club,' he told his son. The slide continued in 1963–64, leading to Ipswich's relegation and their worst ever defeat, 10–1 at the hands of Fulham. Jackie Milburn resigned soon after the start of the following season and then launched into a very public diatribe against Alf. In a *Sun* article headline 'Ramsey Gave Me No Help', Milburn said:

> I want to get one thing clear right from the start. Ipswich are a good club and the directors are gentlemen. But I accuse Alf Ramsey! He gave me neither help nor encouragement when I took over from him. I worked with him for ten weeks and the only advice I got was that I'd have to become thick-skinned to make a go of it. I inherited a team that was over the top and going downhill fast. I knew it, the directors knew it and the most disastrous thing of all, the players knew it too. Ramsey's attitude to me didn't help either. In the first few weeks I was there I was never invited to a team talk! ... Ramsey's attitude convinced me I was on my own in a ruthless jungle.

Milburn's wail would have had more justification if he had not been such a weak manager. Once Alf had left, he had been given the chance to run the team and had failed dismally. A decent man, he was far out of his depth in management. As Ray Crawford puts it: 'He had no understanding of how to get the best out of us, none at all. His team talks were poor. He could not inspire us. He could come in and say anything and nobody cared. To be fair, Alf was a very hard act to follow but Jackie did not help himself.' Jimmy Leadbetter shares that view: 'Jackie was the nicest man you could meet but he was not a manager. I felt sorry for him. He was chicken-hearted. He let people get away with things he shouldn't have.' Andy Nelson is even more harsh. 'From the moment he arrived, it was clear he did not have much idea about what was going on. Alf refused to leave until the club was safe and he was right, because within twelve months Jackie had devastated the place. He was absolutely clueless. He had no tactical sense at all.' Still, Alf does not emerge with any great credit from this episode. There was a cold, jealous streak in him, born of pride and insecurity, that prevented him warming to any of his successors in any job. The same had happened when Danny Blanchflower took over the captaincy from him at Spurs. Years later, he fell out bitterly with England manager Bobby Robson.

Despite relegation problems, Ipswich Town released Alf to preside over England's game against France on 27 February 1963 in Paris. It was a qualifier for the European Nations Cup, the forerunner of today's European Championship. Shortly before the trip to Paris, journalist Ken Jones gave a lift to Alf from central London to Liverpool Street. He was immediately impressed by the new England manager: 'We set off through heavy-afternoon traffic. Alf was amiable; he spoke freely in a precise way, careful with his diction. "I have a great deal to learn about international football," he admitted. "I will have to look closely at players and settle on a system that suits the best of them."' Alf was so open that he revealed to Ken the make-up of most of the team, something that he would never do in future as Alf became more withdrawn. 'I was listening to him speak about various things and I thought I had it all figured out for myself. This is a guy, I was thinking to myself, who has only one objective, who will stand or fall by England's efforts in the 1966 World Cup. As at Ipswich, his thoughts were entirely concentrated on the production of a winning team. The wider aspects of English football, so dear to Winterbottom, held no interest for him.' That was a point that Alf had reinforced when he was appointed manager, stressing that he had no wish to take on Winterbottom's old job of Director of Coaching as well.

The trip to Paris confirmed for Alf the need to ditch the selection committee, who had chosen the team for the game since Alf was not officially to take control until May. Several of them, including Graham Doggart, Chelsea Chairman Joe Mears and Joe Richards of Barnsley, accompanied him on the journey. As Alf told Ken Jones:

I could see right away how difficult things had been for Walter Winterbottom. In their way they were enthusiasts but they had no judgement I could respect. Doggart struck me as a nice man. But none of them could offer a worthwhile opinion. From my first meeting with them, I knew I'd been absolutely right to seek the authority I had been given at Ipswich.

The team the committee picked gave Alf the worst possible start to his England career, though in mitigation it should be said that the big freeze in England had prevented any players gaining much match practice over the previous two months. And the Continent had also been affected by the weather. On a bitterly cold night in Paris, England were beaten 5–2, with goalkeeper Ron Springett giving a woeful performance. Ron Henry, who had been with Alf at Spurs in 1954 and won his only cap in this game, has these memories of Alf's first match in charge:

In his talk before the kick-off, he just said, 'If you behave yourself and work hard, you'll get on all right with me.' He did not talk tactics much that night. He just said, 'Go on, you know what you have to do.' It was an awful night, terrible. We hadn't played for about eight weeks because the winter was so bad. The pitch had a covering of snow. Ron Springett was in goal and he might as well not have been there because he was frozen and didn't move. It was so cold that when we had finished we had to sit around the edge of a big square bath and dangle our boots in the hot water because our laces had frozen solid. Alf could not really say much afterwards but he came round and shook your hand.

Brian Labone, the Everton centre-half, also has unhappy memories: 'Obviously I did not play very well. You have a result like that, you look at the keeper and the centre-half because they're meant to be the backbone of the side. I remember after the game going down to some nightclub and getting really sloshed.' But Bobby Moore was impressed by the new manager in the face of a heavy loss: 'There was none of the ranting and raving you might have got from some managers.'

Jimmy Armfield was Alf's captain that night:

The match should have never been played. You could hardly stand up and the floodlights were poor. I remember in the dressing-room afterwards Alf looked round for inspiration and could not find any. So he walked to me and said, 'Do we always play like that?'

'No.'

'That's the first bit of good news I've had all evening.'

We were on the plane coming back and he said more to me in those three hours than he did for quite a while afterwards. He was on about players, our priorities, what it meant to get a group of players together. He said to me that it was important to get the unit right, that it was not always the best players that made the best unit.

Springett's nightmare led Alf to drop him for the next England match, played in April at Wembley against Scotland. His place was taken by Gordon Banks, the Leicester keeper who, as much as Bobby Charlton and Bobby Moore, was to become one of the catalysts for the greatness of the Ramsey era. But his debut was not a happy affair, as Scotland won 2–1, with Jim Baxter 'strolling arrogantly around Wembley as if he owned the place', to use the words of Banks. It was Baxter who scored Scotland's first, as a result of a mistake by Jimmy Armfield, who hit a square ball across the defence, only to see it intercepted by Baxter and then drilled into the net. 'It was a killer goal to concede on your debut and I took my anger and frustration out on Jimmy, who conceded the mistake had been his,' said Banks. Having endured his second defeat in a row, Alf also confronted Armfield:

After the game he was walking towards me and I said, 'My fault, I know, I know.'
'You're not going to do that again, are you?'
'I'm not, Alf.'
'No, you're not.'
That was the end of the conversation. He could be a bit cutting.

Alf's faith in Jimmy Armfield's defensive qualities was never to be quite restored.

Gordon Banks himself suffered a tongue-lashing from Ramsey after the next game, against Brazil at Wembley. The match,

Ramsey's first since taking up the post full-time, was a creditable 1–1 draw for England, but he was furious with his defence, and especially his keeper, for ignoring his warnings about how dangerous the Brazilians could be with a free-kick near the box. In the first half, Pepe hit a vicious curling shot from 25 yards which went into the corner of the net with Banks completely stranded. Later in the dressing-room, recalled Banks,

> Alf fired daggers at me with those piercing blue eyes of his. 'Don't say I didn't warn you,' he said. 'I gave exact details of what they do from their free-kicks, but you fell for the three-card trick.' I explained that it had moved in the air twice as violently as I had been led to expect, but I could tell from Alf's tight-lipped expression that he thought I should have saved it.

In his own account written in 1970, Alf admitted that

> this was the first time that England players realized I could show anger. Before the game I had discussed repeatedly with Gordon Banks the free-kick technique of their left-winger Pepe. Obviously Gordon couldn't have understood because the first free-kick Pepe took finished in the back of the net. I was furious because I had gone to such lengths to guard against such a possibility ... After the match I went for Gordon. It is most unusual for me to vent my feelings against an individual but in this case it proved its value because he has become the greatest goalkeeper I have ever seen.

A tough Yorkshireman, Banks never resented Alf's approach:

> I admired him enormously. I thought he was a great manager. He went about his job so thoroughly, and put over his

views very well, telling us how we should operate against certain opposition. For instance, there might be a winger in the opposition and Alf would say to me, 'This guy is very, very tricky. He has got a good right foot and can cross a good ball, but if he gets to the edge of the box and cuts in on the inside of the full back, he also has a good shot with his left foot.' So I would be looking out for this. If he tried it, I would be off my line in a shot.

It is a sign of Alf's enormous self-confidence that in the first trio of games in charge, he should feel free to lay down his authority in such harsh terms to captain and goalkeeper. Unlike Winterbottom, he did not flinch from challenging his players. Ray Wilson, who played in those early games, told me this story which illustrates how eager Alf was to exert himself:

I'd had a game with Huddersfield on the Monday night and he came to meet me just outside the changing rooms on the training ground. He walked towards me, stopped me and began to chat.

'Hello, I'm Alf Ramsey,' he said.

'Yes, I know,' I joked.

We talked for a moment and then he said, 'How would you like to play?'

'Well, when I nick the ball off somebody, I then try to find one of our players. I try to keep it as simple as I can. That's how I like to play.'

'You will bloody play as I want you to play.' He had met me, just to let me know that he was in charge.

The central problem for Alf, however, was to devise the best formation in which to use his players. This was the issue that was to preoccupy him for the next two years, until, early in 1965, a mixture of insight and good fortune gave him the chance to create the system he wanted. In the meantime, he adopted the basic 4–2–4 style which Winterbottom had used, with two wingers and two strikers. Greaves seemed the obvious choice for one of the striking roles, but Alf had endless difficulty filling the other, while he also despaired of the talent of England's wingers. He wrote:

> A vital requisite for successful 4–2–4 is two attacking wingers with the ability and speed to take on defenders, to get past them, take the ball to the goal line and pull it back . . . It became apparent that we hadn't got the wingers who could give us this service we wanted.

One of those wingers was Bryan Douglas of Blackburn:

> Alf was a thinking sort of a guy. But not as far as I was concerned. He thought me out of the game. Frankly, I don't think I did the job that he wanted. When he first came into the England set-up, he had a bit of a learning curve. And it was a bit of a joke that he could not get the names of some of the foreign players right – and even those of some of our own players. There might be a chuckle or two when he was going through the opposition. I suppose that was to be expected. But he had a natural authority about him, firm without being bombastic. I did not think he had much of a sense of humour, perhaps because he was a shy man. But then I was used to Walter Winterbottom, who had been a schoolmaster and was used to speaking in front of people.

In the summer of 1963, England went on a three-match tour of Europe beginning against Czechoslovakia in Bratislava. Just after they arrived, Alf made a crucial decision, one that was to have huge long-term significance. Jimmy Armfield, the holder of the England captaincy, was injured so Alf had to appoint a new man to the role. Now the England captain during the 1962 World Cup had been the Fulham midfielder Johnny Haynes, the most elegant passer of a ball in English football, but he had suffered a serious car accident and struggled for much of the season to regain fitness. Nevertheless, many felt that by the end of 1963 Alf should bring back Haynes, who was still in his twenties and had been the lynchpin of club and country for several years. Alf would have none of it. Even a year later, in 1964, Alf still felt Haynes was not fit enough for international football. Fulham's George Cohen, who had established himself as England's right-back, was approached by Alf after a training session.

'How's Haynes?'

'Tremendous. He's snapped back into the game with all his old assurance and bite.'

Alf then shook his head slowly. 'I don't think he's quite right. I don't think he's fully recovered from his injury.'

Later, Cohen told Haynes of the conversation and Haynes just said, 'Alf's right'. Johnny Haynes was never to play for England again. At the end of his life, realism rather than resentment was displayed by Haynes towards Alf. 'He was right because when I returned I had a bit of a struggle. I was sort of playing on one leg,' he told me. What struck Cohen, however, was how shrewd Alf had been in his judgement of a player's fitness. But there may have been more to the Haynes issue than just the physical question. For Alf, a strong believer in the team ethic, may have felt that Haynes was too much of an individualist and perfectionist to be supportive of others. Alan Mullery, who played with him at Fulham, said: 'Johnny Haynes ruined more players' careers than anyone I can remember with his attitude of belittling colleagues. If you let him he would crucify you in the middle of a game.'

With no Haynes or Armfield against Czechoslovakia, Alf turned to the 22-year-old West Ham defender Bobby Moore who had only come into the England team a year earlier. He was England's youngest ever skipper in 91 years of international football. Again, Ramsey's choice of Moore showed remarkably perceptive judgement. He had instantly recognized in Moore that calm, almost regal stature that distinguished him from other players. And he had also been struck by the way Moore handled himself in the defeat in Paris; on the coach to the airport after that game, Ramsey had sat beside Moore, 'asking me a million things about the way things had been done under Walter'. From that moment, Alf came to regard Moore as his lieutenant. In his turn, Moore was only too pleased to take on the captaincy: 'I was thrilled. I liked being a captain. I like the feeling of responsibility, that if something happens on the field I have to make a decision,' he said in 1966. Yet theirs was to be a purely professional relationship, one based solely on mutual respect and not on any deeper friendship. In fact, there were to be times over the next three years when Moore's behaviour off the field would lead Alf to re-examine his decision.

Bobby's reign started in fine style, with a 4–2 win over Czechoslovakia, the mercurial Jimmy Greaves weaving his magic in the penalty box to score two goals. 'It seemed like the start of a new age of hope and ambition for England . . . Somehow England had found a new courage, a head-high pride and an unflinching spirit of battle. If new manager Alf Ramsey has done this, then his achievements are already of high merit,' wrote Desmond Hackett in the *Daily Express*. Before the match, Greaves gained an insight into the character of the new manager. Alf was explaining to the players that the coach would be leaving 45 minutes after the final whistle, and he stressed that the entire party would go back to the hotel together, fixing the players 'with that unblinking stare of his that gives listeners the feeling they are being hypnotised,' in Jimmy Greaves' description. Greaves continues:

There was an uneasy shuffling of feet and I could sense that my drinking pals in the England squad were waiting for me to act as their spokesman. 'A few of us were wondering, Alf,' I said, 'whether we could nip out for a couple of drinks before going back to the hotel . . . ?' Alf studied me for a moment. 'Gentlemen, if some of you want a fuckin' beer, you'll come back to the hotel to have it.' He had made himself perfectly understood. It wasn't said in a nasty way and there was a hint of a twinkle in those cold blue eyes of his as they fastened on to me beneath those rich, thick eyebrows. Alf was just letting me know that he was in charge. From that moment on, Alf had me marked down in his photographic memory as a ringleader of the drinking squad.

But it was Alf's determination to keep his team together that was later to pay such dividends. For Gordon Banks, the Czech match 'did the most to lay the foundations for the club-style spirit that was always in evidence for the remainder of Alf Ramsey's reign as England manager'. The tour continued to go well, as England racked up further victories over East Germany and Switzerland, who were hammered 8–1. *The Times* commented at the end of the trip: 'Here was an England side buoyant, full of confidence . . . May we hope that the tide which has been channelled so successfully will be continued next season and beyond to 1966 and the World Cup. But maybe that is too big a dream.'

It certainly was not for Alf. In the euphoric aftermath of the success of the tour, Alf gave a press conference at which he made a notorious remark that was to hang over him like the Sword of Damocles for the next three years. On his appointment in October 1962, Alf had told the *Express* that England had 'a wonderful chance to win the World Cup in 1966'. But in June 1963 he went far further. 'England WILL WIN the World Cup,' he told the startled journalists. Bryon Butler, one of the most respected of all football correspondents, wrote in the *Daily Telegraph*: 'It was a forecast that might have been anticipated; but Ramsey, a compact, urbane man who speaks slowly and picks his words adroitly, made his point emphatically enough to suggest that he passionately believes it to be true.' In reality, this was far from the case. This was no calculated attempt to boost morale after the Winterbottom era. In a rare moment of incaution, Alf had just blurted out the statement without thinking of the consequences. 'I don't think I really meant it when I said it,' he later confessed. 'The pressures at that time were simply enormous. It was probably just a question of saying the first thing that came into my mind, something I don't normally do.' But Alf felt that his words ultimately did more good than harm. 'Whilst it was an embarrassment over the years leading up to the World Cup because I always had to repeat myself, in a sense it was not a bad thing to have said, particularly from the players' viewpoint because if I showed confidence in them they would have confidence in me.' Ray Wilson certainly is of the view that it helped:

I remember hearing him on the radio when he said, in that voice of his, 'We will win the World Cup.' And like most of the lads I thought, 'For Christ's sake.' It was a hell of a pressure, that was. But Alf was great at passing on self-belief. I think we needed that at the time.

Fortunately for Alf, England's excellent form continued through the rest of 1963, with further wins over Wales, the Rest of the World and Northern Ireland, so the press could not yet taunt him with his comment. Indeed, Alf's first year had been an almost unqualified success. Often cynical about managers, Bobby Moore said of Alf's start: 'For the first time since I'd come on the scene, England were really getting organised. I don't mean that to be disrespectful to Walter but I'd come in at the end of his reign, when he'd done it all. Alf was fresh and full of ambition.' Another admirer was Bobby Charlton, playing on the wing for England in 1963 before his productive switch a year later to an attacking midfield position:

> The most fundamental difference between him and Walter was that Alf talked about the game like a real club pro. He'd been one. He never said an opponent was good unless he was. He was difficult to approach with opinions but that was probably right. The players didn't know best. Alf was never influenced by any player. He was always after what made a team rather than individuals. He made you feel you were picked because you were a good player, and he talked about what you needed. In Bratislava, he made me train in the area of the pitch where I would be playing, try the corner kicks to get the feel of the run-up. He was meticulous.

After the defeat of Northern Ireland, Alf had to wait an awkward five months before his next international. It was in spells like this that he badly missed the day-to-day management of his role at Ipswich. A football obsessive, he disliked being away from the training ground, his sanctuary from the compromises of everyday life. He travelled into Lancaster Gate four days a week, working ten till four in a cramped, starkly furnished office, measuring thirteen feet by eight, 'a room utterly without character. In the days of Regency riches, it might have been part of the servants' quarters,' said the *Daily Mail*, unwittingly reflecting the way the FA Council felt about the new England manager. Trapped in this soulless third-floor eyrie, he struggled to fill his hours. In 1970, he said:

> There were times in the early days when it was so difficult for me to adjust that I could well have walked out saying 'this is no use to me'. I didn't feel involved enough. I wasn't active enough. I sat in my office with practically nothing to do, nothing except think about international football. I looked at players, checked through the files – such as we had – and studied as much as I could about foreign teams and so on. But the biggest contrast to my club days was the fact that I was not dealing with players day in and day out.

Alf's spirits did not greatly revive when, in 1964, England travelled to Hampden Park and lost 1–0, their third defeat in a row to Scotland. This result only fuelled Alf's already ferociously anti-Caledonian spirit, which had burned brightly since his days as an England player. Not since the Duke of Cumberland has any Englishman had a more visceral dislike of the Scots. So strong was this emotion that it broke through his wall of reserve and he became more demonstrative, more voluble. Alan Hardaker, Secretary of the League, left this account after watching an England defeat by Scotland at Wembley:

> Attempting to say something tactful to Alf, I merely observed that if England had to lose I'd rather they lost to Scotland than any foreign team. The effect on Alf was remarkable. His face clouded, he seemed to have difficulty

in speaking and for a moment I thought he was going to explode with rage. He was beside himself but eventually, very deliberately, he ground out his reply, 'I'd sooner anybody beat us than the bloody Scots.

He was just as intense with his players. Barry Bridges, the Chelsea striker, immediately noticed the change when a Scottish encounter was looming:

Alf was not one to show his feelings. But I remember, before we played Scotland in 1965, Bobby Moore said to me, 'You'll see a different Alf today.' And it was true. Alf was fired up, he really was. But after that, when we played the next few games, he was back to his normal self.

The great Derby defender Roy McFarland told me that Alf's passion had not waned by the seventies:

For me, it was the only time I heard him swear. Just before we went out on the field, as we were going out the door, he'd say, 'Come on boys, let's beat these Scots fuckers.' It was a bit of a shock to me. Christ Almighty. It was the first time in my experience that he had shown emotion towards the opposition. He was letting us know what he felt about the game and the Scots. There is no doubt that the Scotland was the game that mattered.

John Connelly, the Burnley winger, has this memory of Alf's anger at any concession to Scotland:

Once, when the ball ran out when we were playing at Hampden, I went and fetched it and threw it at a Scot. They took a quick throw, went down the line and damn near scored.

Watching the film of this afterwards, Alf said to the rest of the lads, 'Just watch this pillock. What do you think of that, running after the fackin' ball for a fackin' Scotsman?'

Alf's antipathy to the Scots did not stop him admiring individual players, as he showed with Jimmy Leadbetter, probably his favourite out of all the footballers he managed. Ken Jones tells this story of a banquet at Hampden after a game: 'I was there talking to Billy Bremner when Alf came past. He looked straight at Billy and said, "You're a dirty little bastard, aren't you? But by Christ you can play."' In return, Bremner was impressed with Alf as a manager when he served under him in a match between Wales and the Rest of Britain, held to celebrate the 75th anniversary of the Welsh FA. 'I could have played for him,' Bremner told Ken Jones.

Jones was present at another moment in February 1968, when he was travelling back to London after England had been held to a draw at Hampden. The sleeper train had not yet left Glasgow, and Jones, armed with a couple of bottles of whisky, walked along to Alf's compartment, accompanied by Reg Drury of the *News of the World*:

Alf is in his pale blue pyjamas and sitting on the edge of his bunk as we go in. Then a Scots fellow comes along the corridor looking for his own berth. He puts his head round the door and sees Alf.

'I thought you were a bit lucky today, Sir Alf,' he says, and then walks off in search of his compartment.

Alf jumps off his bunk, and, still in his pyjamas, rushes out to the corridor and calls out to the disappearing figure. 'I say . . .' The Scotsman turns round and looks at Alf, who continues, '. . . .piss off.'

Alf used even stronger language on the immortal occasion when he and the England team were greeted at Prestwick Airport by the Scottish reporter Jimmy Roger:

'Welcome to Scotland, Mr Ramsey.'

'You must be fuckin' jokin'.'

All of the journalists I have spoken to about this tale have said that it is certainly not apocryphal. Hugh McIlvanney, a Scot himself, says:

Alf would get irritated, but then Scots really can be pests. I fell out with a few of them during my National Service. The story about Alf at Prestwick gains more if you knew Jimmy Roger, who could do a very good impression of Uriah Heep. He was an ex-miner but he spent his whole life trying to ingratiate himself with players and managers. He used to get on my nerves, wee Jimmy.

The defeat against Scotland at Hampden in 1964 was Alf's first since he had taken over in May. Immediately, the optimism of the previous year evaporated, as is so often the way in British sport where wild mood swings prevail and, in the absence of any sense of perspective, the slightest setback can lead to an onset of gloom. The *Guardian* called the performance at Hampden 'pathetic'. And the response of the media and public was hardly improved by a 2–1 win over an ultra-defensive Uruguay in May, with the *Daily Telegraph* reporting that Alf's side were 'booed and slow-clapped by a crowd whose patience had been tested to the limit by slow-motion football'. Alf had the chance, however, to improve the side's reputation during an extensive programme of matches in the summer of 1964, which began with a trip to Portugal and ended with an international tournament hosted by Brazil, known as 'the Little World Cup'. This competition was ideal preparation for the main event two years later, especially because the other three participants were Brazil, Argentina and Portugal, all leading contenders for 1966.

Before the trip began, Alf had to show that he was in charge. He had never experienced any trouble with discipline at Ipswich, largely because, in the words of Tony Garnett, they were 'a well-behaved team'. But with England it was very different, because in the side in the mid-sixties were three of the heaviest drinkers ever to wear the white shirt: Jimmy Greaves, Bobby Moore and Johnny 'Budgie' Byrne, the West Ham forward. John Charles, who was one of the first top black footballers in the League and sadly suffered from alcoholism once he retired, said of the drinking culture that Moore and Byrne inhabited at West Ham:

> We'd go to and from away matches to places like Newcastle by first-class train. By the end of the journey home the bottles of miniatures were piled up in a big heap and we'd thrown half out the window. We were always on the piss. We went from club to pub. Mooro was as good as gold on the field and off the field, but he was a piss-head. He liked a gin and tonic. He liked a lager too. You couldn't get him drunk. He was one of the best drinkers I knew. He was on a par with Oliver Reed! God could he drink.

Another former West Ham player told Johnny Byrne's biographer that

> Byrne was the best in the country by 1965, but he chose to mess about and piss away all that ability. He had all the confidence in the world but he couldn't do what Bobby did. Mooro would come in after a night on the lager and sweat it all off. Budgie wasn't going to have any of that.

This was the culture that Alf decided he had to confront before it infected England. One of Alf's first acts as England manager had been to insist that the entire squad stay together in the same hotel; he said he had been 'really astounded' that London players had been used to sleeping in their own homes while on international duty. 'From a team point of view this had to be changed. And it was.' So the day before flying to Portugal, all the players gathered at White's Hotel near the FA head-quarters at Lancaster Gate. They were then taken by coach down to the Bank of England's sports ground at Roehampton, which was to become the traditional England training venue during Alf's reign. After some light practice, they spent half an hour at the club's bar, with Alf buying the round, and then took the coach back to the hotel for dinner. It was a warm evening, and Bobby Moore suggested to some of the players that they join him for a stroll into the West End. Greaves and Byrne, of course, jumped at the idea, knowing that alcohol would be a key element of the itinerary. They were joined by George Eastham, Ray Wilson, Gordon Banks and, surprisingly, Bobby Charlton, by far the quietest member of the party, The magnificent seven set off down Bayswater Road, had a few beers in a pub near the hotel, and then ended up in a bar called the Beachcomber, a favourite haunt of Greaves. All those involved agree that there was no outrageous drinking; 'nobody was drunk or anything like that,' says Ray Wilson. Accounts differ, though, as to when the group got back to the hotel. Jimmy Greaves claims it was 'nearly midnight', whereas Gordon Banks, perhaps more convincingly, believes that it was 'past 1 am'.

Whatever the actual time of their return, they were all greeted by the same sight when they reached their rooms. Each one found his passport lying on his pillow. It was subtle gesture, but its message was strikingly clear for players who were used to management keeping their travel documents. They all knew they were in serious trouble with Alf. 'It was his way of saying, "Any more of this and you won't be travelling with England,"' recalls Greaves. He had imposed no formal curfew, but it was clearly intolerable for players to saunter back to the hotel in the early hours after a night's drinking on the eve of a major tour. If the players had asked to go out he would have probably refused them permission, but they had not bothered to do so, which made him all the more infuriated. At 11.30 that evening, he had gone round the hotel corridors with the England trainer Harold Shepherdson to check on the rooms and it was then that he discovered the absence of the seven miscreants.

Alf could have confronted the players on their return from Mayfair, but that carried the risk of creating a public scene, which could have reached the press. So he decided on a more sophisticated course of action, one that let the players stew for a while. 'None of us slept well that night,' admitted Bobby Charlton. Alf said nothing the next morning as they flew off to Lisbon on the Thursday. Nor was anything said on their arrival, nor the next day at training. It was not until after training on Saturday that he finally dealt with them. 'You may all go and get changed,' he announced, 'except for the seven players who I think would like to stay and see me.' The rest of the squad walked out, wondering what was happening, for none of the seven had spoken outside their circle about the incident. 'We felt like little boys who had been found scrumping in an orchard as we shuffled with embarrassment in front of an obviously angry Alf,' says Gordon Banks. Once he had the seven in front of him, Alf began in a low-key tone. 'Now what is going on, gentlemen? When you come away with me I don't expect to see you disappearing in the middle of the night.' George Eastham was the first to speak, 'Well, Alf, it's the normal thing. We normally go out and have a few drinks. After all, the game was still four days away.' Alf looked round the room for a moment, and then really let it rip:

You can count yourselves lucky to be standing here right now. If I had enough players with me, I would have sent you all home when we were back in London. All I hope is that you have learned your lesson. I will not tolerate this sort of thing again. You are here to do a job for England and so am I. Gentlemen, the matter is now closed.

This had been Alf at his most ferocious. His anger was certainly not synthetic. Budgie Byrne later remembered it as 'the most severe and punishing reprimand' he had ever experienced. 'His face turned white. He lost it and gave us a right bollocking.'

Alf put all seven players in the side for the game against Portugal. His message about their responsibilities to their country seemed to have been heeded, as Byrne scored a hat-trick and Bobby Charlton one other goal in England's 4–3 victory. Certainly, for the majority of the players, Alf had shown he was the boss, a very different, much tougher manager compared with Winterbottom. 'He went a bit over the top but he was telling us, "I am the man in charge now,"' says Ray Wilson. The news of his verbal assault spread through English football like wildfire, creating his image as an unforgiving disciplinarian. As George Cohen puts it:

He was an old pro, he wanted everybody to know and he was not about to miss a trick. His basic attitude was that if players couldn't act like adults for the limited time they were with the team there was wasn't an awful lot of point in them being there. You couldn't really go on the piss and be sufficiently focused to represent your country.

But there was one man who did not take the reprimand too seriously: his own captain Bobby Moore, a far more complex, difficult man than the blond hero of 1966 mythology. Superficially, there were some similarities with Alf. Both were born into East London working-class families and went on to captain club and country. Both possessed a natural, cool authority on the field. As players, both lacked pace but were tremendous readers of the game and distributors of the ball. Both had a quiet charisma, which could be interpreted as aloofness. Neither man was an easy conversationalist, especially when in the company of strangers. 'There was always a distance. You felt that there was always another door inside him that you could never reach,' wrote Hugh McIlvanney of Bobby, words that could equally have applied to Alf. Both were always immaculately dressed; indeed Bobby was something of an obsessive about his appearance – he even arranged his jumpers in his wardrobe in order from dark to light.

Yet there were huge differences as well. Alf was an intensely private man, whose only two worlds were football and his domestic life with Vickie, whereas Bobby revelled in the glamorous life of a soccer star, especially the drinking and the nightclubbing. Alf rarely visited bars; for Bobby they were almost a second home. Outside football, Alf had an awkward diffidence, and was uneasy with public recognition, whereas Bobby enjoyed his fame in a stylish way. Jack Charlton was once deeply impressed when Bobby took him to a club behind Grosvenor House Hotel. Bobby drove up to the club in his Jaguar, climbed out of his seat, handed the keys to the doorman and went inside. 'I'd never seen anybody do that before and ever since I've always wanted to have a big car and be well-known enough to give the keys over and have someone park it for me,' said Jack. Alf's preferred mode of transport was the underground and the afternoon train to Ipswich. Alf, modest and conservative, disliked being photographed, and was once deeply embarrassed when he was forced to pose for a publicity picture with that tempestuous Hollywood couple Elizabeth Taylor and Richard Burton. 'I wish they wouldn't shoot me from this angle. It makes me look bald,' said Alf to his wife during one of his hated photo sessions. 'Never mind, dear, you're doing very well,' replied Vickie, giving his hand a reassuring squeeze. In contrast, Bobby was only too delighted with his image as a fashionable sixties icon, and after 1966 was regularly photographed by celebrity artists like Terry O'Neill, featuring in magazines with his attractive wife Tina. Alf was not interested in the trappings of wealth and fame; Moore revelled in them. Alf remained a xenophobe all his life; Bobby was a global figure. Alf called the Argentinians 'animals'; Moore embraced Pele.

But perhaps the biggest difference was the streak of cynicism that lay at the core of Bobby Moore, something that Alf utterly lacked. Naïve and earnest, Alf clung to the values of the era into which he had been born. He was no moralizer and was capable of deceit and ruthlessness – as he showed in tapping up Ron Reynolds or in lying about his age – but in his old-fashioned, often derided, way he strove to be an English gentleman. Bobby was far more worldly, more irreverent. Keenly aware of his status, he was capable of inflicting humiliation on others, often through a barbed comment or a withering look. It is one of the paradoxes of this golden era in English football that Moore is seen as the shining knight, the epitome of English decency and warmth whereas Alf is so often regarded as the iron-hearted pragmatist. On the afternoon of the 1966 victory, Moore was pictured kissing the Jules Rimet trophy, a beaming smile on his handsome face, while Alf remained distant and stony-faced. But in truth, beneath his diffident exterior, Alf was a cauldron of seething passion, driven by intense loyalty and patriotism. Yet Moore, behind his front of charm, was calculating, cold, even cruel at times. When he was secretly conducting the affair which ultimately ended his marriage in the early eighties, his wife Tina, unaware of his infidelity but disturbed by his indifference, asked him tearfully why she always seemed to come second to football.

'What makes you think you're as high as second?' replied Moore.

Alf, for all his fixation with soccer, would have been incapable of making such a remark. In fact, once he retired, Alf completely devoted himself to Vickie. Where Alf's distance was caused by a sense of insecurity, Bobby's was due to a feeling of superiority. As Brian James, the former *Daily Mail* chief football writer, says:

> People would gravitate towards Bobby because, in a quiet sort of way, he could be a hell of a mickey-taker. He could be pretty sly in his comments. And around him in the England team there was a London gang, with Budgie Byrne and Jimmy Greaves. They were like the troublemakers at the back of the class, nudging each other and having a giggle.

Nigel Clarke agrees with this judgment:

> Like Alf, Bobby was a bit cold and diffident. But unlike Alf, Bobby was a bit of a piss-taker. It was Bobby's way of showing that he was as important as Alf. He would never detract from Alf's brilliance but sometimes the relationship became a bit strained because Alf was aware that Bobby was sending him up. Alf hated that; he always hated any-

body doing that. Sometimes Bobby would do it in public to get a laugh from the players and that really grated with Alf. His eyebrows would furrow and he would stare at Bobby. Socially, they were completely incompatible.

Bobby's own manager at West Ham, Ron Greenwood, wrote of Moore:

> I even wanted to sack him at one point and our relationship became unhappy and strained. There was an icy corridor between us. He was very aloof, locked in a world of his own. He even started to give the impression that he was ignoring me at team-talks. He would glance around with a blasé look on his face, eyes glazed in a way that suggested he had nothing to learn. It was impossible to get close to him. There was a big corner of himself that would not or could not give. It hurt that he could be so cold to someone who cared about him.

As Tina put it, 'When you were on the icy side of Bobby – on the outside and not able to get in – it was horrible.'

Jeff Powell of the *Daily Mail*, who was probably closer to Bobby than anyone else in football, says that Bobby's early experiences at West Ham under Ted Fenton bred in him a contempt for all managers, a pattern that led to 'an artificial relationship with Alf Ramsey'. Moore's irreverence would occasionally come out in jibes at the England manager, as in the time during the Mexico World Cup, when the England players were trooping into dinner and Alf, worried about infections in the humid climate, asked if they had washed their hands:

'Why, are we not being given any knives and forks?'

Back in 1964, Moore was just as cynical. 'Alf scared the

shit out of most of us! But I'm not sure Bobby bought it. He could read Alf like a book,' said Budgie Byrne. Indeed, according to Jeff Powell, Bobby thought the whole affair was nothing more than a storm in a beer glass. 'It would have been ridiculous if some of the great players had not gone to the 1966 World Cup just because we had a few beers four days before a match.'

Moore, in alliance with Greaves and Byrne, maintained this attitude once the team left London for a match against the USA before journeying to South America for the Little World Cup. On the plane across the Atlantic, Alf initially allowed the players to drink only orange juice. But once he had gone to sleep, Moore and Byrne surreptitiously ordered champagne and gin and tonics. In New York the team was booked into the Waldorf Astoria and immediately on their arrival Alf imposed a curfew. But within the hotel, several of the pressmen were holding a party in a suite on the 25th floor, to which they invited the England team. Barely the moment the first drinks had been served, the England doctor, Alan Bass, acting on Alf's instructions, telephoned the suite to warn that Alf would be there in 15 minutes and did not expect to find any of his players present. It is a reflection of the fear that Alf now inspired, after the Beachcomber episode, that immediately almost all of the players vanished. Typically, Budgie Byrne counselled a show of defiance: 'Forget Alf. If he comes in and finds us all here he can't send all of us home.' But the rest of squad preferred not to take such a risk, and charged back to their rooms twenty storeys below. Byrne was the last to leave.

But even after this incident, Bobby Moore remained as insouciant as ever, deliberately flouting Alf's curfew at the Waldorf Astoria, as Jimmy Greaves, who was sharing a room with him at the time, recalls:

It was about 11.45 pm and Mooro said, 'Come on, we're going out.'

'Where are you going?'

'I want to see Ella Fitzgerald.'

When you're room-mates, you have to go along. Down in the lift we go and we get to this bar where Ella Fitzgerald is performing – we couldn't get in, the place was packed. So we poked our heads around the door so we could say we've seen her sing. We were back within an hour. But it wasn't the best thing to do, and Alf got to know about it and wasn't happy. Mooro got me into a lot of scrapes.

Yet Greaves' tongue could be just as cutting as Moore's towards Alf. One time in the England dressing-room, a discussion arose about the merits of various club chairmen. Jimmy, feeling bored with the conversation, contributed little:

'Haven't you anything to say on the subject, Jimmy?' said Alf.

'Not really, there's little choice in rotten apples.'

'Come on Jimmy, I would have thought you, of all people, would have something more articulate to say. "Little choice in rotten apples?" We are English, Jimmy. We speak English, the language of Shakespeare,' said Alf.

'That was Shakespeare.'

Another time, in 1965, when England were in West Germany, the party had boarded the coach waiting to go to the cinema. Greaves and Moore were standing in the lobby of the hotel, talking to trainer Harold Shepherdson. 'Harold!' shouted Alf, and Shepherdson obediently ran onto the coach. But Greaves and Moore carried on chatting, indifferent to Alf.

'Mr Moore and Mr Greaves, we'll go when you're ready.'

There is no doubt that Alf grew weary of this mocking

double act in the run-up to 1966. Barry Bridges, the Chelsea and England striker, says:

> Alf was great if you were doing the business for him, the straightest guy you could ever meet, but you would not want him as an enemy. If you crossed him, he would not get you straight away but he would get you in the end. You would get your comeuppance. I sometimes wonder if that's what did for Greavsie.

Cohen agrees: 'Greavsie never seemed to grasp the principle of discipline and the value of it and that was always going to be a point of conflict with Alf.' In the same vein, Ken Jones told me: 'I remember after one match in 1963, Moore and Greaves were giggling on the back of the bus about something and Alf, who did not trust either of them, said within my earshot, "I'll win the World Cup without either of those two."'

It is a remarkable line, showing both Alf's confidence about 1966 and his bitterness towards the two Londoners. But there was little sign of England's championship pedigree during the Little World Cup in 1964. Alf's team arrived in South America after thrashing the USA 10–0, a result which wiped away some of the pain of the 1950 defeat. As Gordon Banks recalls: 'Alf got quite worked up in his team talk before this game. He told us how he had never been allowed to forget that he was one of the England team beaten by the United States.' Roger Hunt scored four and Fred Pickering of Everton got a hat-trick, though he was only to play twice more. Pickering says today:

> Alf was great with his players, but he was experimenting a lot then and he obviously decided I was not right for him. There was a great atmosphere in the England camp. He did

not have any favourites. A lot of managers try to alter you, but Alf just let you get on with your game. He said to me that he'd picked me for what I was doing for Everton, so I should go out and play the same way for England.

Maurice Norman, the Spurs defender, was another who saw Alf at close quarters and liked his management style:

I quickly saw how very strong on discipline he was. He would not put up with players who did their own thing outside training. He wanted us to get to know each other and concentrate solely on the next game. Playing for England was for him the ultimate distinction. He demanded more for the team in every way but he also expected more from it. This made you want to give more, to try harder. He made you feel good about yourself, your game; he inspired you to give more. I felt I could have run through a brick wall for him. Many found him cold and aloof but I always got on well with him. He was always fair, never slated you in team talks but took you aside and discussed your mistakes privately. He was a perfectionist, believing that to develop the team's understanding you needed frequent meetings, discussing all aspects of the game and opposition.

These qualities were not enough to inspire victories in the Little World Cup in June 1964, as England were beaten 1–5 by a rampant Brazil in their first game, with three of the Brazilian goals coming from free-kicks. Tony Waiters was England's keeper in that match:

It was a strange game. We actually did very well for the first sixty minutes. The score stood at 1–1 and then the flood-gates opened. Because of the accuracy and creativity that the Brazilians had at free-kicks, it was decided that we put six players in the wall to make it difficult to score. But I ended up trying to get a look at the ball because most of the players were blocking my view. Then suddenly a missile would enter the net.

Waiters, who went on to become a successful international coach, taking Canada to the World Cup finals in 1986, says he learnt a great deal from Alf:

I was in the squad for four years up to 1966 and I saw that Alf was very different in the sense that he was much more tactical than other managers of the time. It was a privilege to see him in action. He was very well-organized in terms of his practices and team talks. I remember Jimmy Armfield, who was with me at Blackpool, saying to me when Alf started, 'This is a bit different.' His talks lasted about an hour. They were never boring. They never lost their tension or concentration. It was all good stuff, very thorough, all given by Alf. Harold Shepherdson, the trainer, would always be there but it was pretty well all Alf. In fact it was a bit of a joke with the players because Alf would say at the end, 'Anything you want to add, Harold?', and Harold would always reply, 'No, Alf.' I had a few good one-to-one talks with Alf and it was nearly always on the tactical side. Like I remember once I had a discussion with him about my throwing. He wanted my throws to go to feet, but I had a way of throwing the ball to the player in front of him so it would reach him right in his stride. He nailed me on it because he feared that such a throw could be intercepted and then we would be in trouble. I would not call him a defensive coach but defensively his teams were very well-organized. What also struck me – from a man-management point of view – was that he gave responsibility to players. So at our hotel in Rio he did not stop us having a beer. In fact, he encouraged us to do so, partly on the grounds that a glass of beer was less likely to do you harm than a glass of water.

Soon after this heavy defeat, Alf and the team watched the key match of the tournament, Argentina against Brazil. Again, Alf saw the volatility of the South American crowds which he had first experienced during the Southampton tour of 1948. 'It was like being front-line observers of a world war,' said Banks, sitting with his colleagues along the touch-line. 'It was one of the roughest games I've ever seen. Before long practically every player on the field was putting the boot in,' said Cohen. The Brazilian spectators grew so incensed at the treatment meted out against Pele that they started to fire rockets into the air and hurl fruit and debris onto the pitch. When a half-eaten apple smashed into Alf's back, he stood up and said, 'Gentlemen, I'm ready, shall we go?', before ushering the team to the comparative shelter of the tunnel exits.

Following a 1–1 draw with Portugal, England then had to face Argentina in their last game of the tournament. Argentina adopted an ultra-defensive, often brutal approach, and managed to win 1–0, having scored with one of their few forays into the England half. George Eastham recalls:

They pulled eight players back behind the ball, and if you got past the first line of defence, down you went. Alf told us not to get involved if Argentina cut up rough, just to look after ourselves. He didn't have to tell me twice. I remember looking up from the floor to see Rattin standing over me. He made as if to stamp on my leg, then stepped over me. Goodness knows to what lengths Argentina would have gone if they'd needed to win the game. It was amazing, really, because they were a terrific team. They let us have most of the ball and won 1–0. In the end, I think Alf was just glad to get out of there. He detested them.

For all his dislike of the Argentinians' methods, Alf knew that there was still a huge gap in class between them and England. They had shown more organization in defence, soaking up the pressure and then scoring on the break. It was a valuable lesson for Alf, who knew he would have to develop the same tight coherence in his England unit if they were to compete against the best. So far he had used 31 players in his first 17 games, no great advance on the vagaries of the selectors, and, to outsiders, he had fixed on neither settled personnel nor an effective system. Danny Blanchflower wrote in the *Sunday Express*:

There has been no gradual build-up to a peak with the conviction growing and getting stronger for the future. I think that Alf is experimenting too much. Of course you have got to experiment from time to time. But not experiment every game. Otherwise you build nothing.

And England's results hardly improved with disappointing draws against Belgium and Holland and narrow wins in the Home Internationals against Wales and Northern Ireland. 'The task Alf Ramsey set himself, to coach the abundant but ill-organised soccer talent to win the World Cup, is facing failure,' said the *Daily Mail* after the game with Belgium. So lacklustre were England's performances that John Cobbold cheekily offered Alf his old job back as manager of Ipswich on the departure of Jackie Milburn. Alf never gave the idea a moment's consideration. 'It was worth the try but Alf's decision did not surprise me – he is not the kind of man to leave a job half done,' said Cobbold.

Even at the highest level, the lack of intelligence and foresight in his players regularly frustrated Alf. Tony Waiters remembers Alf giving Terry Venables a lecture after his debut against Belgium:

> Terry was running from one player to another, trying to pressurize the opposition on his own. And afterwards Alf gave him a bollocking, in a very nice way. He said, 'That's great, Terry, that you're putting so much effort in but it's got to be shared by the team. You do your job and then drop off, let some others come in.

Gordon Banks also recalled Alf fuming after England had been 4–0 up against Northern Ireland in Belfast, and then had conceded three goals in the second half. 'He confronted us in the dressing-room afterwards and demanded to know what had gone wrong. "If you can't cope when you are four goals in the lead, what's going to happen when you are a goal down?"' In mitigation to the England team, however, what had gone wrong was a certain genius called George Best.

But Alf had his own genius from Manchester United: the balding, blond winger Bobby Charlton. During the early part of Alf's reign, Charlton was an enigma, delighting crowds with his surging runs but all too often losing his way in a game. Some questioned whether he would ever fulfil his enormous natural talent. Alf himself grew frustrated at Bobby's carelessness: 'Bobby would listen, talk about my ideas and agree that they would improve his performance. Everything we ha spoken about would last for five or ten minutes on the field then it would go completely out of his head.' Then, aga Northern Ireland in Belfast in October 1964, Alf ma crucial tactical decision, one that allowed Charlton to blossom. He switched him from the wing to an attacking midfield position, something Charlton had already been doing with Manchester United. At a stroke, Charlton was given more freedom – and more responsibility. Charlton repaid Alf's tactical intuition by giving an excellent performance against the Irish, though it was not until early 1966 that he realized his true greatness.

Soon Alf was to make an even bigger tactical move, one that would change the face of British football for ever. After the Northern Ireland game, the *Daily Mail* wrote: 'Ninety minutes of shambles in Belfast ought to be enough to end the eighteen month reign of amiable Alfred. England's team manager should and must feel angry enough to become Ruthless Ramsey.' Alf was about to do just that.

# EIGHT

# *Lilleshall*

The key moment in the Hollywood classic *The Glenn Miller Story* occurs when the lead trumpet player in Miller's band cuts his lip open in rehearsal. Without one of their most important players, it looks like the band will have to abandon its forthcoming programme of concerts. At first Glenn Miller, brilliantly portrayed by Jimmy Stewart, is sunk into gloom. Then he has a flash of inspiration: why not have a clarinet play the lead trumpet's part? Right through the night, Miller sits up re-writing all his arrangements to incorporate the lead clarinet's new role. The next morning, the band rehearses. From almost the first note of *Moonlight Serenade*, Miller knows he has hit upon a unique sound, one that would revolutionize big band music. That night, as the band play in their new style for the first time, the audience stands and applauds. And Miller, as modest and cool as Alf Ramsey, gives a shy smile and an almost imperceptible wink to his wife.

Alf's own Glenn Miller moment arrived on 8 February 1965. He had called the squad together at England's rural training venue of Lilleshall in Shropshire, which England used when based outside London. It quickly emerged that the perennial problem of club versus country, which has dogged English football since the dawn of international competition, had

241

arisen once more. As so often before and since, the League managers had made soothing noises about assisting Ramsey in his task, but it when it came to the crunch, they still gave priority to their clubs. Some felt that Alf was not being tough enough. In the *Daily Mail* Brian James wrote:

> Ramsey should start to demand that he has the entire squad together two days a week to work for England, leaving Wednesday, Thursday and Friday for training with their clubs. Not every manager will accept this easily. But one, who supports Ramsey, told me, 'He has got to start demanding what he needs. He has been too soft. He must start picking fights with people if we are to get anywhere.' If Ramsey is not prepared to fight the hindering legions of 'League Soccer First', then he must select several players from the same side.

The draining influence of clubs was particularly stark this February morning. Alf turned up expecting to work with his 22 players for three days. Yet six of his chosen players were absent, including Gordon Banks, Bobby Charlton, Terry Venables and the skilful Liverpool winger PeterThompson. All six of them were fit, but their clubs had FA Cup ties on the following Saturday. Alf was frustrated at this obvious lack of co-operation: 'Players will have to be available when I want them next season – even before cup ties, if I think it necessary. It is as simple as that.' The mass absenteeism, however, gave the Alf the chance to indulge in tactical experimentation. It is one of the paradoxes of Alf that he was such a conventional suburban Englishman – once, when the Queen was making a visit to Portman Road, he went out and bought a bowler hat – yet such a radical innovator on the football field. He had been the lynchpin of push-and-run at Spurs and the creator of

Ipswich's deep-wing system. When he took over as England manager, he complained about English football being 'so rigid', sticking to 'set ways of playing with a particular player tied to his position'.

For some time, Alf had been dissatisfied with the 4–2–4 formation he had inherited from Winterbottom, which had achieved mixed results and had looked woefully inadequate in the Little World Cup. He had been thinking about the bold departure of playing 4–3–3, using midfielders rather than wingers to mount attacks. For Alf, the great advantage of this method was that it strengthened the defence, since midfielders were much more used to tracking back than wingers. In addition, it allowed more flexibility in attack, given that modern international defences, like Argentina's, covered so well that it was almost impossible for a winger to break through. Alf believed that, since his playing days, 'defenders have tightened up. Nowadays when a winger has got past a full back he is always confronted by another covering player'.

With Bobby Charlton – who still played largely as a winger in the 1964–65 season, despite the successful trial in midfield in Belfast – and Peter Thompson away, Alf told the full senior side to play 4–3–3 in a practice match against the England Under-23s, who were instructed to hold to the normal 4–2–4 formation. The result far exceeded Alf's expectations:

I played what amounted to a rather cruel trick on the younger players, in that I gave them no advance warning of the tactics the seniors were about to employ. The seniors, with three recognised outstanding footballers in midfield – Bryan Douglas on the right, Johnny Byrne in the middle and George Eastham on the left – ran riot with the young lads. They didn't know what it was all about. The senior team enjoyed it tremendously. They were full of enthusiasm.

Contrary to some opinions I was not influenced by the tactics of the Argentinians during the Little World Cup in Brazil in 1964. The Argentines, for me, played with five players, sometimes more, in the middle of the field. Their object seemed mainly to avoid defeat. Mine had always been to win.

The 'wingless wonders', so derided by traditionalists, were born that day at Lilleshall. After two years of frustration, Alf had finally hit upon a system that would challenge the world. He had been far-sighted enough to see which way football was moving, and to devise a strategy to cope with that change. A cold realist, he knew that nostalgia for the era of Matthews and Finney was not going to win England any trophies in the new defence-minded climate of international football. Like the cavaliers of the 17th century, those who called for dazzling wing-play were romantic but wrong. As Dave Bowen, the former manager of Wales, put it:

Of course we've all followed Ramsey. The winger was dead once you played four defenders. Alf saw that and it just took the rest of us a little longer to understand. With three defenders it was different. The back on the far side was covering behind the centre-half so the winger always had space from the cross-field pass. With four defenders the backs can play tight on the winger and he's lost his acceleration space. Without that, the winger's finished. He's got to keep looking for an opening. So it's better to opt for work-rate, for a player who will go again, show his courage and not be confined to the touchline.

Like a spin bowler trying out a mysterious new delivery, Alf was initially sparing in the use of 4–3–3. He was not sure if it would be suitable in all conditions, nor did he want to advertise it too widely. He first unveiled it in a match situation during a brief summer tour of Europe in 1965, when England beat West Germany 1–0 in Nuremburg, with Mick Jones of Leeds, Derek Temple of Everton and Alan Ball of Blackpool playing up front. He then followed this up with a 2–1 victory over Sweden in Gothenburg four days later. As Jimmy Armfield recorded, there was some scepticism in the squad about the new method:

> When he first talked of 4–3–3, a lot weren't too sure, including some of the players. My attitude was to see what happened first. We got into a rhythm with it and handled it well, because prior to that we'd had 4–2–4 with two wide men, but Alf thought we had to move on and you had to move with him. It helped that we all liked him and trusted him. I know he wasn't everybody's cup of tea, he'd have never got a job in PR but he stood up for his players and we liked him for that.

Derek Temple remembers Alf as

> very thorough. He was a deep thinker about the game. He was self-deprecating and could have a laugh against himself about the old days when he played. But when he wanted you to be serious, that was it, you had to be serious. He understood professionals. I was never the most confident player and Alf would always try to build me up. I tell you one thing, he hated unpunctuality. If he told you to be somewhere at a certain time, you'd better not be late. He would get really angry then. A late arrival would get a real rollicking from him in private.

Mick Jones, who made his debut in Nuremburg, was another impressed by the England manager: 'Alf was fantastic; he really made me feel at ease. He was extremely knowledgeable and never got flustered. He simply asked you to do what you did at club level.'

Alf's growing faith in 4–3–3 was confirmed when, in the autumn of 1965, he reverted to 4–2–4, and saw a dismal run of results, including a narrow win against Northern Ireland, a 0–0 draw against Wales and a defeat at home by Austria, Alf's first loss at Wembley since he took full control of the side. This last result prompted an outpouring of indignation from the press, which poured scorn on Alf's repeatedly stated belief that England would win in 1966.

Brian Glanville wrote in the *Sunday Times*:

It was John Wilkes who said that the Peace of Paris was like the Peace of God; it passed all understanding. He might just as well have been talking about Alf Ramsey's teams. He is pursuing a course which is as obstinate as it is inexplicable, a course which leads one to doubt if the team is being picked on any rational basis.

J.L. Manning was just as scathing in the *Daily Mail*:

Mr Ramsey's electioneering is no more relevant than it would be if he went around regularly kissing babies instead of occasionally drilling his team. He will go out as he came in. France knocked his side out of the European Nations Cup in 1963 and be sure some other country will do that in the World Cup in 1966.

But the situation was not nearly as dark as this vituperation suggested. In his column, J.L. Manning argued that 'England under Ramsey is the same as England under Winterbottom. And for good reason. The footballers are all the same.' This was nonsense. Alf was not only changing his tactics; he was also bringing in new personnel. Over the previous two years Alf had been struggling to find the right blend of players, without much success, but by 1965, some of his choices were looking more fruitful. Against Yugoslavia in May, he picked the livewire 19-year-old Alan Ball, the son of a League manager and a player of tireless commitment who was so fixated with football that he did nothing to cure his adolescent spots, hoping that they would drive the girls away and allow him to concentrate on his football. Alf, the ultimate football obsessive, would have understood that. And, like all of the 1966 team, Ball remains today full of admiration for Alf:

Everything I achieved in the game I owe to him. I loved Alf to death. He gave me my opportunity. I remember my first call up to the squad. Before the game against Yugoslavia he took me to one side and said, 'I think it is about time you played for your country. So let's see what you can do.' I thought I had gone on that tour of Europe for the experience, not imagining I would play. But I had great confidence in my ability. I was not nervous on the big stage. I had this drive in me. I wanted to be the best. It got me into lots of shit, lots of bother because I was that keen. But Alf seemed to like that way about me. He liked my attitude. He was a really special man. He was not a big motivational speaker. Not really gung-ho, like some – indeed myself, he was not that type of manager. But he got you to do exactly what he wanted. The only time Alf ever really rocked me back on my heels was in a Football League game against the Scottish League. We were winning at Hampden Park and I thought I was playing really well. We came in at half-time. He was walking over towards me in the dressing-room and I thought he was going to say something like, 'Well done.' He sat down beside me and said very quietly:

'Do you think Bobby Moore can pass the ball?'

'Yeah, sure Alf, he's a great passer.'

'Well then, why do you keep going back and taking the ball off him? If Bobby Moore passes the ball to you 20 yards up the field, you are 20 yards nearer the enemy. And with your passing ability, you can hurt the enemy 20 yards further up the pitch.'

I never, ever went back and took the ball off Bobby Moore again. I always tried to play an extra 20 or 30 yards further on. Alf never had to tell me that again. That is how he was. He knew the best way to handle me, to get the best out of me. When I was younger, I was thirsting for knowledge on the big stage. My father, who was my Svengali, used to say that he could see the influence that Alf had on me. My father said that I was a rough diamond but Alf polished me.

Two other crucial introductions were made in the first half of 1965. By this time, most of the defence had been settled, with Banks in goal, Ray Wilson and George Cohen the full-backs and Bobby Moore in the centre, having dropped back from the midfield position he held at West Ham. Maurice Norman of Spurs had been playing as the other centre-half up until the end of 1964, but Alf was not entirely satisfied with the way the unit was operating. Against Northern Ireland in October, George Best had run rings around Norman, who, according to Banks, 'knew he had not played well in the second half and was very dejected at the end'. Alf brought in the tall Leeds defender Jack Charlton, Bobby's elder brother, having been impressed with the way Jack handled the big Celtic centre-forward John Hughes in a representative match for the Foot-

ball League against the Scottish League. They were the first
siblings to appear together for England in the 20th century
but they could not have been more different in personality or
playing style. Where Jack was obstreperous and opinionated,
Bobby was withdrawn and serious. On the field, Bobby was
all flowing elegance, Jack awkward ruggedness, 'looking
like a big giraffe', said Bobby Moore. Their approaches to the
game were diametrically opposed. Jack's whole outlook was
geared towards stopping goals, Bobby's to scoring them. Jack
was the rebel, regularly in trouble with the authorities as
when he notoriously announced on television in 1970 that he
had 'a little black book' in which he kept the names of enemies.
Bobby was the conformist, rewarded by the establishment
with a knighthood, a directorship of Manchester United and
an exalted role as England's sporting ambassador. They were
not even close as brothers. A bitter dispute arose between
them, caused by a rift between Bobby's wife Norma and his
mother, the Ashington matriarch Cissie. As a result Bobby
drifted away from his family, something that deeply angered
Jack, who claimed that Bobby hardly visited his mother in the
last years of her life.

Jack, who never had the same natural talent as Bobby, had
been a wayward, inconsistent player at Leeds in the fifties. But
he was transformed under the influence of Don Revie, who
arrived at Leeds as player-manager in 1960 and with a mixture of threats and cajoling brought a new discipline to Jack's
game. Even so, few thought of Jack as international class.
Alf, however, always had a deeper insight than a host of more
superficial judges of the game. He saw that Jack was not only
powerful in the air but could be the perfect foil for Bobby
Moore on the ground. Again, Jack's selection highlighted
Alf's belief in the importance of a well-functioning unit, as he
once told Jack over a drink in a hotel bar. The conversation

encapsulates the philosophy of Alf, as well as a certain waspish humour:

> I asked Alf what made him pick me for England.
>
> 'Well,' he said. 'I have a pattern of play in my mind – and I pick the best players to fit the pattern. I don't necessarily always pick the best players, Jack.'
>
> That was his way of boosting your confidence! Later he explained a bit further. 'I've watched you play, Jack and you're quite good. You're a good tackler and you're good in the air and I need those things. And I know you won't trust Bobby Moore.'
>
> I said I didn't know what he meant. Bobby Moore was a tremendous player.
>
> 'Yes, Jack,' he replied with a superior smile, 'but you and he are different. If Gordon Banks gives you the ball on the edge of the box, you'll give it back to him and say, 'Keep the bloody thing' – but if Gordon gives the ball to Bobby, he will play through the midfield, all the way to a forward position if he has to. I've watched you play and I know that as soon as Bobby goes, you'll always fill in behind him. That way, if Bobby makes a mistake, you're there to cover it.'

Jack has this further analysis of Alf:

> He was very much the Boss – you didn't argue with Alf. But he never shouted at us either. If he was disappointed with the way you'd played, he just wouldn't speak to you – and if he came over and smiled, you knew you'd done all right. One of the most disconcerting things about Alf was that you never knew if he was serious or not. That night I talked to him in the hotel bar, for example, I was just standing there having a quiet drink when Alf came in and said, 'We're

still on the pints then, are we, Jack?' I didn't know how to react. I've never been a big drinker and I was just having a quiet pint before going to bed. Maybe he didn't mean anything by it – maybe he did. I never thought he liked me, to be honest. But I learned a lot from him.

Jack Charlton may have felt unsure about his standing with Alf, but that never inhibited him from showing his argumentative side. And Alf allowed him a leeway that he would not have given to others, as Alan Ball recalls: 'He could be contentious. He was never afraid to speak his mind and I think Alf admired him for that.' George Cohen recalls that Jack was

never intimidated. He had tremendous front and on one occasion, after an England work-out at Highbury, he declared, 'Alf, you're talking shit.' Alf's expression didn't change. He paused for a moment before saying, 'That's as may be, Jack, but of course you will do as I say.

Peter Thompson, the Liverpool winger who was in and out of Alf's teams in the sixties, was amused by Jack's quarrelsome attitude:

Nobody ever messed Alf about, except Jack Charlton. Whatever Alf did, Jack would object to it. So Alf would say one night in the team hotel, 'Right, gentlemen, tonight we'll go to the pictures, then come back, have some toast and tea and then to bed. Everybody happy?'

And Jack would put up his hand and say, 'I don't want to go to the pictures.'

Then the next night, Alf would say, 'Gentlemen, this evening we will stay in and watch the television. Everyone all right with that? Yes Jack?'

'I want to go to the pictures'.
We had a laugh.

Also making his debut against Scotland was Nobby Stiles,
another player who was to become a key member of Ramsey's
England. Like Jack Charlton, Stiles was not an obvious choice.
To many of Alf's critics, he was no more than a brutal hard
man, one whose supposed lack of footballing vision was symbolized by the fact that he had poor eyesight and therefore
had to wear contact lenses. But the qualities that Alf admired
in Nobby were his ball-winning ability and the strength of his
passing. With his usual foresight, Alf recognized that Nobby
could be invaluable in feeding the ball to his Manchester
United team-mate Bobby Charlton. And for all his image of
chivalric virtue, Alf did not hesitate to encourage Stiles in his
ruthless tackling. Nobby was first picked by Alf to play for
England's Under-23s against the Scottish Under-23s in Aberdeen, and Alf soon showed his determination to get a result,
even at the expense of fair play. 'At half-time,' recalls Nobby,
'Alf got very specific. He said, "Nobby, Charlie Cooke is giving
us a lot of problems. Sort him out." I asked him what he
meant. "Well, put him out of the game."' Nobby followed the
instructions to the letter. Early in the second half, he scented
the opportunity for a typically crunching tackle and left his
victim rolling in agony on the ground. Satisfied at a job well
done, Stiles marched away from the scene of the assault. Suddenly Norman Hunter, the Leeds defender, came charging up
to him.

'What the fuck do you think you're doing?'

'I'm doing exactly what Alf wanted, taking Charlie Cooke
out of the game.'

'You'd better look again, you stupid bastard,' replied
Hunter.

Before the match, Nobby had realized that he had forgotten to bring his contact lens fluid up to Aberdeen. With his impaired sight, he had gone for the wrong man. 'You didn't do Charlie, you did Billy Bremner.'

Though he had nailed the wrong Scot, Nobby impressed Alf with his ferocious competitive spirit. When he was considering Nobby in the full England team against Scotland, Alf approached Wilf McGuinness, the former United player whose career had been finished by a broken leg. McGuinness had subsequently become a coach at Old Trafford and with the England Under-18s, and Alf respected his judgement.

'Will Nobby be as hard and determined as he was in the Under-23 game when he comes up against team-mate Denis Law at Wembley?' Alf asked McGuinnness.

'No fucking danger, Alf,' was the reply.

And McGuinness was proved right, as Nobby played his heart out in England's 2–2 draw. Gordon Banks said of his performance: 'He came into the team like a tiger. The way he tackled his Manchester United team-mates Pat Crerand and Denis Law made Alf realize that here was a player totally committed to the England cause.' That is certainly the way Nobby felt, saying, 'When I went out in that England shirt, with the three lions, it was brilliant.' And his devotion to Alf is unstinting:

I cannot say enough in favour of Alf Ramsey. I would have died for him. We all loved him. He was such a man of his word. I could not see a single weakness in his approach as a manager. He treated you like an adult. He never hectored or laid down the law. But he was an Englishman through and through. He hated the Scots. I remember, just before I made my debut, asking Budgie Byrne what was the difference between Alf and Walter Winterbottom.

'The difference is that when we're playing Scotland, Alf will say, "Get into these Scotch bastards."'

With the introduction of Jack Charlton in the centre and Stiles as a deep-lying midfielder just in front of the defence, England were now well-organized at the back. The trouble was in the forward line. Though many in the press saw Bobby Charlton as an enigma, Alf had long decided that his genius made him central to the attack. Ray Wilson says that Bobby's welfare was always one of Alf's primary concerns. 'I was generally Bobby's room-mate and I sometimes wondered if I was in the side for my ability to play or for looking after Bobby. So whenever we were leaving the hotel, Alf would say, "Has Bobby got everything? Everything all right?" "Oh yes," I'd tell him.' Alf's real problem was not Bobby Charlton but who would play alongside him. In the three years up to the World Cup he was continually trying different permutations, sometimes with wingers, sometimes without them, but he felt that none quite worked.

His experimentation left some of these forwards disgruntled. The Scots-born Joe Baker, who played for Arsenal was one of them. After a few games in 1965, he found himself out of favour, with the likes of Greaves or Roger Hunt of Liverpool preferred to him.

'I don't know what happened. I just disappeared out of the picture,' said Baker. 'That's what I didn't like about Ramsey, that he didn't explain things man to man. If he'd said, "Look Joe, I've decided on the system I'm playing and I think Roger and Jimmy play it best, I'm the one who gets the stick if it fails, so I am sorry I can't have you," I could accept that but not to get a call or a letter was awful. Like all managers he had his favourites, and my face didn't fit. Maybe he didn't like my accent! But I couldn't relate to him. I call a spade a spade but he wouldn't talk back to you after a game, to tell you what you'd done. He wouldn't say, "Right, you were crap", he'd just quietly drop you out of it without telling you what you'd done.'

Johnny Byrne, the West Ham forward, was another who did not fall under Ramsey's spell. One night, after he had retired, he told Bobby Moore: 'I can hear his talk now. The same old talk. Let's face it, Bob. He didn't hold a candle to Ron Greenwood in his knowledge of the game. Not in the same street.'

But Baker's and Byrne's were hardly representative views. Barry Bridges of Chelsea, who also played in 1965, says that Alf was

a fantastic manager, the best I ever worked with – and I worked with Stan Cullis and Tommy Docherty. I have nothing but respect for him; he was absolutely top-class. He was not a ranter and raver, he was a thinker. I have a story which sums him up. I was picked for the English League game against the Scottish League at Hampden and Alf was in charge. It was the first senior game I played and I remember putting on my shirt in the dressing-room, thinking to myself, 'I've got to be a bit special. If I do well here, I could be playing for England.' I had speed and I could score goals but I was not anything more than that. So I go out in the first half and play like an absolute idiot. I am trying all the tricks, doing all the things I could not really do. So I came in at half time, ready for the team talk. And Alf immediately sat down beside me,

'What are you trying to do, Barry?'

'Well, I . . .'

'Look son, I have picked you to play the way you play for Chelsea. Don't pretend to be something you're not. Just be yourself.' And with that, he walked away. I went out in the second half, got a goal and was picked for England a few weeks later.

Bridges was another who failed to consolidate a place. Indicative of Alf's worries about the front-line is the fact that in the three years to 1966, he used no fewer than nine centre-forwards. There is a view that Alf, if he had embraced flair, would never have needed to feel so uneasy, since he already had one of the finest strikers in the world in Jimmy Greaves, a player who scored an astonishing 44 times in just 57 games for England. Alf's suspicions about the effectiveness of Greaves were allegedly part of his wider dislike of brilliance – or, as Brian Granville once wrote, his 'distrust of genius unless it came wreathed in perspiration'. But it is all too easy to criticize Alf over Jimmy Greaves using the benefit of hindsight. The reality is that in the mid-sixties, Alf was not the only one who feared that Greaves was unreliable. Many journalists and even his own team-mates were disturbed by his fluctuations in form, his reluctance to raise his work-rate and his regular failures on the international stage. Greaves had played poorly in the 1962 World Cup in Chile, when it was written of his performance against Brazil in the quarter-final that 'his only contribution was catching a stray dog'. Alan Mullery, who played with him at Spurs, described him as 'the most undisciplined footballer I have ever known'. Brian James of the *Daily Mail* has this telling analysis:

Jimmy was a smashing guy and a wonderful goal-scorer. But he could be madly unpredictable. I remember covering one League match, when Spurs were playing in Sunderland,

and Jimmy was coming back from an injury. We'd all built this up in the press, saying that this was the match where Jimmy would prove what he could do. On the day, the pitch was like stone because of frost. Jimmy went out, said to himself 'sod this', and did not run a yard. And we were all flabbergasted at the way he seemed not to give a shit about the team. So there was always this feeling, 'Which Jimmy are we going to see today? Is he really up for it?' With Bobby Charlton It was completely different. You never doubted his temperament, that he would give his all. You never saw him walking back slowly when the attack broken down. He never took a rest.

In England's defeat against Austria in October 1965, the *Daily Mail* described him as 'a pale, spasmodic shadow'.

In his drive to create a team of world beaters, Alf had no patience with those who did not give their full dedication in every game. As George Cohen put it: 'Alf liked players who'd take a bad knock but still get up and play, the player who was absolutely knackered but would draw himself up for the next run. He could see through a person's character, which gave him a big edge over other managers.' With his limited application, Greaves was never Alf's sort of player, and when he failed to score consistently, as he did in his last three games of 1965, his position was vulnerable. What made it all the worse for Greaves was that towards the end of the year, he suffered a debilitating bout of hepatitis, which put him out of soccer for three months and left him struggling to regain fitness in the spring of 1966.

For England's final match of 1965, against Spain in Madrid in December, Roger Hunt came in for the absent Greaves. Renowned for his phenomenal dedication and selfless running, Hunt was much more likely to appeal to Ramsey, though he was no mere workhorse – in a 401 match career for Liverpool under Bill Shankly, he scored 245 League goals, while before the Spanish game, he had won six caps for England since 1962 and hit the net seven times. Importantly, Ramsey's England players were big admirers of Hunt. 'There was always this pressure from the southern press about Roger but he was so highly regarded in the England squad,' George Cohen told me. 'He was a terrific guy, a terrific footballer. He never stood still and was quite happy to rough it.' Nobby Stiles says:

> People today are still talking about Jimmy Greaves. But if you asked the squad who they wanted, they'd have said Roger Hunt because Roger just never stopped working. He was very unselfish, always there. He would makes runs across field for other people. Alf knew what Roger was. That was the great thing about Alf: he understood players.

Apart from Alf's psychological gift for reading character, what Nobby Stiles and most of the England squad also admired about Alf was the way his hard, earthy background as a soccer professional would occasionally explode to the surface. They loved his rare, foul-mouthed outbursts because they showed that, beneath the carefully manufactured veneer of gentility, he was really one of them, something Wing-Commander Winterbottom never was. And the cursing was all the funnier because it was such a shocking departure from his usual painfully measured enunciation. George Cohen had two classic examples of this. The first occurred when Alf, his wife Vickie and several of the players were having tea in White's Hotel at Lancaster Gate prior to a foreign trip. George had volunteered to do the serving, but was having some difficulty with the crockery. Suddenly Alf blurted out, 'For heaven's sake Vickie, pour the bloody tea before he scalds us all.' The second incident was far more incendiary. It took place when England were training in Madrid in December 1965, prior to the match against Spain. As was customary, the team was holding a five-a-side game and Alf decided at the last minute to join in. Cohen continues:

It was a bloody cold morning in Madrid and there was some ice in the ground. All I saw was a figure in a tracksuit and I went into the tackle. Unfortunately, it was Alf. I caught him with his feet together. He went straight up in the air and landed bang on his head. He lay on the ground groaning for a while, then he looked me in the face and said, 'George, if I could find another fucking full-back you wouldn't be playing tomorrow.'

Cohen was horrified at the time, fearing he had damaged his chances of appearing in the World Cup, but looking back, he now feels that Alf's authentic reaction only helped to build England's spirit: 'That was Alf, the way he won players over. His occasional swearing brought the team together.'

Gordon Milne, the ex-Liverpool player, has this interesting angle on Alf's language:

He had a ripe tongue at the right time. Sometimes players want their managers to come out and say something. I think his accent somehow worked in his favour. No one expected football sense to come from such a voice, the voice of the FA, and it made his words all the more powerful. The lads sometimes had a snigger but they would love it when he came out with a choice phrase. It was so funny when he would say, 'Fuck it.' It was great for morale, especially when he laid into the press. He did not do it to gain favour with the players but to show them that he was interested in what they said and wrote. He would say to us, 'Well, what does he fucking know about the game? Take no notice.'

Another occasion that caused laughter among the England players occurred after an English League game against the Irish League. The English League won easily, but Alf had been disappointed, towards the end of the game, by the failure of the wall to stop an Irish free-kick requiring a sprawling save from Banks onto the woodwork.

'Gordon, what happened at that free-kick?'

'I touched it onto the post.'

'I know that, Gordon, I'm not fucking blind. I mean what happened to the wall?'

The match against Spain, though a friendly, was seen as a particularly difficult one for England, since the Spanish were the holders of the European Nations Cup. But on a bitterly cold, wintry night in the Bernabeu stadium, Spain were torn apart in daring style, the 0–2 scoreline hardly reflecting England's total dominance. The secret of England's success was the use of the 4–3–3 formation, the first time Alf had tried it since Gothenburg. The trio in England's front-line were Roger Hunt, Joe Baker and Alan Ball, with the midfield comprising Bobby Charlton, Stiles and Eastham. When Alf announced his team, the absence of any wingers was greeted with puzzlement and derision in the press. 'Alf was slaughtered because everyone still believed that the way to win matches was with wingers,' says Nigel Clarke. But the mood changed once the match started and the superiority of England's tactics became apparent. With goals from Baker and Roger Hunt, this was the night that Alf sent a shudder through the football world. 'It was 4–3–3 in all its thoroughness and finest. The Spanish and foreign press particularly were rightly complimentary about our 2–0. I think really this was when it was first registered

firmly in my mind as a system that could win the World Cup,'
said Alf later. The Spanish coach Jose Villalonga almost purred
with admiration: 'England were just phenomenal tonight.
They were far superior to us in their experiment and their
performance. They could have beaten any team tonight.' The
British media, always inclined to see everything in the starkest
black-and-white terms, were just as enthusiastic. Only a month
earlier, Alf had been condemned as a failure. Now he was
being hailed as a genius. One of Alf's biggest critics, the
*Express*'s self-important, bowler-hatted Desmond Hackett,
who combined overblown prose with hysterical switches of
opinion, waxed lyrically:

England can win the World Cup next year. They have only
to match the splendour of this unforgettable night and there
is no team on earth who could master them. This was England's first win in Spain. But it was more than a victory. It
was a thrashing of painful humiliation for the Spanish. Gone
were the shackles of rigid regimentation. The team moved
freely and confidently and with such rare imagination that
the numbers became mere identification marks on players
who rose to noble heights.

In abuse or adulation, Hackett was never taken too seriously
by Alf, who felt – with some justification – that Hackett had
little real understanding of football. Once Hackett was covering an Arsenal match in Oslo, for which the programme had
been misprinted with the wrong numbers on the Arsenal
players. Rather than cause more confusion, Bertie Mee, the
Arsenal manager, told his players to wear whatever shirt
numbers the programme stated, but keep to their normal
positions. At the end of game, Hackett, who never allowed
incomprehension to undermine his self-confidence, wrote,

'Last night Arsenal conducted the boldest experiment in the history of European competition.' He then proceeded to invent a quotation from Bertie Mee. A sharp letter was sent from Highbury to the *Daily Express*: 'We don't mind Hackett making an idiot of himself but don't try to make an idiot out of our manager.' As Brian James puts it: 'Not only did he not know what was going on, he did not even know what he was seeing. There was certainly no love lost between him and Alf.'

On this occasion, however, Hackett reflected a surge of optimism that swept through British football after this result. It is telling that nine of the side that beat Spain that night were to feature in the World Cup Final seven months later. Alf now had the right system – and the right blend. The players themselves recognized that something special had happened in the Bernabeu. 'They settled in that night just as Alf wanted them and you could sense the exuberance and mutual pleasure they got from each other's play,' wrote the trainer Harold Shepherdson. 'Suddenly we all sensed that we had found a style that could win us the World Cup,' said Banks. 'It was a brilliant performance, free, strong and positive,' thought Cohen. Perhaps the most powerful display was given by Alan Ball, just turned twenty, who ran hard and showed huge confidence on the ball. Today, Ball gives this insight into Alf's methods:

What I loved about Alf was that he never told you what to do. He always asked you if you were comfortable doing something. Before the match in Spain, he said, 'Have you ever played centre-forward?'

'No, Alf.'

'Well, do you think you could play with Joe Baker and Roger Hunt as part of a three-man partnership? With your touch, I am sure you can cause them all sorts of problems.

We're not going to hit long balls. We are going to pass the ball to you. I want you coming off defenders and playing around them. Do you think you can do that?'

'Of course I can, Alf.'

So I played right up front in Madrid and we absolutely wiped the floor with them, we really did.

During the match, Alf stuck to 4– 3– 3, even when Baker had to limp off with an injury. Instead of bringing on a winger, he moved Bobby Charlton forward and replaced him in midfield with Norman Hunter of Leeds, who became the first substitute used in an English international. One of the reasons for this move was that he distrusted Bobby Charlton's defensive capabilities. 'I don't want him messing around our penalty area,' explained Alf. For Hunter, the perennial deputy to Bobby Moore throughout most of his career, it was a rare chance to put on the white shirt for England:

I was fortunate that I played under two great managers, Don Revie at club level and Alf Ramsey at international level. They differed tremendously in personality, since Alf was not as intense as the Gaffer, but they had two things in common. The first was their attention to detail. Alf might say, 'Norman, you're playing on the left-hand side at the back. Get out there and familiarize yourself with the pitch. Have a look where you will be spending most of your time.' No-one had ever said anything like that to me before. The second was their man-management. They were both excellent at it. Alf was absolutely top drawer. He was a shy, quiet man but he had great self-confidence; he immediately inspired respect. When he spoke, you listened. He was very brave the way he picked the team, but he knew what he was doing. Tactically, he was very, very good. Nine times out of ten when I turned up for England duty, I knew I was not going to play because of Bobby, but that never bothered me. I just enjoyed being with Alf and the squad. He always made time to talk to me, and would say at the end, 'I know you haven't played, Norman, but thank you for coming.' He made you feel very special. He had a lovely sense of humour. He once gave us the weekend off and described it as a 'bit of remission for good behaviour.'

Alf was so excited with the display against Spain that after the game he invited some journalists for a drink in the Fenix hotel in Madrid to explain his thinking, a rare event given his innate hostility to the press. 'He sat us down in the lounge and I think there were about six or seven of us,' recalls Ken Jones. 'He went through what he was trying to do with 4–3–3 and then answered questions. I never figured out why he took the trouble to do that. There were people there, of course, who did not know what he was talking about.' The more expansive Geoffrey Green of *The Times*, a prodigious drinker, vivid writer and closet racist who was once heard to shout on a train, 'Hitler was right!', left this account of the evening:

As the champagne corks popped so the temperature rose and the verbal exchanges sharpened and slurred. The giant crystal chandelier overhead sparkled like the milky way and Alf was on cloud seven. Laying aside his glass every now and then – every quarter hour on the quarter hour I would judge – he cupped his hands in front of an enigmatic smile to murmur, 'This precious jewel.' Each time he repeated the action I tottered to my feet, raised my champagne goblet and gave a Russian toast, 'Here's to the four corners of this room.' So the wee small hours unwound happily. It was only the next day, following a massive dose of Alka Seltzer, that I came to realize two things. The room I had been toasting was entirely circular; and Alf's 'precious jewel', caressed in imagination, was football!

Alf emphasized that 4–3–3 was not purely a defensive system. As well as the six in the forward line and midfield, the two full-backs, Wilson and Cohen, would take their share of thrusting upfield and of delivering crosses. Bobby Charlton was taken with the offensive possibilities of the new system:

Before Alf, we'd never really had a plan away from home and this new development was really something. When Alf made the switch to 4–3–3 he particularly made the point that we weren't going to become a defensive team, that the three up front wouldn't be alone, that we would have six up front.

Yet, just as had happened earlier in the year, Alf was determined not to play 4–3–3 in every England fixture. Such a move would only reduce its potency and surprise element. It was to be reserved for the biggest matches and, in the meantime, would remain shrouded in secrecy. As Alf explained to Brian James just a week after the Madrid victory:

I think it would be quite wrong to let the rest of the world, our rivals, see exactly what we are doing. I think it is my duty to protect certain players until the time we need them most. This was a step and a very big one in our education as a football party. My job will be to produce the right team at the right time and that does not always mean pressing ahead with a particular combination just because it has been successful.

In early 1966, as Alf reverted to a more conventional style, his England team did not look so impressive. There was a draw in the mud at Goodison against Poland, followed by a dreary 1–0 defeat of West Germany at Wembley, which left the crowd so bored that slow-handclapping and booing echoed round the stadium at the final whistle. In the dressing-room afterwards, as the jeers continued outside, Alf said to his players: 'Listen to them moan. But I'll tell you this: they'll go mad if we beat West Germany by one goal in the World Cup Final.' To the press, Alf adopted his characteristic one-eyed Nelson approach which refused to acknowledge any deficiencies in his side, telling journalists that the crowd had actually been booing the Germans. This failed to convince the *Guardian* which attacked Ramsey for producing 'a travesty of football'. Peter Thompson, the gifted Liverpool winger, had particular cause to regret this game:

> Bertie Vogts marked me. I had about five kicks – and they were all in the warm-up. In the dressing-room afterwards, Alf sat down beside me, put his hand on my knee and just said, 'A little disappointed, Peter.' That hurt me much more than Shankly screaming and shouting. Shanks would throw things at you, ranting, 'You're fucking useless, I'm fucking dropping you.' Alf was the exact opposite. I respected him so much. I can still remember the hurt of those few words that day.

A couple of months later, Alf had the satisfaction of seeing England beat Scotland for the first time under his reign, though he was concerned that England – without Ray Wilson in defence – had conceded three goals in the 4–3 win. A more solid performance in England's last home game before the World Cup saw England beat Yugoslavia 2–0, with goals from

Bobby Charlton and Jimmy Greaves, who appeared to have recovered from his bout of hepatitis.

These mixed results created little sense of euphoria in the run-up to the World Cup. The excitement generated by the Spanish result had evaporated, replaced by a sense of anxiety and even pessimism. 'England will not win the World Cup,' claimed Jimmy Hill. 'But don't blame Alf. No-one could win it with this lot.' And this was mild compared to some of the other commentaries. There has been a trend, since the sixties, to decry Alf's achievement, claiming that England were bound to win the World Cup with home advantage. 'We'd have done bloody well not to win,' wrote Rob Steen in *The Mavericks*. Yet it is fascinating to look back and see how little faith there was in Alf's leadership before the summer of 1966. Chelsea manager Tommy Docherty, perhaps reflecting some Caledonian prejudice, called Alf's World Cup preparations 'chaotic, misguided and full of half-baked theories'. In the *Scottish Daily Mail*, John Fairgrieve argued:

There are those few who contend Alf Ramsey is an unappreciated genius. There are many more who regard the team manager of England as the biggest threat to his country's prestige since Bonaparte. My own view is that England do not have the smallest chance against either Brazil or Italy in July. Against several other finalists, like Hungary, Russia and West Germany, they could not be fancied. And if I were being really harsh, I would say England are lucky to be in the World Cup finals at all. Many Englishmen already believe this and say so. Then, having said it, they seek a scapegoat. Alf Ramsey is the obvious choice and he has been duly chosen.

John Moynihan of the *Sunday Telegraph* wrote this:

Perhaps we of the press and all supporters of England would like rather more communication from him and less of an attitude that the England side is his and his alone. It is not his alone. Haven't we waited long enough for a team to win this competition? Ramsey is not always a man to arouse confidence in the task. Is he trying to build a team with or without Jimmy Greaves; is his plan a mere flash in the pan relying on hard workers, players like Roger Hunt and Nobby Stiles, merely following the plough? England's team will have to be a team of eleven Rolls-Royces, average runners will not do. And surely he must play at least one established winger?

Alf wearied of the febrile attitude of public and press, which never seemed satisfied unless England demolished an opponent in a festival of attacking football. He was particularly exasperated by the widespread belief that he should give up experimentation and instead play the best team in every game. Such a policy, he argued, would provide no basis for long-term planning. 'Since I took over,' Alf said in May 1966 before the Yugoslav game,

> I have insisted over and over again that I have never had a team but merely a squad. It is no use to me having a first team and a number of reserves. They have all got to be ready to step into any match or they're worthless to me. I have picked a team against Yugoslavia because I want to see what certain players and certain combinations can achieve.

Alf learnt two invaluable lessons from the win against Yugoslavia. The first was the effectiveness of Martin Peters on the left side of midfield. The young West Ham player, on his debut in that game, had been a surprise selection, having made just one Under-23 appearance two years earlier and never been mentioned in the press as a possible senior international. But once more, Alf had shown what a superb judge he was of a player. With his excellent control and anticipation, his strength in the air and his perfectly timed runs into the penalty area, Peters was to be the ultimate modern footballer, one who could play in almost any position and was to be famously described by Alf as 'ten years ahead of his time'. Peters now says of Alf, 'he was the very best of managers, a players' man through and through. He had an unrivalled knowledge of the game and could communicate that to players. If you gave of your best to him, he would never forget you, but he had no time for slackers.' The second lesson was the maturity of Bobby Charlton, who had finally grown to be comfortable with his attacking midfield role. Alf said that 'this was the day when the penny dropped, when everything clicked into place.' Alf went on to explain, at one point during the match, 'instead of following the ball, Bobby came back and picked up the danger man working on the blind side of our defence. This was the moment when I thought he became a great player.'

For Alf, the exhausting, drawn-out job of construction was almost complete. But the striking formation was not yet settled, with Greaves still fighting to regain his sharpness after his illness. 'My greatest problem is in attack', Alf told the French press in January 1966. Despite the success of 4–3–3, he was still flirting with wingers like John Connelly of Manchester United and Terry Paine of Southampton. Nor was he fixed on his central strikers – Bobby Tambling of Chelsea, for instance, was picked against Yugoslavia, having won his only previous full cap three years previously. But it was against West Germany earlier in the season that Alf had made his most significant decision about the front-line by bringing in the West Ham number 10 Geoff Hurst. As with other members of the England team, Hurst, who had been converted by Ron Greenwood at West Ham from a right-half into a forward, was hardly a natural selection, and even Hurst confessed he was 'flabbergasted' at his inclusion in the England squad. But Alf saw that his ability to act as a powerful target man, holding onto the ball in attack or making space for others, could be crucial in the more fluid, wingless system. Just as importantly, he had the sort of dedication and discipline which Alf admired and which was so conspicuously lacking in Greaves.

Hurst first met Alf in November 1964 when he was chosen for the Under-23s in a match against Wales at Wrexham. 'The first sight of him was a bit of a shock, for he didn't seem like a football man at all. He was so carefully dressed, so quietly spoken that he seemed more like a businessman or bank manager. He had nothing about him of that casual air you usually find with ex-players,' he wrote later. Throughout the train journey from Paddington to Bristol, Ramsey asked Hurst and his colleagues a barrage of questions about their opinions on football:

I found it a bit frightening. A two-hour quiz when you are not sure what sort of impression you should be making can be very hard on the nerves. Alf didn't make it any the easier with his disconcerting habit of tearing through a gentle conversation with a brutally frank opinion of his own. You would be warming up nicely, describing how such a player had 'done quite well, though of course, some of the tackling didn't suit his style' when Alf would interrupt you with something like: 'The man's a bloody coward.' The fact that this was exactly what you meant, didn't make his direct approach any less startling. I was damn glad when the journey ended. And my first impression of Alf wasn't exactly favourable. This bloke was, I'd privately decided, a bit of a cold fish.

Hurst found his introduction to the full England party in 1966 almost as intimidating: 'Bobby Moore and I, although we were at West Ham, were never close socially. He was slightly older than me. I found it quite hard to settle into the England side at first. I didn't know anybody apart from Bobby. He wasn't a great help.' But Hurst was struck by the respect in which Alf was held, for all his remoteness, 'What surprised me slightly was the manner in which the players accepted Alf's authority. The atmosphere was comfortable, but even Bobby seemed on his guard in Alf's presence. This, I came to realize, was how it was in public places.' And Hurst immediately saw the effectiveness of Alf's man-management once the squad were out on the training ground:

Alf decided to work on set-pieces and wanted a couple of players to help him demonstrate the point that he was making about free-kicks. He looked at the crowd of players around him and began calling out names. I instinctively took a step backwards, anxious not to be selected on my first morning. Alf spotted me. He said nothing at the time but later in the training session, when no other players were near, he said to me quite firmly, 'I've got no use for blushing violets. I've picked you for what I know you can do. It's now up to you.' It was only a small incident but it did a lot for my confidence. It made me realize that I had to have a positive attitude both on and off the pitch. It also demonstrated to me that Alf had belief in my ability. That, more than anything else, convinced me that I was good enough to play for England. One of Alf's secrets was to make players believe in themselves.

Hurst was about to witness the fullest expression of Alf's skills as a man-manager, as the squad were brought together for the final preparations in advance of the World Cup. On 7 May 1966, two days after the Yugoslavia game, Alf named his initial party of 28 players, from which the final 22 would be selected. He then said that, following the FA Cup Final and the end of the domestic season, all the players could take three weeks off, before assembling for intensive training on 6 June at Lilleshall, the sports venue in rural Shropshire. 'I will take them out to the country and brainwash them about what we are going to do,' Alf told the press, a hint of menace in his clipped tones. The menace was justified, for the regime that Alf had planned at Lilleshall was to be the toughest that the players had ever experienced. And out of it would emerge the most formidable unit ever to take the field for England.

Appropriately enough, the start of training at Lilleshall on 6 June was the anniversary of D-Day. The rustic tranquillity of the setting hardly matched the professional rigour that Alf imposed on the squad members, whose number had fallen to 27 with the withdrawal of Everton defender Brian Labone through injury. 'If there was a point when Alf could be said to have changed from second gear into top, and faced the last, hardest lap of all, it was when he met his team at Lilleshall,' wrote Harold Shepherdson. Over the next fortnight, their entire lives were regimented, something of a culture shock for footballers who were used to having their afternoons and evenings free. After breakfast, there would be hard physical training and football practice, followed by a self-service lunch, then non-contact sports like cricket, tennis and basketball. In the late afternoon, the players had a bath, then came down for their dinner, after which they would have a lecture or a film. Nine o'clock was bedtime, for which most of the exhausted party were only too grateful. There was no sense of luxury about the stay. The players were divided into groups of four or five to a room, which they were expected to tidy themselves, while they queued up for all their meals from a self-service counter. They were subjected to frequent medical tests and weight checks, as well as being given advice in all aspects of personal healthcare – even in how to cut their toenails. 'We've got athlete's foot down to thirty per cent of what it was when the players came together,' said one of the England team doctors, Alan Bass. 'And we've got them cutting their toenails properly. There were only five out of the twenty-seven who knew how. It's incredible. You wouldn't get that sort of thing with ballet dancers, yet these fellows get far more money than all the top dancers.'

One of Alf's central aims was to bring his players to the peak of physical fitness, and his assistants Les Cocker, Harold Shepherdson and Wilf McGuinness were each taskmasters in the fulfilment of this goal. As McGuinness told me:

The training was strong and physical for the end of the season. The players were all divided into groups and we passed on each group after 15 minutes of hard slog. Every group was trying to outdo the other in the circuits and in the ball work. It was punishing stuff but the players really took to it. By the end the players knew they were really fit. Alf wanted it that way. He wanted everyone to give everything. Les and Harold were ideal for what was needed. Les came from Leeds, bit of a hard man. Harold had been in the job since Winterbottom's time, very experienced, well-respected.

Dr Neil Phillips, who succeeded Alan Bass as England team doctor after 1966 but who also worked at Lilleshall, says:

I don't think Alf ever trusted Les as much as Harold. Harold was the best number two you could have in an organization. He hated making decisions himself but if you told him to stand on his head three times a day he would do it for you. He would always carry out instructions to the letter. Les was much more confrontational, seeking to discuss things and argue his point.

The regime was certainly effective on the physical side. 'It is the hardest training I've ever done in my life,' says Nobby Stiles. 'Like we would have to run, get to Harold and then jump as if we were heading the ball. Twenty times in a row. Fuckin' hell, that was something else. The fitness was incredible.' Others have the same memories. 'We worked incredibly hard at Lilleshall,' says Terry Paine, the former Southampton winger, now a TV analyst in South Africa. 'When you looked at the England squad, we probably had four or five world-class players, and the rest of the team solved the puzzle. Alf knew how much fitness would tell when it came to the World Cup.' George Cohen remembers Les Cocker continually driving him through the pain barrier:

It was bloody hard work. I was coming back from injury, having had a bad gash at the end of the season and been in hospital for ten days. I loved training but Les really put me through the ringer to make sure I was fit. He was a tough little guy. He would have me bent double, and I would come in from training seeing black and white. Alf had no sympathy. He came by one morning just after Les let me take a breather. He looked across and said, 'George, I don't want you slacking.'

Bobby Charlton was impressed with the way Alf varied the intense routine to prevent monotony:

In the matches, no one played on the same side or in the same position twice; one day for the Reds, the next day for the Whites, one day at inside-forward, the next on the wing. It helped each of one of us to familiarize ourselves with the capabilities of others. To begin with, we were afraid of ruining someone else's chances with an untimely tackle or over-enthusiastic charging. Alf would have none of it. He gave us a dressing down and told us to get on with it. After that we all wore shin guards and played for our lives.

This approach helped to create an ultra-competitive edge, as Alan Ball remembers: 'Whatever task was set, I gave it all my heart. So if it was a team-building exercise, I was always the first to go forward, knowing that Alf was watching every move we made. I was driven by a fear of failure, and I think Alf understood that.' The intensity of competition could lead to friction, but this too only helped to reinforce the team spirit. Like soldiers in the heat of battle, the players were drawn together by the fierce pressure they were under. Geoff Hurst recalls a fiery argument in one training session between two of the biggest characters in the party, Nobby Stiles and Jack Charlton, which for all its abuse helped to inspire a growing feeling of unity.

At half-time these two really sailed into each other. They didn't mince words. It really was pretty brutal stuff. For myself, I was delighted. I realized then that if we had players who felt they knew each other well enough to tear strips off each others' carcasses, then we certainly knew each other well enough to sort out the problems and act together. Alf's reaction during the row was interesting. He could have stopped it with a word as soon as Stiles turned on Jack. He didn't. He could have parted the two when they began again later. He didn't. He let them have a real go at each other, and waited until the insults were starting to come around for the third time before saying, 'Right, I think that's enough. Now let's get this sorted out.' It was, I now realize, a great piece of man-management. If he had cut them off short, the feelings would have bubbled along beneath the surface, resentment would have taken the place of reasoning.

Wilf McGuinness saw the same outcome:

There was many a time I thought to myself, 'This is not going to work.' There would be loud discussions, especially when Jack Charlton was around. Big Jack would disagree with most things, just for the sake of it. He was a bit contrary. And he and Nobby were such competitors on the training ground. It was like a pair of peacocks showing what they were made of. At first I was worried about the effect of their argument but in fact the team fed off their make-up. It helped to build the right spirit.

Yet the unity fostered by Lilleshall was built on far firmer foundations than rows between Nobby and Jack. By requiring all the players to join in every activity, whether it was watching westerns or playing golf, Alf inspired a sense of togetherness that would have been the envy of most League sides. They played practical jokes on each other and adopted silly nicknames. There was endless laughter, as when Alf tried to referee the basketball matches without having a clue about the rules and Nobby Stiles would be barging and tripping up his opponents. Or when George Eastham took the umpire's chair in a tennis match and mimicked a prim Wimbledon official: 'Miss Wilson to sairve . . .' Or when Ron Flowers volunteered to be the local hairdresser. 'I had the worst haircut in my life. Ron had only one style,' says George Cohen. Or the night when the team settled down to watch a new murder mystery and as soon as it started, Ray Wilson called out from the back of the room, 'Oh, I've seen this. Dalby did it.' As they joked and argued, the players developed that rarest of concepts: the club spirit in a national side. This was perhaps Alf's greatest achievement, beyond even his strategic vision and his uncanny judgement of a player. He made England a cohesive unit, rather than a collection of talented individuals. Wilf McGuinness says:

Alf was much warmer than his public image. I found him very thoughtful about the players and the people who worked for him. He felt responsible for us. But he was also a man of natural authority. He might ask my point of view – and would then do it his way. We would have a meeting every evening, going through all aspects of the day's work, then we would gather again the following morning and Alf would say, 'Right, we talked about it last night. This is how it's going to be.' And it all went like clockwork. I think the players felt good about it all.

Dr Neil Phillips, the England Under-23s doctor who would become full England team doctor after 1966, was also involved in Lilleshall. The government had refused to give Alan Bass leave of absence from his post in the NHS for the full period at Lilleshall, so Phillips had to take his place. It was an experience that left him full of praise for Alf:

He was an incredible man. His talks were absolutely unbelievable. He was brilliant at communicating what he needed. As you can imagine, in my profession I have worked with leading consultants and surgeons but I have never, ever

277

worked with someone like Alf Ramsey. He could go through in exact detail any incident that had occurred in a match or training session. Alf was always very keen that the team doctors should be integrated with the players. Whatever they did, we did. When they were training, we joined in. I was lucky because I started with the England team when I was thirty-one. So I was young enough to do some of the five-a-sides and be kicked to death because the players thought it was a big joke to have a go at the doctor. Lilleshall was fantastic because Alf was so well-organized. He just had the four members of staff with him, Les, Harold, myself and Wilf; he knew exactly what he wanted.

It is a point reinforced by Ken Jones:

The great thing about Alf was that he did not feel any need to surround himself with people. Throughout his entire England career, he just had two trainers, Les and Harold. He did not have all the modern huge staff, with coaches, scouts, psychiatrists and all that. Alf did not want any input. He just wanted to control it all himself.

Lilleshall should not be painted as some footballing idyll. For all of Alf's efforts to keep them preoccupied, many of the players became inevitably frustrated with the strict discipline. Jack Charlton nicknamed the place 'the gulag' and later said: 'At times I felt it seemed just like an exercise in pushing the human mind and frame to the utmost level of endurance – and then some. This was a test of stamina, skill and mental ability to cope with.' So desperate were some of them to get out that they cast envious glances at the Catholics like Nobby Stiles who were allowed out for Mass on Sunday. Their yearning for freedom stronger than Anglicanism, they asked Alf if they too could go to church on Sunday. 'No need for that,' said Alf. 'The warden of Lilleshall happens to be a lay preacher. If you want, I shall arrange for him to conduct a service.' With those words, the enthusiasm for religious worship suddenly disappeared. Another possible escape from the prison was across a nearby golf course to the club-house bar. Alf had allowed a visit there by the entire party, but it was normally out of bounds. Surprisingly, Nobby Stiles and Alan Ball, two of Alf's most dedicated young players, joined the Lancastrian John Connelly on a furtive trip for a pint one evening, a decision that Stiles now looks back on with horror: 'Like schoolboys playing hookey, we sneaked off to the bar but, of course, we had no sooner got there than we started feeling guilty. We swallowed our pints, turned on our heels and headed back to the training complex and the authority of Ramsey.'

Unfortunately for the trio, Wilf McGuiness was waiting at the door for them.

'Where the hell have you been?'

Ball and Stiles owned up to having a pint. 'We just drank it down and came straight back.'

'You ought to know you're in deep shit. Alf knows all about this. He wants you to go to his room.'

Panic-stricken, Ball and Stiles made their way there, followed by a surprisingly relaxed John Connelly. Alf came out of his office with a solemn expression. Ball and Stiles looked at their feet in shame. 'I didn't say you couldn't go to the bar. I didn't say you shouldn't go. I just expected you wouldn't go. We are here on serious business and I thought you all understood that. We are going to win the World Cup.' Ball and Stiles were uttering profuse apologies, begging forgiveness for their abject error and promising that nothing of the sort would ever happen again, when John Connelly butted in:

'What the fuck are you two talking about? We only had a pint, which isn't going to do us any harm after all the training we've been doing.'

'Get out of here, all of you. Get out,' Alf exploded.

Ball and Stiles spent a sleepless night, wondering if they were about to be sent home, their international careers ending in disgrace. But Alf was a far shrewder pragmatist than his tough image sometimes suggested. An excellent reader of foot-ballers' characters, he could see the regret that overwhelmed Ball and Stiles. The very fact that they were so embarrassed was an indicator of their respect for him. There was nothing to be gained by upsetting his carefully laid plans for the World Cup just to prove a disciplinary point. Alf contented himself the next morning with this warning to the assembled players. 'We are here for a purpose. I just want to say that if anyone gets the idea of popping out for a pint, then they will be finished with the squad for ever.' No one tried to put that statement to the test.

On the last day at Lilleshall, Alf had to whittle down the squad from the original 27. The final 22 would then undertake a brief tour of Eastern Europe – in which Alf promised that all of them would get a game – before the commencement of the World Cup itself on 11 July. The knowledge that five of them were facing the axe created a degree of nervousness in the camp, as Les or Harold went round summoning the unlucky ones to Alf's room:

It must be a terrible thing for a manager to have to do,' says Terry Paine. 'Look at what happened with Glenn Hoddle and Paul Gascoigne before the 1998 World Cup.* Nothing

---

* Gascoigne launched into a tearful drunken diatribe against Hoddle on hearing that he had been left out of the squad, and even threatened the England manager with a table lamp.

like that went on with Alf, of course. We all respected him too much. The funny thing was that when you went up to your dormitory, you sort of wanted to hide in the cupboard. You just didn't want to hear that knock. And there was a huge sense of relief when you realized you had not been called.

The unfortunate quintet were Keith Newton, Peter Thompson, Johnny 'Budgie' Byrne, Bobby Tambling and Gordon Milne. Today, Milne still has a clear memory of how Alf broke the news:

Alf had this way with him – a bit like a headmaster, a bit cold. What he had to say was over in a couple of minutes. Maybe my disappointment made it seem colder than it really was. But certainly it was pretty clinical. It all stemmed from his simplicity. Later, when I became a manager myself, I saw that there was no room for sympathy. You had to take your decisions and give the player a few words of explanation. Some managers waffle on too much and miss the whole point of what they are trying to get across.

Peter Thompson recalls his personal sadness alleviated by a typical moment of Budgie Byrne humour:

I thought it was an honour to be in the 28. Alf was firm, knew the game inside out and was a great tactician. Like all top managers, he had a ruthless streak, which meant that we were all a little bit frightened of him. He did not rant and rave but you always listened to what he said because you knew that's what he meant. You could argue with Shanks, he was effing, all the players were effing. Alf just told you and you accepted it. He had that bit of steel about him. It was one of my biggest disappointments to be left out of the 22. The five of us trooped into his office and he just said. 'Thank you so much for turning up and for working so hard. But I have made my decision.' The thing was that at Lilleshall all of us had been given our England kit and sports jacket, plus a white Burberry mac. So we were standing there and Alf was about to finish. 'I know you're all disappointed but that is my verdict. Any questions anybody?' Budgie Byrne immediately piped up:

'Can we keep the coats, Alf?'

Before he finished at Lilleshall, Alf had one, more pleasant, task to perform. He summoned Dr Neil Phillips and Wilf McGuinness, both of whom thought they had finished their duties with the England camp and would not be involved in the actual tournament. But Alf had other ideas.

'I want to thank you both for what you have done for the England team to get us to the stage where we are now. When we get to the World Cup Final, I shall send for you two because I want you there when we win it.'

'But Alf,' replied Dr Phillips, 'you can't be sure we're going to win.'

'I am sure we're going to win. And I shall send for you both in the last stages of the competition.'

# NINE

## *Hendon Hall*

The name Bobby Moore has become synonymous with the summer of 1966. So it is amazing to think that in the weeks leading up to the World Cup finals, Alf had quietly given the impression that he was planning to drop Moore, not just from the England captaincy, but even from the national team. Alf's trust in Moore had been badly undermined by the events of 1964, when Moore proved rebellious over discipline and training. The incidents at the Beachcomber Bar in Mayfair and the Walfdorf Astoria in New York had been compounded by a row during the Little World Cup in Brazil, when Moore attacked Alf for imposing too big a burden on the players with his harsh training schedules. As leader of a recalcitrant clique, Moore approached Dr Alan Bass to complain that the team was being over-worked after a long season. To Alf, this smacked of little short of an open challenge to his authority, especially as Moore had not shown the courtesy to speak to him directly.

But Alf, still feeling his way in his job, was not yet powerful enough to abandon one of his most talented, publicly admired players. He therefore tried to reach an accommodation with him. That autumn, after a game against Northern Ireland, he took Moore aside to discuss the role of the England captain in the build-up to the World Cup. 'Alf asked me to join him for a few minutes. We talked about being ready to commit ourselves to the objective of winning the World Cup in 1966. We sorted out our priorities on and off the pitch and agreed we would back each other up. Alf made it clear he expected the captain as well as the manager to conduct himself in a responsible manner and that was that. No problem as far as I was concerned.'

Well, not for a while anyway. But by the beginning of 1966, Moore was slipping back into his old ways of cockiness and complacency, especially when in the company of his East London drinking partner Jimmy Greaves, who said of Moore, 'there are not many footballers who could match him in a drinking contest; he's got hollow legs'. Alf grew irritated when the two of them would sit at the back of the England bus and start to sing, 'What's it all about, Alfie?', the hit Burt Bacharach song of the time from the Michael Caine movie of the same name. He was also disturbed by the high priority Moore attached to his own monetary value. Every year, Moore was the last member of the West Ham squad to sign his annual contract, a form of financial pressure that ensured he received the largest possible salary increase. Alf, brought up in the age of the maximum wage and post-war rationing, had no empathy with this kind of free-market bargaining. In the period before the World Cup, this situation was proving serious for England, since Moore was being more difficult than ever about his contract, hinting that he might move to another club.

Frustrated by Moore, Alf decided that he had to be taught a lesson. In May he was left out of the England team for the match against Yugoslavia, with his place taken by Norman Hunter and Jimmy Armfield, playing only his second game in three years, assuming the captaincy. It was widely assumed that Moore was merely being rested, but when England began their tour of Eastern Europe in June with a match against Finland in Helsinki, Moore was again on the sidelines and Armfield was captain. Sadly for Armfield, he broke a toe towards the end of the game, was sidelined for the rest of the tour and never played for England again, though he remained part of the 1966 World Cup squad. Alf never talked to Armfield or Moore about his plans for the tournament, but he did nothing to dampen speculation in the press about Moore's future. Brian James of the *Mail* recalls: 'Bobby had not been playing that well and when they went on the tour of Europe, there was a shadow over him. I don't think there is any doubt that Alf by then had had enough of Bobby's nonsense and smirking and was considering dropping him before the World Cup.' Alf certainly fed this line to some journalists, and Bernard Joy, the former Arsenal centre-half, ran a story in the *Evening Standard* saying that Bobby's position was under threat. But many writers think Alf was only giving Bobby a warning, and never seriously contemplated going into the World Cup without him. Hugh McIlvanney told me:

Alf's relationship with Bobby was quite strange. Bobby was a bit of a mickey-taker and this annoyed Alf. There were widespread suggestions before the World Cup that Alf was thinking of not playing Bobby. Bernard Joy, who was big on ingratiating himself with people who he thought would do him good, was claiming that Norman Hunter would play instead. And I believe that Alf was quite happy for this idea to be spread because of the way that Bobby was irritating him. In Alf's eye, Bobby was inclined to take his status for granted, treated the whole business of the World Cup too lightly and joined in the piss-taking with Jimmy Greaves. But I told Bernard that there was no chance that Bobby would not play. It was part of Alf that he would spread disinformation. There was no chance Alf was going to drop Bobby. It was so obvious. He liked to give the impression he was considering dropping him but there was no way he would do it. Bobby was a strange case. He was smashing in many ways, but you could not really have a proper conversation with him – he just asked questions all the time. You could not get to know him. He would keep you off balance. I introduced him to Joao Saldanha, the Brazil manager, and they sat together on the plane. I saw Joao later, and asked him, 'How did that go?'

'I don't know much about Bobby Moore but he knows a lot about me.'

Alf's tactic worked brilliantly. Bobby Moore was shaken by his exclusion for two successive matches. As he later confessed:

It made me sit up. From that day, I never expected to be in an England squad until the letter from the FA dropped through the letter box, never took it for granted that I would be in the team until I saw my name on the sheet or heard Alf call it out. Alf was driving home to me that there are always enough players for any team to get by without any one player. I was so disappointed. So sick. I'd gone through all those games. The preparation had become really intense during the training camp in Lilleshall.

Bobby was all the more worried because England easily beat Finland 3–0, with the defence looking solid. So he was relieved to be brought back for the next game against Norway in Oslo. 'No one was more on his toes,' Moore said. Except, perhaps, Jimmy Greaves, who had also been left out against Finland. For the first time in a year, Greaves looked back to his sparkling best, hitting four goals in a 6–1 win. 'Out of chaos came football of a quality that has eluded England for so long,' trumpeted the *Guardian*.

Greaves' position as the leading striker seemed all the more secure when, in a 2–0 win against Denmark in Copenhagen, Hurst gave a woeful performance, showing poor control on a dry, bumpy pitch and failing to combine well with Greaves. For Ken Jones, the aftermath of Hurst's sorry outing again highlighted the originality of Alf's thinking:

The ball was bouncing all over the place and Geoff could hardly get hold of it. The next day I was walking with Harold Shepherdson across the concourse to catch the plane.

'What did you think of him last night?' said Harold.

'Who?'

'Geoff Hurst. He'll never make an international player, never make it.'

For me, that just shows what a special manager Alf was. He did not write off Geoff. He took the conditions into account and the way Geoff had to expend such an enormous amount of energy just getting hold of the ball.

Hurst, however, was left out for the final match of the tour in favour of Roger Hunt, when England took on Poland in Katowice, a grim industrial town typical of the bleak communist Eastern bloc in the sixties. The team's journey there tested their resolve almost as much as Lilleshall had done; it involved a flight to Warsaw, followed by another flight to Cracow, and then a seven-hour road trip by a battered old coach through a series of bleak villages in a grey wasteland. At one point on this meandering, laborious voyage, the Polish interpreter made the mistake of trying to engage Alf in conversation.

'And what do you and the team plan to do later in the evening, Mr Ramsey?'

'Get to Katowice – I hope,' he replied.

When the bus finally arrived at its destination, and the stiff players clambered out, Jimmy Greaves took one look at the depressing skyline of tower blocks and chemical plants, over which hung an acrid yellow smog, and said, 'OK, Alf, you've made your point. Now let's piss off home.'

But there was little room for joking about this game. The players were convinced that the team chosen was Alf's first eleven, the one that would take the field at the start of the finals themselves. That was good news for Roger Hunt, who had initially seemed to be out of favour, lagging behind Hurst and Greaves, but was picked against Poland in place of Hurst. When Alf had announced his squad of 22 to the press on 17 June, Jimmy Greaves had been at Number 8, Bobby Charlton at 9, Geoff Hurst at 10 and John Connelly at 11, while Roger Hunt had been given the Number 21 shirt, implying that he was only seen as a reserve. 'I am not making the slightest criticism of Alf, who always treated me fairly and did what he thought was right for the team. But I had done pretty well as Jimmy Greaves' deputy and especially after the Scotland game, I fancied I might be in the first team,' says Hunt. When he saw the shirt numbers, he felt a wave of disappointment but received no explanation from Alf. 'That wasn't Alf's way. He probably thought I'd be delighted just to be there.'

The misleading impression that Alf gave with the squad numbers was just another example of Alf's campaign of disinformation, designed to leave everyone – press, opposition and his own team alike – guessing about his intentions. And he pulled off another surprise at Katowice when he named Martin Peters, rather than John Connelly, at number 11. Alf had decided to use 4–3–3 for the first time since Madrid the previous December, and the long-striding, versatile Peters, who could play equally well in attack and defence, was perfect for the role on the left-side of midfield. But Alf was not about to give away anything to the media about his tactics. When he announced the team at a press conference, he made a theatrical pause before stating the name of Peters at number 11. There was an audible gasp of surprise among the journalists, given that Peters had won just two caps previously. Then Frank Magee of the *Daily Mirror* asked:

'Can you tell us the thinking behind the selection of Peters?'

'No Frank,' replied Alf with a wry smile, before walking out of the conference. A lot of the reporters did not see the amusing side of Alf's brusqueness, and complained about his being deliberately awkward. But Ken Jones felt it was 'the way the England manager should behave. He shouldn't be expected to give indications of what he intends doing before the game.'

Both Peters and Hunt played well in a strong England performance, which saw them win 1–0. It was Hunt who scored the only goal with a 25-yard shot hit sweetly on the half-volley, prompting a moment of rhapsody from Desmond Hackett – 'this thing of splendour', he wrote in the *Express*. Hunt's brilliant strike, his twelfth goal in just thirteen appearances, appeared to confirm him as the partner for Greaves. England's victory gave them a 100 per cent record on the tour and their seventh consecutive win, their best run since 1950. Against Poland, Bobby Moore gave a masterly performance, banishing any doubts that he might not play in the World Cup. The defence had conceded just one goal in four games, emphasizing how settled it had become. Ray Wilson, one of its stalwarts, says:

I would go into games for England and for half an hour I would not even have a touch of the ball. That's how good the system was. What we did was that we each had an area that we played in, and when an opposition player moved into someone's zone, we made sure he was picked up. We would talk to each other a lot, 'Have you got him? He's coming across.' It was a zone of about twenty square yards; that was your area and whoever came into it, you picked him up. You never let anyone get behind you. As long as you could keep your back four across the field, you would be all right. We would not break until about thirty yards from goal. We didn't really mind if someone tried to shoot from that distance. You couldn't imagine anyone beating Gordon Banks from there.

For Wilson, the trip to Eastern Europe had been crucial: 'The tour made me realize we could do it. We'd moved into a different league.' His fellow defender Jack Charlton felt the same: 'Among the England team, there was a tremendous spirit of confidence as the aircraft skimmed through the skies towards home, and the real thing at Wembley.' Ron Flowers, the Wolves midfielder, agreed. Turning to Jimmy Armfield after the Poland game, he said, 'Jim, I can't see anyone beating this team.'

On their return to England on 7 July, the players were given a two days off by Alf to see their families, and then instructed to reassemble at Hendon Hall, the hotel in north-west London which was to be the team's base throughout the tournament, chosen for its proximity to Wembley and its oak-beamed tranquillity. The one disadvantage was that it was a long coach ride across London to the training venue at the Bank of England's sports ground in Roehampton. Fed up with the traffic, the players formed a delegation to ask Alf if he could switch to a training camp nearer Hendon Hall. He politely but firmly refused. There was more to this than mere stubbornness. Alf reckoned that keeping the players together, even in the jams on the North Circular, would deepen their sense of mutual belonging. At other times, Alf simply laid down his authority. It was almost four years since his appointment, and, after a number of difficult incidents, he had shown clearly that he was in charge. 'Alf Ramsey was the common denominator,' says Geoff Hurst, 'the cement that bound us all together. He was all powerful and one of the things that made his job possible was the willingness with which we all accepted his authority.' A good example of this occurred over the England squad's formal attire. The players had been issued with heavy grey flannel suits, totally unsuitable for the summer months. So Bobby Charlton, who was the senior member of the squad, was persuaded to approach Alf to ask if the squad might be allowed to travel to and from training in lighter, more casual gear. 'I'm always open to suggestions,' said Alf. He then paused for a while before telling Bobby, 'We'll stick with the suits.' On another occasion, at a banquet following a home international, Alf approached Bobby Moore: 'Robert, I think we ought to go.' Bobby pleaded with Alf to allow the players one more round. With a nod, Alf agreed. The beers were ordered and the players sat chatting away until they had finished their drinks. Moore then went over to Alf again to tell him the squad was now ready to depart. Without a word to Moore, Alf summoned the waiter and ordered himself and Harold Shepherdson a pair of large brandies, forcing the players to hang around longer. 'Alf knew exactly how to put us in our place. The next time he said it was time to go, we would not be asking for another drink,' says Alan Ball.

It is easy to imagine that in the days before the opening ceremony, the England of 1966 was gripped – as it would be today – by a mood of World Cup fever, with a carnival atmosphere spreading across the country. We now look back on the event through the prism of history, imbuing the World

Cup with the spirit of the sixties' liberation. It is now part of an uplifting narrative that takes in the Beatles and Carnaby Street, a moment when the nation threw a giant party to celebrate the abandonment of the starchy class-ridden, oppressive values of the fifties. Mini-skirts were in. Deference was out. Like that other cockney lad Michael Caine, Bobby Moore, East End working-class and proud of it, is now regarded as one of the symbols of this exciting social change. 'England in the summer of 1966 was a good place to be,' says the actor Terence Stamp.

But it did not necessarily feel like that at the time. Britain was still a fundamentally conservative country in the middle of the decade. The sense of social revolution has been exaggerated. With all his insecurities and anxieties about correct behaviour, Alf Ramsey was far more representative of the British public than, say, John Lennon. Indeed, as the historian Douglas Sambrook has pointed out, the influence of the Beatles has been hugely overblown. *The Sound of Music* sold twice as many copies as the Beatles' most popular album, Abbey Road, while Cliff Richard had 38 top-twenty hits compared with just 22 for the Fab Four. Britain in 1966 was a place where homosexuality and abortion were still illegal, drug-taking was almost unknown and the vast majority of teenagers were virgins. It was an overwhelmingly white country, where 20 million viewers tuned in every week to watch *The Black and White Minstrel Show* and few troubling questions were asked about national identity or monarchy. Capital punishment had been officially abolished only a year earlier, a decision deplored by the great majority of the public. It was a land of Morris Minors and Angus Steak Houses, of Vickers Viscounts and Blackpool boarding houses, of Sunday closing and corner shops.

In the Britain of the mid-sixties, public emotion was still

frowned upon, something that Alf understood well. The sombre dignity of the crowds at the state funeral for Winston Churchill in 1965 was in stark contrast with the mass hysteria that surrounded the death of Princess Diana almost 33 years later. And football largely reflected that restraint. It is amazing to look at the footage of 1966 and see how many of the male spectators are dressed in collar and tie. With little violence on the terraces, there was no need for segregation. Nor was football the business juggernaught it later became. The FA's organization for 1966 bore the whiff of amateurism, a reluctance to exploit commercial opportunities. The organizing committee failed to find any sponsor for their ticket and sales brochures, one million of which were distributed in 1965. The official mascot, a cartoon lion wearing a Union Jack, known as World Cup Willie, was a puerile, half-hearted design that failed to inspire the public, as did the feeble song 'World Cup Willie', performed by the fifties skiffle artist Lonnie Donegan, which sold well in Japan but nowhere else. There were also an array of souvenirs, like World Cup Willie stockings for women and a five-foot-high glass Wellington boot, though, in the words of one retailer, David Walker, 'It was crap merchandise.' Poor security led to the World Cup trophy itself being stolen on the eve of the tournament when it was on display at a stamp exhibition. Understandably, there was severe embarrassment within the FA, which changed to relief when the trophy was found by Pickles the dog in a bush in south London. The absence of any marketing consciousness was reflected in the absurdly low prices of seats. It was possible to buy a block of tickets for the best seats at all ten London games (nine at Wembley, one at White City), including both the semi-final and the final, for just £25*, which even then was not much

---

* Only about £250 in today's money.

more than the average weekly wage of £20, while a season ticket to stand on the terraces cost just £3.87. But football was living in the past, refusing to exploit its potential earnings from gate receipts and television rights; it was still possible in 1966 to watch a game for only five shillings. In consequence, the players' pay was far lower in real terms than the earnings of today, despite the abolition of the maximum wage. During the World Cup finals, the match fee per game was just £60.

Nor was football the dominant cultural force it was to become by the end of the century. It was not *de rigeur* for politicians to take an interest in soccer. The TV schedules were not filled with evening games – indeed, FA Cup games were often the only televised games in a season. To parts of the establishment in the media and civic life, football was just a working-class pursuit of little wider consequence. It was not woven into the fabric of society as in Italy, Spain or Brazil. Brian James of the *Daily Mail* gives this insight:

> Until 1970, sport was confined to the back pages. It was not taken seriously at all. Football writers were just called 'Sport' at the *Daily Mail*, in tones dripping with contempt. It was an attitude of condescension. And it was not until after 1966 that big business had any idea about football. Then marketing men woke up to the importance of football. After '66 I was constantly being asked for advice from companies about sponsoring players. It was often absurd. You'd go to a meeting in the boardroom and a director would say, 'Now we ought to get one of these players on board. The man I know is Matthews, Stanley Matthews.' The whole thing was bizarre.

The lack of media interest in soccer was graphically illustrated by the *Daily Mirror*, by far Britain's biggest-selling paper, on the day of the World Cup Final. 'This is the crunch. This is judgement day,' screamed an editorial on the front page. But the paper was not talking about a football match; it was referring to the government's economic policy. The lead story, filling most of the page, was about the Economics Minister George Brown's attempts to uphold a pay, prices and dividends freeze. The World Cup did not feature until page 13.

Initially, some of this indifference extended to the footballing public itself, with many of the matches outside London played in front of disappointing crowds – just 24,000 turned up to see Hungary against Bulgaria at Goodison Park in Liverpool. Even England's first match of the 1966 campaign, against Uruguay on 11 July, was nowhere near a sell-out. With 87,000 spectators in the stadium, Wembley was 10,000 short of capacity.

England's preparations before the match were interrupted by two administrative problems. The first was that Bobby Moore had still refused to sign a new contract with West Ham, and was therefore technically ineligible under FIFA regulations to play in the finals. In the midst of all his other work, Alf was not pleased by this distraction, especially because he had to conduct frantic negotiations with Moore and FA to find a solution. The difficulty was overcome by Moore agreeing to a temporary one-month contract to cover the tournament. Ron Greenwood was summoned urgently to Hendon Hall, where he was greeted by an impatient Ramsey. Pointing to a dark, panelled room off the foyer, Ramsey said, 'You can have him in there for just one minute.' Moore signed the relevant form in seconds, saying barely a word to Greenwood, who then hurried back to Upton Park.

The second, more heart-stopping, problem arose barely an hour before the kick-off. The Hungarian referee, Istvan Zsolt, came into the England dressing-room and asked to check the

FIFA identity cards of each of the team. These little red cards, similar to passports with the name and photograph of the holder, were intended to stop teams surreptitiously fielding ineligible or suspended players. To Harold Shepherdson's horror, he realized he had forgotten to confirm with the players that they were carrying their cards. And sure enough, seven of the eleven had left them behind at the Hendon Hall hotel. 'I am sorry, Mr Ramsey,' said Zsolt, 'but these seven cannot take part in tonight's match.' Alf remained astonishingly calm amidst the mounting drama, and, with the co-operation of the police, instructed one of their motorcyclists to go to the hotel to pick up the missing cards. Typically, Jack Charlton relieved some of the tension: 'Man, they don't need identity cards at Leeds. Everyone knows me up there.' The police rider returned with just forty minutes to go, having travelled most of the route on the wrong side of the road to avoid the heavy traffic around Wembley. Harold Shepherdson's admiration for Alf was only increased by the way he handled the incident: he wrote in 1968, 'Although this was my fault, for after all I am the team's baggage master, there was no time for recrimination, and to this day Alf has never given me the right rollicking he should have done for forgetting such an important item'.

It was an inauspicious start to the evening, and the match was hardly more inspiring, once the opening ceremony was out of the way and Alf, looking his usual dapper self in a charcoal grey suit, had presented his team to Queen Elizabeth. Alf had warned his players that the Uruguayans, winners of the World Cup in 1930 and 1950, would be difficult to beat. 'They are very good at getting men behind the ball but more important is what they do when they get there. They engage you. They don't just let you have the ball, they come for you and force you into mistakes,' he said in his pre-match talk. His judgement was correct. The Uruguayans, having set out to achieve a draw, packed the defence. It was a frustrating experience for England, who never really looked like scoring. Alf had played a version of 4–3–3, with Stiles, Bobby Charlton and Alan Ball in midfield, and Hunt, Greaves and Connelly in the front-line. Martin Peters' replacement by Connelly was the only change from the Poland game on the European tour, Alf believing that a conventional winger might be more successful in cracking a side bent purely on stalemate. Connelly said:

I was surprised, and glad, to be back in the team because I knew Alf had an admiration for Peters, who was a very good player. But Uruguay was a bad one to come back for. They were determined they weren't going to lose. I hit the bar and scraped the post. The crowd had applause for Bobby Moore, playing at the back with Jack, and I remember thinking, 'He should try it up here.' Up front, we were three against eight some of the time. I couldn't believe it.

The match ended 0–0, the first time England had been goalless at Wembley since 1938. 'We ran relentlessly, but only into an ever deepening road-block,' says George Cohen. The players trooped off the field in disappointment, the boos of the crowd ringing in their ears. Yet again, Alf showed his gift for man-management once they were back in the dressing-room. Instead of the rollicking they were expecting, he gave them whole-hearted encouragement:

You may not have won, but you didn't lose, and you didn't give away a goal either. Wonderful, we didn't give them a kick. How many shots did you have to save, Gordon? Two? That's the stuff. Whatever anyone says, remember you can still qualify, provided you keep a clean sheet and don't lose a game.

Ray Wilson remembers: 'These were the words we wanted to hear, the sentiments that really counted. The fans and critics could talk all day. Our faith was with the manager.'

In public, Alf said he was 'disappointed with the result, but not the performance'. It was not a verdict shared by much of the press. Ken Jones recalls that the outcome sparked bitter abuse against Alf, long seen as too arrogant in his behaviour and too rigid in outlook. 'Answering my press-box telephone, I heard a *Mirror* executive say, "You can hear what the people think about this man's team and his bloody playing tactics, so take him apart."' The foreign press were just as dismissive. *La Stampa* of Italy believed that 'this was a bad England team. They did not look like scoring tonight.' The Dusseldorf paper *Sport Informations Dienst* predicted, 'England will not win the World Cup.'

Alf recognized that relaxation would be better for his team than yet more training, so the day after the Uruguay match he took them for a visit to Pinewood Studios. At a buffet lunch where the wine and beer flowed generously, the players mingled with stars such as Sean Connery, Yul Brynner, Britt Ekland and Norman Wisdom. Bobby Charlton chatted to the rotund Robert Morley, who was 'amazed that our wives are not allowed to stay with us'. Afterwards they gathered to watch the filming of a scene from the new James Bond movie *You Only Live Twice*. A well-lubricated Ray Wilson took a seat off camera just a few yards from Sean Connery. Silence fell on the set as the cameras began to roll. Then, half way through the scene there was a loud clatter. 'Cut,' shouted the director. All eyes turned on the sprawling figure of Wilson, who had toppled backwards and smashed his chair against the floor. Wilson and the rest of the England party looked at each other sheepishly as the shot had to be re-taken. When it was time to leave, Alf strode onto the set, and gave a few words of thanks to the studios and Sean Connery for their hospitality. Unfortunately, this was one of those classic moments when Alf's mixture of unworldliness and artificial elocution let him down. Instead of pronouncing Connery's name correctly, he said, 'Thank you, *Seen*.' Inevitably, Bobby Moore and Jimmy Greaves could not resist having a laugh. 'Now I've *shorn* everything,' said Moore.

It was soon back to the serious business, as England prepared for their next qualifying match, against Mexico on the 16 July. Alf stuck with 4–3–3, but he made two changes to the team, with Peters coming in for Ball and Terry Paine replacing Connelly, who had lacked penetration if not effort against Uruguay. Because of his fiercely competitive fiery nature, Ball could not easily handle rejection. When Alf had broken the news of his exclusion, he returned to his room uttering all sorts of curses against Alf. After collecting some winnings from a bookmaker, recalls his room-mate Nobby Stiles, Ball came in, 'throwing fivers on the floor and dancing on them, saying "Fuck Alf Ramsey".' Ball even spoke for a while about walking out of the England squad. Jimmy Greaves helped to talk him out of such a drastic move. 'Ballie was sick with Alf but over a lager we helped him see the sense of staying on.'

For the first half hour against Mexico, it looked like England were heading for the same dismal result as against Uruguay. The Mexicans had shown their intentions right from the start, hoofing the ball straight from the kick-off deep into England's territory, then retreating into defence. But in the 38th minute, the deadlock was broken by a moment of magic from Bobby Charlton, the player that Alf had regarded as his potential match-winner from the moment he had been appointed England manager. Charlton picked up the ball in midfield, kept advancing, switching the ball from foot to foot as he surged past the Mexicans, and then suddenly unleashed a thunderbolt of a shot from 25 yards, which screamed into the net past a bewildered keeper. Charlton hit the ball so hard that it was still rising like a rocket even as it crossed the line. 'The nearer it got to goal the more it seemed to speed up,' says Ray Wilson. 'If the keeper had tried to save it he would have been carried straight through the net and into the back of the stand.' It was a moment of genius that pulled England out their torpor and set the crowd alight. The ever reliable Roger Hunt, whose run had opened up space for Charlton by dragging a defender with him, added a second goal fifteen minutes from the end. The England campaign was finally under way.

But for one member of the England team against Mexico, the World Cup was over. Terry Paine had enjoyed even less luck than John Connelly:

I got hit in the back of the head when I went up for a ball. I was badly concussed but there were no substitutes in those days so I played on. I must be the only guy who played in a World Cup but cannot remember much about it. I did not actually wake up until I was sitting on the table in the dressing-room itself; then things came back into shape. But I was groggy for a few days after that and Alf was one of those managers who ruled you out if there was a suspicion of an injury. I suppose if I hadn't had that injury, things might have been different. That is something I would never know and Alf would never tell.

So Alf ended up trying a third winger, Ian Callaghan of Liverpool, in England's final qualifying match. A draw against France would almost certainly be enough to carry England through to the quarter-final, and Jack Charlton claims that 'we were never really worried about this game'. Nevertheless, England played poorly, their football lacking any rhythm.

Callaghan was no more effective on the wing than Paine or Connelly had been, while Greaves, for the third game in a row, looked out of touch. In fact, just twice in his last ten games for England had he been on the score-sheet. His poor form was made all the worse by a nasty shin injury he received from the boot of Joseph Bonnel. Though Greaves, like Paine, had to carry on playing because of the absence of substitutes, he later received four stitches in the wound. It was only through two well-taken goals from Hunt that England secured their victory. In public Alf praised his team's march to the quarter-finals. In the privacy of the dressing-room, he was more critical, singling out Ray Wilson. 'There were one or two people tonight who thought they were good players. And you were one of them,' said Alf. Wilson thought for a moment of arguing back, but quickly decided that would be pointless. It was, he thought, just Alf's way of trying to puncture any complacency.

Yet in the dressing-room Alf had avoided any mention of a far more serious miscreant, Nobby Stiles, who had perpetrated an outrageously late tackle on the skilful French midfielder Jacques Simon. In the last quarter of the game, Stiles hacked Simon down after the Frenchman had received the ball from a throw-in, turned and passed it on to a colleague. 'I was aware that it was late, a terrible tackle,' says Stiles. George Cohen, who was nearby, calls it 'the tackle from hell, one that from the moment of its inception was destined to land somewhere between the Frenchman's thyroid gland and his crotch. I recall grimacing and saying to myself, "Jesus, that looked bad." It was. Jacky Simon had to be carried from the field and France were down to ten men. Strangely, England were not reduced to the same number, for the referee did not even book Stiles for the challenge, never mind send him off.

The incident cast a shadow over England's victory. There

was uproar in both the British and international press, with Stiles accused of having heaped embarrassment on the hosts. Alf's arch-enemy, Danny Blanchflower, claimed Stiles had 'ruined the game'. Joe Mercer, later to succeed Alf as temporary England manager, said Stiles had committed a 'terrible foul, one to shame English football'. FIFA was moved to announce that 'if this player were reported to them again by a referee or other official, they would take serious action'. For many critics, the incident also reflected badly on Ramsey. Stiles was seen as emblematic of his sterile, negative managerial style, where work-rate was cherished above artistry. For the FA councillors this was a golden opportunity to put their unaccountable manager in his place, having had to endure years of his dismissiveness. Alf had caused them offence on his very first overseas tour in the summer of 1963, when, at the end of the trip, he mockingly thanked them for 'staying out of my way'. And he had continued in the same vein, sneeringly referring to them as 'those people'. The commentator Kenneth Wolstenholme recalled an incident when he asked Alf about the arrangements for accommodation at a certain match. 'The players will be at the Hilton, so will I. I don't know where the FA officials are staying. They are nothing to do with me.' Nobby Stiles remembers an incident on tour in Sweden, when he realized he had run out of contact lens fluid. Alf immediately phoned Denis Follows, Secretary of the FA, and made arrangements for more fluid to be put on the next flight to Gothenburg. While Alf was giving his orders, he was interrupted by an FA councillor, asking him about an official reception. Instantly, Alf barked: 'To wear his contact lenses Nobby needs this fluid. That is important. Receptions and cocktail parties are not.'

Now, thanks to Stiles, Alf was summoned to Lancaster Gate, where the International Committee was ready to grill him. Alf bristled with indignation as he went into a meeting which he regarded as an utter waste of his time. If the FA thought that Alf might be on the defensive and willing to give some ground, they were mistaken. Prompted by the public outburst from FIFA, the Committee members told Alf that Stiles was an embarrassment to the good name of English football and should be dropped, if not for the rest of the tournament, at least for the next game. Alf fixed them with his coldest of stares:

'Most certainly Nobby Stiles can be thrown off the team,' he said, 'but I must tell you that I see him as a very important player for England, one who has done very well since he was first selected, and if he goes, so do I. You will be looking for a new manager.'

That brought the meeting to a sudden close. Soon afterwards, unsurprisingly, rumours of Alf's threat to quit reached the press, forcing Alf to issue a statement of denial, in which he claimed, rather unconvincingly, that 'at all times I have received the utmost co-operation of the members of the Senior International Committee'. For the rest of his reign as England manager, he maintained this stance, saying in 1970, for instance, that 'there was no pressure on me to eliminate anyone at the time. And I don't remember having a disagreement throughout the competition.' But in an interview in 1991, long after he had retired, Alf finally admitted the truth as he poured out his bitterness against the FA:

It was quite extraordinary. It seemed that they could not accept Stiles as an international and made it clear that they didn't want him. I just told them that if Stiles was to be dropped, they could find a new manager. And I meant it. I would have walked out there and then.

None of this was known by Stiles or the rest of the England team, who carried on with their preparations for the quarter-final against Argentina. On the Friday morning on the training ground at Roehampton, Alf pulled Nobby to one side and asked him a simple question:

'Did you mean it?'

'No Alf, I didn't. I mistimed the tackle.'

'You're playing tomorrow.'

Then Alf, just to rub it in with the FA, made a powerful public defence of Stiles, calling him 'a great young Englishman who is proud to play for his country and has done it very well. He is not just a good player but a great player.' Nobby told me that when he heard Alf's words: 'I felt tears coming to my eyes. The press had been slaughtering me all week, that's the way they are. Then Alf defended me. He was a great man, such a strong man.'

Loyalty is perhaps the most precious commodity any leader can enjoy. But it has to be earned. It cannot be demanded. And with his robust support for Nobby, Alf had earned it from his team. They knew that when he talked of loyalty, he really meant it. He had put his job on the line for one of his players. He had unequivocally sided with his team against the media, the FA and FIFA, giving his players a powerful boost to morale. In pressurized situations, a siege mentality can be beneficial for team spirit. 'Everyone felt that was great,' said Bobby Moore. 'All right, we were biased. All right, Nobby was there first and foremost to spoil, to mark people, to niggle and upset people. But he could still play the game.' Stiles was primarily a defensive player, whose central job was to win the ball and give it to Bobby Charlton. Indeed, Nobby argues that the system Alf played was not 4–3–3, but 4–1–3–2, with himself as the linkman between the defence and midfield. Because the opposition had been so geared to holding out for a draw in the first games, Nobby had not had the chance to shine in the tournament. But Alf knew he would be vital in the harder rounds against more attacking sides.

Apart from standing by Nobby, Alf had two other important decisions to make before the Argentina game. The first was about the formation. Alf had tried three wingers in three different games, none of whom had made much impression. With Argentina likely to be far more creative than any previous opponent, Alf believed he had to strengthen the midfield, so he brought in Alan Ball in place of Ian Callaghan. Gordon Banks says that Ball and Peters were the perfect pair to operate within a 4–3–3 system:

> I thought at the time that the decision to dispense with wingers was a good one. Alan Ball and Martin Peters were highly intelligent players. They worked tirelessly, dropped back and helped out in defence, were good when going forward, and, particularly in the case of Martin Peters, could make quality crosses into the opposition penalty area. Possibly their best assets were their lungs, which must have been like sides of beef, so much ground did they cover.

Today, Ball remembers how Alf approached him on the Friday before the game:

> He came up to me on the training ground and said,
> 'How are you, young man? You don't look as if you are enjoying yourself.'
> 'Well, Alf, I've missed my chance, I suppose. I'm very, very disappointed. I don't think I played that poorly against Uruguay. I can understand what you have done. But I'm still disappointed.'
> 'Well, I wouldn't be. Because you're going to play

tomorrow. I'm, giving you a job on the right hand side. They have a very good young full-back, Marzolini, and you are going to stop him. I don't think he's the fittest of their players and that will suit you right down to the ground. Do you think you can do that?'

'Alf, I will die doing that.'

Silvio Marzolini was a really good player going forward and Alf wanted me to stop him. No disrespect to Terry Paine, John Connelly and Ian Callaghan, who were all wide right players, but Alf thought I was the person to be a nuisance to this guy, get up his nose and get around him.

The other key duty of Ball, working alongside Stiles, was to open up opportunities for Bobby Charlton, England's most creative player. 'Don't forget,' says Ball, 'Bobby was not a big tackler or ball winner. We scrapped so Bobby could live. Nobby and I worked all day just to get the ball to him in the right areas, knowing that Bobby would produce.' At Roehampton, Alf illustrated this with a canine metaphor.

'Do either of you have a dog?' he asked the pair.

'I do,' said Ball.

'You know how when you throw a ball your dog chases after it? Well, that's what I want you both to do for Bobby. Win the ball and give it to him.'

Alf's second big decision was more straightforward. Jimmy Greaves' shin injury had, in his own words, 'opened up like a red rose towards the end of its bloom'. There was no way he would be able to take the field. But it is doubtful he would have done so even if he had remained fit since, in Alf's view, his lack of goals had already ruled him out. When Greaves was not scoring, he was not contributing. Alf later stated, 'Jimmy Greaves had not shown his true form to substantiate his position in the England team and would not have been selected for the Argentina match.' In Geoff Hurst, Alf had a replacement who would not let him down in terms of commitment. Though playing in a revolutionary wingless system, Hurst was in one respect a throwback to the English tradition of the strong, bustling centre-forward. Jimmy Armfield recalls a late-night conversation with Alf at Hendon Hall which centred on this very issue:

Harold Shepherdson, Alf, myself and Bobby Moore were sitting up one night, talking about the old days, and I happened to say, 'You know, all the times I have watched and played with England teams, I have never really seen a successful side without a big target man, an old-fashioned centre-forward.' I quoted the example of Bobby Smith, and we mentioned others like Dixie Dean and Nat Lofthouse. Then I said that the only big striker we had in the squad was Geoff Hurst. The simple truth is that Roger Hunt was a workaholic; Bobby Charlton was a workaholic; Alan Ball was a workaholic. Alf had the runners but he needed someone who could hold the ball. Geoff had always been able to do that. I played against him and I knew what it was like when he had his back to me, a big bulk that you couldn't get round. I said, 'Well, that's my opinion,' and I just left it. Bobby Moore, who knew Geoff well, said, 'No, it's a good idea.' Ironically, Geoff was in soon after that conversation.

Argentina were the team that Alf most feared in the World Cup finals, partly because of their magnificent skill on the ball, partly because of their epic cynicism. He had long regarded them as more likely champions than Brazil; during England's tour of Eastern Europe just before the finals, Alf had taken the chance to watch Brazil in action in Sweden and had returned to the England camp with the news that 'Brazil are no danger.

They're too old.' Disorganized and demoralized, Brazil failed to qualify for the quarter-finals, though they were subjected to savage treatment at the hands of Portugal, with Pele literally kicked out of the tournament. Argentina, however, were a more daunting prospect, an intimidating mix of the ruthless and the sublime. Having watched them in action in the Little World Cup in 1964, Alf sensed that they would be England's toughest opponents. As his captain Bobby Moore put it: 'We knew how difficult it would be to beat them. From all we'd seen of them, we knew they were often scruffy and untidy, but that they had enormous skill.' On the Friday afternoon, Alf gave his usual purposeful team talk. Nobby Stiles gives this insight into the way he promoted a feeling of inclusion:

Alf went through their side, and then said, 'But the player who really makes them tick is Ermindo Onega. Do you think we should man-mark him?' All the lads said, 'Yes'. Now we did not usually man-mark with Alf, using zonal marking instead. Alf continued, 'So who should do it?' Ray Wilson was the first to say, 'Nobby.' That was Alf. He was going to do it anyway but he wanted to give us the feeling that we all shared in the decision.

Harold Shepherdson also talked privately to Nobby at Hendon Hall that night, giving him a lecture about his duty towards Alf. 'I told him that he owed a great deal to Alf, who had stood by him against very strong newspaper criticism, and that if he did anything silly, he would be letting down the man who had faith in him.'

After all the criticism and apathy of the previous few weeks, the public mood appeared to have swung in England's favour once the team reached the quarter-finals. From villain, Nobby was transformed into national hero. As the England bus approached Wembley, a banner could be seen bearing the slogan 'Nobby for Prime Minister'. In the dressing-room, however, the atmosphere was more sombre. 'We accepted in our guts it was going to be hard. Maybe brutal,' said Bobby Moore. Just before the kick-off, Alf confined himself to one harshly realistic sentence, 'Well, gentlemen, you know the sort of game you have on your hands this afternoon.' But no warning from Alf could have prepared England for the depths to which Argentina sunk. Potentially a fine team, they simply refused to play football and instead tried to foul their way to the semi finals. The hardened professionals of England, used to the physical contact of the League, were surprised at the naked hostility they encountered. 'I quickly discovered that whenever I beat an Argentinian I could expect to be tripped, body-checked, spat at or dragged to the ground,' said Bobby Charlton, one of the most chivalrous performers in international football. 'Never, in any other match, had I been kicked when the ball was at the other end as I was now. I'd look round, and one of their fellows would make a gesture of innocence! It was the worst behaviour I'd ever experienced,' argued Roger Hunt. His companion up front, Geoff Hurst, compared it to 'walking down a dark alley late at night in a strange town'.

Ankles were kicked, hair tugged, eyes poked. 'The tackles were flying in, and so was the spittle,' jokes George Cohen. In the 36th minute, the match reached boiling point. The Argentinian captain Antonio Rattin, one of those naturally commanding players, like Bobby Moore, who always seemed to have time on the ball, had spent much of the game arguing with the German referee, the balding, diminutive Rudolf Kreitlein. The last straw for Kreitlein occurred when Rattin, described by Cohen as 'a natural bully', began yet another dispute over one of his decisions. The German's patience suddenly snapped, he reached for his notebook, waved his right arm and ordered Rattin from the field. The Argentinian could hardly believe it. For a full eight minutes, he stood in front of Kreitlein, alternately threatening, pleading and remonstrating. A sense of anarchy prevailed over Wembley, as other Argentinians joined in the protests. Bobby Charlton described the scenes as 'degrading' and a 'nightmare' as the 'Argentinians went berserk. They all piled into the ruck, arguing, gesticulating, pushing, shoving and fighting among themselves to get in on the act. The referee was disgracefully manhandled and at one time I thought the match would have to be abandoned.'

As Hugh McIlvanney memorably commented, this was 'not so much a football match as an international incident'. Rattin eventually left the field but his departure did not make the game any easier for England, as the ten remaining Argentinians rallied in defence and kept up their spoiling tactics. It should be said England were not above retaliation and indeed, during the game, they were deemed by Kreitlein to have committed more fouls than the Argentinians. Even Bobby Charlton was booked for the only time in his international career, when he ran to the aid of his brother when he saw Jack being assaulted. There were moments when Alf grew worried that Nobby would lose his composure in the mayhem. After Nobby was spat on for the seventh time, Alf buried his face in his hands, fearing the worst. He then looked up to see Nobby being led quietly away by Ray Wilson. 'There was more to it than just relief. Regardless of Nobby's will to win, the tremendous job he did for England, those people would have happily kicked him out,' said Alf. In all it was an ugly, dispiriting spectacle, 'the worst I have ever seen England involved in,' said Harold Shepherdson. The match looked to be heading for a draw when, in the 77th minute, Peters picked up the ball, went down the left wing and then hit a curling cross towards the near post. Geoff Hurst, who had timed his fifteen-yard run to perfection, met the ball with a glancing header, sending it across the keeper and just inside the far post. It was a beautifully worked move, simple yet devastating, one that Peters and Hurst had practised thousands of times on the West Ham training ground. 'We'd worked on near-post goals till it became an automatic action,' says Peters. 'I wouldn't even have to look. I knew Geoff would be there.' The West Ham connection was another advantage of Hurst's presence over Greaves, just as the Manchester United partnership of Stiles and Charlton worked so instinctively for England.

Hurst's goal decided the result. England were through to the semi-finals. But Alf's mood was one of outrage rather than pleasure. The Argentinians had confirmed all the negative views he had held about the over-excitability and underhand methods of South American football since he had first toured Brazil with Southampton in 1948. In his fury, he let his usual mask of impassivity slip, giving an almost unique public demonstration of the fire that burned within him. When he saw George Cohen about to swap shirts with his opposite number, Alberto Gonzalez, he ran twenty yards onto the field, grabbed the sleeves and, with real venom in his voice, told Cohen, 'George, you are not changing shirts with that animal.' Alf's outburst was fully justified, given the behaviour of the Argentinians once the game was over. First of all some of them were so threatening towards Kreitlein that he had to be escorted from the pitch by a quartet of police officers. Once they were off the field, they kept up their antics, urinating in the corridor outside their dressing-room and threatening to smash down the door of the England dressing-room. 'Let 'em in. I'll fight them all,' shouted Jack Charlton.

Alf was still seething when he was interviewed on television by Kenneth Wolstenholme, and his bitterness was to prompt one of the most infamous remarks of his career: 'We have still to produce our best and this best is not possible until we meet the right type of opposition and that is a team that comes out to play football and *not act as animals*.' The implication that Argentina had acted like animals caused uproar in South America and consternation in FIFA and the FA. Just days after the Nobby Stiles affair, Alf was in serious trouble with the authorities again. When the disciplinary committee of FIFA met, they first decided on some tough punishments for Argentina, including an £85 fine and the suspension of Rattin for four matches, then turned their attention to Alf. It was agreed to write to the FA, drawing attention 'to the unfortunate remarks made by Mr Ramsey in a television interview'. In FIFA's view, 'such remarks do not foster good international relations and it desires the FA to take appropriate disciplinary measures'. So soon after being bitten by Alf over Stiles, the FA were not prepared for another full-scale confrontation and merely asked secretary Denis Follows to have a quiet word with the manager. Anxious to avoid more distractions, Alf gave an apology in a half-hearted way, one that revealed his unease at dealing with the press: 'I was unfortunate in my choice of words. I am placed in the position of answering questions under the conditions because of my job. It does not excuse my choice of words.'

That was good enough for the FA. But Alf's comments would haunt him for the rest of his time as England manager, reinforcing his image as sour, insensitive and undiplomatic, and creating a well of resentment against him in Latin America, which would work against him in the 1970 World Cup. For the South Americans, his outburst smacked of old-fashioned British imperialism, a not entirely unjustified belief in Alf's case; as Brian Glanville once wrote of him, 'his own xenophobia was a kind of cloven hoof, which he could not help but show'. So offended were the Argentinians that the British

Ambassador in Buenos Aires, Sir Michael Cresswell, had to be given a special police guard. On a deeper level, the row strengthened the South Americans' belief that the entire 1966 World Cup was biased against them. For the first time in history, all four semi-finalists were European: England, Portugal, West Germany and Russia, while the refereeing – typified by Kreitlein – was said to favour the Europeans. In one respect, this represented a clash of football cultures. Tactics which the Europeans regarded as abhorrent, such as arguing with the referee, diving or spitting, were quite normal in South America, whereas the Latins were appalled at the northern referees' leniency towards brutish tackling, especially from behind.

Alf did not care what Argentina or FIFA or the FA thought. He was unconcerned about wider developments in world football. All that ever mattered to him was his team, and now they were though to the last four, a far greater achievement than his critics had suggested was possible. That Saturday night in Hendon Hall, he allowed his players to celebrate: 'It was a smashing night. We had a few bevvies and a big sing-song. Most of us got pretty drunk, but Alf didn't say a word, he just sat in the corner.' Alan Ball remembers. 'It was that night, over a few drinks, that we began to realize the enormity of what we had done.'

# TEN

# *Wembley*

'I knew there was a certain cynicism among fans and critics alike at the early stage. Not a lot of people gave us any great chance of winning,' says Ray Wilson. Reflecting on this climate of negativity, Brian James, the *Daily Mail*'s former chief football writer, tells an extraordinary story which illustrates the huge prejudice in the press against Alf that existed in the summer of 1966:

> Half-way through the tournament, I was taken for a walk in Hyde Park by Jim Manning, then the sports columnist on the *Daily Mail*. He was acting on the instructions of the Editor, who had told him, 'Brian has got to stop saying that England will win the World Cup because he is making us look stupid. He's backing the wrong man. And you can tell him that if England do not win the World Cup, then he may have to look for another job.'

In part, this was because quite a few journalists simply did not understand what Alf was trying to do with his wingless formation. Trapped in their stereotyped thinking about W–M, the old guard in the media turned their incomprehension into scorn. 'Alf, you give me the World Cup Willies,' wrote

314

Desmond Hackett. But the deeper reason was that Alf made it so obvious that he viewed the press largely as an irrelevance. 'If they get in touch with me, it's always because they want something – there's nothing I ever want from them,' Alf said. It was players, not public relations, that achieved results. His unco-operative attitude left journalists aggrieved, but it actually strengthened the spirit of his team, as Nobby Stiles recalls:

He could not give a shit about the press, really, it was great. Budgie Byrne told me that when Walter Winterbottom was in charge and England were training, the interviews with journalists could drag on for two hours. But with Alf, it was very different. When we were at Roehampton, the press would be gathered there, wanting interviews and photographs. And Alf would say to the lads, 'How long should we give the press, half an hour, twenty minutes?' 'Twenty minutes,' we'd reply, though Ray Wilson did not want to give them a second. 'They know fuck all,' he'd say. So Alf goes to the press, 'Gentlemen, before we start, you may have twenty minutes with the lads.' At the end of that time, Harold Shepherdson would blow the whistle and that was it. It didn't matter if you were in the middle of an interview. Alf understood that we didn't want to be wasting energy talking for hours to journalists. You can lose energy that way. I'm sure the press didn't like that but we loved Alf for it. Under Walter, the press would rule. Under Alf, he was in charge.

Contrary to the widespread gloom in the press before the 1966 finals – and again after the Uruguay game – Alf had taken England further than they had ever been before. In fact, his team was in the middle of a phenomenal run, having lost just one of their previous 21 games, and conceded just one goal in their last nine. If not the most elegant or explosive side, they had almost become unbeatable. Sepp Herberger, who had managed West Germany when they won the World Cup in 1954, said that 'England are justified in reaching the semi-final. As a team, they have no weakness, which is rare.' With the introduction of Hurst, Alf had achieved exactly the right balance in his team – it had strength, industry, hard-running and attacking options. For all the moans about the 'wingless wonders', Alf had really lost nothing down the flanks, since Martin Peters and Alan Ball were so industrious and such good users of the ball. The two full-backs, Wilson and Cohen, were also exceptionally quick when going forward, though the quality of Cohen's crosses left something to be desired – it was joked that the spectators behind the goal should have been given gum shields because they were in more danger than the opposition keeper. In an interview in 1978, Alf explained the thinking behind his dropping of orthodox wingers:

Terry Paine, Ian Callaghan and John Connelly all had one game each. To accommodate them, I had to leave out either Alan Ball or Martin Peters. And when it came to the moment of decision, I felt I needed the best players regardless of their acceptable positions. A manager's job is to pick his best available team. That is exactly what I did for the quarter-final against Argentina. What I will readily admit is that I do not favour old-fashioned wingers, the type who were stationed out on the touchline and waited for the ball to be served up to them. To have two players stuck out on the flanks is a luxury which can virtually leave a side with nine men when the game is going against them.

Ray Wilson has this analysis of the tactical success of Alf's system:

Most of the England team was solid. The goalkeeper and the back four never changed. We were always secure there. Once Alf had established the defence, we were there for ever. The only guy Alf gave any freedom to was Bobby Charlton. Every other player on the field had a job to do. They all had to come back; they all had to put defenders under pressure; they had to tackle, making the opposition play square balls. But Bobby was allowed to run loose – and quite right. Who else could have scored a goal like his against Mexico?

Ray Wilson further argues that the arrival of Hurst made a big difference:

Jimmy Greaves was bloody useless in the air. The chances we were going to get at Wembley would be mainly in air because the other teams were so outrageously defensive. There comes a time, in that situation, when you have to start hitting 50–50 balls. And that's where Geoff was so good. You could hit balls up to him and he would hold on or knock them down for people like Martin Peters or Bobby. The change from Jimmy to Geoff certainly suited me because it meant that if I was under pressure, with two opponents against me, I could get it to Geoff and he'd keep it, putting their defence under pressure. Jimmy couldn't do that.

Alf's long-period of team building, sticking with the same team – especially in defence – also paid dividends. Jack Charlton gives this example: 'With George Cohen, you knew that if anyone took him on the inside, he struggled. But over a year, you learned how to cover for that sort of thing.'

England's progress was based on more than just a constructive tactical approach. Since his appointment, Alf had laid great stress on building a team of strong personalities. It was not enough to have technique or skill. A player with Ramsey's England also had to have the right temperament, one that would not buckle under fire or put self-interest before the needs of the team. In the band of brothers he forged, there was no room for show-offs, slackers or complainers. Roger Hunt says:

It strikes me that every member of that team was an honest trier, irrespective of ability. It seems clear now why Alf chose the men he did and it is a tribute to his acumen and judgement of character. Alf knew that, no matter what the circumstances, he could rely on a certain level of performance.

Character was a central feature of Ramsey's England, and his final eleven in 1966 reflected the values that he cherished: honesty, dignity, application, courage and selflessness. Several of them had come through harrowing personal ordeals: Bobby Moore survived testicular cancer at the age of just 23; Bobby Charlton saw the loss of most of his mates in the Munich air crash of 1958. Others had been written off, an experience that only added to their steeliness. Alan Ball, for instance, was twice rejected by other clubs before finding fame at Blackpool, while Jack Charlton had been told by Don Revie at Leeds, 'You'll never do for me,' a comment that only made Jack determined to prove Revie wrong. Most of them had experienced tough upbringings which hardened them as men: Gordon Banks' father was a Sheffield foundry worker, Hurst's an Essex toolmaker. This tribute from Nobby Stiles to his colleagues George Cohen and Ray Wilson perfectly captures the essence of Alf's side. On Cohen, Stiles says:

If there was ever a better-hearted, fitter, harder-running, more professional footballer than George Cohen, well, I never got to play with him. I have never met a more honest, more decent man, and the fact that he so quickly became an integral part of Alf's grand plan can be easily explained. Alf knew that, if he asked him to, George would run through a brick wall, partly for fun. He gave so much strength and energy along the right side.

Of Ray Wilson, he says: 'He had moral courage to burn. I never saw him do once what most of the greatest players I have played with or against have done from time to time – he never blinked or flinched at a moment of heavy pressure.'

By the World Cup finals, Alf was at the peak of his powers as a manager. He had come up with a formidable blend of players operating in a strong defensive system. After three years in the job, he had established a masterful authority over all his players. Partly as a result of his own naturally reticent personality, he had pulled off the rare feat of maintaining his distance while incurring affection. Among the players, fondness and respect for Alf were mixed with a degree of fear. One time Geoff Hurst was wearing his official England suit, but had decided not to wear the enamel England lapel badge with it, sensing this would make him look like a school prefect. Alf spotted the omission immediately:

'Geoffrey, where's your badge? You're improperly dressed without it.'

'Sorry Alf, I think I lost it.'

'Not to worry, Geoffrey.' Alf dipped into his pocket, pulled out another badge and pinned it to Hurst's lapel. 'Now don't lose that one.'

At Hendon Hall, when he told the players at night that it

was time to go to bed, he encountered no arguments, as Hurst remembers:

> At 10.30 each evening Alf walked into the TV lounge, where the players spent most of their time after dinner. 'Good night, gentlemen,' he used to say. That was enough. Very often we'd be at the critical stage of a movie but everyone got up and went to their rooms.

On one occasion, Alf allowed the players' wives to come up to Hendon Hall briefly in the evening – though there no question of any visiting their husbands' bedrooms. Tina Moore recalls:

> We were all having a chat in the players' lounge when Alf came in.
> 'Goodnight ladies, goodnight gentlemen.'
> 'Why, Alf, are you going to bed?' said Bobby.
> 'No, gentlemen, you are.'
> So off we were all swept. Alf looked dour but there was often a sparkle in his eyes. He delivered his lines with this deadpan voice, but behind that façade there was real humour.

Tina says that she found Alf

> always very courteous and polite. Generally, I thought he was great. He was charming but words never gushed out of him. Bobby and Alf were different people, but they both aspired to what they considered were the finer things in life. Bobby, like Alf, groomed himself. I think Alf was very aware of his image and how he came across. He wasn't totally natural and everything he did was studied.

She believes that by mid-1966, the relationship between Alf and Bobby was on much stronger ground than it had sometimes been in the past. 'There was a mutual respect between them. Bobby would talk to me about Alf. He admired him as a man and liked him though he did tease him, as in that time with Sean Connery.'

Alf's dry humour could also come out on England's training ground at Roehampton, as Ron Springett, the deputy goalkeeper found:

Jimmy Greaves had asked him if he could nip home but Alf refused. 'We are a team', he said, 'and we are going to stay as a team.' I pointed out that I lived no more than fifty yards from the Bank of England club at Roehampton, so one day, after a training session, Alf said, 'You can go home for a cup of tea.' I took him up on his offer but, knowing Alf, I didn't stay longer than it takes to drink a cup of tea. When I got back to the Bank of England Club, the first shot that came my way went right through my legs into the net. 'That's the last time I'm letting you go off home for any tea,' was all Alf said.

It was at Roehampton that Geoff Hurst gained another insight into the sensitivity of Alf's man-management. At West Ham, Hurst was in the habit of training in a tracksuit, so that when it came to match day, he felt much lighter. But with the England squad, he was sure that Alf, a stickler for correct dress, would not allow this; all the players trained in red and white bibs. When he was out of the team, Hurst had not bothered too much about this, but once he had replaced Greaves, he felt he had to ask for permission to train in his tracksuit:

Alf looked at me for what seemed ages, then said quietly, 'All right, Geoffrey, if this matters to you, go ahead.' I should have trusted Alf to know the difference between someone just trying to be awkward and someone genuinely worried about breaking an old habit.

Back at Hendon Hall, Alf had arranged for special television lines to be installed, so the squad could watch whatever live match he chose. Predictably, the players always wanted to view the most potentially exciting games, such as Brazil against Hungary at Goodison, but he insisted on matches involving their opponents. 'By the time we played Germany in the Final, we had seen them several times and we knew what every player would do. It was as simple as that,' said Bobby Charlton. On other evenings or free afternoons, Alf preferred to make a group trip to the local cinema, not only because he retained a child-like affection for westerns and adventure films, but also because he felt it was a good bonding exercise for the team. Sometimes, as Jimmy Armfield remembers, Alf's announcement of a cinema outing could be quite abrupt;

We would be sitting in Hendon Hall Hotel after lunch or dinner, then Alf would suddenly say, 'Harold, John Wayne is on at the Odeon.'

'Very good, Alf.'

'I think we should go. What do you think?'

'Yeah.'

'Then tell the lads we're going to the Odeon.' By then, he's picked up his gear, got his coat and is almost out the door. And we have to run up the stairs, get our coats, and then chase him to the Odeon. So we have the sight of the England football team running down the hill after our manager. As he gets to the ticket office, we would all pile in behind him. And he would say, 'I want 26 seats.' We would always go upstairs. It was dark, the film would often have started and we would be noisily clambering into our seats and Alf would say, 'Shut up, John Wayne's on.' That was Alf. He loved his Westerns.

As they fought their way into the last four, the team of 1966 were aware of their huge debt to Alf. Gordon Banks reflects on his qualities:

He was in a class of his own. Some managers are tactically aware. Some excel at coaching. Others are good at motivation and man-management. Alf was superb at everything. That's what made him so special. Always fair to his players and scrupulously honest, he was a man of unyielding integrity and absolute loyalty. Alf put his job on the line for Nobby Stiles after the game against France, as he would have done for any of us, and his loyalty was reciprocated. He was devoted to the team ethic, yet at pains to point out that no one was indispensable. He bore no grudges and had no favourites.

Even those who were outside the final eleven, like John Connelly, were filled with admiration:

He did what he thought was right and Alf was almost always uncannily right. He was a brilliant manager. It was he who fostered such a spirit among the lads and he made sure that being in the squad was just like being in a club. He was out on his own when it came to man-management. He knew every one of his players inside out, their strengths and their weaknesses. What is more, he knew exactly how to get the best out of his players. Alf never took anything for granted. He believed you never got anything without working for it. I've heard it said that he was sometimes a bit aloof with the lads. Maybe he was, but you knew that he would never let you down. All of us respected him. He was a brilliant tactician and he wasn't afraid to experiment. He was such a brave manager, determined in his own selection and then determined to make his selection work.

In the build-up to the Portugal game, Alf had no selection problems. With Jimmy Greaves' recovery not yet complete, there was no question of his playing. The only issue of immediate controversy was the venue. It had originally been stipulated that if England won their quarter-final, they would travel to Goodison for the semi-final, but at the last minute, FIFA decided the game should be played at Wembley because of its bigger capacity. The move led to anger on Merseyside and more accusations of favouritism towards England. But Alf was pleased not to have to leave Hendon Hall, where he had established a well-ordered regime.

Before the tournament, Portugal had not been thought likely to qualify from a group which included Brazil and Hungary, but they had marched through with a mixture of expansive skills and occasional brutality. Their biggest threat was their striker Eusebio, the 'Black Panther' from Mozambique, who was already the tournament's leading scorer. To counter his power, Alf again gave Nobby the job of shadowing him.

'I want you to mark Eusebio,' said Alf.

'Do you mean for life, Alf?' joked Nobby with a gap-toothed smile.

As it turned out, Nobby did the job superbly, closing Eusebio out of the game by continually forcing him to operate on his weaker left foot. 'Nobby had his best game for England. Eusebio got so fed up he went out on the wing,' says George Cohen. But this was no repeat of one of Nobby's more violent earlier performances. In fact, after the horror shows of England v Argentina and Brazil v Portugal, the match was played in a magnificent spirit, and it was not until the 23rd minute that the first foul was committed. Portugal did not even concede a free kick until the 57th minute. Moreover, Portugal's emphasis on attack, by opening up space across the field, freed England from their shackles. For the first time in the finals, England proved they could play captivating, positive football. Bobby Charlton, all grace and elegant power, was at the top of his form, revelling in his freedom to burst through from midfield. 'This was the best match we played because it was against a team that allowed you to play football. The game flowed from end to end,' said Charlton. It was Charlton's dynamism that brought England both their goals. The first came in the 31st minute, when he seized on a rebound from the keeper Pereira and stroked the ball across the lush Wembley turf into the net. The second, which came in the 79th minute, showed the importance of Geoff Hurst to the side. Hurst took a long pass from Cohen near the byline, beat one man, held the ball up for a moment, then hit it neatly into the path of Charlton who struck it first time without breaking his stride. It was a goal of simplicity and beauty, highlighting both Charlton's genius and England's team ethic. 'It was a wonderful education to play alongside Bobby Charlton. He was the greatest footballer I ever played with,' says Alan Ball, 'That night against Portugal, Nobby and I got the ball to him all the time and he was incredible.' In the dying minutes, Portugal gained one back, when Jack Charlton handled in the area and Eusebio scored from the spot. Twice more they almost equalized, Stiles making a crucial tackle and Banks pulling off a finger-tip save. But the score-line finished 2–1. England were through to the Final.

Because of his focus on the team, Alf rarely singled out individuals for praise. But he was so moved by Nobby's subjugation of Eusebio that he broke with the long-held practice of his management. In the privacy of the dressing-room, he said: 'Gentlemen, I don't often talk about individuals. But I think you would all agree that Nobby has today turned in a very professional performance.' Critics of Ramsey might point out it was Nobby's defensive display rather than Bobby Charlton's attacking one which earned Alf's most effusive approval. Back at Hendon Hall, Nobby was not able to join in the alcoholic celebrations for England's victory. He had been accidentally punched in the head by Gordon Banks when going for a high ball, and Dr Alan Bass had given him an injection to prevent the development of a cauliflower ear. But Nobby clearly remembers Alf's words to his triumphant team as they gathered round the bar:

Gentlemen, congratulations on a fine performance and on making the final. Tonight you may have two pints – and I mean two pints. Not like last Saturday night after the Argentina game when, how shall I put it, some of you were rat-arsed. But not tonight, gentlemen. Just two pints. Because on Saturday, you are going to win the World Cup. And when you do, I shall see to it that you are permanently pissed.

For the first time, the country was gripped by World Cup fever. The manner of England's victory over Portugal had created a new mood of excitement and expectation. As the football historian Clive Leatherdale wrote: 'Before the semifinal, patriotism had been blurred by doubt. After it, the clouds lifted and a buoyant nation could barely wait for Saturday to arrive.' Amid the rising enthusiasm for Alf's team, a debate was raging as to whether the manager should bring back Jimmy Greaves. This was widely seen as by far the toughest decision of Alf's three-year-reign, and Alf later admitted that it was his 'most controversial'. After all, Greaves was England's finest goalscorer of modern times, a far more naturally talented player than the pedestrian Hunt or the laboured Hurst. With his awesome acceleration over a short distance, his uncanny positioning and swiftness of shot, he could transform a game with a moment of sublime skill. 'He was the best goalscorer we ever had. I played behind him for England and he would be running at the opposition and it was as if they were opening up to let him through,' Jimmy Armfield told me. Most of the southern public and London press favoured the return of Greaves. This piece by Brian James in the *Daily Mail* was typical:

> The game is bound to be hard, and though I do not think it will be dirty, strength will be vital. Yet for all that, I would play Greaves. His skill is undeniable. Only his application has ever been suspect, and in a World Cup Final EVERY-BODY works . . . today, for the first time in this tournament, England can only win if they are more skilful than their opponents.

There is no doubt that Greaves had fully recovered. He had been training hard without any ill-effects; Harold Shepherdson wrote that 'when it came to the Final, Jimmy was completely fit and raring to go'.

The problem for Greaves was that England had been playing better without him. The team had looked more balanced, solid, and dangerous. 4–3–3, or, more accurately, 4–1–3–2, was a style that required the hard running of Hunt and Hurst rather than the mercurial unpredictability of Greaves. Moreover, both had proved effective in front of goal, Hunt scoring three times in five games, Hurst once in two. In the England camp, there was a near universal feeling for the current striking pair, though Bobby Moore did stick up for his room-mate and fellow East Londoner. Bobby Charlton, with a rare degree of stridency in his voice, thought that the Greaves debate had been 'blown out of all proportion and I was confident that Alf would do the right thing. Hurst was better suited to the competition as it was. I don't think Greaves' reputation meant so much to Alf – that was part of Alf's quality.' In another interview, in 1973, Bobby was even more scornful of Greaves:

Jimmy was a bit of a luxury, I always felt. He'd score five if you won 8–0, but in matches where a single goal would decide, it was better to have someone like Hurst. You never saw Jimmy much in a game, he was waiting up there to score, and I suppose that's why he never materialised for Alf.

Alan Ball echoed Bobby's sentiments: 'With Geoff, I could always bounce the ball off him, build something. He would help to get you into the team. With Jimmy, you had to play for him. Geoff could do more for our team.' The German manager, Helmut Schoen, agreed with this assessment, as he later told Ken Jones:

Was Greaves still in the picture? He was a brilliant scorer, a quick dribbler, with outstanding anticipation, but he was not a good team player. And he'd missed two games with an injury. My feeling was that Ramsey would select the team that defeated Portugal.

In an interview with the BBC in 1995, Alf said: 'Jimmy was a good player and I admired him. He came from Dagenham, like me, but I had to decide if I was going to leave out one player for him. I probably spent four or five nights worrying about it.' This is an unconvincing exaggeration. Alf had probably decided to keep with the winning team as soon as they left the field against Portugal on Tuesday night. There was no chance he was going to refashion a side that had brought him to the brink of glory. It is telling that at training on Wednesday and Thursday, Alf kept the same first eleven separate from the remainder of the squad. Alf had already decided to drop Greaves before the Argentina game, even without any injury. He had no reason to bring him back now. In an interview with the commentator Kenneth Wolstenholme, Alf explained his thinking:

> The team had performed magnificently in his absence. We had beaten two fancied teams in Argentina and Portugal, so I could not have asked for anything more. Geoff Hurst, who had come into the side, had done a great job. It was him or an injured Jimmy Greaves. After a lot of thought, I decided to leave well alone. As they say, if a thing isn't broken, don't try to mend it. I had a clear conscience. I had to make a decision, and a decision that was best for the team and their chances of winning the World Cup.

In his heart, Greaves had known that he was doomed: 'At the end of the semi-final I felt in my bones that Alf was not going to select me for the Final. My dream of helping England was about to be smashed.' Greaves sensed the truth about his omission all the more strongly on Thursday when he was sitting beside Harold Shepherdson on the coach back from training: 'I said casually, "I suppose it's going to be difficult to get back" and he turned away and looked out the window. I was close to Harold, he'd been there ever since I came into the squad. Alf had obviously confided in him and he was too embarrassed to answer me.' Years later, in his retirement, Alf was sitting watching a game with Roy McFarland, one of the most intelligent footballers of the seventies. McFarland asked him why he didn't play Greaves. And Alf replied: 'I was thinking to myself one day that I had played Jimmy Greaves with Geoff Hurst, with Bobby Smith, with Roger Hunt and many others. It had never quite worked. Then I realized that the problem was with Jimmy Greaves, not the man he was playing with. That was the conclusion I came to.'

In the first three days after the Portugal game, Alf had said nothing to any of his players about the team selection. It was a period of mental agony for several of them, especially Hurst and Hunt, who both feared that they might have to make way for Greaves. Hurst wrote:

> I wanted nothing more in my life more than I now wanted to play for England in this Final, I wanted it so badly I literally ached at the thought of not being in. I found myself watching Alf with a sort of scared fascination, to see if I could get some tiny hint of encouragement. He had only to pass me the sugar at tea to start some fantasy about wanting to build up my strength for Saturday; he had only to leave a newspaper on the chair beside me for me to snatch the sports page to see if he was trying to break the news through a hint in some reporter's guess that I was about to be dropped.

On the eve of the Final, Alf brought the torture to an end. The squad travelled by coach to the local Odeon to watch *Those Magnificent Men in Their Flying Machines* and, as the players stepped into the theatre, Alf discreetly told each of his selected team that they would be appearing the next day against West Germany. As Alf later revealed:

I varied the way I told them. To one or two I said, 'If it will help you to sleep tonight, you'll be playing tomorrow.' To Nobby Stiles I said, 'Well, are you ready for tomorrow?'

'I hope so,' he replied.

'You bloody well better be.'

Alf asked the players to keep the information confidential, but inevitably some of the room-mates, like West Ham colleagues Peters and Hurst, could not resist telling each other. 'Risking instant death at the hands of Alf had the rooms been bugged I blurted out, "Martin, old mate, I'm in, I'm playing." "Great," he replied, "And so am I." We rolled over and looked at each other, then together we had one great whoop of utter jubilation,' said Hurst.

One man whom Alf did not inform was captain Bobby Moore. This was partly because it would have been such a formality – 'If Bobby Moore didn't know he was playing without me telling him, he's not the Bobby Moore I know,' said Alf, but more importantly because Moore was actually a doubt for the Final, not because of form but because of fitness. Soon after the semi-final, Moore had contracted tonsillitis, a potentially serious health problem. Fortunately, it was diagnosed early by the team doctor Alan Bass and, with the right treatment and diligent care, he had recovered by Saturday. 'If we had let matters go for a day, the tonsillitis would have got such a hold on Bobby that it would have taken five days to clear up. That is how near he was to missing the Final!' wrote Harold Shepherdson. The players were kept in the dark about Bobby's ailment, and remained so for years afterwards. It was at a reunion in the mid-nineties, after Bobby Moore had died, that George Cohen revealed how, one evening in Hendon Hall, he had overheard Alf in discussion with Harold Shepherdson and Les Cocker about Bobby's prospects of playing. According to George's account, Alf had asked Les, 'How do you think Norman would do?' Geoff Hurst, among others, greeted this news with astonishment. 'None of us at the time realized how close Bobby was to losing his place in the team.' But the reason for these talks was misinterpreted. Alf was not thinking of dropping Moore; instead, he was hoping for his recovery but preparing for the worst.

To Alf's relief, Moore was fine by Saturday morning. But Jimmy Greaves was shattered. He had gone down to breakfast and had sensed Alf being 'very distant' with him. He knew then he was out. He went back up to his room and started packing his bags.

'What are you doing, Jim?' asked Moore.

'Just getting ready for a quick getaway once the match is over.'

'You can do that tomorrow morning. We'll be on the bevvy tonight, celebrating our World Cup win.'

Greaves could not bring himself to say any more. At midday, Alf confirmed his fears, when he told Jimmy that he was going with an unchanged team. But, according to Greaves, Alf expressed the hope that Jimmy would understand his reasons for doing so. 'Sure Alf, they'll win it for you,' said Greaves. 'I think so,' replied Alf, who then disappeared to talk to other members of the squad who had not made the final XI. As Greaves later recorded: 'Alf couldn't have said a lot more to me. He knew I was choked and disappointed but he was doing what he thought was right for the good of the team.'

Greaves has always maintained that he felt no bitterness towards Alf for the decision, yet he has often given out contradictory messages. Sometimes, he has said that he could not have played in the Final because he was injured, while at other times he has accused Alf of using fitness as an issue to drop him. The journalist Nigel Clarke has this fascinating recollection, which differs from some of the accounts Greaves has given:

> After 1966 the relationship with Alf was never the same again. That killed Jimmy. I was on holiday with him in Portugal sometime around 1970. He was a funny little man in some ways because his wife Irene ruled the roost. I think she was fundamental in turning Jimmy against Alf. Jimmy is an honest lad but he also had a big ego and he thought he could have done the same role as Geoff did. He told me in Portugal that he could not get over the fact that Alf had said to him, 'I don't think you're fit.' He felt that Alf used the injury as an excuse. Jimmy thought Alf should have been more honest and told him he was going to use a certain system which worked better with Geoff. I remember Jimmy said: 'Alf should have just come out and told me straight. He hid behind the fact that I'd had that shin injury.'

Geoff Hurst, who played at West Ham with Greaves after 1970, says that during their time at Upton Park, 'Jimmy was still impishly humming the tune "What's It All About, Alfie?" I don't think he ever forgave Alf for the way he discarded him.' Despite denials from Greaves, it cannot be disputed that Alf's decision had a disastrous effect on his career. He won just three more caps and was finished with England at the age of just 27. He soon went into premature retirement and then plunged into chronic alcoholism, which saw him regularly getting through 18 pints and a bottle of vodka a day, though he subsequently fought a heroic battle against the grip of drink to become a much-loved TV personality.

For all the controversy surrounding Greaves, it had been a straightforward tactical decision for Alf to make, purely on a football level. But in terms of public relations, it was much harder, because of the huge following for Greaves. It would have been easy to court popularity by picking Greaves, yet Alf was a strong man precisely because he wasn't interested in popularity. If he had got it wrong, if Hurst and Hunt missed a string of chances, he would have been crucified. A weaker manager might have regarded the selection of Greaves as his personal security blanket in the event of defeat. With his remorseless focus on the interests of his team, such considerations would have never occurred to Alf. He was the personification of the epigram of the American football coach Vince Lombardi, 'Winning isn't everything. It's the only thing.'

Apart from his moral strength, one of Alf's other attributes was his almost Zen-like calm in moments of the most intense pressure. Though not a religious man, he could have almost been a Buddhist monk for the aura of stillness that enveloped him. 'If he was at all nervous or tense during the tournament, he did not show it, but then he has amazing self-control,' said Geoff Hurst in 1967. No one in British sport had ever experienced the burden that he was under in the days before the World Cup Final, yet he gave no indication of any anxiety or any doubt about the outcome. Instead, he was a man at peace with himself. On the Friday evening, he sat happily through *Those Magnificent Men in Their Flying Machines*, describing it as 'the greatest film he had ever seen'. In his room at Hendon Hall, he enjoyed a restful, contented night: 'My own job was done. The responsibility was now theirs, and I was able to sleep well that night – even though I normally don't sleep well in strange beds away from home.'

On the Saturday morning, he went through a final briefing with the team. Again, he was his usual cool, authoritative self, running through the opposition without undermining the confidence of his own team. 'As always,' says George Cohen, 'Ramsey avoided loading up the pressure – or bombarding us with his sure-fire master plan. His concern was always to make sure that individuals were in the best possible frame of mind, alert but not weighed down with responsibilities.' Alf was not deceived by the fact that Germany had never beaten England since the nations had first met in 1901, nor could he have found it reassuring that, since the Second World War, no hosts had won the Cup. A well-organized, combative outfit which had beaten Spain and thrashed Uruguay 4–0 on the way to the final, the Germans had several outstanding players, including Willi Schulz as sweeper, the resourceful captain and striker Uwe Seeler and the tall, powerful winger Lothar Emmerich, who had a ferocious left-foot shot. But from Alf's point of view, the most worrying player was their young wing-half, Franz Beckenbauer, already emerging as one of the stars of European football. It is testament to the threat of Beckenbauer that Alf gave Bobby Charlton the job of making sure he had no freedom of movement. Conversely, Helmut Schoen, the German manager, was so concerned about Charlton that Beckenbauer was instructed to mark him. In the game itself, therefore, these two maestros cancelled each other out, though this ultimately worked to England's advantage.

After his talk, Alf then led the players in for a light lunch of chicken, poached eggs or beans on toast, though the growing tension meant that few of them were hungry. At 1.15 the bus left the hotel for Wembley. Along the route, thousands of people came out to cheer and wave their Union Jacks, something that had never happened before at an England international. The urge for victory was almost palpable. As they looked out on the vast throngs packed along Wembley Way, the players could feel how much this match meant to the country. Bobby Charlton was struck by the 'incredible enthusiasm generated by a traditionally conservative people. Fire engines rang their bells, factory sirens hooted and car horns blared; it seemed as if the whole of London wanted to be in at the kill.' At 1.45 the bus arrived at the ground. While some of the team went straight to the dressing-room, others walked out onto the pitch to savour the atmosphere. Already the terraces, full of eager fans, were buzzing with anticipation. The volatile, stormy weather matched the nervous electricity pumping through the stadium. One minute the sky would darken and crackle with thunder, the next Wembley would be bathed in warm sunshine.

Alf might have been calm, but the England dressing-room was not. In the hour before the kick-off, it was packed with the TV crews, officials, reporters and well-wishers. Even the man who made the tea at Wembley was wandering around with an open autograph-book. At 2.15, chaos still prevailed, with scores of people milling around the players. Geoff Hurst was surprised that Alf, usually so attuned to the needs of his team, did not throw out the whole circus. 'It was very un-Ramsey like,' he says. Moore was equally shocked, though he felt Alf may have had an ulterior motive in allowing the bedlam to drag on: 'Perhaps he hoped it would give us something to occupy our minds.' But Moore was disgruntled that he had not been allowed his usual period of quietness to collect his thoughts.

Just before 2.45, as the team prepared to go out, Alf shook each one by the hand and said, 'Good luck.' In their red shirts, the players then went along the tunnel and out onto the field, their entrance greeted by a deafening roar from the 97,000 capacity crowd. They were followed by Ramsey, who was wearing his blue England tracksuit, white socks and strange black semi-brogues. The presentations to the Queen and various other dignitaries went on for what seemed an interminable fifteen minutes, heightening the tautness of the players. There was a sense of relief when the referee, Gottfried Dienst of

ABOVE: Champions of the World, July 1966: Alf with the eleven men who made English sporting history.

ABOVE: A round of golf with his assistants Harold Shepherdson and Les Cocker at Lilleshall, England's training camp before the World Cup.

LEFT: Labour Premier Harold Wilson and Sports Minister Denis Howell seek some reflected glory from Alf.

LEFT: Not so much a football match as an international incident. England v Argentina, World Cup quarter-final, 1966.

BELOW: 'You are not changing shirts with that animal,' exclaimed Alf at the final whistle of the Argentina game.

LEFT: 'What's it all about, Alfie?' Star striker Jimmy Greaves never recovered from the disappointment of being left out of the World Cup Final team.

LEFT: 'We thought we'd blown it,' says Ray Wilson. Wolfgang Weber equalizes for West Germany in the dying seconds of normal time in the World Cup Final.

RIGHT: Alf remained utterly impassive throughout the Final, even at the moment of victory.

LEFT: It's all over. Hurst scores his hat-trick and England are top of the world.

RIGHT: 'This is your day. You have done this,' says England's self-effacing manager, reluctant to join his team's celebrations at Wembley.

BELOW: With the World Cup on the balcony of the Royal Garden hotel. The players preferred the Playboy club to the official FA banquet.

BELOW: Alf was always at his happiest on the training ground.

LEFT: From Dagenham labourer's son to Knight of the Realm. Alf with Lady Victoria at his Buckingham Palace investiture in 1967.

LEFT: Alf with Nobby Stiles, Jack Charlton and Barry Bridges.

RIGHT: Alf on the bench at the start of the 1970 campaign to retain the World Cup in Mexico.

BELOW: England line up against Brazil, 1970.

The greatest save in history? Gordon Banks turns away Pele's header in the match against Brazil.

Quarter-final disaster. West Germany's Gerd Muller volleys home against the hapless Peter Bonetti to make it 3–2, and England are out of the World Cup.

'I aged 15 years in that afternoon,' said Alf later, seen here trying to comfort a distraught Bobby Charlton after the German defeat.

Never at ease with public relations, Alf proved even more abrasive with the press than usual on his return from Mexico in 1970.

Peter Shilton looks bewildered as Poland take the lead in the crucial World Cup qualifier at Wembley, October 1973.

Harold Shepherdson puts his arm around a shattered Emlyn Hughes after England's exit against Poland. Kevin Keegan and Norman Hunter are equally disconsolate.

The end of the road as Alf congratulates Poland's manager Kazimierz Gorski. His grimace can barely conceal his inner turmoil.

Another goal in the back of Ramsey's net, this time at England's training ground at Roehampton.

Alf had a brief spell as media pundit for ITV during the 1974 World Cup, working alongside Brian Moore, Malcolm Allison and Brian Clough. He never cared for the loudmouthed Clough.

ABOVE: With fellow Dagenham lad Terry Venables in 1996. Tragically, Alf's Alzheimer's was already well-advanced by then.

Lady Ramsey at the unveiling of the statue of her husband outside Ipswich's ground.

Switzerland, finally blew up for the start, with Alf looking stony-faced from the bench. The Germans soon saw the power of Hurst as he went up for a high ball and collided with the keeper Hans Tilkowski, leaving him badly winded. It was England, however, who in the 13th minute made the biggest early mistake. A long innocuous ball hit upfield by Siggi Held seemed to be going nowhere except out of play, when Ray Wilson inexplicably and uncharacteristically headed it straight into the path of Helmut Haller, whose tame shot was deflected off Bobby Moore and squeezed into the net between Jack Charlton and Gordon Banks. It was the first goal England had conceded in open play during the tournament, and, as Alf said later, the first error made by Ray Wilson in four years. 'I made a right bollocks,' he told me. 'I was back-pedalling and I could not get enough height on the ball to get it away. It was a poor header. I read now that the only thing the matter with Ray Wilson was that he was poor in the air. That is nonsense. I was brilliant in the air for a small man.'

On the bench, Alf's expression did not change. There were no histrionics, no scowls. In his certainty of victory, he later revealed he felt no great concern. 'I was not particularly worried when they scored their first. It was a bad goal defensively but these things do happen. It meant nothing in the fact that the Germans had not actually beaten the defence.' Alf's optimism was justified when, six minutes later, England were given a free-kick. Bobby Moore quickly took it and hit the ball into the penalty area, where Hurst, making another of his perfectly timed runs, nodded it into the corner. It was another goal made on the West Ham training ground. Alf still sat poker-faced on the sidelines. For the rest of the half, England looked increasingly dominant, mixing a short passing game in midfield with long crosses into the box. But after 45 minutes the score-line was still 1–1. In the dressing-room, Alf was as calm as ever during the interval. 'He agreed with our consensus that we should be winning,' says George Cohen. 'Alf's main concern was the mood of excessive optimism that seemed to have gripped the forwards. No doubt if a long shot had gone in, he would have been delighted, but he felt that we were giving away the ball too easily on such a sticky day. Retaining possession was one of his reigning principles.' He took Roger Hunt, who'd had a quiet game, aside for a word. As Roger Hunt recalls: 'Alf wanted to know what was going on and why I was not doing as I was told, pushing up on the German sweeper. I didn't actually blow up but I replied that I wasn't getting involved. Then Bobby Moore stepped in and said to leave it as it was.' As the players went out again, Alf gave them another word of encouragement, 'You're doing very well, but you can improve. And if you do, you will win the World Cup.'

Yet in the second half, England still struggled for a time to translate their ascendancy into goals. Only half-chances were presenting themselves. But with just 12 minutes remaining, Alan Ball, whose non-stop running was exhausting the German defence, took a corner. It reached Hurst, who fired a speculative shot from outside the penalty box. The ball spun off the boot of Horst Hottges, looped up in the air and as it fell to earth was met on the volley by Martin Peters. 2–1 to England. It seemed that England must win now. With four minutes to go, Alan Ball sent yet another superb pass through to Hunt, who raced towards goal and then laid it off for Bobby Charlton. But the great marksman scuffed it. 'Hunt's pass was too square and my shot too weak,' he said. As the hands on the clock ticked by, it did not seem to matter. England were still ahead with one minute left. Then West Germany were awarded a free-kick when Jack Charlton was deemed to have leant on Siggi Held. England for once seemed to lose their concentration, making a mess of the wall and the marking. Emmerich hit his kick into the area; it bounced around like a pinball before reaching Wolfgang Weber who side-footed it over the outstretched leg of Ray Wilson and the diving hands of Gordon Banks. 'Ray tackled fresh air, I grasped at nothing and the ball shot over both of us into the net,' recalls Banks. 2–2.

According to Harold Shepherdson's stopwatch, there were just four seconds left from the restart. After just one kick from England, referee Dienst blew his whistle. Not since 1934 had the World Cup Final entered extra time. Soaked in perspiration, their socks round their ankles, most of the England players slumped to the ground. Their morale had been broken. Bobby Charlton looked close to tears. 'We thought we'd blown it,' says Ray Wilson. Roger Hunt remembers:

> I think we were all in shock. No one could believe what had happened. There was an immediate feeling of emptiness. We thought we had it won and then it was snatched away at the death. Stamina had always been one of my strongest suits but now I felt unbelievably tired.

'It was like being pushed off Everest with just one stride to go to the top,' says Banks. As dejection, weariness and bewilderment spread through the team, the figure of Alf Ramsey could be seen striding purposely across the turf.

In the lives of most successful leaders, there is a single moment which can define the essence of their heroic stature. One statement or an action, usually made in the burning heat of crisis, can crystallize the qualities that made them triumph. For Alf Ramsey, that moment occurred at 4.50 pm on 30 July 1966, when he knew that what he said to his team could fix the destiny of the World Cup. The paradox was that Alf's chances of lifting his crestfallen players depended entirely on his ability to find the right words, yet all his life he had been fighting a running war with the English language. He was a man more renowned for his silence than his eloquence. Today, however, the fate of the great non-communicator depended on communication.

Alf reached deep inside himself. Always more confident with footballers than anyone else, he found the words. This was to be his finest hour, when the power of his speech changed the mood of his team. He was resolute, defiant, inspirational. 'Get up, get up,' he said calmly as he arrived among his bedraggled troops. As they rose to their feet and gathered round, he looked them in the eye. 'Forget it. Forget what's just happened. You've been the better team. Look at the Germans.' The team glanced over at the white-shirted figures stretched out in the other half. 'Look at them. They're finished. They've had it. They're gone. Down on the grass. Having massages. Flat on their backs. You're fitter than them. They can't live with you, not for another half hour, not through extra-time.' And then he concluded with the immortal line, 'You've won the World Cup once. Now go out and win it again.'

Alf's message transformed the atmosphere. Weariness was replaced by determination. The men had been made ready for battle once more. George Cohen says:

Perhaps we might have crumbled but for Alf. He was angry and magnificent in those spirit-dredging moments before extra-time. He was animated in a way we had never seen him before. Animated, urgent and emphatic. As he spoke, you could see little Bally's eyes shining and Nobby's redoubled determination and you could see a whole team's shoulders lifting at this confirmation of what they felt in their bones to be true.

Alf had hit exactly the right tone, banishing any lingering sign of self-pity or resignation. 'Make no mistake,' recalled Hurst, 'if the wrong thing had been said during those tense seconds, we could have lost the Cup.' Even the normally detached Bobby Moore was won over. Moore had feared that there might be a note of recrimination for conceding a last-minute goal: 'If he'd gone on about that right then, he could have killed half our team stone dead. They were gutted enough as it was. You never know absolutely and for certain how people are going to react until the really big moment comes. Alf was unbelievably good.' Alf later explained that he had deliberately suppressed his anger as he marched onto the pitch:

I was absolutely furious. I knew exactly how many chances of scoring we had missed. But I knew that I must not show my anger. I also realized that I must not indicate either by word or expression the least degree of sympathy for the team because they had to go on playing. I knew they could do it; they knew they could do it. But even a casual 'hard luck' might have put doubt in their minds.

The thirty minutes of extra-time were Alf's justification as a manager. All the months of preparation, the long, hard hours in 'Stalag Lilleshall', paid off as England comprehensively out-ran the Germans, with Alan Ball setting a wonderful example in endeavour. 'I could have run until nightfall,' he says. It was Ball, typically, who provided the England breakthrough, chasing a long ball in the 100th minute, curling a low cross into Hurst, who pulled it down, turned and then shot, the ball hitting the underside of the crossbar and then bouncing down in the region of the goal-line. After consulting the Soviet lines-man Tofik Bakhramov, the referee pointed to the centre spot, much to the Germans' angry despair. Whether Hurst's second goal should have actually been given has been debated ever since, and neither contemporary testimony nor modern technology has been able to settle the issue, though it does appear unlikely that the whole of ball crossed the line. Nevertheless, it stood. England were 3–2 ahead. Both sides were almost spent. Nobby Stiles told me of this incident with just eight minutes to go, which shows his depths of exhaustion:

> I'll never forget it. I went on an overlap with Ballie. He was the best player on the park in that last period. He plays me a ball, just level with the six-yard box, and as I went to strike it, I felt my legs go whoosh. Honest to God, I'll never forget it, I thought I'd crapped myself. And the ball trickled off my foot. Everything had gone. I had nothing left. And I heard the crowd groan. But instantly Ballie was there, shouting, 'Move you bastard, move.' Honest to God, I felt like I was running in slow motion, like when you're in a dream and your legs are made of lead.

With just seconds remaining, Bobby Moore, still composed even after 120 minutes, took the ball deep in his own half. But instead of trying to 'belt the fucking thing' into the stands, as Jack Charlton was urging, he looked up, saw Geoff Hurst near the half-way line and hit him a beautifully weighted 40-yard pass, the sort that epitomized Alf during his playing days at Spurs. Hurst ran most of the German half, chased heroically by Wolfgang Overath, and then, with his last dreg of strength, hit the ball into the top left-hand corner. It was the final kick of the match. England were emphatically the world champions. Immediately, the crowd began to chant '*Ramsey, Ramsey*'.

But the labourer's son from Dagenham remained impassive as tens of thousands of voices shouted his name. Even at the moment of Hurst's hat-trick, he had shown no sign of emotion, while all around him the England squad erupted with joy. His only words were, 'Sit down, Harold', directed at Shepherdson for obscuring his view of the goalmouth. Alf was the personification of the masculine ideal in Kipling's 'If', keeping his head while all around him were losing theirs. When Moore and his team had lifted the trophy, to an ecstatic roar from the crowd, Alf still refused to take part in the celebrations. They tried to persuade him to join in their lap of honour, but he refused, telling them, with more modesty than truth, 'This is your day. You have done this.' The journalist David Miller, in his excellent history of the summer of '66, wrote, 'It took my mind back to that spring day in 1963 when I had given him a lift back from Crystal Palace to catch his train home to Ipswich and he said self-effacingly, "It's not my team, you know, it's England's team."' George Cohen has this theory:

My own feeling was that Alf was mentally and emotionally done in. He was drained of everything he had because he had done what no one in the country believed he could. He had taken on the FA, handpicked his own players and been absolutely unswerving in his convictions. Everyone in the stadium was jumping about but he sat still, gazing into the middle distance. He had done, as one of his heroes once said, what a man had to do.

In fact, Alf was full of emotion at the moment of victory, but his extreme self-consciousness meant that he was incapable of showing it, as he later confessed: 'I realized I had to be sensible but inside I was completely drunk. I was dancing.'

There was one other member of the squad who displayed little joy: Jimmy Greaves. 'Even in this moment of triumph I felt a sickness in my stomach that I had not taken part in the match of a lifetime. It was my saddest day in football,' he later wrote. Instead of joining in the celebrations that night at the official banquet in central London, Greaves went home and got drunk. Alf told Moore that he felt Greaves had deliberately snubbed him, though Greaves said that was far from the case: 'I did not want to spoil his moment of glory by seeing the hurt in my eyes.'

Once his triumphant team had reached the dressing-room, Alf became more open. Ever the perfectionist, he lectured Bobby Charlton about giving away the ball: 'What the bloody hell do you think you were doing out there? Shooting when you should have been looking around for other people. We should have sewn it up,' he barked. As Charlton later told Ken Jones: 'You don't expect a rollicking after winning the World Cup. I mumbled something about the ball being wet, but Alf was in no mood for excuses; he never was.' Having got that off his chest, he then started to beam with pleasure and to congratulate the players fulsomely, as Geoff Hurst recalls:

He wandered about the dressing-room slapping players on the backside and grinning at them. This was a bit flamboyant for Alf, though by the time the press burst in twenty minutes later he was standing there accepting congratulations as calmly as though he'd just won third prize at a flower show.

Indeed, Alf's equanimity in front of the press that afternoon was remarkable. Four years earlier, when Ipswich had won the title, he had merely said that he felt 'fine'. On 30 July 1966, he was no more excitable in front of the microphones and cameras. When asked to describe his feelings, he replied in his usual deadpan voice: 'I don't know. The tremendous desire to win the Cup rubbed off on the players. You have this tremendous feeling of satisfaction and I thought that extra-time might prove which team was the fitter.' Then a journalist asked him, 'You are the hottest property in football. You are the man who trained the World Champions. What about your future?' Alf replied, 'I have not thought about it. And when you said that I am the hottest man in football, that is certainly true, with all these lights in front of me.' The final, perhaps most revealing, exchange went:

'Do you feel you have been misjudged, that there was any malice towards you?'

'I am not sure there was any malice. Yes, I have been furious with people but if you carry these troubles on your shoulders, you'll get a stoop. I'll always remember that after a year at Ipswich, the chairman said to me, "As a manager, you'll have to learn to grow a few extra skins." This I have done.'

But Alf was not going to let all the journalists off so lightly. As he walked out of Wembley, one of his more persistent critics, drunk with euphoria, said to him, 'Well done Alf, I always knew you would do it.' Alf fixed him with a cold glare: 'That's not what you said before the competition.'

The England squad went back to Hendon Hall to change into their formal suits. While they were there, they all drank a huge jeroboam of champagne which Alf had been given by a well-wisher. 'It was really terrific. We had a lot of laughter and fun before we piled into the coach,' he recalled. They then travelled to Royal Garden Hotel in Kensington, where the official banquet was held. London was in the mood for a gigantic party. Tens of thousands gathered round the fountains in Trafalgar or thronged the Royal Garden Hotel, while all along the route between Hendon and the West End, people cheered the England coach until they were hoarse. There had been nothing like it in the capital since VE Day. The little jig that Nobby Stiles danced at the end of the match perfectly captured the feeling of the country. Alf later gave this description of the coach trip:

> Everywhere there were people lining the pavements and waving and shouting. There were more and more and more as we neared the centre of London. One man stood in the middle of the road with his arms in the air and ran towards us until we had to stop. Then he climbed up, put his head through a window and all he could say was, 'I love you all, I love you all.' It was about fifteen minutes before we could move on. He was quite a chap. Further along, our way was barred by a car parked slap across the road like a barricade and a young girl in a very bright red mini-skirt danced on top of it. And there was a public house with about forty customers outside; everyone one of them holding up a pint mug of beer in a toast. I felt the excitement then and there is nothing quite like it.

Alf later told Nigel Clarke that out of the whole amazing day, these were the moments when he was at his happiest:

> Alf never wanted to say much in public because of his shyness. But when the public did show him affection, he was genuinely, terribly moved by it. He said to me, 'I shall never, ever forget that journey. That meant as much to me as winning the match, the fact that our team had given so much happiness. That was the thrill.'

At the Royal Garden Hotel, Alf and the players appeared with the Jules Rimet trophy to greet the acclaim of the massive crowd. That prince of political opportunists, Harold Wilson, also muscled his way into the scene. 'The government wanted to milk the situation for all it was worth, with Harold Wilson out there blowing bubbles,' says Terry Paine. For the players themselves, the banquet was something of a dampener. Not only was it packed with FA officials and their hangers-on, the 'unnecessary' type that Alf despised, but, more depressingly, their own wives were not allowed to attend and were catered for in a separate dining room. It was a cruel, class-ridden act typical of the male-dominated conservative British establishment in the mid-sixties, and one that would be unthinkable today. Understandably, the players themselves thought it was a disgrace, having seen their spouses only once in the previous six weeks – as George Cohen jokes, 'after such a long period, even Jack Charlton starts to look attractive'. It was with some relief that they left the stuffy occasion and trooped off to venues like the Playboy Club and Danny La Rue's nightclub, though Jack Charlton – whose wife Pat was at home in Leeds expecting a baby – went out on a bender with the journalist Jimmy Mossop and ended up in a stranger's house in Leytonstone.

The Playboy Club was not exactly the sort of venue that would appeal to Alf. Instead, he stayed on the Royal Garden later than his players, chatting to some of the genuine football folk that he admired. It was not until two o'clock that he arrived back at Hendon Hall, where Vickie was waiting for him – she had gone there straight from Wembley. It was almost the first time he had seen her in two months. He and Vickie sat up talking and drinking for two more hours, and did not finally get to bed until about four. As he later revealed, Alf was not the automaton he was often portrayed as: 'We could not stop talking. I don't know what I thought as I lay in bed that night. I know I didn't sleep much. I can't remember my thoughts – they were just a jumble. I kept wondering if it were really true and if we really had done it.'

It was no dream. The next day Alf and Vickie, accompanied

by Tanya, were the guests at a celebratory lunch organized by television company ATV at Elstree, at which the Jules Rimet trophy stood proudly in front of the top table. The rest of the England team attended and after the meal was over, Bobby Moore, all past differences forgotten, proposed a toast 'to the greatest manager in the World'. Alf looked suitably embarrassed. Later that afternoon he returned with Vickie to their modest house in Ipswich. As he arrived home, he was overwhelmed by total exhaustion. Having held himself together for so long under such remorseless pressure, he was unable to face the world. For seven days he cloistered himself with Vickie:

We put the telephone in a little room where it was difficult to hear it and we determined that we wouldn't answer it for a week. We probably lost a lot of calls we would have liked but it couldn't be helped. It was the only way we could get any peace. We could hear a faint buzz all day every day and there was a television team camped outside the door for 48 hours but we didn't want to see anyone. We opened letters and enjoyed reading them together and answering them. When there wasn't anybody about we went out. It wasn't too difficult.

It was typical of Alf that he should retreat into seclusion after masterminding the greatest triumph in the history of British sport. But one footballer, Peter Osgood, who was to play for England in the next World Cup, had this prophetic insight: 'I remember thinking as I watched Alf's amazing self-restraint during the celebrations after the game, "Enjoy it, Alf, because it doesn't get any better than this."'

# ELEVEN

## *Florence*

Two incidents that took place on the Sunday after the World
Cup Final illustrate the contradictions of Alf's character. The
first occurred just before the ATV lunch at Elstree, when Alf
arrived with Vickie and Tanya. As Alf walked towards the
studios, he was approached by three journalists: Ken Jones of
the *Daily Mirror*, Brian James of the *Daily Mail* and Clive
Toye of the *Daily Express*. This trio had been Alf's most loyal
advocates in the press over the previous three years. When all
the rest were sneering at his promise to win the World Cup,
they were defending him. They had understood, far better than
anyone else in the media, what Alf was trying to achieve. So,
not without some justification, they believed that Alf might
reciprocate their support. Ken Jones was the first to speak,

'Well done, Alf. We were wondering if we could ask you a
few questions?'

Alf's reply was perverse in the extreme, given that he was
dealing with his three most loyal voices in the press: 'Sorry,
it's my day off, and I've been working for nine weeks.'

Jones pointed out that they had been working just as hard.
Vickie, standing nearby, rolled her eyes, a gesture that seemed
to make Alf relent.

'All right, just a few minutes then.'

Later that day, Alf, Vickie, the players and their wives were taken to a small theatre at Elstree to watch a Pathé news film of the World Cup Final. The team, of course, were engrossed in the footage, reliving England's glory, but Kay Stiles, wife of Nobby, saw a discreet gesture from Alf which showed him at his most chivalrous:

> Kay noticed that early in the running of the film, Alf got up and went to the elderly lady usherette who had shown us all to our seats. She was standing to one side. All the seats had been taken. Alf took her by the hand and led her to his seat. He watched the rest of the film standing up.

The quality that helped him become such a great manager, his rare combination of passion and detachment, could also make him appear contradictory. Alf could either be graceless or charming, well-mannered or hostile, depending on his mood and the situation. During England's visit to New York in 1964, before the Little World Cup, the team was staying in the Waldorf Hotel and the US team boss Joe Barriskill was waiting to be introduced to him. After he had sat there for 20 minutes, Alf appeared. But he barely acknowledged Barriskill, sweeping past him with the single phrase, 'Hot, ain't it?' On the other hand, Alf's former tailor in Ipswich, Peter Little, tells this story which illustrates Alf's courtesy and modesty, even after he had won the World Cup. 'I came back from lunch one day to my premises to find two men on the landing, both of them wanting fittings. One was Sir Alf. The other was a young man for whom I was going to make a wedding suit. I went up the stairs and said, "Oh gentlemen, I am very sorry for keeping you waiting there."

"That's quite all right. We have not been here very long," said Sir Alf. So I unlocked the doors to my office. But I was in a terrible dilemma, wondering which of them should go first. So I decided to let them decide.

"Gentlemen, to whom should I give the first fitting?"

The young man said, "Sir Alf Ramsey was here before me."

Alf said, "I have finished my work for the day. No doubt you have to get back to yours. You should have the first fitting."

Boy did that stick in my mind. Sir Alf Ramsey waited in my foyer while the young man was fitted. How many others would have done that? But Sir Alf was that sort of man. I said to him afterwards, "That was very nice of you."

"It was absolutely fine."'

The journalist Brian Glanville, who was never a Ramsey enthusiast, was working in Italy in 1962, soon after Alf had been appointed England manager. Through his work there, he had grown close to Gerry Hitchens, the former Aston Villa centre-forward who was playing for Inter Milan and had recently appeared for England in the 1962 World Cup. When Ipswich were playing AC Milan in the European Cup, Hitchens went with Glanville to see the game, partly because he wanted to remind the new national boss of his presence.

'Must say hallo to Alf and wish good luck to the lads,' he told Glanville. So Hitchens went down to the Ipswich dressing-room.

'Hallo, Alf.'

'Oh yes,' said Alf condescendingly. 'You're playin' in these parts.'

As Glanville recorded: 'Gerry couldn't get over it. He sat beside me during the match in which, under teeming rain, Ipswich were thrashed 4–0, muttering, "Prat! Prat! Playin' in these parts." He never played for England again.' Stan Cullis, the iron manager of the great Wolves side of the fifties, also complained that Alf could appear witheringly condescending.

'One has the feeling when talking to him that he is a brilliant mathematics professor explaining a mundane problem to one of his duller pupils.'

Once more, however, England youth coach Wilf McGuinness and Neil Phillips, England's doctor after 1966, tell of a very different side of Alf during the World Cup. After Lilleshall, Phillips and McGuinness had gone back to their respective jobs, as a Middlesbrough GP and an Old Trafford trainer respectively. But just after the semi-final, they were both surprised to receive a call from Alf, fulfilling his promise made at Lilleshall to ask them down to Wembley for the Final. 'With everything else that was going on,' says Neil Phillips, 'for him to remember that he told Wilf and I four weeks previously that we would be invited down to Wembley was unbelievable.' Today McGuinness confesses:

I worship Alf. I found him such a thoughtful man, especially what he did for me in the World Cup. He phoned me up and asked me and my wife to come down for the final. My job was to look after the players' wives and on the Friday night we all went off to see the West End musical *Charlie's Girl* with Joe Brown – it was bloody awful. But Alf insisted I be with the players, have breakfast with them on the Saturday and come into the dressing-room after the game. Alf was much warmer than his public image. I found him very caring about the people who worked for him.

Alf could be sensitive, as when Gordon Banks' father died during an England trip to South America in 1969 and Alf made the arrangements for Gordon to fly home for the funeral. 'Alf was very understanding. He offered me comfort and condolence. He was a fabulous guy.' When Alan Ball was sent off against Poland in Katowice, Alf showed him nothing but sympathy. 'He sat up half the night with me. He realized how distraught I was. He just knocked on the door and he was there. He knew how I felt and he did something to ease it. A marvellous man.' But even with footballers he knew well, he could be hurtful, as Eddie Baily, his old colleague from Spurs, recalls:

I did not see Alf for a period of time until he won the World Cup. At one stage I was in a restaurant at Wembley and Alf came through. I was rather disappointed in him that day because he never came up to me and said, 'How are you going?' I would not say that he ignored me but he gave me nothing more than a nod. He had been my mate for years at Spurs. I think he was carried away by whatever was going on around him and he had a different group of people with him. Years passed, and I would excuse it, but I must admit I was a bit disappointed in him that day.

At Ipswich he could be caring on one occasion, distant the next. When the club held a dinner at the Savoy Hotel in London to celebrate winning the League, Alf insisted that all the staff be invited, including the youth players and even two old-age pensioners who swept the ground. 'I don't care that other clubs only invite the players. Everyone's coming to our dinner. If they don't, then I won't go,' he announced. Yet Pat Godbold, the manager's secretary, has this memory of Alf's unsociable side:

Jackie Milburn had taken over as manager and was talking to one of our staff, Freddie Blake, when Alf drove into the ground. 'Look, there's Alf, he'll probably come over and talk to the boys.'
　　'He won't, you know,' said Freddie.

And Alf didn't.

Geoff Hurst left this description of Alf's behaviour at Lilleshall:

> His attitude to visitors was curious. People in football, managers, coaches and some journalists, were greeted in a friendly enough manner. Alf would soon be sitting down with them talking about the game, nothing else. But the others, the officials, the foreigners, the people outside the game, would be greeted with very correct respect, dealt with efficiently and politely, then edged smilingly on their way. I doubt whether they would have been made to feel like long lost brothers exactly.

It was the press who probably felt most keenly his enigmatic, contradictory nature. As Mike Langley of the *Sun* put it: 'He is rude and polite. He is uncommunicative and a great talker. He's deep and straightforward. He's aloof and friendly. He's relentless and relaxed.' His natural suspicion was tempered by good – if fluctuating – personal relations with several leading journalists. Ken Jones, who was at the receiving end of his rudeness at ATV, gave me several examples of Alf's personal kindness:

> In the summer of 1973, the England team were making two trips to Eastern Europe, first to Czechoslovakia and then to Poland and Russia. We had only been back a day in Czechoslovakia when my father died. So I obviously cancelled the trip to Poland and I flew out to Moscow after the funeral. It was a sunny day and I was sitting on the steps of the hotel in Moscow. Alf came up to me:
> 'I was very sorry to hear about your father.'

He was very comforting, sympathetic, though he had so much else on his mind. On another occasion, my oldest daughter Lesley was desperately ill with a burst appendix and peritonitis, and the doctors feared that she might not live. I was due to take a trip to Madrid with England at the time but I had to cancel that. And Lesley came through the crisis when she responded to penicillin. My wife suggested that I go to Madrid to take my mind off it. So I flew to Madrid and got to the hotel just before the England team were leaving for the ground. I saw Alf in the courtyard of the hotel and he gestured to me to come over:

'Why are you here?'

'I've come to see the game.'

'You should be at home. There are more important things in life than football.'

It turned into a sort of mild bollocking. But that is the sort of caring person he could be, unlike so many other managers, who just live in their own hermetically sealed world.

Brian James was another who saw the friendlier side of Alf most of the time:

He was always a mixture of shyness and self-confidence. He never enjoyed being in the public eye but I rarely found him unco-operative. I could not understand why people were always complaining about how horrible he was. Like in the 1970 World Cup, he allowed a British press team to play against England, though I made one of the biggest mistakes of my life when I shouted, 'Don't worry about fuckin' Hurstie, I've got him,' just as Bobby Moore passed Geoff the ball. Geoff went straight through me and it took about twenty minutes to re-assemble the pieces. So Alf was not difficult there. I got quite close to him in the 1974 World Cup, after his sacking, when we were both staying in the same hotel on the outskirts of Frankfurt. We used to have breakfast together and he was always very polite. He was reasonable company, never a bundle of laughs but always interesting about football. He had an amazing knowledge of the world game and could give insights into almost every player in the tournament.

But James could also find him exasperating, writing in the *Mail* in 1973 after a difficult tour of Europe:

The writers do not know what he is trying to achieve with his teams for he seldom theorises and never explains. Equally, he is so absorbed in his own function that he simply does not pretend to comprehend the pressmen's pre-occupation with deadlines, communications or their nagging necessity to have something fresh to write about every day.

Brian Glanville of the *Sunday Times* once saw a playful side of Ramsey:

I recall sitting in a railway compartment with him and several other reporters. 'I don't know why you telephone me,' he said and went round the carriage. 'I never telephone you, I never telephone you, I never telephone you' – till it came to myself – 'you never telephone *me*!'

When he was a starting out as a journalist with the *Daily Mail*, Jeff Powell had this exchange with Alf outside Hendon Hall during the 1966 World Cup.

Alf was quite fun to have around. You could have your jousts with him but you had to be prepared to give as good as you got. The first time I spoke to him was after Bobby Moore had hinted to me that there might be a slight fitness problem with Bobby Charlton. So just as the players were boarding the team bus, I went up to him.

'Mr Ramsey?'

'Yes.'

'I'm Jeff Powell from the *Daily Mail*. I wonder if I could have a minute.' Alf looked at his watch.

'It's now down to 50 seconds.'

'There is a thought that Bobby Charlton might be injured.'

'Is there? I never discuss the injuries or personal situations of my players. We are now going to the cinema.' And off the bus went.

Yet, because of his defensiveness, Alf's career was littered with less friendly altercations. Alf himself admitted, when he had long been in retirement: 'I probably did not do too well with the media. I made a lot of enemies, although it may well be that some of them were intentional. But if I had my life over again I think I might do better in that department.' Once, during a row with Eric Cooper, the *Daily Express*'s 'Voice of the North', Alf stood up from his seat, started to take off his jacket and invited Cooper to step outside. Cooper declined the offer. In January 1966, Alf travelled to London to give a television interview about the draw for the World Cup. The TV company sent a representative to meet him at Liverpool Street Station and take him to the studio. As Alf came down the platform from his train, the young man went anxiously up to him.

'Excuse me, are you Alf Ramsey?

'What's that got to do with you?'

The *Guardian* and *Sunday Telegraph* writer John Moynihan was travelling to Sheffield by train to watch Wednesday play Everton, a game in which the Everton winger Derek Temple, on the verge on England honours, was likely to be prominent. Moynihan entered the restaurant car and was surprised to find that Alf was the only other guest:

As the landscape turned into the industrial tattoo of the north, Ramsey gazed out of the window at the fields and factories, giving the waiter a slightly embarrassed smile when he was recognized. I asked Mr Ramsey if it was indeed Temple he was going to see. He looked up at me as if I was mad. The coffee cups tinkled and tried to sprint across his table. He looked just as edgy. 'Could be,' he said in a slightly refined tone. 'Now, if you'll excuse me.' He rose and walked away towards his compartment. 'That's Alf Ramsey,' said the dining-car attendant. 'I know,' I said.

Elsewhere, Moynihan wrote that Alf's 'cold, withdrawn expression, as impersonal and mysterious and vaguely hostile as a duty officer marching up to inspect a fire piquet, hides a burning fanaticism and surely a trace of anxiety'.

While England were winning in the sixties, Alf's relations with the press were largely an irrelevance to his position. Results gave him a wall of protection. But once the tide turned in 1970, he grew more vulnerable to criticism and hence even more hostile. A classic example of this prickliness occurred at the press conference on his return from the Mexico World Cup, when he was asked about his dealings with the media. Visibly angry, his nostrils flaring, he spat out his words:

Have I been rude to you at press conferences? Can anyone turn round and say to me that I have been rude to them?

Tell me what approach has been made. It seems to me that I am told I am rude, yet I am treated with rudeness. They stick their faces in front of me. They stick these microphones in front of me, yet I am being rude. I don't think there has ever been a word invented to describe some of the mannerisms I have been confronted with. Yet I am rude.

Little wonder that Bobby Charlton, one of Alf's greatest admirers, described his public relations as 'pretty diabolical'.

Because of his xenophobia, Alf could be even colder with foreign journalists. During an England tour of Latin America in 1969, Alf was at a party in Montevideo, when he was introduced by a British reporter to a cultivated Brazilian writer.

'You know Jose Werneck, Alf, don't you?'

'Yes, he's a pest.'

It was remarks like that which led the *Sunday Times* to comment that 'on his travels, the England manager is liable to seem more like Alf Garnett than Alf Ramsey,' drawing a parallel between Alf and the notorious cockney bigot created by the TV writer Johnny Speight.

It was Bryon Butler, one of the most respected journalists in British football, who said that 'at best Alf could tolerate journalists, at worst he would cut them off at the knees'. But Butler believed that this attitude was born out of an underlying shyness. Rob Hughes of the *Sunday Times* has this analysis:

He frightened the life out of me. He answered my questions but he had no warmth at all. The wall between him and us was almost unbreachable. It would be almost impossible for him to do the job today, trying to shut the door on the whole media. Before he was ill, a foreign journalist had to do a story for his paper. I said to him, 'I'll tell you where

Alf lives in Ipswich, but that is the furthest you'll get.' So he went along, knocked on the door, spoke to Lady Ramsey, who invited him in, spent three hours with him, showed him some scrapbooks. And just as he was leaving, he heard a sound in another room. He realized that Alf was there and he said, 'Can I speak to him?'

'No, no, he's far too shy with foreigners.'

So he never got the interview. He only got the ambience of the home and place, and this delightful woman, and there was Alf in the back room, presumably with his ear pressed against the door. He was a man of his time. Not one player ever complains about being mistreated by Alf. It is the press who complain.

Part of the reason for this contradiction was that Alf's instinctive diffidence was combined with his overwhelming devotion to football. He had such strongly held feelings about the game, such deeply fixed ideas, that he could not tolerate what he regarded as sloppy or ill-conceived opinions, especially from those who had never played international or professional football. At such moments, his politeness came into conflict with his intensity. Hugh McIlvanney has a good illustration of this:

Alf liked a drink and he could get quite bitter when he was arguing about football. He liked to go to war. He was always utterly convinced of his case – and with good reason: he was a great manager in any sense. My biggest row with him was after a Sportsman of the Year lunch in Fleet Street and Alf was about to get a train back to Ipswich. I knew Alf was seething with me about something I had written criticizing his relationship with the press. I disliked the way Alf picked and chose who he'd talk to, though they all do that; I mean Bobby Robson was always with Bob Harris, a great big blunderbuss of a man. So this time I knew Alf had been saving up for this row. He was getting very worked up and said:

'How many caps did you ever win?'

'Alf, I was never within light years of a cap. No one respects experience more than I do – but experience is only relevant in relation to the intelligence which is exposed to the experience. If you send a turnip round the world, it will still come back a fucking turnip, not an expert in geography.'

'Words, words, words.'

'Alf, you'll find that they are very handy if you want to say something.'

That was about as bitter as it got. It was sharp, but did not become anything silly.

Another problem was his insecurity. He had diligently constructed an outward image, with refined voice and immaculate appearance, to protect himself. But when he felt that his armour of civility was being punctured by a well-educated journalist or FA official, he would react with brusqueness. He was always more relaxed with footballers because he felt no social threat from them. This is why Alf remained such an intensely private man, happy only in management or domesticity or the provinciality of Ipswich. Venturing beyond these confines brought risks to his self-esteem. Early in his England career, he and Vickie considered buying a house in London nearer Lancaster Gate, but he eventually rejected the idea, fearing he would always be ill-at-ease in the more sophisticated atmosphere of the capital. At heart, for all his polished veneer, he was still the rural Dagenham lad. 'I can't accept that people on newspapers, on radio and on TV have the right to criticise me as a private person,' he said in 1970. 'I value privacy enormously and it is fortunate that I can go virtually un-molested in Ipswich, where we have been living for the last fifteen years. I am accepted there. I can walk out in the street without anyone worrying me. They are used to me.' To further protect his privacy, Alf put his phone number ex-directory and grew a high hedge at the front of his Ipswich semi-detached house. 'Occasionally we see coaches stop outside our house and go slowly past the windows. We get a lot of people peer-ing in, but it doesn't worry us because they don't see us anyway.'

World Cup glory did not bring the slightest alternation in Alf's character. He relished victory for its own sake, not for any kudos it brought him. 'In football, he's obviously changed, because from a player to a manager the responsibility is so much greater. But personally and around the home, no, he has not changed at all,' said Vickie in 1969. Luxuries were of no interest to him. The FA awarded him a bonus of £6,000 for winning the World Cup, and he used the money to pay off the mortgage on their house in Valley Road, though he also had to pay a crippling tax bill of £3,350 on the sum, which would have done nothing to undermine his innate conservatism. Away from football, he and Vickie led a very quiet existence, partly because he had few interests outside sport and the idea of a hectic social life repelled him. He revealed in an interview in 1967:

I always make a point of being home on Sunday. I am away so much that I feel that my wife should be able to rely on me being home for one day a week; this is the least I can do. When I am there we don't do anything very much. She is fond of gardening and I am not; but I like to see a garden tidy. We potter about together.

During the week, unless he was involved in a match, Alf would generally commute back to Ipswich in the early evening. 'The best part of the day is the first half-hour when I get home. Then we have a drink, generally a glass of sherry, and we sit in armchairs and talk.' Inevitably, football was usually the subject. 'My wife knew nothing about football when we first met but she takes a tremendous interest in it and now she has certainly more knowledge than the average fan,' he said in 1967. Like many shy people, Alf found it easier to demonstrate affection for his dog than for most humans. His beloved pet was a little dachshund called Rusty, which he took for long walks around Ipswich and the local golf club. 'I didn't like dogs before we had him, but he's a lovely little fellow. He hasn't a bad thought in him,' he told the *Dagenham Post* in 1971. Alf's fondness for Rusty meant that his favourite newspaper was the *Daily Mail*, because of the Fred Bassett cartoons.

When he and Vickie went on holiday in the summer, it was generally to Majorca or Kyrenia in Cypus. Alan Odell, who was in charge of the International Section at the FA, remembers Alf's fondness for the latter resort:

On Alf's recommendation, my wife and I used to go to Kyrenia. The first time we went, our holiday overlapped with Alf's and we shared some evening meals together. He and Vickie went there a lot because it was quiet and peaceful and not many people knew who he was, which is what he liked. He hated to be hounded by the press or the public. He did not enjoy the trappings of fame at all.

In London, he would occasionally go to a good restaurant, though usually for the purposes of work. Ken Jones recalls:

When he had a tie-up with the *Sunday Mirror* I would take him out to lunch at the Eccentric Club in St James. Some of the members were extremely eccentric but Alf liked it because the members would not bother him; he would not be pestered. He never had any small talk. It was always football. I never heard him express a political view. Over lunch, he liked a gin and tonic and some wine. He loved a glass of port. He was always immaculately turned out: waistcoat or three-piece suit, shiny shoes. He was always very proper. I'll never forget the time we were coming out of the Eccentric Club one day and a very smartly dressed man with a walking stick shuffled up to him.

'I say, it's Ramsey, isn't it?'

'Yes it is.'

'Ramsey, I saw you play in the 1927 FA Cup Final. Good luck to you, sir.'

The receipt of a knighthood in the New Year's Honours in 1967 did not change Alf either. A genuinely unassuming man, he debated with Vickie for some days as to whether to accept it. But eventually, he decided to accept, convincing himself that it was an honour for the whole of the game. Besides, it was not very likely that Alf Ramsey, the conservative patriot, would turn down the Queen. Alf was only the second professional England footballer in history to be knighted, after Stanley Matthews in 1965. 'I shall clobber the first player who calls me Sir Alfred on a football pitch. I accepted this honour because the fact that somebody else in the game is now a "Sir" should lift the whole of football a little bit,' he said. For his visit to the Palace, Alf was determined that he should adopt absolutely the correct morning attire, so he went to his tailor Peter Little for advice. Little then approached Moss Bros and the official trade organization Tailor and Cutter, and they both came back with the same written instructions as to what Alf should wear. As Little recalls:

> They wrote to say that although Sir Alf might feel he was not dressed properly, this in fact was true sartorial correctness. What Alf wore were the usual striped trousers and black tail jacket, but two things were different: first, a black waistcoat, not a silver one, and second, a black silk hat not a grey one. We had to practise a few times with the top hat – it had to be worn exactly the right way, not at a jaunty angle. At the final fitting, just before he left for the Palace, he said to me, 'You know that letter from Moss Bros. Can I have it for my top pocket, so I can touch it when I get there and see all the others dressed differently? I can tap it and think I am dressed properly.' That is the way Alf was. He wanted everything done correctly. And the day went off perfectly. All the headlines said he was 'immaculate'.

Peter Little, a gold-medal winning tailor, has several other interesting memories of Alf, including details of his dimensions:

> I made suits for him for about ten years. Alf had a difficult figure. He was powerful on top, a big-square-shouldered man with a great chest and big chunky legs. I still have his measurements from the mid-sixties: 42-inch chest, 37-waist and 44-inch hips. The thing about Alf was that he liked turn-ups on his trousers, though I tried to persuade him not to have them. When he asked why, I explained to him, 'Because you have not got very long legs, and our height is really determined by the length of our legs. So if you have turn-ups it tends to give an illusion of a shorter leg.' He also liked a centre-vent in the back of his suit. I told him that this was quite old-fashioned, more in keeping with a sports

jacket or an old hacking jacket. But that's what he wanted. I would have said he was a shy man, but he was such a gentleman he commanded automatic respect. I never had to tell Alf anything. There are some people who don't know how to wear clothes. Alf was not one of them. He was wonderful to work with. He relied on me in the sense that if I said, 'Shall we take a quarter of an inch off the sleeves,' he would just say, 'If you're happy, then I'm happy.' I did not have many clients like that. Others were far more demanding. Some of our fittings would take about half an hour and we would have a chat – usually about football. He was very good with my two boys if they came into the workshop, signing autographs and such. He gave them one of his World Cup badges. This man, Alf Ramsey, he was my hero, I just loved him so much.

For a knight of the realm and a World Cup winner, the depth of Alf's modesty was astonishing. He never put on any airs, never revelled in his position. On Wednesday afternoons he regularly visited his elderly mother Florence, who continued to live in Parrish Cottages in Halbutt Street after the death of Alf's father in January 1966. Like her son, Mrs Ramsey guarded her privacy even after his success. Maintaining her frugal lifestyle, she shunned the limelight, and never gave interviews or attended football functions. One neighbour of Alf's from Dagenham, Joyce Rushbrook, remembers: 'I worked in a clothes shop near Halbutt Street and would see Alf most Wednesday afternoons as he waited for the bus to go back to the railway station. He would stand there, in his fawn raincoat, and he always looked quiet, respectful. You would not have known how famous he was.' Ken Jones recalls that Alf was not too proud to get his hands dirty:

I was giving him a lift back from Manchester Airport when I got a flat tyre. That did not faze Alf at all. We got out, he jacked up the car and changed the wheel at the side of the road. That is not something you could imagine Alf doing but he thought nothing of it. That's the way he was, very modest.

Alf's own office at Lancaster Gate reflected his asceticism. It was a small, bare-walled room, without a single cup, souvenir or photograph. Apart from a desk and a chair, all it contained were some newspapers and back copies of FIFA reports.

Alf may have frequently clashed with journalists and officials, with whom he felt under constant scrutiny, but his own staff within the FA testify to his essential decency. Margaret Fuljames, née Bruce, was his secretary for many years at Lancaster Gate, earning just £11 a week when she started in 1967:

I worked directly with Alf, doing all his correspondence and paperwork. He was brilliant to work for, absolutely brilliant. He was lovely. I cannot tell you how nice he was. He was reserved, quite old-fashioned, but ever so thoughtful. He would come in, sit down and have a little chat with me. When the team was abroad, he would send me a postcard. When I was getting married, he gave me a cheque as a wedding present, which I thought was brilliant. He answered every single piece of correspondence, unlike dear old Joe Mercer, who came in afterwards and would just glance at some of them and say, 'Oh, bin those.' Alf sometimes dictated letters, but would more usually handwrite them out. I have to say that his handwriting was not very easy to read. He was well-organized. I never knew him to miss an appointment. You always knew where you were with Alf because he was so calm, whatever he was doing. People were in awe of him but he was really very modest. My brother once saw him at a restaurant in Liverpool Street. So, after a little hesitation, he went in and spoke to Alf, explaining that I was his sister. And he later told me that Alf was really nice and polite. But Alf was a very strong man. If he did not like someone, he would leave no doubt in your mind about it.

David Barber, now the FA's chief historian, with over 100 book titles to his credit, started work as an £8.60-a-week clerk in the FA's international section in 1970. At the time the FA was still a slim-line operation, with only around 30 staff, compared with 250 today. Barber recalls:

Alf used to come in Monday to Thursday by train from Ipswich, getting the tube from Liverpool Street to Lancaster Gate. He would arrive about ten and I would make his tea, which he always had in a pale green cup. He would then read all the papers. We would get the regional ones as well so Alf could check on the scores and see who was doing well. Right from the start, I was not in the slightest bit overawed by him. He was very down to earth. He was the most famous man in football at the time, but he treated me like a colleague, not an office boy. He was uncomfortable with the press and FA Council members, but with people like me, who worked with him on a daily basis, he could not have been more friendly. He was well-organized but he was not a paperwork sort of person. The only piece of paper I ever actually saw written by Alf would be the squad, which he would handwrite out in pencil and then give to us so we could officially inform the press by letter. One thing I remember about him was that he walked very slowly. I always thought he looked a bit like Jack Benny who walked serenely across the stage. There was an air of grandeur about it.

David Barber's immediate boss, the man in charge of the International Section, was Alan Odell:

I always equated my role to that of a secretary at a football club, with my club the England team. Alf was obviously responsible for picking the team and training, while I was responsible for the administration: the hotel bookings, flights, liaison with the other associations and so on. It was more difficult in those days before modern communications, especially dealing with the Eastern Bloc countries, who could take weeks or even months to respond to a letter or cablegram. From 1969, I travelled with Alf all the time. The FA was not flush with money, so we always went by scheduled flights, never by charter. He was very meticulous and a good organizer, though I would not have said that he was demanding. He just told us what he wanted and we got on with it. He was always very appreciative. He would say thank you to everyone for anything they had done. He was well-liked in the FA offices, though he was not a big mixer. I would say that he did not make friends easily. Anyone he met, he initially treated with a bit of reserve or suspicion. On away trips, the FA staff would share a table with Alf. He enjoyed a drop of wine or a glass of brandy. Football was the great passion of his life. I don't think he was interested in anything else apart from that and his family. I never heard him say anything about current affairs, though there was so much happening at the time: strikes, Northern Ireland, the Vietnam War. He certainly could swear. He had quite a good turn of phrase and would sometimes fly back into Dagenham talk. He was not a good public speaker, mainly because he detested the press, apart from one or two journalists, like Ken Jones.

Alf's problem at the FA was not with the staff but with the councillors, whom he treated with disdain. Alan Odell says:

He felt that most of the Council were a bit of a waste of space. He did not have much time for them and did not think much of their knowledge about football. And I supposed they resented the way he had taken away their power.

David Barber thinks that much of Alf's attitude was justified, given the incompetence and irresponsibility of many of the FA's leading figures. 'We used to send out the agenda for the international committee meetings and once Maggie Bruce accidentally stapled a copy of a *Woman's Own* article to the papers of Len Shipman, the Leicester City Chairman. He did not even notice. We called J.W. Bowers 'Jumping Jack'. I once had to spend the night in his flat in Wanstead because he got so drunk at an amateur game at Vicarage Road that I had to take him home in a taxi. Dick Wragg was a terrible scrounger. Very jolly, friendly, but always going to banquets and receptions where he could get pally with foreign dignitaries. Denis Follows, the Secretary of the FA, was known as Big D. He was a throwback to an earlier age. He was like a schoolmaster and we were his pupils.

In fact, the FA's contempt for its staff was reflected, not just in the dismal rates of pay, but also in other offensive gestures. Neil Phillips, the England doctor, is scathing about the attitudes that prevailed:

Even after 1966 we were treated as upstarts who did not know anything. Alf's relationship with Denis Follows was awful from the start. There was so much petty jealousy in the FA. The conflict went on all the time and it was just ridiculous. It stemmed from the central problem that Alf had been used to running the whole show at Ipswich but then found at the FA that lots of things were being kept from him. And Denis Follows took great delight in keeping it that way. To give you one indication of what was wrong, several months after we had won the World Cup, Alf, Les, Harold and myself were in the bowels of the FA putting away some England kit. Alf pointed to some blue, gold-crested boxes on the shelves and then, moments later, Denis Follows came in.

'Denis, what's in those blue boxes?' he asked.

'Oh, those are the table mats we had made for the World Cup.'

'What table mats? I didn't know there were any table mats.'

'Oh yes, Alf. We had aerial photographs taken of all the World Cup grounds in England and then we had them made into table mats. And we had drink coasters made as well to match them. In each box, there are eight place settings.'

'Can I see a box?'

'Yes, of course.'

So Denis got down a box. And inside there were these absolutely magnificent colour photographs sealed into the mats. They were superb. There must have been more than a hundred of these boxes on the shelves. So Alf said,

'Could you give each member of my staff a set?'

'Oh no, Alf, you and your staff don't qualify. These mats are only for the directors of the Football Association and visiting dignitaries. You can't have any.'

That was that.

Remarkably, Dr Neil Phillips was not even paid a penny by the FA for his work as team doctor. During the 1970 World Cup, he had to take unpaid leave to join the England team in Mexico. He got £2 a day in expenses, so his 42 days brought in £84. But he also had to employ a locum in his practice, for which the FA promised to pay the wages but failed to do so promptly:

> In the fourth week out in Mexico, my wife rang me up and said, 'We have a problem. I have paid out four weeks' salary to the locum but I have not received anything yet from the FA, even though I have sent them the receipts.' So I had to ring up the FA to make sure my wife was not destitute while I was away.

Phillips reveals that Alf, towards the end of his reign, grew fed up with this absurd, unpaid situation and approached the FA Chairman, Andrew Stephen, demanding a change:

> On an England tour in 1973, I saw Alf and Andrew Stephen huddled in a corner. Alf beckoned me to go and join them.
> 'Neil, Alf has been telling me he thinks you should get a salary for the England team job.'
> 'Yes, that's right, I've discussed it with Alf.'
> 'But Neil, even if we paid you £30,000 a year, you could not do a better job than you are doing now. So why should we pay you?'
> There's no answer to that.

And Phillips never did receive a salary until he left the job in disillusion when Revie took over.

The FA's bizarre attitude to money was further demonstrated by the fact it made a profit of over £3 million from the

1966 World Cup, yet handed over most of this to the Treasury. There was a bonus of just £22,000 for the 22-strong squad, which the players decided to split evenly, ending up with just £1,000 a man, a sum further eroded by the 80 per cent super-tax rate. 'I told my father I was never going to vote Labour again,' says Alan Ball.

It is little wonder that Alf, with all his insecurities, felt no affinity with the FA's rulers. And he could make his annoyance explicit when he wanted. After Alan Mullery was sent off during a pre-World Cup tour in Mexico in 1969, three FA councillors had a meeting with Alf and one of them, Sid Collings, asked if he might have a report on the incident in writing. Alf blithely said, 'No' and then, looking over at Denis Follows, continued: 'He's the secretary. He can deal with your report.' Francis Lee, the Manchester City striker, recalls that that

> one thing Alf liked was putting the FA in their place, if he got the chance. The blazer brigade used to come into the dressing-room before the game. When I made my debut against Bulgaria in 1968, I was Number 7 and Nobby Stiles was Number 6. Nobby had just put his boots on and gone to the toilet. And this guy from the FA came in, looked at the programme and said, 'Who's 6?' This was about Nobby, a World Cup winner. Alf would say, 'Right, gentlemen, hurry up please, thank you.' He had no time for them.

Ken Jones, who witnessed some of Alf's behaviour with the FA, says: 'At times I thought Alf was deliberately provocative. Some of it was unnecessary. He made it obvious that he did not think the FA councillors made any useful contribution.'

Nor did Alf take any interest in wider FA issues beyond the immediate needs of the England team. Unlike Winterbottom, he played no role in development, as Allen Wade, the English director of coaching at the time, who had also been appointed to his job in October 1962, recalls:

> He was always courteous but I was never made to feel that he was keen to share his thoughts. Alf never once asked me about the work I was doing. He never showed any inclination to speak at our courses. He wasn't interested in coaching as such, just playing ideas. He was keen to find out how the game was developing in other countries and he had this trick of putting a provocative question so that he could count on an objective response. And if Alf had his teeth into something, he could be brusque to the point of rudeness, if anybody intruded upon the conversation.

Wade was once surprised, however, that on one of their few lunches together in London, Alf – 'in that clipped way of his' – expressed his anger at the lack of professionalism among many of the players touted by the press as potential internationals. 'It bothered him that some of those who were up to standard had a poor attitude. It was beyond Alf's comprehension that a footballer could not be relied on to give every last drop of sweat for his country.'

Alf's self-containment, allied to his enormous self-confidence in football matters, meant that he bristled at any interference with the England team. But it also meant that he could easily cope with the pressure of making decisions. Without any army of hangers-on, he felt no need to consult widely. Selection and tactics were entirely in his hands. He once gave this insight into the way he worked:

> There is this feeling of loneliness about my job. It's not like being a club manager at all. There, you have regular

matches. In my case, there are frequent lulls. I pick England teams on the basis of what I see in many matches. It isn't a hurried or last minute choice. Headlines don't influence me at all. I do it myself and have no hesitation in dropping a player if I feel it has to be done.

In another interview, with Brian James in 1965, Alf explained:

Sometimes the team comes quickly, sometimes it takes days. I make a lot of decisions on the train from my home in Ipswich. I don't talk my teams over with anyone. I just think the problems out myself. I have grave doubts, of course. Grave doubts. I make mistakes and I know it. But often thinking back on what I am sure has been a mistake, I know that I would have to do the same thing again.

It is one thing to reach the summit; it is another to stay there. As he had shown at Ipswich, Alf was always better at building a winning team than maintaining its championship status. Indeed, soon after 1966, Alf, reflecting on his future, said, 'It would be rather fun to build up from scratch like I built Ipswich and England.' But there was no chance that Alf would give up the job he loved by going into club football again. Besides, he wanted to prove that England under his leadership were the best team in the world, wherever they played. 'There is another World Cup in four years' times. You see, we had the advantage of playing in this competition at home. It would be rather nice to have a go elsewhere,' he announced at the press conference on 30 July 1966. In addition, Alf had a point to prove to his critics in England, whom he felt had failed to recognize the extent of his achievement and preferred to focus on the negativity of his methods. 'I can't help thinking that there are people in England who did not want us to win the World Cup,' he once complained. And he was absolutely right. Alan Hardaker, the pipe-smoking, opinionated, Hull-born, Secretary of the League, recorded that an FA official told him on the eve of the World Cup finals, 'If England win this championship, it may be the worst thing that could ever happen to English football.' Such a grotesque outlook was based on the belief that the premium Alf put on organization and stamina would close down the robust, open physicality of the English game, and, even worse, would destroy the role of wingers. And Hardaker himself was no supporter of Alf. He virtually suggested that the World Cup was an irrelevance to English football and, on a more personal level, said of Ramsey: 'I have never met another man quite like him in the whole of my career. He was difficult to work with and difficult to understand.'

But it was the blinkered attitude of the Football League and their managers that continued to impede Alf's determination to keep England at the top of world football. Within less than a year of England winning the World Cup, clubs were bleating about players being released for international duty. Bowler-hatted Len Shipman, Chairman of the FA's International Committee, in a statement which sums up the lack of co-operation that has bedevilled English football, said in early 1967, 'Although the League clubs are completely behind England, they must look after themselves first.' This spirit infected the biggest names in football. During their time as club managers, Don Revie tried to stop Norman Hunter playing for England, while Matt Busby of Manchester United once slammed the phone down on Nobby Stiles when he stated his preference for England duty rather than turning out for United. Clubs continually complained about lack of consultation, but when Alf organized a meeting in late 1969 of the eleven leading clubs – from which most of England's players were drawn –

to discuss mutual problems, just three of them turned up. In the *Daily Sketch*, Laurie Pignon wrote that this showed 'a complete disregard for the man who has laid the golden egg. Ramsey deserves better support than this. Football at every level has cashed in on the World Cup win.' Alan Hardaker himself, the League Secretary, was at the centre of obstructionism, complaining about Alf's belief that he had 'divine rights'. In the run-up to the 1970 World Cup, Hardaker said:

> I do not regard Sir Alf as God. He is a very good colleague, a good manager, but he's got to realize that other people have problems as well. The whole thing is very simple. There's all this talk by the FA and Sir Alf, but the whole thing comes back here – where we decide the fixtures – whether they like it or not. I am prepared to do everything I can to help but it does not mean that the Football League programme is going to be set aside for the whim of any international match.

Apart from problems with the League, Alf was also hindered by the break-up of his superbly cohesive unit of 1966. George Cohen and Ray Wilson both had to bow out of international football because of injuries. Early in 1968, Roger Hunt also told Alf of his wish to retire from England, unable to commit himself to another World Cup. 'By then I would be 32 and I didn't have the burning ambition to go through it all again. My role in the 4–4–2 system was taxing and I didn't really relish it. It offered invaluable experience but was very hard to fulfil, both mentally and physically.' When Hunt told Alf of his decision, 'he accepted it graciously and thanked me for all my efforts in the past. There was no extravagant reaction. He didn't show any emotion and I wouldn't have expected any. That was never the nature of the man.'

There was a less amicable departure when Jimmy Greaves told Alf he did not want to be considered for international service any more. After 1966, Alf had included Greaves in several of England's squads, only to leave him out of the final eleven. Having won just three more caps in 1967, Greaves grew fed up with this. 'What I said to Alf during my last training session with his squad at Roehampton was that I would rather not be called up unless I was going to play,' explained Greaves. Alf found it intolerable that any player should seek to impose a condition on his playing for England. Throughout most of 1968 and 1969 Greaves' high scoring for Spurs led to pressure on Alf to include him. Eventually in March 1969, after complaining with a degree of self-martyrdom that the 'campaign to bring back Greaves is crucifying me,' Alf revealed the truth that Greaves 'did not want time away for training without having a game'. Greaves admitted that this is what he had told Alf. He was never picked for England again and left Spurs at the end of the 1969–70 season.

But there were brave competitors coming into the England team at this time, like the midfielder Alan Mullery of Spurs, who gradually supplanted Nobby Stiles, and the bustling, sharp, intelligent Francis Lee of Manchester City up front. Mullery says:

His man-management was absolutely superb. He did it extremely well. He was very sincere and extremely close to his players, closer than some club managers were to their men. The greatness of Alf lay in his simplicity. I remember we were once at Wembley Town before a home international, practising our free-kicks. He was watching us from the side, doing our ball work, and we were trying out various types of kick: we had one type at Tottenham, Bobby Moore had another at West Ham, Alan Ball had a certain method at Everton. Eventually Alf came onto the field and said, 'Gentlemen, you look as if you are a bit confused. Why don't we tonight, instead of trying a West Ham one, or an Everton one, instead just knock it square to Bobby Charlton.'

'Okay, Alf.'

It came to the evening. We got a free-kick 25 yards out. Mooro said, 'We'll do the West Ham one.' Alan Ball weighed in, 'No, the Everton one.' Then quiet Bobby Charlton said, 'Shouldn't we just do the Alf one first?' So we did. And Bobby smashed it into the back of the net. That was Alf Ramsey for me. He worked out things simply where the players complicated it.

His language could be quite strong. We were coming in from Troon to play at Hampden, and there were all these Glaswegians, giving us the fingers and swearing at us. I was not a good traveller and I was sitting next to Alf. As we went through all these places like Kilmarnock, I kept looking at my watch. Eventually Alf said, 'Alan, if you don't stop looking at your bloody watch, I'll stop this coach and you can get out and walk. You're driving me mad. We'll get there on time and we'll beat this lot.' I stopped looking at my watch for the next 25 minutes.

Francis Lee made his debut against Bulgaria in 1968:

He took me aside and said, 'I want you to play for my team in exactly the same way you play for Manchester City. That is the reason I have picked you.' That's all he said, nothing else. Later on, all his talks followed the same pattern. He would speak to Banksie about the forwards, who was good in the air and so on, then he would deal with the back four and the midfield. Then, to Geoff Hurst and myself, he would often say nothing more than, 'Geoffrey, Francis, I don't need to tell you anything. You know what you are doing.' His manner was slightly arrogant, to be honest, though he knew how to swear. The funny thing was – and Jack Charlton will never admit this – when we had seven- or five-a-sides, the next to last player picked was always Alf. And the last was always Jack. Jack would go mad, but it was a way of winding him up, 'We'd rather have Alf on our side than you, Jack.' Alf would enter into the spirit but you could only go so far with him. He had his rules that kept you in place. Once I was having a great run in the England team during the Home Internationals, and I was getting good write-ups in the press. Alf took me to one side and said, 'I don't know whether you are a player who gets big-headed but if you are I'll drop you like a stone. Forget how well you've done and think about the next game.' He was a disciplinarian. He would often say to me the next time we met after an international:

'I had a report that you were in Tottenham Court Road the night after the game.' There were a couple of clubs there.

'It wasn't me, Alf. I went home.'

'Are you sure?'

'It must have been someone who looked like me.'

But he always had this doubt in his mind that I was out clubbing after games, which I wasn't really. He did not approve of players going out getting bow-legged, though he did not mind them having a few drinks.

Francis Lee was impressed by Alf on the training ground and on trips: 'He stood there watching, assessing what you were like in skill and pace. Until you actually watch players close up, you don't really know what you are getting. When we were travelling, Alf would move you around, make you share with different players. He disliked cliques developing.' But he also remembers that Alf could be ruthless:

I once took two penalties in succession for England and missed them both. Previously, I had not missed for five seasons. I took one against Portugal at Wembley in 1969. The ground was very loose and I did not even hit the photographers – I missed them. Then in the Home International against Wales I hit the underside of the crossbar and saw it bounce out. I could not believe it. After the game, Alf came up to me and said, 'Francis, I don't believe that taking penalties is your vocation any more.' Fair enough. If you miss two in a row, you have to pack it in.

Yet Alf, Lee found, was no dogmatist and could listen to a player's viewpoint:

Malcolm Allison at City was a great tactician, analytically brilliant, even better than Alf. He would see things that no one else could. I learnt a lot from him. I remember once England were playing Scotland and though we were winning at half-time, Alf was still worried.

'We have to do something about Charlie Cooke. He is running riot. He's here, there and everywhere. Someone has to pick him up.'

And I said, 'To be honest, Alf, he is getting the ball deep in his own half on the right-hand side and he is running across players to wide on the left and vice-versa. He has not had a shot yet – and he has not made a cross yet.' That is the way Malcolm would have analysed it.

'I take your point, Francis.' But part of me feared that I had overstepped the mark.

Like Francis Lee, Mike Summerbee, Manchester City's forward, made his England debut in 1968. He comments:

Alf was a quite remarkable man. He was a one-off, very much a players' man. I had my first game against Scotland. It was pretty nerve-racking playing in front of 100,000 people but Alf made me feel at ease. We were all equal under Alf, no matter how many caps you had won. He was certainly no lover of Scotland. I remember on the bus into Hampden he said, 'We're going to beat these Scottish bastards.' He was someone you instantly looked up to. When he came into a room, he had that aura about him. On the training ground, he would watch and then whisper something in your ear. 'Never give the ball away' was one of his lines. He was a very funny man, a dry man. When we were at Roehampton, we used to have a great roast beef lunch. Then we would go into this room to hear a tactical talk from Alf. It was cold outside; the heat was on in the room and we were sitting in these beautiful, big, plush leather chairs. Bobby Moore would be feeling the effect of the lunch and the warmth. Alf was talking and suddenly he said, 'By the way, Michael, could you wake up Bobby so we can include him in this.'

Brian Labone, the Everton centre-half, is another who remembers Alf's sense of humour. He had recovered from his traumatic game against France in 1963 and was a regular by 1968, often taking the place of the ageing Jack Charlton:

Alf was the archetypal Englishman. His man-management was superb. He seemed remote to everyone, especially journalists but he was warm and loyal to his team. He would take you to one side and let you know what he wanted you to do. He kept things simple. He didn't give out a ten-page dossier like Don Revie, but he would let you know what he expected. He would extol your virtues rather than the guy you were up against. One of the funniest things I remember about Alf was when we were playing Scotland at Wembley in 1969. We were watching the experts on TV: Joe Mercer and Jimmy Hill. They were saying that Alan Gilzean of Scotland would give me a hell of a hiding and that Alf had made a big mistake in picking me. The pundits were giving me 5 out 10 before I had even stepped onto the field. But we thrashed Scotland, Gilzean was taken off and I had a pretty good game. I remember coming off the pitch and Alf grabbed me and said, 'Some fucking mistake I made.'

In a previous game against Scotland, this one at Hampden, the Everton keeper Gordon West had been drafted into the side. Always a nervous individual, who dropped out of the 1970 squad because of homesickness, West had been going to the toilet when, to his horror, he saw the bus leaving the team hotel. He eventually caught up with it as it stopped soon afterwards. But then, on reaching the ground, he realized that in the rush he had left his boots behind. 'Sir Alf did not bat an eyelid but promptly despatched someone back to the hotel. With just five minutes to go, I got my boots,' recalled West. Alf later said to Brian Labone, tapping his head, 'Is Westy a bit slow up there?'

One less happy introduction was that of Mike O'Grady, the prolific Leeds striker, who won his only cap under Alf against France in 1969. He is one of the rare group of players who was not enamoured of Alf's style:

I never disliked him but I found him a very serious guy, very dour. I don't think he had much of a sense of humour and he never seemed to smile much. I was quiet myself and I think Alf, even though he was dour, liked people who were a bit extrovert and more outgoing than himself, such as Jack Charlton. I could not understand why I was only picked for that one game. After all I had scored the first goal in a 5–0 win. What annoys me is that I was the only player in that game who was never, ever selected gain. Alf never said anything to me. When I later went to Wolves from Leeds, the first thing the manager, Bill McGarry said to me was, 'I was at that game. I can't believe that was your last for England. When I next see Alf, I'm going to ask him. Apparently Alf's answer came back that I only tried when England were in front. That's what I was told. I said to Bill, 'That's a bit odd, cos I scored the first goal.' I just feel Alf disliked me. It might have been my name.

The passage of the World Champions in the period after 1966 was not an easy one. In only their third game after the World Cup Final, England were beaten 3–2 by Scotland, with Jim Baxter giving another of his sensational performances. It was a result that was particularly painful to Alf, given his loathing for the Scots. After that setback, he led an FA XI – though it was virtually the full England team – for a tournament in Montreal to coincide with the Expo 67 World Fair, held to mark the centenary of the Dominion of Canada. The trip threatened to descend into a fiasco because of the dismal quality of the soccer facilities and the accommodation. Alf was shocked to find that he and his squad, most of them World Champions, had been put up in a college for divinity students. For eighteen people, there were just three toilets, three urinals and three showers in a communal room. On his first arrival in this residential hall, Alf went into the toilet area where he found a Mexican washing his feet in one of the basins. 'How bloody appalling,' he remarked as he walked out. 'This isn't good enough, we're going home,' he told Harold Shepherdson. But he could not carry out the threat, since there was no spare hotel accommodation available in Montreal, nor any seats on any flights back to England for three weeks. So he told the team that they would just have to put up with it. But the fiasco deepened when he saw the state of their pitch, which only three weeks earlier had been used for a circus and was covered in elephant dung. 'Doctor,' he called out to Dr Alan Bass, 'can players get tetanus from elephant shit?' Only after some urgent repairs was the pitch brought into a state fit for play. Then, in training, Alf was firing in some shots at makeshift goalkeeper Ray Wilson when he misjudged a kick and badly sprained his ankle, leaving him hobbling about for days, though fortunately no bone was broken. 'I hit the ball correctly. It is just that the ground was too high!' claimed Alf, only half joking. There was one moment of humour on the tour, when Alf was handing out daily expenses to the players in brown envelopes. Ray Wilson insisted on the players lining up, army style, to receive the money, giving Alf a salute as they did so. Ex-Sergeant Ramsey entered into the spirit of the occasion, giving a smart salute each time in return, though he did not have a clue what to do when George Cohen decided to salaam him in Arab style.

Despite the elephant dung, the FA XI won the tournament, beating Borussia Dortmund 3–2 in the final. But Alf was only too relieved to get home. The following season, 1967–68, England still struggled to set the football world alight. They were beaten by West Germany for the first time, in a friendly in Hanover, when Alf was furious with several of his players for wearing new boots, the gifts of their sponsors, which ended up blistering their feet. As Peter Thompson recalled, 'When Alf saw our feet afterwards, he just said, "If anyone ever wears new boots for England, I'll never pick them again."' England did better in the 1968 European Championship. The Home

Internationals of the previous two seasons had been used as the qualifiers and even after their defeat by Scotland, they still sailed into the final rounds. In the two-legged quarter-final again Spain, England won 1–0 at home, with Gordon Banks making a miraculous save in the last minute, and then triumphed 2–1 in Madrid. The victory in Spain was all the more impressive because England were without several key players, including Geoff Hurst, who had a poisoned toe. The Hurst injury led to a rare row between Alf and the team doctor, Neil Phillips, who had taken over from Alan Bass. During the trip to Spain, Phillips felt that his job was to be with England, but to his surprise, Alf acceded to a request from the FA chairman Sir Andrew Stephen that Phillips attend a reception hosted by the Spanish Football Federation. When Hurst cried off on the morning of the match, Alf asked him why he had not reported the condition earlier. 'I tried to but I couldn't find the doc,' was Hurst's reply. Instead of feeling defensive, Phillips had a go at Alf, 'It was the first time I ever went against him, but it was his fault and I let him know that he should have told Andrew Stephen that my place was with the team, not at the reception. "Don't ever do that again," I said.'

After the Spanish game, Alf was so thrilled with the performance of England that he made another of his ill-judged, overblown statements. Wondering aloud whether this was the best team that England ever had, he asked, 'This must end some time. But where, and who is good enough to do it?' He was about to find out. In the semi-final in Florence, England took on Yugoslavia. It was a bad tempered, often vicious game, which England lost by a single goal. Alan Mullery became the first English player to be sent off while playing for his country, though the reaction of Alf, supposedly the stern disciplinarian, was interesting. Mullery became fed up with what he called the 'strong-arm tactics' of the Yugoslavs and, as he recalls:

My concentration finally cracked when Bobby Moore played a pass to me and an assassin called Trivic, who had been kicking lumps out of us the entire game, went right down the back of my legs with his studs. I cracked and with the referee only five yards away, kicked him straight in the groin.'

The referee, Mullery admits, had no alternative but to send him off. After Mullery had reached the dressing-room, 'I was expecting the biggest roasting any player has had, when the door burst open and Alf came in, grim faced. He looked at me and shouted, "If you hadn't done it, I would have."'

Afterwards, fuming about what he saw as a raw injustice, Alf said, 'I have never seen anything like that. I don't think even the Argentines in the World Cup were worse. We *are* hard – when we go for the ball. But the ball is always there to be won. These people do their worst when the ball is away. It is evil.'

There was little sympathy for England. Many felt that, given the record of the likes of Jack Charlton and Nobby Stiles, they only had themselves to blame. Even the FA Chairman Andrew Stephen admitted: 'I am afraid our reputation precedes us into these matches, that our opponents are so scared of what they have heard about us that they come out to meet any trouble more than halfway. All football is moving to a bad and dangerous position.' Indeed, the entire mood about the national team turned sour in 1968 as England stumbled. As so often, the British public and the press showed themselves to be remarkably fickle. The glory of 1966 was quickly forgotten as Alf came in for a barrage of criticism over his approach. He was seen as too defensive, too unimaginative, too dour, encouraging brutality rather than flair. Far from being a moment that invigorated English football, the World Cup win was followed by a prolonged spell of introspection, in which Alf was blamed for undermining football as a spectacle. Goals were drying up thanks to Alf, it was said, while defences and midfields were packed. In 1961, when Spurs won the title, they scored 115 goals. In 1969, Leeds won the Championship after scoring just 62 goals. Denis Law, the Manchester United and Scotland striker, claimed that though 'you can't blame Alf for the decline of British football, you must blame the people who followed his example'. Law believed that England had largely won the World Cup because of home advantage:

> The system worked in that limited context for England, in favourable circumstances, but to play football like that on a permanent basis would be fatal. With no wingers, attacks were coming just from midfield, negative to watch and negative to play. The year of 1966 saw the start of eight or ten years of bad football. It took a couple of seasons to work its way thoroughly into the League system, but within a few years, British football had become, for the most part, boring and predictable. Skill was stifled at birth.

In the same vein, J.L. Manning wrote this article in the *Daily Mail* in January 1969, headlined 'Ramsey's Company Far Too Limited,' which coldly analysed Alf's record:

> There is a mounting case against Alf Ramsey's football methods. In 1965, his teams never scored three goals in any match. Since 1966, three goals were scored only once against a foreign side – Sweden at Wembley in 1968. In the past ten matches, there have been 11 goals, and only four were won. Performances in all but two of the World Cup matches were disappointing and since then 30 goals have

been scored in 19 matches. Those are the facts. Ramsey drives in low gear. In addition, the public is losing enthusiasm for his methods. In game after game opponents are gobbled up without being swallowed. Ramsey's players merely chew the cud of football.

Jimmy Greaves, not of course an unbiased critic, believed that Alf had undermined originality through his emphasis on hard professionalism: 'Each player had a job to do within a game-plan. There was no place for a player who might want to stamp his own idiosyncratic course on the game, no place for a maverick with a penchant for playing to the crowd.'

The nadir was reached in March 1969, in a friendly against France, when England were actually booed onto the field after two dull draws against Romania. The subsequent 5–0 win for England did little to stifle the jeers. The only way of doing that would be to retain the World Cup in 1970.

# TWELVE

## *Leon*

A few months before the England team left for the 1970 World Cup in Mexico, Alf had a staff meeting with his loyal lieutenants: Harold Shepherdson, Dr Neil Phillips and Les Cocker.

'We have a problem,' said Alf.

'What's that?' asked Phillips.

'Some of the players from London have been doing promotional work for various companies and, as payment, they have arranged for their wives to be flown out to Mexico.' The four players concerned were Geoff Hurst, Martin Peters, Bobby Moore and Peter Bonetti.

As Neil Phillips recalls:

Well you could have knocked us down with a feather. We were absolutely shocked. I will always remember Les Cocker saying, 'You shouldn't pick them, Alf. Think of the effect it is going to have on the rest of the squad, when just four wives appear and all the others' wives are back in England, with no chance of their coming out. I just don't think it should happen.' But Alf said that there was nothing he could do because it had all been arranged and in any case it was a private matter.

Besides, Alf was on weak ground, because his wife Vickie was due to fly out to Mexico with a friend, though she would not be staying with Alf in the England headquarters.

Today, when players are encouraged to bring their partners on international trips, it may seem odd that Alf's aides were so concerned about the presence of four wives in Mexico. But the fact is that the England management saw them as a distraction to the team, with the potential to break the harmony and concentration of the outfit. Geoff Hurst, who says that 'tact was not high amongst Alf's list of qualities', recounts an incident when he and his wife Judith ran into Alf during a trip to Belgium in February 1970:

> He turned to Judith and poking her in the chest with his finger, said, 'I hear you're going to watch us in Mexico this summer. I want you to know that we're not going there for your enjoyment and we're not going there for my enjoyment. We're going there to bring back the pot and I don't want any interference from you or anyone else.'

And events were to justify these fears. The anxiety caused by one wife in particular was to help lose England the World Cup.

What was aggravating about this issue for Alf was that he believed that he had assembled the best-prepared squad ever to leave these shores. He knew that they would be facing an arduous tour in alien conditions in Mexico, especially because the intense heat and high altitude would undermine the English players' stamina, one of their greatest strengths. To counter this, Alf had taken a number of steps. First of all, he arranged for England to undertake a tour of South America in 1969, so his team could acquaint themselves with the conditions. They first flew to Mexico City, where Alf managed, typically, to incur local hostility by complaining about the Mexicans' lack of respect for his team, which was demonstrated, he claimed, by the absence of a promised motorcycle escort for the team bus and the unfriendly reception accorded to the England players in their first match against a Mexican XI. It was Alf at his most pompous, sounding almost like a colonial governor. Trying out two substitutes in that game, he ordered Alan Ball and Martin Peters to run themselves into the ground in the first half, before he replaced them with Bobby Charlton and Alan Mullery in the second. Unfortunately, Mullery was again sent off for retaliation, and this time Alf was not so sympathetic. 'You always have to put your big nose in. You've always got to be there. It always has to be you. Why don't you keep away from trouble? Anytime anything is going on you have to be part of it.'

After drawing 0–0 with the full Mexico side, England moved on to Montevideo, where Alf experienced more problems. Gordon Banks' father suddenly died so the keeper had to return home, though he returned before the game against Uruguay. Again, the flight only deepened Alf's contempt for the FA, when he discovered that Banks had made the trip economy class, while an FA official had gone first-class. 'Is it any wonder I have no respect for these people?' he was heard to mutter. But Alf's own public relations did not help. His notorious 'animals' remark after the Argentina game in 1966 was still reverberating on the continent, and the arrogant, insular image of his England team was reinforced in Uruguay, when almost all the players refused to eat any food at a barbecue laid on by the Uruguayan football federation, the fare including such local delicacies as sheep's kidneys and entrails. Jack Charlton was the only exception, and he was sick for the entire day afterwards, thereby justifying his colleagues' caution. But some of the Uruguayan hosts were deeply offended, and soon exaggerated rumours circulated about the Englishmen's loud and drunken behaviour at the event. Alf attacked the stories as nothing more than the 'products of a vivid imagination', a view supported by Mullery who said that they were 'ridiculous' and 'blown out of all proportion'. There was another difficult moment in Rio, just before England's final game of the tour, against Brazil, when Alf was furious at attempts by the Brazilians to delay the kick-off for their own advantage. It was a trick that had been pulled on him in 1964 during the Little World Cup, but Alf was not going to put up with it a second time, as Francis Lee remembers. 'A Brazilian official came up to Alf and said, 'The team is not ready yet. It will be another ten minutes before they can come out.' And Alf replied, "You can tell them that if they don't fucking well come out now, there won't be a game."' The match started on time. But Alf's undiplomatic approach had not enhanced his international reputation.

On the football side, England beat Uruguay 2–1, and then, in another impressive performance, lost narrowly to Brazil 2–1 in front of 200,000 fans in the Maracana, with both the Brazilian goals coming late in the game. Alan Mullery recalls this incident, which gives an insight into Alf's understanding of his players:

Just before the kick-off in Rio, I was walking up and down the dressing-room and Alf stopped me and said,

'Are you OK, Alan?'

'Yeah, I'm fine.'

'You look a bit nervous.'

'Well, I am bit nervous. You've given me the job of marking Pele, the greatest footballer in the world.'

'Look Alan, if you weren't the best player at doing this job in the country, you would be sitting at home watching this game on television. I know you're good enough. So get yourself out there and do the job.' And I went from five foot five to six foot five.

The central reason for England losing their early advantage against Brazil was simply exhaustion. So severe was the heat that Bobby Moore, who heroically played in all four games on the tour, was physically sick after the final whistle, while Mullery and Bobby Charlton also suffered badly. It was useful experience, however, for the main event the following year. At first Alf had not been too worried about the heat, believing that the World Cup matches in Mexico would be played at a cool time of the day. But then, to his annoyance, he learnt that they would be played around noon when the sun would be at its peak, in order to satisfy the scheduling demands of the European TV companies.

For Alf, this made it all the more important that the England team had exactly the right medical back-up; he therefore instructed Dr Neil Phillips to make whatever arrangements were necessary. At first, Dr Phillips was somewhat daunted by the task, especially after a visit in 1968 to Romania, who would be drawn in the same group as England. Phillips had been to the Romanian Institute of Sports Medicine and had been amazed at the quality of the facilities and the number of staff focused on the needs of national sides.

I went back to the hotel and spoke to Alf. I said to him, 'Alf, I've had a wonderful morning. I've learnt that Romania has 22 full-time doctors looking after their national team. And I am a part-time GP on my own in Redcar. How on earth can I provide the England team with the same sort of cover as the Romanians get? It is impossible. I just cannot do it.'

Alf's eyes narrowed into that steely look he had from time to time and he said, 'I don't mind how you do it, but just make certain that our medical preparations and cover are far better than the Romanians'.' Alf was one of those people who could make you feel terrible if you ever let him down. I have worked for surgeons and at times I have made a mistake and it has not really bothered me. But if you made a mistake with Alf, it was something that really hurt.

Determined not to disappoint Alf, Neil Phillips set about his task with zeal. He spoke to the Liverpool School of Tropical Medicine about diseases in South America and to Roger Bannister about altitude training for athletes. He sought out advice from Griffith Pugh, who worked at Hammersmith Hospital and had been the physiologist on Hillary's climb of Everest in 1953, and from St Mary's Hospital in London on conducting blood tests. 'Would you believe that before 1968, no one had ever carried out proper blood tests on England players?' The London School of Tropical Medicine assisted with the provision of vaccines and immunizations. Phillips continues:

> Another thing we did was get a consultant from the National Orthopaedic Hospital to examine the teeth of all the players because we did not want them visiting Mexican dentists while they were out there. One of the England internationals had eleven, yes eleven, decayed teeth in his mouth; he had not been to a dentist since he left school.

But what concerned Neil Phillips most was the loss of salt in the tremendous 110-degree heat in Mexico. And then he had his greatest stroke of luck. Alf was being interviewed one evening on television about the problems his team would face in Mexico, particularly salt deficiency caused by fluid loss. It so happened that the interview was watched by Hugh De Wardener, the professor in the renal unit of Charing Cross Hospital. De Wardener had been working for some time on a revolutionary new tablet to counter salt loss, since one of the consequences of a dialyser is to remove not just waste products but also salt from the body. De Wardener rang Alf the next day at Lancaster Gate and was immediately put in touch with Phillips, who went down to Charing Cross Hospital. He was deeply impressed with the prototype salt pill that De Wardener had developed. It was like a miniature honeycomb of salt cells, with the walls made of a soluble material. Because the walls were of variant thickness, the salt would be released into the body at different times. De Wardener hoped that this tablet would save dialysis patients from having to be put on a saline drip. But it was also perfect for footballers, because it would allow them to absorb salt over a period. 'We worked out the best absorption pattern and found the maximum effect came from taking the tablet two or three hours before the game. We never had any problems with salt deficiency during the World Cup.' Dr Phillips remembers Alf taking a keen interest in the medical side of the preparation. 'I used to sit down with him and explain everything. He was very, very bright. I had absolutely no problems in discussing medical matters with him from a technical point of view.'

Alf's biggest influence, of course, was on the selection of the squad. Again, as in 1966, he picked an initial 28, which would be whittled down to a final 22 in Mexico. With Cohen and Wilson gone through injuries, and Jack Charlton fading, only Bobby Moore remained from the iron defence that had won in 1966. Those vying for places at the back in 1970 included Terry Cooper of Leeds, Emlyn Hughes of Liverpool, and the Everton trio of Brian Labone, Keith Newton and Tommy

Wright. Gordon Banks had firmly established himself as the world's finest keeper by 1970, so barring a disaster his deputy Peter Bonetti of Chelsea was unlikely to play. Bobby Charlton, Alan Ball and Martin Peters were still at the core of the midfield, with Mullery now filling the role of Nobby Stiles, though Alf still insisted on bringing Stiles along to Mexico, mainly as mascot to raise the team's spirits. 'Nobby is good for the party, good for the team,' claimed Alf. But the news of his selection inspired little enthusiasm. 'It takes no great imagination to capture the world-wide groan of dismay as the news was released in a dozen languages,' wrote Brian James in the *Daily Mail*. Since 1966, Alf had generally been playing 4–4–2, and he planned to use Hurst and Lee as the two main strikers. There were other contenders up front, such as Jeff Astle of West Bromwich Albion and Peter Osgood, the flamboyant, individualistic star of Chelsea. Alf was never sure what to make of Osgood, a perplexity that gave ammunition to the critics who claimed he was suspicious of brilliance. Brian James recalls this incident when England were training at Roehampton:

> Alf had this habit of occasionally sitting down beside me to discuss football. We were watching England practising and Peter Osgood was out there, doing something extravagant and silly, beating men, then keeping the ball up in the air. And Alf turned to me and said,
> 'What the fuck am I going to do with this Osgood?'
> 'Well Alf, he can play.'
> 'I know he can play, but he's a bloody idiot.'
> Alf just could not get his mind around someone who enjoyed fooling around. Can you imagine Alf fooling on the training ground? Never. Training was a serious matter for him.

Osgood remembers Alf tackling him directly on the subject during one of his first spells in the England squad in 1969.

> I was stepping off the coach for morning training when he greeted me with, 'Well, Ossie, how do you fancy training today?'
>
> 'Not a lot, Alf,' I unwisely but truthfully replied.
>
> 'Well, you're going to fucking well enjoy it!' he told me in those clipped, plummy tones. I was shocked. It was like catching the Queen kicking one of the corgis up the arse.

Allan Clarke of Leeds was another potential striker. In fact, he had first been called into the squad in 1967, yet by the time of Mexico he was still waiting for his first cap. He had gone on the tour to South America in 1969 without playing, his strongest memory being Alf's words to him on the plane journey to Mexico. Alf came up to him in the cabin of the aircraft and asked Allan if he was enjoying himself.

'Yeah, Alf, great, thanks.'

'Don't, son. You're here to work.' Allan took this as an example of Alf's sense of irony.

Ian Storey-Moore, a winger and a lethal finisher with Nottingham Forest, made his debut against Holland in early 1970 and would have won more than his one cap if it had not been for injury. 'I was with the squad and the Under-23s a few times,' he told me, 'and I found Alf very knowledgeable, mild-mannered, never seemed to raise his voice.' Despite Alf's renowned dislike of wingers, Storey-Moore found Alf more flexible than his rigid image:

> I was always a winger, but unlike John Robertson, who stuck to the touchline so tightly he had chalk on his arse, I used to have a wander every now and then – that is how

I scored so many goals. Alf said to me, 'I know you're playing Number 11, but just play how you do for your club.' So I had a licence to roam, which was comforting. Alf was very quiet in the dressing-room. He would have a talk on the morning of the match, setting out what he wanted. Then he would come round, talking to people individually. As you went out, he shook you by the hand and wished you luck. I had enormous respect for him, though I was very surprised when I first got in the squad and found that Jack Charlton talked to Alf as if he were his best mate. 'Come on, Alf, we're ready for you now,' he'd say. I think Alf liked that. I did OK against Holland at Wembley. It was probably the worst surface I played on because it had just been used for the Horse of the Year show. I did OK, had a goal disallowed and could have scored another couple. Alf said I had done well and would soon have another game, but then I had a bad injury.

Ian Storey-Moore's injury prevented his selection in the initial squad of 28, Peter Thompson serving as the only genuine winger.

Among the other inclusions was Peter Shilton of Leicester City as one of Banks' deputies. He remembers:

He made me feel welcome. From the moment I met Sir Alf I knew he was someone special. He had something different about him. He had that presence that dominates a room. Any decision he made, you knew he made it for the right reason. What I really liked about him was he treated international players properly, with respect and intelligence. I have been in England squads where players are screaming and shouting and banging doors, all that sort of thing. But that never happened with Alf. It was a composure thing. You went out focused. I remember, though, one time I did see Alf really riled. We were on an Under-23 tour in Europe and we were travelling to Russia. We got to our hotel at about three in the morning, but the Russians appeared to have made a mess of the bookings. We were standing around the lobby for ages, waiting to go to our rooms, when suddenly we were told that we'd been taken to the wrong hotel. It almost seemed as if the Russians were trying to make us as late as they could. Alf completely blew his top. He had a right go, saying 'Bastards'. It was the first time I had seen him like that. It was brilliant in a way because you felt Alf was really sticking up for you. He turned the whole situation around, made us even more determined.

Some of the players of 1966, like Nobby and Jack Charlton, may have been in decline, but several of England's biggest stars, including Banks, Bobby Moore, Alan Ball and Geoff Hurst, were at the zenith of their careers. Alf always maintained that the 1970 England team was actually stronger than that of 1966. 'I find myself thinking that it's going to be hard, tremendously hard for us out there. Then I think about what we've got and I say to myself, "It's going to be bloody difficult for anybody to take this World Cup from us,"' he told Hugh McIlvanney.

In the weeks before departure, England's spirits were raised further by the release of their World Cup single 'Back Home', which flew straight to the top of the charts. Most of such records, like Lonnie Donegan's dire 'World Cup Willie' of 1966, are instantly forgettable, but 'Back Home' was of a far higher standard because of the strength of its melody and lyrics. Written by the successful duo of Bill Martin and Phil Coulter, who had previously created such hits as 'Congratulations' for Cliff

Richard and the Eurovision Song Contest winner 'Puppet on a String' for barefooted Sandie Shaw, it managed to evoke the poignant heroism of wartime. This was the songwriters' aim, as Bill Martin explains:

> As a good Scotsman, I was not interested in England. But before the 1970 World Cup I thought to myself that there had never been a song done by a football team. 'World Cup Willie' had been a lot of nonsense. So I said to Phil: 'We should do this. We should write a song that shows England as World Champions going off to war, like troops.'

So the pair sat down in their office in Denmark Street in London, and soon Martin knew he had a winner on his hands. But if it was going to be a success, it would have to be sung by the England team – and that meant winning the support of Alf Ramsey, not a man renowned for his love of pop music.

But Bill Martin, an amusing, twinkle-eyed Scot, felt he had the ideal card to play if Alf proved uncooperative. Alf's brother Albert, he sensed, was the England manager's vulnerable spot. Bill Martin understood a bit about the Ramsey family because his father-in-law, the advertising manager of the *Daily Sketch*, knew about the seamier side of East London and had told Bill stories about Albert's drinking and gambling. Albert's behaviour had long been a source of unease for Alf. It was rumoured that Albert occasionally would turn up at Portman Road, when Alf was manager there, begging for cash. Just to be rid of him, Alf would send him away with a tenner. Tony Garnett, the Ipswich journalist, says: 'Alf could wash his hands of people. He did not really want to know his brother Albert, the dog man. He was embarrassed by him.' Bill Martin had seen Albert in action himself. One evening he called on a pub in Dagenham, having been with the singer Sandie Shaw, who hailed from that district, and to his astonishment he thought he saw the figure of Sir Alf Ramsey slumped up at the bar. He could not resist going up to the man, who turned out to be Albert 'Bruno' Ramsey:

> He was the absolute double of Alf. Once I saw it wasn't Alf, I thought it must be his twin. We got drinking and talking. He did not say a word about Alf but then drunks don't talk family. Having the most famous brother in England meant nothing to him. He did not want to talk about Alf, only himself.

Soon after this experience, Bill Martin used his friendship with the top football agent Ken Stanley to arrange an appointment with Alf and the England team at Hendon Hall.

> Ken Stanley ushered me in to see him. The minute I opened my mouth, Alf knew I was Scottish and he didn't like me at all. He did not get out of his seat or shake my hand. He just sat there. I said,
> 'I've got this idea for a song for the World Cup.'
> 'How dare you come to the England hotel to discuss show-business with my boys who are World Champions.'
> 'It might be good for them and we could all have a laugh.'
> 'We don't have laughs,' continued Alf in that very slow, deliberate voice. 'I have no idea why you have even entered this room. Ken, I'm amazed you have brought this man along.'
> 'Alf, I'll tell you what. I had more fun with your brother Bert the other night in the pub, even though he fell over and was lying in the gutter when I left him.'
> Alf replied immediately, 'I beg your pardon. Go and see the boys. I have absolutely no interest in this conversation.

Speak to the footballers.' Alf cut me short because I recognized his Achilles' heel, his brother who was a serious drunk.

Martin then went to see the players, who turned out to be much more receptive to the idea of the song, especially when Bill told them he could guarantee that it would get to Number One and be on *Top of the Pops*. As Martin predicted, 'Back Home' became a massive hit, at one stage selling over 100,000 a day just before the World Cup. The players, who appeared on *Top of the Pops* in their tuxedos, adored it as much as the public, and it became their anthem on the journey in Mexico. Sir Alf, however, remained unmoved. Martin says:

> He did not join in any of this. He did not want his picture associated with it in any way whatsoever. He never, ever spoke to me again. I met him a few times afterwards and he always gave me the cold shoulder. He wanted nothing to do with me at all. Showbusiness and Scots were not for Alf. Funnily enough, John Lennon once told me how much the song meant to him, that it made him think of home in Liverpool. I got more from John Lennon than I ever did from Alf Ramsey.

England arrived in Mexico on 4 May, almost exactly a month before the tournament began on 2 June. These four weeks, felt Alf, would be vital for players to acclimatize to the altitude and baking climate. Based in the Parc de Princes Hotel in Mexico City, 7,349 feet above sea level, the team started gently with some cricket and golf at the Reforma Sports Club, as well as their own mini-version of the Olympics, which was hardly a competitive success as super-fit Colin Bell, the Manchester City midfielder, won all the events. But even Bell felt the strain of the conditions: 'It was very hard to breathe. It was a week before you could think about training. You'd run ten yards and put your hands on your knees, you couldn't go for a one–two. It was frightening.' Alf took other measures to deal with the problems. The players were only allowed brief spells of sunbathing by the pool; they would lie on one side for fifteen minutes, then Harold Shepherdson would blow a whistle, and they would turn over and lie on the other. It was a faintly ludicrous arrangement but, as Geoff Hurst put it, 'Alf had absolute power. He was the boss, his authority was never questioned and his word was law.' Not quite. Peter Thompson once went up to the roof of the hotel for some illicit sunbathing, only to find Bobby Moore up there in sun-glasses and trunks, showing his customary indifference to Alf's injunctions. To combat dehydration, the players each day took a litre of an American drink called Gatorade. Mexico had imposed an import ban on Gatorade in liquid form, but the US company that made it gave Neil Phillips a large supply of crystals which could be mixed with water. The task of producing the Gatorade in drinkable form each day fell to Neil Phillips:

> Every day we were in Mexico, I used to get buckets of ice delivered to my hotel room at six in the morning. We had taken with us 25,000 bottles of Malvern Water and I would make up 30 litres of Gatorade, using the crystals and the Malvern Water, pour them into thermos flasks and then pack them in ice in the bathtub before taking them training.

But it was Alf's elaborate preparations that were to land England in serious trouble. Fearful of stomach upsets, Alf had decided to import not just Malvern Water but the squad's entire food supply for duration of the tournament. He had negotiated a deal with the frozen-food giant Findus, whose shipment to Mexico included 140 pounds of beefburgers, 400 pounds of sausages, 300 pounds of frozen fish and ten cases of tomato ketchup. Many other countries were following this pattern, giving their players the diets they were used to. Helmut Schoen, the German manager, explained after the tournament, 'we took along our own chef, sent enormous quantities of equipment months in advance to cover any contingencies and generally turned our hotel into a small German province'. This was exactly the same insularity that was so condemned in Alf. But the huge difference was that the Germans did not make a virtue of it, whereas Findus, for commercial reasons, boasted of their work with England. Feeling slighted, the Mexican authorities announced that no meat or dairy products could be brought in from England because it was a foot and mouth country. A vast bonfire was held on the quayside of all the steaks, beef, sausages and butter. 'I had to go down to the docks and certify that it had all been burnt,' says Neil Phillips. For the rest of the tour, England had to subsist on ready meals and fish. 'It was absolutely dreadful. All the time we were having fish-fingers with salad or fish-fingers with chips. You know I have not had a fish-finger in my life since then,' says Alan Mullery. One of the leading TV commentators of the time, Hugh Johns, thought Alf was to blame for the fiasco: 'England did not do themselves any favours at all. It was all "the nig-nogs the other side of the channel", "don't drink the water", typical Anglo-Saxon nonsense and, of course, the natives didn't like it and I don't blame them.' Alf worsened the mood in other ways. He decided to import England's own team bus, the unintended implication being that the Mexicans were still struggling to come to terms with the internal combustion engine, then found that the British vehicle struggled to cope with the intense heat. And he also imposed a strict ban on any of his players speaking to the press, which only encouraged a siege mentality. At one stage, when a gaggle of Mexican journalists came into the England dressing-room, he threw them out, ensuring their exit was accompanied by some Dagenham vernacular. Nor did Alf bring with him any Spanish-speaking press officer, an oversight that only widened the gulf. 'We were about as popular with the Mexicans as an outbreak of plague,' said Bobby Charlton.

If England hoped a change of scenery would enhance their standing, they were mistaken. The team flew down to Colombia for further acclimatization, training and two friendly matches at an even higher altitude than Mexico City. But it was in Bogotá that the greatest off-field drama of the tour took place. England were based at the Hotel Tequendama and soon after their arrival, the squad were milling, in rather bored fashion, around the foyer. To pass the time, Bobby Moore, Bobby Charlton and Dr Neil Phillips went into a small jewellery shop near the reception, Charlton thinking that he might find a present for his wife Norma. But all the gifts were too expensive, so the trio walked out and sat together on a settee opposite the shop. Suddenly, the glamorous young assistant, Clara Padilla, came rushing out, started rummaging between the cushions on the settee and then openly accused Moore of having stolen a bracelet. She was quickly joined by the shop-owner, who made the same accusation against Moore. Dr Phillips jumped to his feet: 'You two stay where you are. Don't say anything. I'll go and find Alf.' Phillips was immediately suspicious, because the night before a jeweller had come into the England hotel in Mexico City, flogging his wares, only to claim that an Omega watch had been stolen. Alf, anxious to avoid a scandal, had offered to pay for it himself, but instead the players had held a collection to meet the cost. By the time Alf reached the scene of the alleged crime in the Hotel Tequendama, the place was buzzing with police officers, cameras, curious by-standers and England players. Simply by his authoritative presence, Alf calmed down the situation. He spoke to Moore, Charlton, the shop-owner and the police, arranged for statements to be taken, stressed that the players believed it was all a misunderstanding and, it seemed, brought the issue to a close, with Moore apparently left a free man. 'Alf handled it like an expert and everyone thought it was done and forgotten the minute Bobby and I finished making our formal statements to the police. But there was something about Alf that made me feel that he was upset. He already sensed that something was up. Felt it there and then,' said Moore.

Alf was right to sense some foreboding. England played their two friendlies, beating Columbia 4–0 in Bogotá and Ecuador 2–0 in a match played in Quito at 9,300 feet; the results showed that the players seemed to be adapting well to the conditions, though Alan Ball spoke of the continuing difficulties caused by altitude. 'Normally, Alan Mullery makes a lot of noise on the field, always shouting. Well, when he tried that out there all that came out was a sort of gurgle and a mouthful of froth. Nobody had enough breath to run, let alone shout. I thought the talk about altitude were crap, me. But I found out different today.'

Any reassurance Alf felt about these two results was soon shattered by an almighty row about the naming of the final 22 players in the squad. For one of the few times in his career, Alf decided to co-operate with the press, yet the behaviour of the papers only succeeded in reinforcing all his prejudices. Alf felt he owed the journalists a favour, because of the restraint they had shown so far over the Bobby Moore bracelet story; not one word of this potentially enormous scandal had so far been printed. But his generosity backfired horribly. In order to meet weekend deadlines made difficult by the eight-hour time difference, he gave the football writers on the Sunday papers the names of the six men who had been left out – Peter Shilton, David Sadler, Ralph Coates, Bob McNab, Peter Thompson and Brian Kidd – on the strict understanding that no comments would be sought until he had spoken to the six players involved. The sports reporters themselves did not break this embargo, but the news-desk of the *Sunday Mirror* immediately contacted the wife of Dave Sadler, the Manchester United defender, asking for her views. Inevitably, she was straight on the phone to her husband. As Sadler recalls:

I basically heard from my wife that I was out of the squad. I was playing well, felt good, was optimistic. It was a blow, a real downer. I went straight to confront Alf. I caught up with him and we had words in front of people. I was blazing, very angry. I was fairly handy with the language. Alf was defensive, of course, and was at pains to say, 'Come on, let's go and talk about this in private.' We did. We sat in a room. He explained what had happened. He was big enough to apologize, as you would expect in a man of his standing. I was starting to calm down a little bit. I realized he had done it to try and help the press, but once again they had let him down, confirming all he thought about them. We sorted it out. The official announcement was made and I fully accepted that it was the last thing that Alf would have intended. My relations with Alf were fine after that. It was not in my nature to fly off the handle and I think Alf accepted my situation.

But Alf's relationship with the press was never to recover from this incident. And his mood worsened as the international explosion over Bobby Moore erupted. After defeating Ecuador, England planned to fly back to Bogotá, and then on to

Mexico via Panama. At a staff meeting in Ecuador, Neil Phillips suggested that the flights should be rearranged to avoid Bogotá and the Bobby Moore problem, which had still not been satisfactorily resolved. According to Phillips: 'Alf went off to discuss this alternative with Bobby. But the two of them agreed that such a move would only encourage a belief that a bracelet really had been stolen.' So the team, accompanied by the press, flew back to Bogotá, and even returned to the Hotel Tequendama during a five-hour gap while changing planes. A film showing of the old American Civil War epic *Shenandoah* was arranged for the players, while the press party was taken on a visit to the tourist attraction of a local salt mine – 'perfect for you lot,' joked Jack Charlton. During the film, two plain-clothes officers from the Columbian police entered the room, tapped Bobby Moore on the shoulder and beckoned him out-side. The players thought that he had just been instructed to carry out another of his duties as England captain and con-tinued watching the movie. Even when they left the hotel and made their way to the airport, they were still only dimly aware of Bobby's absence. But they were more disturbed when Alf turned up on his own shortly before take-off. Once the plane was airborne, he gave them the news that Bobby had been formally charged with the theft of a bracelet from the Green Fire jewellery shop at the hotel. The team was thunderstruck. It was unthinkable that Bobby Moore, a man of supreme dignity, England captain for seven years, leader of the World Champions, would descend to such a petty crime. 'Alf might just as well have said that Mother Teresa had been arrested for child abuse; it was that outlandish and unbelievable,' says Gordon Banks. When the news filtered down the plane, the journalists were equally shaken, though their distress was caused by the fact that they were sitting high in the air, unable to handle the biggest football story for years. Peter Batt of the

*Sun* thought to himself that 'all the agencies are going to have this story, oh my God. The news-desks will think we have sat on it. By now I'm having the last will and testament.' After the shambles over the squad announcement, Alf could not have cared less about the professional fate of the pressmen. Ken Jones watched Alf as the plane flew towards Panama: 'He's sitting there, transfixed in his seat, impassive throughout the whole flight. Never said a word.'

When the plane stopped in Panama for refuelling, the press rushed out to try to phone London, while Alf went deeper into introspection. 'Alf was a man possessed. He paced the airport like a caged lion, his face inscrutable but his mind obviously on the fate of his captain,' recalled Banks. For all his past differences with Moore, Alf knew he could not afford to lose him on the eve of the finals. But as he paced the departure lounge, Moore was holed up in Bogotá, awaiting further questioning. Because of the special status of the prisoner, the Columbian courts decided that Moore could be placed under house arrest rather than thrown into jail. So he was allowed to stay in the home of Alfonso Senior, the Director of the Columbian Football Federation, with two armed guards by his side. 'I felt like the captured hero from one of Alf's westerns,' he later said. It was not an unfair analogy. Moore showed true grit in coping with his ordeal, never once giving the slightest indication of the pressure he was under, joking with his guards and going for early morning runs to keep himself fit.

If Alf thought the storm could be contained, he was badly mistaken. On arrival at Guadalajara, which was England's base for the opening round, Ramsey's party were greeted by scenes of mayhem, with reporters and TV crews rushing across the tarmac towards the plane. What made it all the worse was that Jeff Astle, never a good traveller, had spent most of the long journey drinking to calm his nerves, and by the time of his arrival he was, to quote Brian James, 'pissed out of skull'. A few England players tried to hide his state of inebriation from the Mexican press, propping him up as he went down the steps and then covering him up in the lounge with a coat, but it was a hopeless task. 'He was looking as if he had not changed his clothes for a fortnight,' recalled Gordon Banks, who also felt that in the midst of the crisis, 'Alf was not his normal cool, calm self.' The next day, one of the Mexican newspapers described England in a headline as 'a bunch of drunks and thieves'. Ramsey later told Ken Jones that the whole sorry business had been the worst thing that ever happened to him in all his years of football.

England were staying at the Hilton Hotel in Guadalajara. Though well appointed, it was in the centre of the city, meaning that it could easily become the focus for the anti-English sentiment that was sweeping through the country. The string of difficulties, from burnt meat to Bobby Moore, only fed Alf's instinctive hostility to foreigners and the press. At times, he was in danger of being gripped by a form of paranoia, as he muttered about secret plots against his team. And he may not have been wrong in the case of the Moore bracelet, for the evidence points to an attempted set-up by the shop to extort money. Soon after Moore's arrest, Joao Saldanha, the former Brazil manager, explained that a similar trick had been pulled on him when he was in charge of the Botafogo team. 'The jewellery had been hidden in a drawer. It was an attempt to embarrass us into paying up to avoid a scandal. The allegations against Bobby Moore are disgraceful. This is slander,' argued Saldanha. The flimsiness of the case against Moore was exposed when he was brought back to the hotel jewellery store for further cross-examination. Ms Padilla claimed that Moore, clad in his England suit, had slipped the bracelet into his left-hand pocket. Triumphantly, Moore raised his left arm to show that his suit had no such pocket. Ms Padilla also changed her story about the bracelet's value. Faced with such evidence, the Columbian judges eventually decided that he would not have to stand trial. On 29 May he was granted conditional release and flew up to Guadalajara, though the case was not formally dropped until 1972.

The story of the set-up always seemed the most likely version of events, but the journalist Jeff Powell revealed after Moore's death that the truth may have been more complicated, for Moore had said to him, 'Perhaps one of the lads did something foolish, a prank with unfortunate consequences.' Rodney Marsh also claimed that Moore had confirmed this story to him. There are several younger players who might have fitted the role as possible culprit; Emlyn Hughes and Peter Thompson both said that they went into the shop at some stage that afternoon, and Thompson actually told Alf that he was the third man. 'They're not after you, Peter, it's a set-up,' said Alf coolly. Peter Osgood was another who says that he followed Charlton and Moore into the store, but dismisses the idea that he was the thief as 'complete and utter bollocks'. All this speculation is treated with great scepticism by the two people who probably were closer to the truth than anyone else. The first is Tina Moore, who was still to be married to Moore for another decade:

All I know is that when I was with Bobby, we did not have any secrets. Bobby told me that there was not a bracelet. And would Bobby really have allowed himself to be put under arrest, with no certainty that he would be released in time to play for the World Cup, just to protect a kid who had played a prank? Why would he let himself be slammed up it if he knew someone else did it? It is ridiculous.

The second is Neil Phillips, who was actually in the shop with Moore and Charlton at the time of the alleged theft and thinks claims of another player being involved 'are a load of codswallop. I was there with the two of them. There was no one else in the shop whatsoever.' Phillips is a particularly reliable witness because, as a doctor, he was used to taking notes.

Alf had said to the press that 'you won't see a smile on my face until I see Bobby Moore'. Nor had he had the slightest doubt about Bobby's total innocence. 'I should have thought that the integrity of this man would be enough to answer these charges. It is too ridiculous for words.' When Bobby walked into the Hilton on the 29 May, Alf gave him a greeting that was as close to a hug as he could manage. Yet for all the mutual respect that had developed between them, Moore confided to Jeff Powell that he had been a little disappointed in his manager, leaving him in Bogotá to be supported by Denis Follows, the Secretary of the FA, and Andrew Stephen, the FA Chairman. 'If there was a man I believed was as important to me as Alf said I was to him, then there's no way I could have walked on to that plane without him.' After the 1970 World Cup, Bobby reflected on this sense of mild disillusionment:

Despite what the outside world thought, I would never regard myself as being the same as Alf. Not at all alike. The only Alf I knew was the football manager. We were together maybe a total of a month or two out of every year. That didn't mean I knew him as a person. Alf never drew me into his social company. It became quite clear that Alf and I were different personalities outside our working relationship. Apart from football, Alf would never talk in depth about anything at all. In company the conversation might flit across the usual small talk about cars and holidays but would invariably settle on football. Socially, I like people who are interested in what you do but can also relax you and take your mind off your own line of business once in a while. Alf had just two worlds: his players and his home. And they were kept strictly apart.

But Moore, who had a good understanding of human psychology, recognized that Alf was far more sensitive than his hard public image: 'Unless you knew him closely, you would not have noticed when he was hurt. He had great control of his emotions and never showed it outwardly when he was under stress. He would just carry on. Yet you sensed he was hurt. Alf would be deeply upset if a member of the press expressed a damaging opinion.' And Moore always retained a profound admiration for Alf's ability as a manager: 'He was a players' man. We were attracted by his loyalty. He shared our desire for success. Alf's first thought was for his players so there was never any problem about getting the players to do what was asked of them.'

After all the problems of the previous weeks, it was a relief for England when the competition finally got under way on 31 May. England were drawn in a group containing Brazil, Romania and Czechoslovakia, none of them easy opponents; England had not beaten Brazil in six encounters since 1956, while there had been two dull recent draws against Rumania, the same result that had been achieved in their last game against Czechoslovakia in November 1966. Nevertheless, two sides went through from the qualifying round, so England were not facing any great obstacle on the path to the quarter-final. The first game, against Romania on 2 June, was a brutal, uninspiring affair, with England winning by a single Geoff Hurst goal and Keith Newton having been forced off by a vicious challenge. The next day, the England team went to watch their next opponents, Brazil, demolish Czechoslovakia 4–1. The skill and verve of the Brazilians left a deep impression on Alf. 'By Christ, these people can play,' he told Ken Jones.

On the Saturday night before the crucial game against Brazil, a large crowd of Mexican and Brazilian supporters gathered outside the Hilton, where England were accommodated on the 12th floor. In the sultry tropical air, for hour after hour, the crowd kept up an incessant racket, blaring horns, banging drums and blowing whistles. The Mexican police did nothing to move on the trouble-makers. 'It sounded like a thousand West Indian cricket supporters in full cry,' said Emlyn Hughes. Unable to sleep, the England players started throwing water and cartons of milk at the crowd. When that failed to achieve anything except to pump up the volume, they moved to different rooms at the back of the hotel, but the noise still penetrated. 'We didn't get a wink of sleep,' said Brian Labone. Bleary-eyed, the England team reported on Sunday morning for their final talk with Alf, who had lodged a formal protest with FIFA and the Mexican government about the previous night. Alf began his address in cryptic fashion, 'Do you like gold, boys?' Puzzled looks were exchanged round the dressing-room; Alan Ball thought Alf was making a reference to a possible win bonus. He was soon disabused of that idea. 'Well, the ball's a lump of gold today. So don't give it away.'

As Alf ran through the opposition, one player sat disconsolately in the corner, barely able to listen to a word. Having come on as a substitute for Francis Lee, Peter Osgood believed that he had a strong chance of making the starting line-up against Brazil, especially because he felt in good form and had worked hard in training. Moreover, during the week Bobby Moore had confided in him that he was likely to be in the side. So when Alf announced that 'the team to face Brazil will be the same team that finished against Rumania', Osgood was overjoyed. But his excitement soon turned to confusion as he listened to Alf referring to the role of Francis Lee against the Brazil defence. Bobby Moore immediately spoke up for Osgood, 'Excuse me, Alf, you're talking about Francis, but Ossie came on for Francis and he finished the game against the Rumanians.' Alf looked over at Osgood and just said, 'Oh, I'm ever so sorry Ossie, I meant to say that the team which *started* against Rumania will play against Brazil', before calmly resuming his talk. As Osgood later recalled:

I was devastated and wanted to walk out there and then but I felt paralysed. That evening, against all the rules, I hurried out of the hotel alone and hit the first bar I could find, and then the next, and the next. I got myself paralytic with drink and have only vague memories of sharing my misery with the groups of England fans. In the morning, I would not get out of bed and missed training. Alf tried to see me but I shouted at the door. 'Go away. Don't say a word. You can't excuse what you have done to me – you slaughtered me in front of the entire squad – just leave me alone!'

The incident showed how preoccupied Alf was with the endless series of crises on the tour. Normally so good at man-management, he had been casually insensitive towards Osgood, though there is little doubt that the player also over-reacted. Alf was never to pick him again after Mexico. The altercation was the precursor of an increasingly difficult time Alf would have with the self-styled mavericks of seventies football.

England's reputation was at a low point as they took the field against Brazil at noon in the shirt-drenching, 98-degree heat. But they went some way to rebuilding it with a magnificent performance against the Brazilians, today widely regarded as the finest team in the history of soccer. England were undaunted, with Moore giving the performance of a lifetime and Banks producing a heroic save at the far post when he dived full-length to stop a powerful Pele header. Pele, who shouted 'goal' the moment he connected with the ball, called it the greatest save he had ever seen. England actually finished the game more strongly than the Brazilians, and should have equalized when Jeff Astle, who had come on for Lee, missed a sitter with an open goal in front of him. From the stands, Osgood muttered that he would have never missed a chance like that. But even in defeat, England had shown the quality of champions. 'It really is what the game at the top level is all about. There was everything in it, all the skills and techniques, all the tactical control. There really was some special stuff played out there,' said Bobby Charlton.

England only needed a draw in their final game against Czechoslovakia to go through to the quarter-final. Several of the players were feeling the heat – Alan Mullery lost 12 pounds against Brazil – so Alf decided to rest Hurst, Ball, Lee and Labone. But after reaching the heights against Brazil, England plumbed the depths with a laboured display against the Czechs. Clad in unfamiliar light-blue shirts, they continually gave the ball away and only scraped through 1–0, thanks to a penalty from Allan Clarke, who was finally making his England debut after spending three years in the squad. Today Clarke recalls:

> The day before we played Czechoslovakia, Alf comes over
> – I will remember his words to my dying day – and says,
> 'I'm going to play you tomorrow, Allan.'
>   'That's great,' I replied, feeling elated.
>   'Yes, because I think you're ready now.'
>   'Alf, I've been ready for three years.'

In the dressing-room before the kick-off, Alf asked presciently about penalties. No hands went up so Clarke volunteered. 'Good lad,' said Alf. When the moment arrived in the match, Alf turned nervously to his trainer Les Cocker, who also worked at Leeds. 'Will he score, Les?'

'Put your mortgage on it, Alf.'

England had hardly emerged triumphant from the opening rounds, scoring just one goal in open play. For Danny Blanchflower, their lacklustre methods epitomized the worst of their manager; he wrote: 'There is no way that Sir Alf Ramsey or anyone else can justify the present England tactics. He has found a way to destroy the game rather than glorify it ... Ramsey makes a potentially good team look like a bad one. They survive despite their tactics – not because of them. The team has lost the sense of going forward.'

Whatever the disappointment caused by their industrious style, England had reached the last eight, and were due to play their old rivals West Germany in Leon on 14 June. But it was now that England's trip really began to fall apart, partly due to a series of organizational oversights by Alf and his staff. For someone who was usually so meticulous about his preparations, Alf had been strangely slapdash about certain aspects of the Mexican adventure. He had obsessed on one issue, the medical arrangements, yet had overlooked others or made poor decisions. He admitted, for instance, that he had been wrong to choose light-blue shirts against Czechoslovakia, because, in the burning glare of the Mexican sun, they were virtually indistinguishable from the white of the Czechs. But, as the quarter-final approached, he was guilty of far more serious errors. Remarkably, given that England were the reigning World Champions, Alf had neglected to ensure that any accommodation or flights were booked beyond the opening rounds. So instead of flying to a comfortable hotel in Leon,

England had no choice but to accept the accommodation organized by FIFA. Moreover, the Mexican authorities refused England permission to fly into Leon on the grounds that the runway was too short to take a large aircraft. This was plainly nonsense, since the Germans had flown to Leon two weeks earlier. It was just another example of the extreme anti-English sentiment that Alf managed to provoke abroad. But Mexican obduracy meant that England had to make the 170-mile trip to Leon by coach, another strain on the squad's already over-stretched nerves. Dr Neil Phillips believes that the shambles over the transport was another consequence of the poor relationship between management and the FA:

> The Mexicans insisted we travel by coach, which was ludi-crous, absolutely ludicrous. But we did not have any power with the local Mexican authorities because Denis Follows was in Mexico City looking after Lord Harewood, the President of the FA. Alan Odell tried to sort it out but he did not have the standing that Denis would have had as Secretary of the FA. And our hotel was reputed to be terrible. Bulgaria had stayed there and it was said to be surrounded by prostitutes.

Having heard these rumours about the dismal standard of their hotel, Alf instructed Harold Shepherdson and Neil Phillips to travel ahead by taxi to check out the place and report back to him by phone. As always believing that he should be with the players, Phillips strongly objected: 'I didn't like the idea of not being with them on that road journey.' But Alf insisted, so at 4 am Harold and Neil left Guadalajara for Leon. As it turned out, Neil's presence was badly needed back in the England camp, for Gordon Banks suddenly went down with a severe bout of stomach poisoning. He managed to stagger onto the bus and hold himself together for the journey. 'I sat at the back of the coach praying for it to end. I was suffering from terrible stomach cramps and in imminent danger of letting go at either end. I was in a clammy sweat yet shivering with cold,' says Banks. As soon as he arrived in Leon, he went straight to bed, though he did not get much sleep, spending most of the night on the toilet. As his room-mate Alex Stepney, the Manchester United keeper, later remarked, 'Montezuma was extracting his revenge with the strike power of a cobra.' England players, including Bobby Charlton, Keith Newton and Peter Osgood, had suffered before with stomach upsets on this trip, despite all the medical precautions. But this was on a different scale. And both the violence of the ailment and the importance of the player gave rise to all sorts of rumours about a conspiracy against the England team. Becoming more paranoid by the day, Alf himself did not discount the theory that Banks was the victim of a sinister overseas plot. Nigel Clarke recalls Alf once telling him: 'It may have been done by the CIA, those American people or whatever you call them. I know Gordon was got at because we took all our own water and food.'

But Neil Phillips believes the truth is more prosaic. He fears that Banks may have been struck down as a result of England's own celebrations after the victory over Czechoslovakia. With Alf's permission – but Neil's disapproval – the players held a small party at their hotel, to which the four wives were invited. An infected sandwich or beer consumed at this event may have been the cause of the trouble, as Neil told me:

I wasn't too happy about that party. Months later, I ran into the Leeds manager Don Revie, who had been working out in Mexico as a pundit. He said to me, 'Neil, never blame yourself for what happened out there. The players, contrary to your instructions, were having sandwiches delivered to their rooms. I know what you had told them: no drinks or sandwiches in the rooms. You can take it from me, Neil, that some of them had room service.' I did not see any of this myself. Gordon Banks was of the opinion that someone put something, maybe ice, in one of his drinks.

Neil Phillips feels that if he had been able to treat the infection, then Banks might have recovered quickly, as Charlton and Newton had done. Sadly, he was not on the bus.

The less disciplined atmosphere of the England team, compared to 1966, was reflected in the aftermath of that party. Hurst took his wife Judith back to her hotel, though Alf warned him that he had to be back by midnight.

'Geoffrey, you do know when midnight is, don't you?'

'Yes Alf, we know,' said Judith with a withering look. 'It's when both hands are pointing upwards.'

That was a curfew hour that Emlyn Hughes was unable to meet by some margin. After going out drinking with his father and drowning his sorrows over his non-selection for the England side, he did not stagger back into the hotel until 1.30 am. Following training the next morning, Alf gave him a dressing down:

'What were my instructions to you last night, young man?'

'You're right, Alf, I was out of order. But surely you must understand how I feel. I'm here and you know how much I love the game and how keen I am, how much I want to play.'

Alf looked at Hughes coldly and said, 'I understand your feelings perfectly, young man. I pick the team. I pick the subs. I am the boss of this outfit. You'll do as I say, or, believe me, you'll be on the next plane home. Now piss off.'

'Look Alf, I have let you down. I really am sorry. It won't happen again.'

'Son, you haven't let me down. But if any of the journalists had been just a little bit naughty they could have written a hell of a story about England players drinking after a curfew. You would have only let yourself down.'

On the eve of the quarter-final, Alf had a far bigger problem than the consequences of Hughes' misbehaviour. The loss of England's premier goalkeeper through illness would be a disaster. Alf was so desperate to retain Banks that on the morning of the match, he and Harold Shepherdson gave Banks the most feeble of fitness tests. Banks told me:

> It was so silly, it was no test at all. It was just a bit of jogging for a few yards, and then Harold Shepherdson rolled a ball either side of me. I was just picking it up, not even diving. 'How do you feel?' said Harold. 'OK', I replied. But I had been expecting someone to be banging in balls at me.

At the subsequent team meeting, Banks suddenly felt ill again and had to retire to his room, where he was violently sick. It was obvious that his deputy Peter Bonetti of Chelsea would have to play. Bonetti had been put on standby the night before, as his room-mate Dave Sadler recalls:

> You could just feel the tension coming into Peter when he realized he might have to perform. He'd had the odd game, but by and large, he was happy to be second string to the best keeper in the world. When he was told he might have to go in, the nerves started immediately.

Those nerves were exacerbated by the anxiety gnawing away at Bonetti over the state of his marriage. It was in the enforced selection of Bonetti that the foolishness of bringing wives to Mexico damagingly revealed itself. Though they stayed in separate hotels, they were undoubtedly a distraction for the four players involved. This was partly because the players, understandably, wanted to make regular contact with their wives, and would often get on the phone straight away once they had returned from training – Peter Osgood recalls that Geoff Hurst 'seemed preoccupied as to where Judith was at any given time'. Just as importantly, the cohesion of the team was fractured in a way that never occurred in 1966. Those who were unaccompanied would regularly tease the quartet, as Neil Phillips remembers:

> When the players were trying to ring their wives, the others would take the mickey out of them. 'Oh, they're still in bed' or 'They're swimming nude in their hotel pool, having a whale of a time – why would they want to speak to you?' It was all jocular stuff. But it showed that the 18 players in the squad without their wives were not happy with the other four.

Of the breakdown in unity, Alan Ball said to me: 'As a squad, I thought 1970 was miles stronger, but not as a team. All-round we were definitely stronger, but not as a team.' And any sense of togetherness was not helped by the fact the Mexican press, eager to acquire any dirt on the England team, sought to exploit any tales of exuberant partying. Brian James has this interesting memory:

> The Mexicans loved spreading rumours, telling the players, 'Your wives are screwing everybody at the hotel.' I got friendly with some of the Mexican journalists out there and one of them rang me one day, saying 'I have a good story.' So I went to see him and he told me, 'At their hotel, the wives of the England players are hanging out with loads of

men. We are going in tonight with some lads, and a few photographers, and we're going to get some pictures of them. It will be a big front-page story tomorrow.'

'Oh, fuck.'

So immediately I ran out, got into a taxi and made my way to their hotel. Sure enough, there were the wives at the poolside bar – where they usually were. I went up to Judith Hurst and explained what was happening. She understood immediately and grabbed Cathy Peters and Tina Moore. 'Right, we've got to get out of here, go, go, go. Come on.' And the Mexicans turned up thirty seconds later, gigolos, girls, cameramen. It was all a set-up.

The uxorial problem was particularly acute with Peter Bonetti. A devout Roman Catholic, he did not take easily to the dressing-room banter about his wife's hotel activities. 'Peter was a much more sensitive person and could not laugh it off the way others could,' says Neil Phillips. But his anxiety was not entirely unfounded, as Brian James explains, 'Frances Bonetti was very, very pretty but she was one of those girls who used to come on to everybody. I think it was just her nature.' James continues: 'Peter was very upset when he heard people talking about his wife. On the night before the big match in Leon, he was tearing round looking for her.' Jeff Powell confirms that 'without a doubt, Bonetti was distracted because he had heard rumours that something might be going on. Frances lost the plot. The other footballers' wives, like Tina, were used to travelling, they kept their head, but Frances lost control of her emotions.' From the England camp, Dr Neil Phillips says he remembers that Bonetti was 'genuinely upset' about what he had heard. And Allan Clarke told me that the rest of the side were aware of the reports of frolics:

Yeah, we heard the rumours. Billy Bremner and Johnny Giles were fronting the World Cup coverage for ITV, and they were staying in the same hotel as the wives. Billy came to me and said, 'We're having a great time at our hotel. There's a great night life. Mooro's wife, Peter's wife, they're all there.' It seemed that they were having a better time than we were. Alf would have been worried bloody stiff if he had known.

Geoff Hurst doubted whether Peter Bonetti was in a fit mental state for such a crucial encounter. 'Peter was no slouch between the posts, but he had never played in a match as remotely important as the one now facing him. My own feeling at the time was that Peter's mind was not wholly on the job. It was across the city, with his wife Frances. Peter was a man who took his family responsibilities seriously.' If Alf had known Bonetti's predicament, he might have played Alex Stepney of Manchester United, regarded by many in the England squad as a better keeper than Bonetti. 'I thought on the day that Alf would have played Alex Stepney, because he was more of a big-time keeper than Peter. He had played through a European Cup Final, so he was more experienced in the big time atmosphere,' argues Francis Lee. 'I agree with Franny,' says Nobby Stiles. 'Peter was very nervous that day, great lad, smashing lad, but very nervous. I remember Denis Law saying to me that the difference between Peter and Alex was that "Peter will dive for the ball, whereas Alex will get across if he can. Every time Peter dives, I'll be in."' In fact, as Neil Phillips revealed to me, Alf himself had real concerns about Bonetti's big-match temperament. 'I remember discussions taking place between Alf and Dave Sexton, the manager of Chelsea. Dave would be saying what a marvellous keeper Bonetti was and Alf would reply, "Yes, when he's playing for Chelsea but I have real doubts about him when he's playing for England."'

The doubts about Bonetti turned out to be fully justified. England played superbly for the first 50 minutes against West Germany, going 2–0 up with goals from Peters and Mullery, who was having the game of a lifetime. No England team under Ramsey had ever lost from such a position and once more, as in 1966, the threat of the finest German player, Franz Beckenbauer, had been nullified by his duties in marking Bobby Charlton. 'When the second one went in I ran round the field shouting to the Germans, "Goodnight, God bless, see you in Munich,"' recalls Alan Ball. The celebrations were premature. Ramsey's team appeared to be cruising into the semi-finals. Then, with just 20 minutes to go, England suffered a dramatic reversal of fortune. Beckenbauer, breaking free for a moment from the shackles of Charlton, advanced towards the penalty box but was driven wide by the wonderfully dogged Mullery. It seemed like the attack had gone nowhere when suddenly Beckenbauer tried a shot. It was a vapid strike, one that should have been easily saved by Bonetti but somehow, as he dived, he allowed the gently rolling ball to squirm under his body. Bobby Moore was later scathing about Bonetti's error: 'Franz's shot was nothing special. If Peter is going to be honest with himself, he had to be disappointed. Psychologically, it was a desperate goal to concede. It was the sort of goal which cut your confidence from the back.'

It was soon after Beckenbauer's goal that Alf made probably the most controversial decision of his reign as England manager. With England still 2–1 up, he brought off Bobby Charlton, replacing him with Colin Bell. Alf's aim was to save Bobby, then 32, for the semi-final but the move backfired. Charlton had kept Beckenbauer quiet for two successive World Cup ties. Suddenly the great German, one of the most gifted playmakers of all time, was liberated. As Beckenbauer proceeded to dominate, England grew increasingly ragged and exhausted. To shore up his side, Ramsey brought on the hard-tackling Norman Hunter in place of Martin Peters, hoping to counter the insurgency of Jurgen Grabowski. It was too late. In the 76th minute the inevitable happened. From a mis-kicked England clearance, Uwe Seeler flicked the ball with the back of his head over Bonetti, who was left flailing in no-man's land. 2–2. 'England are throwing it away,' bellowed BBC commentator David Coleman. The game was about to enter extra-time.

There is a compelling symmetry about the 1966 final and the 1970 quarter-final, given the score-lines after 90 minutes, only in 1970, Alf could not produce the same inspirational rhetoric at the full-time whistle. By definition, a finest-hour speech can only be given once in a lifetime. By 1970, the grandeur of Alf was fading. He made a half-hearted attempt to rouse the troops, telling them, 'You did it in 1966, you can do it again,' but this time Alan Mullery, England's star of the match, said cynically, 'Yeah, but it wasn't 100 degrees in the shade at Wembley.' Mullery was instantly ashamed of his comment: 'I don't know why I said it and I have regretted opening my mouth ever since.' But his words summed up the exhaustion of his team. England could cope with the heat when they were winning. After conceding two sloppy goals, they were broken. In extra-time, Gerd Muller, 'der Bomber', won the game by hooking a close-range volley past the hapless Bonetti.

England were out of the World Cup. It was an unbelievable result, given England's total superiority for most of the first 90 minutes. Alf gave a rather forced handshake to the German manager, Helmut Schoen, and then retreated with his distraught side to the team hotel in Leon. Like most of his players,

Alf was barely able to speak. 'I never want to go through that again in my life,' says Alan Ball. 'Alf was as shell-shocked as the rest of us. We were so, so disappointed.' Brian Labone told me that 'losing that game was the most upsetting time of my life. It was thirty-five years ago, but it is still with me to this day.' Francis Lee has always refused to watch any video of the game:

I would find it too painful. Even now I look back on that day with real regret. The atmosphere after the German game was absolutely terrible because we knew we had them down and should have finished them off. Alf was so morose after the game. He was terrible. I saw him shaking hands with Helmut Schoen and he hardly knew what to do. On the coach back to the hotel, we hardly spoke. We hardly spoke for two days. It was the worst anti-climax of all time. It still affects me to this day.

Ken Jones tracked Alf down to the hotel two hours after the final whistle. He was sitting disconsolately at a table on his own. 'I couldn't think of anything to say. Nothing would have made any sense,' says Jones.

'Do you want a drink?' asked Alf. Jones nodded.

'Pour it yourself,' he said, handing over an opened bottle of champagne.

'You were so close . . .' said Jones. Alf was not listening.

'I still can't believe it. Of all the players to lose, it had to be him.' Alf was, of course, referring to Banks. In 1973, Alf gave this vivid description of his feelings after the final whistle:

I think I lost 15 years of my life in one afternoon. I was shattered but I couldn't show that in front of the players. I remember forcing myself to go and congratulate the German manager Helmut Schoen. It was necessary to do that but, by goodness, it wasn't easy. Our dressing-room was like a morgue. My job was to pick the players up off the floor. Jack Charlton wasn't playing that day but I can hear him now, telling me to let myself go. I couldn't. It's not in me to do that.

In the tortured aftermath of the game, Alf came in for a deluge of criticism about his substitutions. If he had not taken off Charlton, it was averred, Beckenbauer would never have been free to move forward. There is some truth in this. Alf had made the fatal mistake of planning for the next game before victory had been achieved. Beckenbauer himself added support to this view: 'When England were leading 2–0, we were completely dead. After I scored what I thought was a rather soft goal, Alf Ramsey decided to substitute Bobby Charlton, who we felt was the heart of their game. Ramsey made such a mistake in taking him off.' It was a view that captain Bobby Moore shared: 'As soon as Bobby Charlton walked away, it was like a ton weight had been lifted off Beckenbauer.' Not usually prone to confessing his errors, Alf privately admitted that he may have got it wrong. He told Bobby Charlton on the plane back to England that it was 'a mistake I shall always regret' to have taken him off. According to his secretary at the FA, Margaret Bruce, one of Alf's first actions on his return to Lancaster Gate was to express his annoyance at what he had done. 'He told me that he rued the moment he took off Bobby Charlton. "I shouldn't have done it," he said.'

But Alf was being too hard on himself. The reality is that, in the context of the match, his substitutions were perfectly sensible, given the boiling conditions of Mexico and the age

of Bobby Charlton. Far from undermining England, the introduction of Bell and Hunter could have reinvigorated the side.
As Alan Ball says:

When Alf took Bobby off, I thought to myself: 'Great, fantastic, Alf, bit of help in the middle of the pitch.' They were
fabulous substitutions at the time. Colin Bell and Norman
Hunter were two great lads in the middle of the park, great
runners, great lungs.

Bobby Charlton himself said he 'never blamed Alf for the
substitution. When he pulled me off, I did not doubt if for
a minute. I was disappointed only in that I felt really full of
running.' Francis Lee believes that the 'effect of the substitutions has been overdone. Colin came on and played well and
at that heat and altitude you have to use the subs.'

In truth, the entire debate about the substitutions is something of an irrelevance, for England would have almost certainly
won 2–0 if Banks had not been indisposed. No matter how well
a team plays, if the keeper makes a series of howling errors, they
are doomed to defeat. And that is what happened in Leon. 'No
way would we have lost with Gordon in goal,' says Ball.
'Gordon would not have allowed the first to go in and he would
have caught the cross on the second. I felt sorry for Peter but
ultimately he cost us.' From the press box, Brian James agreed:

Going back to the England hotel was almost like attending
a funeral. There was not anything you could say. I avoided
Peter Bonetti's eye. People blame the substitutions. It was
nothing to do with the substitutions. In fact the substitutions
were quite right. Bobby Charlton had worked his bollocks
off in the heat. The goals were the keeper's fault. Alf cer-

tainly believed that Peter was so shaken up before the game because of the rumours about his wife.

Tommy Docherty jokes that Bonetti acquired the nickname 'The Cat' because 'he was always pissing in the back of the net' and that was the way some England players felt about him in June 1970. 'Peter's role in our downfall is beyond argument,' says Geoff Hurst. Similarly, Brian Labone, according to Osgood, 'slated Catty', while Allan Clarke teased the Chelsea keeper.

> We'd been away from home for more than six weeks, which is a long time. Peter was as sick as a parrot, but I actually went up to him and said, 'Thanks a lot, Peter.'
>
> 'Why's that?'
>
> 'You've got us all home early.' I made him feel even worse.'

Alf also blamed Bonetti, though he would not say so in public. Nigel Clarke remembers this revealing conversation when they were working together on Alf's column in the *Daily Mirror*:

> He told me that he had not seen how England could lose to West Germany. He said to me, 'I knew my biggest test was coming up in three days in the semi-final and I had to have fresh legs. And Bobby was not getting any younger. But what I did not bank on was Peter throwing in two goals.' There was a pause and then Alf said, 'You're not going to put that in, are you?'
>
> 'Not if you don't want me to. It's up to you, Alf.'
>
> 'Well, Peter did throw two in but I would hate to put that in print.'

So Alf went on shouldering the blame for the defeat because of his substitutions.

As so often, the brilliantly perceptive Hugh McIlvanney went to the heart of the matter, writing in the *Observer*:

Sir Alf Ramsey's team are out because the best goalkeeper most people have ever seen turned sick, and one who is only slightly less gifted was overwhelmed by the suddenness of his promotion. Those who ranted smugly in distant television studios about the tactical blunders of Ramsey were toying with the edges of the issue. Errors there were and Ramsey in private has acknowledged one or two but the England manager is entitled to claim that his side were felled by something close to an act of God.

Such wise words brought little reprieve. Alf came home to an inevitable torrent of criticism. He had been a manager who lived by results, not by quality of football, and for the first time in his career since taking over at Ipswich he had experienced a real setback. If he had been better at public relations, he might not have been so vulnerable. But now the vultures were circling. He was condemned for his stubbornness, arrogance and negative tactics. When he said at a press conference on his return that England had 'nothing to learn from the Brazilians', he was only stating an objective truth, in the sense that everyone knew that Brazil, the winners of 1970, were the outstanding team of the tournament. But it sounded like gross provincial complacency. Joe Mercer, manager of Manchester City, complained that Alf had ignored him throughout his stay in the same hotel in Mexico: 'It's the art of a manager's job to foster friendship. As a public-relations man Alf is the worst in the business.' Malcolm Allison attacked Ramsey's caution,

especially in the game against Germany. 'If you play defensively, the opposition start getting confidence, they start to feel
you aren't so fearsome after all. So instead of saying, "We're
the champions, come and take it off us", you're saying, "We're
as worried as you are."'

Alf had to hope that he could improve England's performance. But he was entering new territory. For the first time in
his international career, England would have to qualify for the
World Cup finals.

# THIRTEEN

## *Katowice*

England players of Alf's era love to tell of the moments when he appeared to rebuke them for taking their places in the national side for granted. Gordon Banks says that after playing Yugoslavia in May 1966 he breezily called out to Alf in the Wembley car park, 'See you next time, Alf,' only to be greeted with the stern reply, 'If selected, Gordon.'

On another occasion, Ken Jones was giving a lift to Alf and Geoff Hurst. Alf was, as usual, left at Liverpool Street station, and as he stepped out of the car, Geoff said to him, 'See you at the next game, Alf.'

'Yes, Geoffrey, I'll send you a couple of tickets.'

Such statements have usually been taken as examples of Alf's determination to prevent his players becoming too complacent about England duty. Gordon Banks said of Alf's remark, 'It was a lesson to me that I had to fight for my England place no matter how well I had played in previous games.' But the greater likelihood is that they were only a demonstration of Alf's dust-dry sense of humour. The truth is that Alf remained almost obsessively loyal to the footballers that had brought him success in the past. Rather than experiment, he preferred to surround himself with those he trusted. This inability to rebuild, to create a long-term culture of continuing success,

was one of his weaknesses as a manager. It had happened at
Ipswich, where the failure to replace ageing limbs or change
outmoded tactics saw Ipswich in severe danger of relegation
only months after winning the title. And in the early seventies,
following the shock exit in Leon, the same process started to
happen with England. Alf built one great side for 1966, but
he struggled to do so again for 1974.

Alf is often portrayed as a ruthless, cold-hearted realist,
whose expressionless face reflected his inner hardness. But this
is a false picture. In fact, Alf was something of a sentimentalist.
There was little of the cynic about him. The love of westerns,
of his family and of his nation showed a man of simple but
profound feelings. And he extended that mix of nostalgia and
affection towards his teams. In 1963, for instance, when he
had to drop his favourite player, Jimmy Leadbetter, from the
Ipswich side, he was distraught. 'This was a terrible moment.
After all Jimmy had done for this team, he took it well, better
than I did,' said Alf. Like Prime Ministers, managers have to
be good butchers, but Sir Alf was too loyal to be one. Loyalty,
of course, had been one of the virtues that helped to create the
spirit of 1966. 'Loyalty was his massive strength. It served him
well for years. It won him the World Cup,' says Alan Ball. But
once the Cup had slipped from his grasp, he still remained
cautious in his selections and systems, reluctant to embrace
wholesale change. As Peter Osgood put it, 'After 1970, he
should have started to rebuild right away, because if we qualified for 1974, it was obvious that Bobby Moore would be too
old, and Mullery, Hurst and Lee weren't going to be around.
He left it too late. Mooro played until 1973, which was too
long.'

There was some inevitable speculation that, after the failure
in Mexico, Alf's position might be in question. But the FA
quickly quashed any of that talk. 'We acclaimed Sir Alf in

1966 as probably the best team manager in the world. As far as I am concerned, I have no reason to alter my opinions in view of our performance in Mexico,' said Sir Andrew Stephen, Chairman of the FA. And Alf himself had no intention of resigning, telling a press conference that any talk about his departure was 'pure invention on the part of newspapers, television and radio commentators'. But what the press were clamouring for was not a change in manager but in playing personnel. 'Now, not next year or the year after, is the time to look at fresh faces,' wrote Frank Magee in the *Sunday Mirror*.

In Alf's first competitive game after Mexico, against Malta in Valetta in a qualifier for the European Championship, Alf did make a few introductions of new players, though the spine of the team was still built around Banks, Ball, Peters, Hunter and Mullery. One of the enforced changes was Roy McFarland of Derby County for Bobby Moore, who had been suspended by his club for a late-night drinking session on the eve of an FA Cup tie. McFarland immediately sensed the spirit of loyalty that Alf had built in the England camp. 'The bond with the players had to be close because of the World Cup, but it was easy to come into it. You felt so much part of the camaraderie. There was a real bond there. Perhaps that was part of Alf's problem. Maybe he was too loyal for too long. Maybe he took longer than he should have done with the transition to younger players.' For all that, McFarland was deeply impressed with Alf as a manager from the moment he came into the squad.

Alf would come and speak to you privately on the training ground. The only piece of direct coaching advice he gave me, which really helped me improve as a player, was this, 'Roy, I have noticed that when you run and jump to head the ball, nobody will beat you. But from a standing jump, people do beat you. Practise doing it and you will improve. You may work with light weights and practise springing, but you have to do it from a standing position.' That shows how good Alf was. He honed in on one problem. He did not give long team talks. He spoke in the same manner in the dressing-room as everywhere else, no great emotion. I did not find him aloof. For me, he was quite warm. He was very modest, never boasted, never gloated about what he had achieved. His focus was completely on the players – that's why he would get annoyed with the press. When you were away with England, one person could not go off on his own. Whatever we did, we did together. If we went to the pictures, we all went together. He loved his cowboy films. I remember one hilarious time when we were going to see *Hang 'em High*. Alf just could not get the words out properly. He kept saying 'Hang Hem High' or 'Ang Em Igh'. He must have done this about a dozen times, until Ballie said, 'Oh come on Alf, for fuck's sake, it's *Hang 'em High*. Now let's get to the pictures.'

England were expected to enjoy a rout against Malta, but on a grassless, rutted pitch, they limped to a 1–0 win. So poor was the pitch that when Gordon Banks went to make a save, he ended up with a badly cut leg and torn shorts. Paul Reaney, who won the third of his three England caps in this game, remembers how Alf dealt with this problem:

It was an awful, dreadful pitch, rock hard. I will always remember Alf saying before we went out, 'Gentlemen, I understand the situation. If there is anyone who does not want to play, please tell me now before you go out.' Of course no one put their hand up. But Alf was ensuring that no one could come in making excuses at the end. It was a good tactic to stop the moaning. That was typical Alf. There was no ranting.

But the quality of the ground was of no concern to Alf's critics. The pressure on him was ratcheted up another notch. It was then eased somewhat as England proceeded to enjoy a string of decent results for the next 14 months. This better form saw England reach the quarter-finals of the European Championship, hammering Malta 5–0 at home, defeating Greece home and away and remaining unbeaten against Switzerland. Much to Alf's pleasure, Scotland were also crushed 3–1 at Wembley in May 1971. The worrying point, however, was that these performances had largely been achieved by the old guard. When England defeated Switzerland in Basle in October 1971, for instance, seven of the side – Banks, Cooper, Mullery, Moore, Lee, Hurst and Peters – were of pre-Mexico vintage, while England's 1–1 draw at Wembley in November against the Swiss prompted more complaints about 'Alf's old faithfuls not doing it any more'. In the *Daily Mail* Jeff Powell wrote of the need for Alf 'to pump fresh blood into his ailing team . . . The alternative is for all of us to sit and watch a once great international team dying slowly on its feet.' Despite qualification, a campaign of assassination against Alf was in full swing by the end of the year. 'Sir Alf would have to be stone deaf not to hear the knives being sharpened, the ammunition stacked and the verbal damnation being rehearsed,' wrote Ian Wooldridge in the *Mail*. 'You can hardly glance at a sports page or tune into a radio or TV debate without hearing the man demolished as though he were Public Enemy Number One and his methods dissected as if they were wholly responsible for the loss of the Empire.' And Wooldridge concluded prophetically: 'What you are witnessing, I suspect, is a classic story of the human race: of people waiting for the man who went up to pass them on the way down again. Had Sir Alf spent a little more time on personal relationships down the years, it might all be reading differently.'

Much of the press were clamouring for Alf to inject more excitement, youth and adventure into the team by promoting some of the daring individualists, like Osgood, Alan Hudson of Chelsea, or Rod Marsh of QPR, who were setting League football alight with their dazzling skills. Alf's refusal to integrate them into his side was widely seen as another indicator of his inherent dourness. Once more, it was said, he was putting a higher premium on industry than artistry. When Alf sent Marsh on for seven minutes in the home qualifier against Switzerland, Frank Harrington ruefully commented in *Reveille*, 'It's like putting a stopwatch on Casanova.' Waxing about Marsh's ability, Harrington described

how the crowd love those weaving figure-of-eight dribbles, that shrug of the hips that sends defenders shuffling the wrong way. If Alf has a fault, it is perhaps that he is too professional, that he has forgotten what draws spectators. Ramsey must experiment, chance his arm. Now is the time to go not only for style but youth.

Yet the picture was more complicated than the simple image of brilliant stars damned by a stubborn, blinkered manager. The reality is that in almost every case, Alf was willing to give these mavericks a try, but felt let down by their indiscipline, self-indulgence and absence of any team ethic. Alf knew that trophies are not won by a few crowd-pleasing moments but by hours of sacrifice for the team's cause. At the highest level, mere colourful talent was not enough. It had to be allied to professionalism, determination and moral courage. And this was not the judgement of Alf alone. Alf's successors with

England, and other club managers often shuddered at the self-destructive irresponsibility of these men, as did their fellow professionals. As Geoff Hurst argued: 'With the greatest respect, there's flair and then there's genius. And perhaps Alf didn't think they were the right sort of characters for him and his side of secure, solid, tougher players. The flair players of the seventies weren't in the same class, and he couldn't trust them with a free role in the way he could Bobby Charlton.' It was said of Peter Osgood, for instance, that he would not run five yards for the ball but he would run fifty for a fight. Mike Doyle of Manchester City, the club which Rodney Marsh joined in 1972 from QPR, blamed Marsh for losing City's title bid in 1972–73: 'It was clear he just wanted to do his own thing. You don't win anything with players like that in your side.' Malcolm Macdonald has this memory of Alf's fury at Marsh during a match against Scotland: 'I was substitute that day and I could see Alf fuming on the bench. He was getting madder and madder until you could practically see the steam coming out of his ears. In the end, he couldn't contain himself, "Harold, get that fucking clown off!"' Perhaps the most extreme example of petulance came from Alan Hudson, whom Alf tried to pick for the Under-23s in 1972. Annoyed at being left out of the full side, Hudson told Ramsey over the phone he would not join the Under-23s for a tour of Eastern Europe because he was putting his home life and club first. 'I was damned if I was going to put him before my family if that's the way he was going to treat me,' said Hudson later. Alf told Hudson: 'Your problems are no concern of mine. Be there in the morning. You'll take the consequences if you don't come.' To which Hudson replied, 'In that case, you'd better start now, because I won't be there.' Hudson never played for England under Alf. According to Ken Jones, he was no great loss, since he was an overrated footballer in the early seventies as a result of an injury: 'In 1970 he missed the Cup Final, missed Mexico and was never the same.' Moreover, Hudson showed a monumental indifference towards his personal fitness, sometimes drinking a bottle and a half of vodka and six pints of beer in the evening before going training the next morning. 'He was phenomenal, absolutely phenomenal,' says his Chelsea team-mate Ian Hutchinson of Hudson's capacity for drink. It was not a gift that Alf appreciated.

Nevertheless, it is fair to say that Alf felt far less connection to the colourful stars of the seventies than he had to the more solid, mature figures of the mid-sixties. There was an affinity of outlook between Alf and men like George Cohen, Ray Wilson and Bobby Charlton. They had all done military service for their country and experienced the maximum wage. Modest and dignified, they had a sense of privilege about earning their living as a professional footballer. They belonged to an era when extravagant emotions were frowned on. But Alf was a man out of time by the early seventies. His fifties demeanour, clothes and voice had looked reassuringly old fashioned in the mid-sixties. A few years later, he was in danger of becoming an anachronism. The fabric of Britain was starting to change dramatically. Authority was collapsing in every aspect of society, whether it be in the classroom or on the bloody streets of Belfast. The old post-war consensus broke down, with the trade unions asserting their own power in an unprecedented, often bullying manner. Politicians of all parties seemed impotent and bewildered. The country was in a state of near permanent crisis, reaching the nadir under Edward Heath of the three-day week in 1973, designed to cope with the shortage of power supplies. The traditional family unit was under threat, with divorce and lone parenthood on the rise. And Britain was on the road to becoming a multi-racial society, provoking an often anguished debate about national identity that continues to this day.

Questions of national self-confidence and authority had never troubled Alf before. Now he was in an alien environment, one that had infested football. Believing in hard work rather than hedonism, sacrifice rather than self-indulgence, he could not relate to a new generation that mocked the conservative values he held dear. Long hair and kissing on the field were an anathema to him. His enemies suggested he disliked flares just as much as flair. 'We used to take the mickey out of Alf Ramsey for being so straight and proper but not to his face because he didn't have a sense of humour, or at least not one I could see,' said Rod Marsh, the prince of the seventies glamour boys. 'As players became more affluent and they had outside interests, advertising and boutiques, I don't think Alf ever adjusted to that. I don't think he adjusted to the pop-star image of footballers. Alf and myself didn't get along.' A new amoral football culture was being built, one that was a world away from the stability and fidelity that Alf understood. As Neil Phillips put it: 'The attitude of players throughout the League was changing. A lot of them had picked up the showbiz thing and were therefore harder to discipline.' Ian Hutchinson of Chelsea once related that his manager Dave Sexton told his players to refrain from sex the Friday night before games:

> On Saturday morning, Ossie would promise that he hadn't made love the previous night, omitting to mention the fact that he'd got his leg over with an air hostess that morning. Free love, it was the in-thing. We went to a party in Sweden after playing Atvidaberg in the Cup Winners' Cup and our full-back bedded three different birds in one night.

As Arsenal's Peter Storey recalled: 'From the first time I kicked a ball as a pro, I began to learn what the game was all about. It's about drunken parties that go on for days: the orgies, the birds and the fabulous money. Football is just a distraction, but you're so fit you can carry on all the high living in secret.' It is impossible to think of any statement which more violently differed from the essence of Alf. His puzzlement at modern attitudes was beautifully captured in June 1972 when he picked the young Huddersfield striker Frank Worthington for the Under-23s. Worthington turned up at Heathrow Airport in high-heeled cowboy boots, red silk shirt, black slacks and a lime velvet jacket. Peter Shilton, also on the trip, recalls that Alf took one look at Worthington and said, 'Oh shit, what have I fucking done?'

The mood of self-interested rebellion sweeping the country was mirrored in football, where top clubs became ever more defiant of Ramsey's needs. Players were withdrawn from the England squads not just for major League and Cup games, but even for less important tournaments like the League Cup and the forgotten Texaco Trophy. Throughout this period, Alf had to conduct draining, sometimes bitter negotiations with club managers over the availability of their internationals. Norman Hunter says that Don Revie 'often found ways of keeping his players back from international matches'. Alf later claimed in an interview in 1986 that once, when he was on the phone to his wife from the England hotel, 'I heard Norman Hunter pleading with Revie to release him for England. Revie refused. Hunter broke down in tears.' In November 1971 after his preparations for the European qualifier against Switzerland were badly disrupted by a number of League Cup ties, there were rumours that Alf was so angered by the endless squabbling that he was on the verge of resignation. In an interview with Frank Magee in the *Sunday Mirror* he denied this but made clear how difficult his job had become. Having explained that he wanted to 'bring the right attitude in soccer about international football', he said, 'It is easy to say "I'm fed up" and quit. It is far more important to establish for the future the right of the England manager to have first call on the services of any player.' The *Daily Mail* was sympathetic to Alf's plight: 'At a critical time in English football development, Ramsey is pinned to the doorposts of his Lancaster Gate office by a number of very sharp league knives.' Even Alan Hardaker, the parochial League Secretary, admitted that Ramsey 'did not get a fair crack of the whip', though he also said that Alf 'failed to appreciate that there were times he also had to co-operate'. An indication of Hardaker's dismissive attitude towards Alf was reflected in this exchange, when Hardaker was making the case for the Newcastle striker Malcolm Macdonald to be allowed to play for his club rather than England.

'But you're not qualified to pick an England team,' said Alf.

'Well, after reading this morning's papers, I gather you're not either,' replied Hardaker.

Taking their cue from the League, several young players showed scant respect for an England call-up. Tommy Smith and Chris Lawler of Liverpool were selected for an Under-23 tour but said they wouldn't go, because they were too tired after a long season. As Smith recalls: 'Alf called us a couple of prize prigs. I'm afraid all we did then was go around the corner after he'd gone and have a good laugh.'

The nadir for Alf was reached in April 1972, when England played West Germany in the home leg of their European Championship quarter-final. Shortly before the game, the Derby manager Brian Clough withdrew Roy McFarland from Alf's squad, claiming he was injured. Yet just 48 hours later McFarland played in a crucial championship match for Derby. Alf was furious: 'This man calls himself a patriot but he has never done anything to help England. All he does is criticize us in the newspapers and television.' Because of the huge differences in their personalities, it was unlikely that Alf would have ever been close to the theatrical, alcoholic, loud-mouthed socialist, but after this incident, Alf barely spoke to Clough again. In McFarland's place, Alf picked Norman Hunter to play alongside Bobby Moore, but this left the central defence unbalanced because Moore and Hunter did not easily comple-ment each other, particularly because Moore was uncomfort-able at being asked to play the kind of hard-tackling, aerially powerful centre-half role that Jack Charlton used to fulfil. 'I was made uneasy by the lack of cohesion between Mooro and Hunter,' said Banks later. But England's other difficulty was directly Alf's fault. Ignoring the threat of Günther Netzer operating from an advanced midfield position, he failed to give anyone the role of marking the brilliant but erratic young German. According to Francis Lee, Netzer's name was barely even mentioned in the team talk. But on the night, he tore England apart with his precision passing and incisive runs. At one stage he was wreaking such havoc with England that Hunter yelled at Moore, 'Let me have a chance to get the bastard,' only for Moore to reply, 'This is the way Alf wants it and that's how it's going to be,' a demonstration of how Moore still respected Alf's authority.

West Germany won 3–1, England's worst defeat at home since Hungary in 1953. 'They murdered us, they couldn't do a thing wrong,' said Alan Ball. Alf's strategy and selection were now under severer attack than at any time since he was appointed a decade earlier. 'Have the methods of the only man to win the World Cup for England become as dead as a dinosaur? Does not Ramsey's ponderous system based on prodigious work-rate, no wingers and endless, top-speed run-ning also burn up players?' asked Alan Hoby in the *Sunday Express*. Francis Lee, who played his last game for England that night, agreed that Alf's tactical rigidity was undermining the team's effectiveness:

We were still playing 4–4–2 in the seventies. I don't think Alf was trapped. He just believed in 4–4–2. By then the system was becoming outdated. I am a great believer at international level that you have to play with three at the back and five in midfield, because you cannot have your four at the back marking one player. You must have three at the back to give you the flexibility in midfield. You'd have a great player like Cruyff who would start off in the front, then drop back, giving the Dutch six in midfield and he would have freedom. That is where we did not readjust. We could have played three at the back and had more strength in midfield. The reason we got beaten by Germany at Wembley was because we got murdered in midfield. It did not matter how much effort the lads put into midfield, because they were outnumbered. And when you are outnumbered by class acts, there is a problem.

Alf's next move only further damaged his already plummeting reputation. When England played the away leg of the German tie in Berlin in May, Alf appeared desperate merely to save face rather than gain the substantial victory that was needed. To resolve the midfield problem, he brought in Peter Storey, one of the toughest, most cynical tacklers in the game, as well as shifting Norman Hunter from central defence. To Alf's critics, it was the distillation of everything that was wrong with his stodgy, joyless, narrow approach, with its emphasis on closing down opponents rather than encouraging good football. Predictably, the game ended in a goalless draw. Afterwards, the Germans complained, with some justification, about the violence of England's methods. 'The whole England team has autographed my leg,' said Günther Netzer.

Many thought that the German defeat should have spelled the end of Alf. 'Most managers have a finite usefulness and

Ramsey was no exception,' wrote Brian Granville. 'By 1972, he was not the same man. This was plainly the time for Ramsey, who had achieved so much, to go.' But Alf was not a man to walk away from a challenge. From his earliest days in Dagenham, he had battled against being tainted by failure. The next World Cup represented the chance of redemption. Besides, he still retained the support of most of his players. Rod Marsh had little time for Ramsey, saying that 'I didn't feel suited to play in the England set-up; Alf wanted me to be another Geoff Hurst, and that wasn't me at all,' but Marsh was very much an exception. The noise from the press and public only drew the Ramsey camp closer together. 'The knives were out for Alf,' recalls Peter Shilton. 'I did not think within the team there was any decline in his authority. I personally did not see that at all. There was still great loyalty and respect for him.' Mike Summerbee, who played in most of the games in 1972, strongly disagrees with Marsh about Ramsey: 'Rodney is that type of person and he does not like the disciplinarian thing. I don't feel that Alf was out of touch. He was still a great manager, still in tune with football. I always found him very supportive, very loyal to his players. He was a person you always looked up to.' Younger players who came into the side also testify that there was little sign of Alf's influence on the wane. Colin Todd, who won the first of his 27 caps in 1972, told me: 'His style was not outdated. There was a tremendous authority about him. As a youngster coming into the dressing-room, I found him wonderful: calm and controlled. While I was with the England team under him, it was like a close-knit family.' Joe Royle, now manager of Ipswich, won two caps under Alf, the second of them against Yugoslavia:

Alf said something in the team talk which really lifted me. He reminded the players that while I was a centre-forward with a decent head, I was equally receptive to the ball played to my feet. So we must not get pulled into a long-ball game just because we had a big striker who could head the ball. That made me feel really good about myself. It shows his gift for saying the right thing. He was a man of few words but every word counted. He was a very calming influence, a very dignified man. He hid his passion well but there is no doubt that he was a passionate and proud man. I was not intimidated going into the England set-up. Everyone was met with a smile and a handshake. He always made a great play for reminding players that they were in the England team because of what they did for their clubs. Therefore, because you were playing for England, you did not necessarily have to do anything different to what you did for your club.

Ray Clemence, the Liverpool goalkeeper who made his debut in 1972 against Wales, felt that Alf still had

a very tight squad. It was still a very tight community. There was no sense of Alf losing his authority. When you went into the team, you realized what a great man he was, with so many top players holding him in such high regard. He was a gentleman, but I was definitely in awe of him.

Sadly for Alf, it was not the views of the players that counted, but public opinion and the press. And by the end of 1972, the press were whipping up a frenzy against Alf. Such was the depth of feeling against Alf that a few knowing smiles were exchanged in the Wembley press box after the German defeat, as several journalists took pleasure in thinking that their arch enemy was on the slide. What Alf was experiencing was a new form of journalism, raw, sensational and personality-driven.

The days when Hugh Cudlipp at the *Mirror* thought it was the duty of his paper to raise intellectual standards were long gone; the new breed of tabloids wanted to appeal to baser instincts, creating a new climate of near permanent excitement with one noisy campaign after another. Sports coverage succumbed, as newspapers woke up to the huge public interest in football. For the first time, soccer reached the front pages. Brian James gives this description of the change in atmosphere at his own paper, the *Daily Mail*:

> There was a lot of pressure going on. Charlie Wilson, my editor, was kicking arses all the time. He was a hard man who thought we sports reporters were all soft. He thought England should be going out and winning 10–0 every game and if they weren't there was something wrong with the manager. And he believed that we should be getting scoop after scoop, not just covering matches. So he'd say to me, 'I want you to go and see Alf Ramsey and offer him £50 to tell you the next England team.' I told him it couldn't be done. Wilson couldn't comprehend who we were dealing with: 'What do you mean, he won't tell you?' The next thing, Wilson sends our golf correspondent out to Alf's home in Ipswich to get the team. So there is our golf reporter, banging on Alf's windows, trying to get an answer. Of course, Alf refused to say anything.

Joe Royle, who as a long-serving, successful manager, has himself experienced the cauldron of media pressure, feels that Alf was the victim of this changing trend in journalism: 'Before the seventies, managers would often socialize with the press. But by the end of Alf's reign, it was a 'them and us' situation. It grew from a murmur to a grumble to a roar. Alf was very poorly treated by the press, there's no doubt about that.'

Perhaps even more serious for Alf than the press was the growing antagonism towards him within the FA. For ten years, he had treated its leading members with contempt and his obvious disdain had rankled with them. On one occasion during an England tour, an FA official had turned to Alf and brightly said, 'Aren't we doing well?' To which Alf responded: 'What do you mean, we? The players are doing well. You're just here for the cocktails.' Mike Pejic, the Stoke defender, was part of Alf's squad in 1973 and 1974. He remembers this incident during a trip to Russia:

We were on the coach waiting for some of the FA officials who were still hanging around the hotel. Alf sent Les Cocker inside with the instruction to tell the FA men that, 'If you are not on the bus in two minutes, then you're going to have to catch taxis.' Next thing you saw the FA officials running down the steps and racing each other to get on the bus. Alf was really about to say, 'Off we go.' It was one of the sort of things that probably cost him in the end.

Peter Shilton gives this account of Alf's annoyance during an Under-23 trip:

I was sitting with some of the lads enjoying a drink with Alf when one of the FA's blazer brigade strolled up and engaged Alf in conversation.

'We played very well tonight, I think,' said the official.

'Yes, these boys did very well,' agreed Alf.

'Yes, very well. What's-his name at number 9, did very well.'

'Joe, Joe Royle.'

'Royle! That's the one. Did well. And the goalkeeper too. Had a very good game.'

'Peter, Peter Shilton.'

'Shiften. Yes. Very good. So well done to you all,' said the official, making his exit. Once he was out of earshot, Alf turned to us.

'Bloody silly sod,' he said. Alf took a sip of his gin and tonic and sighed, 'And there, with the likes of him, gentlemen, hangs my job as England manager.'

The silly sods were now planning to strike back, and for the first time they had a leader who was determined to pull down Ramsey. Professor Sir Harold Thompson, the FA's vice-chairman, was a formidable intellect. An internationally renowned chemist and Oxford don, he had been a tutor to the young Margaret Thatcher, as well as one of the founders of the famous Pegasus amateur side of the 1950s. But his academic achievements, combined with a natural booming self-confidence, made him a figure of almost suffocating pomposity. The normally restrained Alan Odell, secretary of the FA's international section, says that

Harold Thompson was a bastard. He was a brilliant man, but as a person I could not stand him. He was one of the very few people I have met in my life that I detested. He treated the staff like shit. No one liked him. He would offend people so much. He was one of those old public-school, upper-class lot. He would come in and say, 'Odell, do this.' There was never a 'please' or a 'thank you' or an attempt to call you by your first name. It was always a barked surname, even if he was talking to Alf or international players.

As well as being pompous, Thompson was priapic. He had an appalling reputation for sexually harassing women, and British European Airways once made a formal complaint about his trying to touch up a stewardess. 'No girl was safe in a lift with him,' says David Barber of the FA. One club director described to me this incident on tour:

> We went to a reception at the British Embassy. There were two 20-year-old girls on the staff and they came up to me and said, 'Could you do us a favour?' Sir Harold Thompson and some other FA directors have invited us to a casino tonight and we think that they have an ulterior motive. Could you chaperone us?'
>
> 'You're joking.'
>
> 'No, we went out for dinner last night. While they kept offering us red wine, they were pouring theirs on the carpet. So please come.' So I did chaperone them to make sure there were no unwanted advances from Thompson and the rest.

Thompson's domineering, authoritarian manner was particularly loathsome to Alf, whose insecurity always rose at any hint of condescension: 'He always referred to me, even to my face, as Ramsey, which I found insulting.' Two incidents highlighted the deep antagonism between the two men. The first occurred in October 1972, after England's 1–1 draw with Yugoslavia at Wembley. 'Thompson was standing 10 yards away. He turned up his nose, implying it was a bad performance, a bad match. I looked at him and turned away.' The second occurred eight months later during a trip to Prague for a friendly against Czechoslovakia. It was Thompson's first trip overseas with England, and in common with the other FA officials, he was having breakfast with Alf and the England players in their private dining room at the hotel. 'He was smoking a cigar over breakfast,' recalled Alf, 'although no England player ever smoked during a meal. With him, it was always a cigar. He never seemed to be without one in his mouth, even when talking to you. I turned to Dick Wragg, the chairman of the senior international committee, and said, "Do you mind if I have a word with Sir Harold Thompson and ask him to put out his cigar?" Wragg did not object so I went over to Sir Harold Thompson and said politely that my players didn't smoke and that his cigar was unpleasant for them. I explained that he could either put it out or eat in another room.' Thompson put the cigar out, but he had never been treated that way by an employee before. Alf's fate may have been sealed in that Czechoslovakian breakfast room.

As long as Alf had been delivering results, his position was safe. But the twin German disasters made his position precarious. And misfortune continued to dog him. In October 1972, his team suffered the disastrous loss of Gordon Banks through a car accident that destroyed the sight in one eye and finished his career. Peter Shilton was a ready replacement, but he lacked Banks' experience. Alf continued to struggle to find forwards who could match Geoff Hurst. Apart from Joe Royle, others he tried included Allan Clarke and Martin Chivers, who won 17 and 24 caps respectively under Alf, as well as Tony Brown of West Brom, Mick Channon of Southampton and Kevin Keegan, the busy Liverpool striker who first played against Wales in 1972. Keegan found the transition from Liverpool to England difficult:

I don't think Alf rated me as a player at the time. I have a feeling that pressure from outside influenced his decision to call me into the squad. Alf put me alongside Rodney Marsh and Martin Chivers, and until a manager experiments with a new blend of players, he cannot possibly know whether it will work. I just might have been able to bring something out of Marshie, and he done likewise for me, but it did not happen. When I moved inside for England, both

Marshie and Chivers stood still, leaving me nowhere. I ended up wandering out on the wing, feeling frustrated and disillusioned.

On Alf as a manager, Keegan says:

We were never close. We did not have time to get to know one another, but I found him fairly predictable. He rarely surprised people and if anyone annoyed him he would dismiss them tactfully and without a fuss. A manager has to lean towards his players, something the press do not seem to realize. If he gravitates towards the press at the expense of his players, he has no chance of success. Alf was only concerned with his players. He was probably wrong to be quite so emphatic about this, but he did, at least, win the respect of the players.

Malcolm Macdonald, the Newcastle striker, was another he tried. It might be imagined that Macdonald, one of the most explosive, charismatic players of the seventies, would have the same negative opinion of Alf as some of the other extroverts like Marsh and Hudson. Nothing could be further from the truth. Macdonald was a huge admirer of Alf's from their very first meeting, when Alf picked him for an Under-23 squad against Scotland in 1970: 'I found him one of the most polite men I have ever met in my life. He thanked me profusely for putting myself out and making the journey, and he hoped I hadn't been prevented from doing anything important. In fact, he made me feel like a million dollars!' In the next couple of years in the Under-23s, Alf remained 'a great supporter of me as a player for exactly what I did at club level. That message came through loud and clear at team meetings and half-time talks. He was always urging people to get their heads up to look for my runs and knock me in, so it was obvious for me to not stop doing that.' Once he reached the full squad, Macdonald was struck by the thoroughness of Alf's team talks:

> Once he got going there would be no stopping him. He would go through every position in the England team, every player in the opposing team, how generally he expected us to play against them, what we had to watch out for them doing to us. He would go through corner-kicks, free-kicks and who went in our wall, even to the extent of establishing who would be at one end and who would be at the other. He was absolutely meticulous in his planning. He never referred to any notes, either. It all just came out of his head.

Macdonald was part of the England team which beat Scotland 1–0 at Hampden in 1972, when Alan Ball's provocative antics aroused the ire of the Scottish players and crowd. Ball's hatred of the Scots matched that of Alf's – he called them 'skirt-wearing tossers' – and towards the end of the game, as England hung on grimly to their lead, he took the ball to the corner flag, sat on it and gave the V-sign to the Scots. Predictably, he was soon hacked off the ball and England won a free-kick. Moments later, he got hold of the ball again, took it to the corner flag and sat on it. By now, 120,000 Scots were going beserk, their rage made all the greater when Alan stood up, kept his foot on the ball and proceeded to wipe his nose on the flag of St Andrew which stood on the corner spot. Seconds later, the final whistle went, and England dashed for the safety of the dressing-room. 'I have never been so fearful', says Macdonald. But what was fascinating was Alf's reaction. 'Alf walked in, and with a big grin on his face, said, "Alan, Alan, you really are a very naughty boy."'

Victories over Scotland, no matter how satisfying, were not

going to keep Alf in his job. Only a successful World Cup campaign could do that, and England appeared to have a comparatively straightforward passage into the finals in West Germany in 1974, having been drawn in a small group against unfancied Wales and Poland. England got off to a solid, if not dazzling, start, beating Wales 1–0 in Cardiff, but then were held to a 1–1 draw at home by Wales at Wembley in January 1973. Given that the Welsh side included three players from the Second Division and one from the Third, it was a shabby performance by England, in which their defence looked insecure and the front-line powerless. Keegan, Chivers and Marsh again failed to impress, while England's goal actually came from an opportunistic 25-yard shot by Norman Hunter. Towards the end, England were slow-handclapped by the Wembley crowd. It was to be Marsh's last game for England, his downfall assisted by a cheeky remark he made within Alf's earshot. Before the match, Alf went up to Marsh and said:

'I've told you before that when you play for England you have to work harder. I don't care what you've done at Manchester City or QPR but that's what you have to do for me. In fact this is the last chance I'm going to give you. In the first 45 minutes I'll be watching you and if you don't, I'm going to pull you off at half-time.'

'Christ!' muttered Marsh, 'At Manchester City all we get at half-time is a cup of tea and an orange.'

It was a typical piece of cockney wit, which Marsh thought the unworldly Alf would not understand even if he heard it. But Alf knew enough to know that Marsh was mocking him. And he was not a good enough player to get away with such sarcasm.

After dropping points against Wales, it was vital that England avoided defeat in Katowice in June 1973. By now, relations between Alf and much of the press were almost at freezing point. They sunk below zero when the journalists arrived in Katowice, only to find out that they were being kicked out of the hotel they had originally been booked into, the Hotel Silesia, which was also being used by the England party. They now had to stay in the much more downmarket Hotel Katowice. The decision had obviously been taken by Alf and the FA. What made it even more insulting was that the 50 rooms vacated by the press were filled by travelling England fans. 'What it comes down to is that Alf would rather have his players surrounded by yobs in rosettes, yelling for autographs, than us,' said one reporter. Alf did nothing to assuage the press's anger at a conference he gave on the eve of the game. In a diary kept by Brian James, he left this record:

More than 80 English and Polish press and TV are waiting as Alf arrives, stone-faced. To the first question, 'Can you give us the team?' he replies, 'I will deal with this very quickly. The team will be announced tomorrow. Probably. Around lunchtime. Probably.' There's a grim silence, then Frank Magee of the *Daily Mirror* asks with careful politeness, 'Could you tell us why you are delaying naming the team? Is it a matter of tactics, or are there practical reasons, like injuries?' Ramsey stares back and snaps, 'Do I have to give you reasons? I have already told you what I am going to do.' There is a long, dreadful, embarrassed silence. Englishmen stare down at their feet, acutely aware that the insulted Magee has probably been Alf's greatest supporter over the past 10 years. The conference drags on for a further 10 minutes, time for Ramsey to complain about not being offered 'even a glass of water' and 'Polish TV teams with their hot uncomfortable lights'. As he leaves, a hostile silence is broken only by derisory handclaps from three Polish writers. Magee is visibly upset. 'I consider this man to be a friend. But I was both embarrassed and outraged by what he did in there.'

The gloom which hung over the England entourage only deepened as Alf's team gave one of most disappointing performances of his reign. The pessimism of the press seemed to have infected the players. 'Somehow, I didn't feel the old confidence,' recalled Alan Ball, who was winning his 64th cap. Within seven minutes England were 1–0 down, conceding a goal from a free-kick which sailed between Moore and Shilton. It was a sloppy goal, the kind that infuriated Ramsey, who was always meticulous in his planning at set-pieces. The second was an even more grievous, self-inflicted wound. Just after the start of the second half, Bobby Moore gathered the ball near the half-way line. As he looked round the field with his characteristic assurance, the Polish forward Lubanski quickly advanced on him. Moore casually tried to side-step him, lost his balance and gave away the ball. Lubanski gleefully charged down the field and flashed a shot past Shilton. England never looked like recovering. With just fifteen minutes to go, Ball took out his frustration on the midfielder Cmikiewicz, grabbing him by the neck and jerking a knee towards the Pole's groin. The referee had no alternative but to send him off.

Alf's empire was crumbling into incompetence and indiscipline. As one-eyed as ever, Alf suggested to the press afterwards that England had actually been the better team. He was fooling no one. 'Ramsey had picked the wrong players in the squad, and from that squad chosen the wrong team,' wrote the *Daily Mail*'s Brian James. 'Ramsey had instructed his players badly, and had failed to reinforce them with substitutes when he needed to do so. Ramsey had thrown away England's best chance.' In a way, this was an even worse result than Leon, when England has lost a 2–0 lead thanks to goalkeeper errors. In Katowice, England had not even looked like scoring. That night, most of the England players gathered in Bobby Moore's room for a drink of commiseration. They were discussing the game, and Peter Shilton remembers being struck by Bobby Moore's lack of any self-pity: 'Bobby came over as aloof but he was special in his own way. I learnt so much from him that night, seeing how he could handle such a big disappointment. That is how I saw his greatness on the field.' As the players talked, suddenly there was knock on the door. It was Alf. This was something of a surprise, since he usually kept a social distance from the team. 'Mind if I join you?' he said. The discussion began again, and immediately Alf started saying that he was at fault for the first goal because he should have ensured that the space behind the wall was covered. Colin Bell then tried to take the blame, claiming that he should have been there but Alf would have none of it. As Roy McFarland recalls: 'Alf blamed himself and would not listen to us. He had one beer and then said, "Thank you very much for the drink" He then got to the door and repeated, "It was still my fault. Goodnight, gentlemen." I could see then why all the players loved him and loved working with him.'

It was a tired and morose England team that left Poland the next morning for Moscow for the next leg of their summer tour. There were to be two further matches, one against Russia and one against Italy in Turin. They boarded the BAC-111 and as the plane took to the sky, the newspapers were brought out by the stewardesses. Jeff Powell recalls:

It was one of those aircraft with some seats facing forwards and some backwards. I was sitting in an aisle seat facing forwards and Alf was further up the plane, facing back down the plane. Alf was holding up the *Daily Mail*, his favourite paper, and I could see the headline above my report on the back page, RAMSEY'S PLANS BETRAY ENGLAND. Alf, of course, was an intense patriot. So as I saw those words I thought to myself, 'Bloody hell.' He turned over the paper to look at the back. He lowered it, glared at me and then raised it again. He did not speak to me throughout the journey or for sometime afterwards. Only over some drinks after the game against Italy did he come up to me and say, 'Well, we'll put that behind us now.' We chinked our glasses and Alf was OK.

David Lacey of the *Guardian* has a happier memory of this trip to Moscow, when Alf was trying to build some bridges after his icy behaviour in Poland:

A few of us were having some beers outside the team's hotel, the Metropole, in Moscow. Alf joined us and unwound completely about the match in Katowice and Bobby Moore. In a memorable phrase, he told us that 'If Bobby Moore had wept, we would have all wept with him.' I found Alf a very human type of guy and you could see why all the players liked and respected him. But he did not like being questioned. He would join in a conversation but he would freeze up if he thought an answer to a question might go on the record. He was old-fashioned in the sense that he thought writers should report the match. All the rest was intrusive to him. One of the most important aspects of our job was to know the team. He once pulled a fast one on us there before a game at Hampden. The journalists had been battering him all Friday about who would be playing. He stonewalled everything. Then, in the early evening, most of the journalists had done their pieces for the day. Some were having a few drinks, others had gone to the cinema. Then

Alf got on the phone to the Press Association to ring through the team. That showed a sense of humour.

The England tour ended sadly. After a narrow victory in Moscow, England were beaten by Italy in Turin, the first time the Italians had defeated England in 40 years. But of far more concern than records was qualification for the World Cup.

Alf's international career would be heading to a close unless England beat Poland at Wembley on 17 October 1973. The match was to be the biggest in England since 1966 and England warmed up satisfactorily by beating a weak Austrian side 7–0. But Alf knew this result meant little for the Polish encounter. Shortly before the vital game, he flew to Holland to watch Poland. Ken Jones travelled with him and took this account of Alf's reflective conversation:

I have been through all the emotional hazards that go with this job. I've known success and failure, elation and disappointment. When England win, everything belongs, quite rightly, to the players. They are the people who have made victory possible. When England loses, it is my responsibility. But football management is a double-edged thing. On one hand, the manager gets too much credit, on the other, he takes too much of the blame. I have never looked for praise. It makes me uncomfortable.

The game was vital, not just to Ramsey's future, but to the future of English football: 'This October match is the thundercloud hanging over the new season. Failure would bring the sort of cataclysm not seen since Ramsey's last match as an international right-back, the 6–3 slaughter by Hungary 20 years ago,' wrote Mike Langley in the *People*. Yet, typically, the League remained as purblind as ever, refusing to cancel the fixtures for the Saturday before the game. In a statement of breathtaking complacency, Alan Hardaker said: 'If England do lose against Poland, the game is not going to die. It will be a terrible thing for six weeks, and then everybody will forget about it.' While Hardarker puffed on his pipe in his self-satisfied way, Alf had to endure further rounds of criticism of his management style, with Brian Clough, Tommy Docherty and Malcolm Allison taking to the airwaves to question his approach. But on the night itself, Clough had no doubt that England would emerge victorious, since the Polish keeper Tomaszewski was nothing more than 'a clown'. Clough was reflecting the growing public optimism that England would pull through because of home advantage. For all the abuse that Alf had endured, it was worth noting that England had only lost four times in 27 games since Mexico in 1970. 'On form and ability, England should win comfortably,' wrote David Lacey, though he added prophetically: 'The main doubts will concern the ability of the front three, Channon, Chivers and Clarke, to snap up the fleeting chances that come their way.'

Peter Shilton remembers Alf's team talk before the match because of its unusual intensity: 'It was the most passionate talk I ever had from him. You could really tell that he had gone up a level. He was not shouting but he was letting the players know how important it was to him to get a result.' For one of the few times in a competitive match since 1962, England lined up without Bobby Moore, who was relegated to the substitutes bench, the captain's armband being taken by Martin Peters. Alf felt it a severe wrench to leave out the player with whom he had shared so much, both in glory and defeat, but he knew that Bobby's powers were fading. 'It was a bad moment for me. Bobby was shattered,' said Alf.

As the match got under way, the chances were more than fleeting; they came in wave after wave, but somehow the England forwards failed to find the back of the net. Tomaszewski proved himself anything but a clown as he pulled of a series of acrobatic, sometimes eccentric saves. England were also desperately unlucky, frequently shaving the post or the crossbar. For Alf, it was horribly reminiscent of the most agonizing game of his playing career, when England laid siege to the USA goal in 1950 without being able to convert any of a string of chances. And like the Americans, the Poles scored with one of their first attacks. In the 57th minute, Norman Hunter went to meet a Polish clearance down the right-hand side as the balding winger Lato also rushed to the ball. Usually, Hunter would have just belted the ball – and the man – into touch. But this time, he failed to go through with the tackle and lost possession. It was almost a carbon copy of Moore's error in Katowice. Lato ran forward, paused, then threaded the ball to Domarski, whose shot skidded off the lush Wembley turf and underneath Shilton's diving body. 1–0 to Poland. Today, Norman Hunter is open about his error:

> I should have just come across and tapped it out of play with my left and then defended. But because we had to win the game, I tried to keep it in with my right foot. To tell you the honest truth, I was waiting for a crunching tackle. I was setting myself for that. But then the winger actually started to slow down so I thought, 'I'll try and keep this in play and nick it round him. But it went straight under my right foot.' I should have known better than to go with that one. That's how it happens. That's the end of it.

Peter Shilton also admits to having made the wrong decision:

> What I should have done was make a blocking save, or parry the shot away for a corner. But I tried to get hold of the

ball by scooping it into my body and retaining possession. It was the speed of the ball coming off the turf, together with the fact that I had been momentarily unsighted when Domarski actually struck it, that beat me.

England now had to score twice. The attacks became more feverish, but still the ball would not go in. Given the number of chances, England's inability to score defied the law of averages. 'How we did not win that by four or five I do not know. It was unbelievable,' says Hunter. In the 60th minute, England managed to claw one back, thanks to an Allan Clarke penalty. The bombardment intensified, with Channon, Clarke and Tony Currie all missing good chances or being denied by the spectacular Tomaszewski. 'It was the most one-sided international I have ever played in my life,' says Allan Clarke, who saw one of his efforts miraculously tipped over the bar. 'I half-turned, thinking it was about to reach the back of the net.' With just fifteen minutes to go, the score was still 1–1. Bobby Moore on the subs bench started to urge Alf to send on Kevin Hector, the Derby striker. All Alf did was push Norman Hunter forward. The Polish goal somehow remained intact. 'As the minutes unwound, seemingly faster and faster, there he sat with the substitutes on the sidelines. What fires were burning inside him, one perhaps will never know. But he sat there immobile, while his men out on the field drained themselves of their last ounce of energy,' wrote Geoffrey Green in *The Times*. Then with just two minutes left, Alf finally relented and put on Hector in place of Chivers, who'd had a poor game. Despite its extreme lateness, the substitution almost did the trick, Hector seeing one of his headers scrambled off the line in the dying seconds. Alf's tardiness over Hector might seem like another example of his obduracy, but according to Nigel Clarke there was a bizarre chronographical explanation:

Unbelievably, his watch had stopped and he did not realize that there were only two minutes to go. He said to me, 'I suddenly realized that it had stopped. I know people will wonder why I did not rely on the stadium clock. But I always used to go by my own watch. The stadium clock could be far slower.' He always went by his own timing. He would never call out to Harold, 'How long left?' Bobby Moore was at his side saying, 'Alf, you've got to get someone on.' Bobby started to tear at Kevin Hector's tracksuit bottoms before Alf had given the word out. Then Alf realized that his watch had stopped and he shoved Kevin on immediately. Afterwards, Alf said that he 'shivered about it'.

'A little neglect may breed mischief. For want of a nail the kingdom was lost,' went the 18th-century maxim. Hector's intervention was too late. The match was drawn. England had failed to qualify for the World Cup for the first time in history. Disconsolately, the England players retreated off the Wembley turf, Bobby Moore putting a consoling arm around Norman Hunter. 'I've never been in a dressing-room like it. Players were crying,' said Roy McFarland. Tony Currie recalled: 'It was an accumulation of bad finishing, lucky goalkeeping and good goalkeeping and fate. We all sat in the dressing-room afterwards and not a word was said. Everyone was in shock.' Yet even in this, one of the saddest episodes of his managerial career, Alf could spare a thought for others. He ordered the shattered players to wait in the dressing-room, for a presentation was due to be made by the FA to Harold Shepherdson for his long service to the England cause. Typically, the FA did not show the same sensitivity as Alf. Not one of their directors bothered to show up for the ceremony, even though Shepherdson's wife had come down especially from Middlesbrough. Neil Phillips gives this account:

All the players in the dressing-room were completely and utterly dejected. Some of them were in tears because they knew they would never have an opportunity again of playing in a World Cup. Alf insisted that they stay until the directors presented Harold with his silver salver. So we were all sitting round the dressing-room, really dejected. We sat there for three-quarters of an hour and not one FA director came into the dressing-room, not one. In the end, Alf went away to find out what was going on and came back and said, 'I'm sorry but the directors are not coming down because they found the area was too crowded.' The crowds had not stopped them coming down after the 1966 World Cup final.

A pall of despair hung over Ramsey's footballers. Even today, many of them are still pained at the recollection of the game. 'I was meant to be doing a commercial the next day at my house in Leeds for the Nat West Bank and I just could not do it. It took me three weeks to get over the disappointment,' says Allan Clarke. 'It was awful. It was devastating. It was the lowest I have been in football. Driving home that night was miserable,' says Roy McFarland. On the surface, the FA appeared to share this sorrow. On 5 November 1973, the Council passed a resolution expressing 'sincere regrets to Sir Alfred Ramsey that the England team had been eliminated from the World Cup' but adding that he had 'the unanimous support and confidence of the Senior Committee'. But Professor Sir Harold Thompson, still brooding about being told what he could do with his cigar, was not happy about this. He saw the Polish defeat as the ideal chance to be rid of Ramsey. So at the next Council meeting on 26 November, he put it on record that the previous Minute 'did not represent the feeling of all members of the Council and whilst he agreed that the Senior Committee were perfectly within their rights in recording the view expressed in the Minute, he felt it should not preclude a wider discussion by the Council or some other select group at a later date'. The language might be bureaucratic, but Thompson had made it clear that he had decided Ramsey's days were numbered.

Apart from elimination from the World Cup, what was also making Alf's tenure less secure was the fact that his contract was up for renewal in June 1974. He was presently rewarded with a pitiful salary of just £7,200, lower than some Third Division managers, and understandably wanted a rise. But from the viewpoint of his enemies in the FA, the end of his contract provided the ideal opportunity to force his departure, especially given that Alf would be 58 by the time of the next World Cup.

Furthermore, Alf faced another threat from within the FA, in addition to the bullying Thompson. Following a heart-attack, brought on by the hectoring of Thompson, Denis Follows had retired. He was not a man whom Alf liked or admired, but he was too weak to be able to challenge Alf seriously. His successor, however, was very different. A former pilot and Charlton Athletic footballer, Ted Croker had been a highly successful businessman and he now sought to apply the commercial ethos to the Association. Dynamic and resourceful, Croker was appalled at what he found when he took up his post at Lancaster Gate in September 1973. In the previous twelve months, there had been 42 changes of staff, despite the fact that the FA only employed 56 people. Ludicrously, the organization also made it difficult for the public to buy tickets for England's home games, since the FA's number was ex-directory. Royalties and TV rights were bringing in just £104,000 a year, compared to £2 million when Croker was at his peak at the beginning of the eighties. But there was one aspect of commercialism that Sir Alf despised, and that was

Croker's plan to seek sponsorship for the England shirt, which was estimated to be worth £15,000 a year. Alf, the nostalgic, romantic, conservative English patriot, thought the white shirt should never be sullied in this way. It was like tampering with a symbol of nationhood. Alf's devotion to the traditional shirt was almost physical, as Nigel Clarke recalls:

> He threw me an England shirt once and said 'What do they want me to put fancy badges on it for? Isn't it beautiful?' He even rubbed it against his cheek, continuing, 'Isn't it soft, isn't it lovely?' It was just a white shirt but to Alf it was almost a sacred garment. It was something that he adored, 'What do they want to put stripes on it for? How can they want to make money from it? I can't believe these people.' That was the sort of man Alf was, terribly proud to be English, terribly proud to be manager.

It was a sense of pride that stopped Alf from resigning. If the FA wanted him out they would have to force him. He would not voluntarily leave to satisfy them. So he remained in charge for a friendly at home, against Italy in November, which saw another defeat. It was Bobby Moore's 108th and last game for England. Alf played him as a sweeper, showing that he was at last willing to innovate from a cast-iron 4–4–2 system, but it seemed like a forlorn gesture. On 14 February 1974, the FA decided to set up a committee to 'consider our future policy in respect of the promotion of international football'. In reality, there was only one issue the committee was considering: the future of Alf Ramsey. As Croker later remarked:

> The decision to remove Sir Alf Ramsey from his post was effectively taken on St Valentine's Day 1974. There was a feeling within the FA that we had to bow to popular opinion

as represented in the newspapers. Nearly all the critics wanted him out and it appeared that we could no longer think of offering him a new contract when his present arrangement expired in June of that year.

Croker now had his own motive in wanting to get rid of Ramsey, who was seen as a block on the road to commercialism and better public relations.

The committee was headed by FA Chairman Sir Andrew Stephen, who had made supportive noises towards Ramsey in public but in private doubted the wisdom of renewing a con tract for a man who would be 58 at the time of the next World Cup. Sir Harold Thompson, Alf's most implacable foe, was inevitably the dominant figure. Because of his autocratic manner, there was little chance that the other committee men would mount any defence of Alf, even if they had wanted to, which was doubtful. Bert Millichip of West Brom and Brian Mears of Chelsea were open to persuasion. Only Len Shipman, President of the League, and Dick Wragg, Chairman of Sheffield United, were opposed to dismissal, but even Wragg despaired of Alf's public relations and thought that his two lieutenants, Cocker and Shepherdson, should go. Alf was not invited to the committee meetings, an omission which made a mockery of its stated purpose to examine 'the future of football'. In fact, he only found out about its deliberations when he noticed a draft minute on a desk in another FA office. 'How could a committee discuss England's future without talking to England's manager?' Brian James asked him.

'Maybe that's the point,' replied Alf.

While Thompson plotted, Alf continued with his job. There was a blinkered, defiant side to his nature that often refused to recognize reality – as in 1953 when he claimed that England should have beaten Hungary – and early in 1974 he seemed to convince himself that he had weathered the storm. In response to criticisms, he tried to improve his relations with the press. 'In his last months, he was communicating more freely,' wrote Jeff Powell. Colin Malam, another distinguished football writer, told me he was surprised by Alf's openness on an England trip to Portugal in April 1974:

I had heard all the stories and had been led to believe that Alf was some kind of ogre, especially towards the press. But to my utter astonishment, he invited us over to enjoy tea at the England hotel outside Lisbon. He could not have been more charming. He just chatted away about football. I wondered where the ogre had disappeared to. I was so awe-struck. It may have been, however, because he was stuck with the International Committee he was delighted to see the cavalry coming over the hill.

On that Portuguese trip, Alf also showed his willingness to change at last, selecting no less than six new caps: Trevor Brooking, Martin Dobson, Mike Pejic, Phil Parkes, Stan Bowles and Dave Watson. Sir Trevor Brooking says that even at this late hour

there was no sign of authority draining away from Sir Alf. He had fantastic respect from all of us. He did not convey to us that he was under any pressure when we met him. His whole emphasis was on looking to the future, on giving opportunities to new players. I could see in that one game what made him so special. He was very precise. He came across as this very quiet individual, who looked like he never got excited or irate, but in his own way, got the message across very clearly. He was very good on discipline and what role he wanted you to play.

Martin Dobson, the Burnley midfielder, has a similar memory:

> He was very thorough in his preparation. He knew how he wanted to play. Basically, he was trying to take the pressure away from me. He told me to enjoy it, get a good touch of the ball early on and play as I did for Burnley. He did not complicate things. He kept it simple. Burnley had just got promotion. We were doing well. He said, 'You're captain at your own club, taking responsibility. Well, you've 10 captains around you now. Enjoy it.' I know he was under a bit of a cloud but he did not seem distracted to me.

Mike Pejic has this wonderful example of Alf's dry humour, too little recognized by the public:

> After a spell with the Under-23s, I broke through to the first team. And we were down at Lilleshall for training. One morning he had called training for ten o'clock. At the time I was very interested in ornithology, and Lilleshall is great for that because it is surrounded by woods. So after breakfast that morning, I thought to myself, 'I've got a bit of time to spare before training, so I'll go into the woods.' I came back at about half-nine, and Les Cocker immediately ran up to me, saying, 'You'd better get down to the training ground quickly. Alf's brought forward the start time. They're waiting for you.'
>
> 'Oh shit.'
>
> All the top players were there, Bobby Moore, Alan Ball, and this was my first training camp. I ran to my room, got my gear and then ran back down to the training ground. But when I arrived, there was no one on the field. There was a pavilion overlooking the pitch and through the window I could see the heads of some of the players inside. I walked

over to the pavilion, went through the doors and found everyone sitting down inside. Alf was standing at the back of the room. There was complete silence. I felt so nervous, this on my first morning of training with the England team. Alf says,

'Mike, where have you been?'

'I've been bird spotting.'

Immediately the whole room collapsed in laughter. The lads had told Alf and he'd set up the whole thing. He knew exactly what was going on.

Far from feeling that he was at the end of an era, Mike sensed the beginning of a new one: 'I had been with England for two years, and I felt he trusted me. I felt I was part of the next batch coming through.' That is exactly what he told the team before the game in Portugal, according to Malcolm Macdonald: 'You are England's future. We have got to start with the next World Cup as our target and that's precisely where I'm starting from, as of today.'

The result did not match this exciting rhetoric. England drew 0–0. And there was to be no England future for Alf Ramsey. The Stephen committee met in mid-April and decided not to renew Alf Ramsey's contract. Effectively, he was to be sacked with three months notice from the 30 April. Parading his own guilt in the process, Brian Mears later revealed that the committee was split on the decision and the chairman's casting vote fixed Alf's fate. For all the self-assurance of Thompson, it had been a close affair, with Wragg, Millichip and Shipman only in favour of changing the management structure rather than the manager. Mears relates that 'Three voted for Alf, three against. Sir Harold Thompson was adamant that Alf had to go and I'm afraid I got carried away with the tide but I felt, when I came away from that meeting, a sense of shame. Here was a man who had won that coveted trophy for the first time in our history and I had been part of a committee that had decided he should go. It should never have happened.' Len Shipman, inadvertently admitting the role of Thompson, said, 'What can you do when your hand is forced?'

On Friday 19 April, Alf was summoned to Lancaster Gate to be told of the decision by the chairman. He had no inkling of the momentous news he was about to be given, and asked for a day's postponement because he was preparing for England's summer tour of Eastern Europe. So the meeting was fixed for 10.30 am on Saturday. Alf later left this description of the encounter:

Sir Andrew was nervous. He paced round the office, rubbing his hands and smacking his lips. 'I'm thirsty. Do you fancy a drink?' I declined. 'You won't mind if I have one,' said the chairman and took a bottle of tonic water from the cocktail cabinet. I watched while he struggled for several minutes to remove the cap. Finally he gave up, placed the bottle on the desk and revealed why he wanted to see me. He said it had been the unanimous decision of an FA subcommittee that I should be replaced. The chairman seemed relieved to have got that off his chest. For he picked up the bottle again and opened it first turn. I made no comment. I was shattered but not entirely surprised.

The Executive Committee of the FA met on 22 April to rubber stamp the decision. Alf asked for the public announcement of the decision to be delayed until 1 May, so he would have time to inform his family and friends. The FA agreed to that request but, contrary to several reports, Alf was never offered the chance to resign. It was a plain, brutal sacking. 'We had come to a very final conclusion. There was no way out for Alf, no room for manoeuvre,' said one council member with an air of defiance.

Alf cleared his desk and said his farewells to staff at the FA in the week of 21 April. The devotion that Alf could inspire was shown in the moment of his departure. Alan Odell, Secretary of the International Section, vividly remembers his feelings on hearing the news. 'When he told me he'd got the bullet, well, I just couldn't believe it. I drove home to Uxbridge, parked the car, went inside, sat in the kitchen and told my wife that Alf had been sacked. I just sat there and cried, I was that upset. He meant so much to me, he was such a loyal, faithful sort of bloke.' Margaret Bruce felt the same way: 'He was a huge part of my life. Working with him had been so special. I cried my eyes out I was so upset.' Peter Little, his Ipswich tailor, happened to be making Alf a suit for England duty when he heard the news on the radio in his workshop. 'It was a real blow. It was hard to think for a moment. I had tears in my eyes. I could not help it. I could not believe what I was hearing.' Even some hard-nosed professional footballers, used to managerial changes, could not avoid such emotions when Alf's sacking was publicly announced on 1 May. Mike Pejic says:

I can remember the day well. I pulled up in my car outside our house and the news came on the radio. I could not believe it. I cried my eyes out. I don't for one second feel any embarrassment over that. I kept crying, even when I went inside the house. It was instant. Alf somehow built up this rapport with you, this trust, this feeling for him. When he was in charge, you did not want a penny for playing for England. You would have paid him.

It is often the way in Britain that public figures are only lauded when they have gone from office. That is certainly what happened in Alf's case. For almost four years, there had been an unceasing campaign for him to go. Yet now that he had been sacked, there was a great outpouring of affection for him; meanwhile the FA were vilified in many quarters for the way the whole issue had been handled. Ted Croker confessed that he was

amazed at the reaction. The people who had pilloried him now made him a martyr. It was probably Alf's simple honesty that caused the incredible turn-around in press opinion when he was sacked. The critics may have felt that they had played their part in bringing him down, but were not prepared to share blame, if there was blame to share. The public reacted in a similar way and the mood was quite definitely against the FA.

By the time the announcement was made, Alf had gone with Vickie to stay with their friends, the Knott family in Southampton, to escape the attentions of the press. A close friend of theirs from Ipswich, Donald Gould, Chairman of the Leek and Westbourne Building Society, described Alf's mood in this period:

He is a very sad man. The trouble with Alf is he is too polite and too charming to speak out for himself. I knew there was something on his mind. He has been brooding a lot lately. Then eight days ago Alf and his wife came round for dinner to my house and he had a heart-to-heart talk with me. Obviously he was very upset, but he is a man who can control his emotions. Alf feels he has been cheated. The Football Association has let him down and treated him shabbily.

In his first interview after his sacking, on 12 May, Alf explained what happened in those traumatic days:

> I didn't hide in a disguise, as has been suggested. We simply had a week on the coast with close friends. We went for many walks and were seen by a lot of people who no doubt respected that I sought peace and privacy. Vickie and I had 11 years of pressure and we wanted time to think and plan. For I had died a thousand deaths since being informed of my dismissal.

In a statement made in response to the public outcry, Sir Andrew Stephen, Chairman of the FA, explained that Alf had been dismissed because

> he was intransigent. When we failed to beat Poland we quickly realized that it would be ruinous for our football if we again failed to qualify for the World Cup finals – by hook or by crook. We had to look at the quality of our game and we realized we had been falling behind the rest of the world, particularly since 1970.

Len Shipman added that England needed a manager who was 'flexible enough in his attitude and outgoing enough to sustain a healthy dialogue with all the managers and coaches in England'. Stephen was probably right that Sir Alf's time was up. Eleven years is a long time in any job, and international football was changing rapidly in the mid-seventies. Alf had shown little inclination to adapt. And the failure to qualify for the World Cup or advance in the European Championship had been disastrous blows, with the FA estimating that it cost them £500,000 in lost revenues. Even his staunchest supporters say that he could not have continued long in the job.

'When I look back now and think long and hard, without blinkers – because I really liked him – I can see the faults,' says Nigel Clarke. 'To be honest, I think he was starting to lose it completely. I think he became too rigid. He did not understand how football was changing and how it was being played in a different manner.'

What angered his supporters, however, was not so much the dismissal itself as the way it was handled. After years of modest, poorly rewarded service, Alf was given a meagre golden handshake of £8,000, with a pension of only £1,200 a year; to add insult to injury, when Don Revie was appointed his permanent successor, he was paid £25,000 a year, more than treble Alf's salary. Moreover, no attempt was made to utilize Alf in any other role in the FA, such as a coach, advisor or ambassador, despite his vast professionalism. The day he walked out of Lancaster Gate after his dismissal was his last contact with the FA. Alan Ball summed up the anger felt by many:

> The FA could have given him another job, like educating the next generation. In the typical English way, he was just gone. All that knowledge, all that expertise was lost. He should have been a central part of our football set-up. How can you sack a knight, a man like that, without giving him any other role? To me, it is the most incredible thing that ever happened in English football. The most successful manager in the history of our country was just sacked by the amateurs of the FA.

Alf's standing with his players was highlighted when a testimonial dinner was held for him on the night of 30 July 1974, the eighth anniversary of the World Cup victory. Guest speakers included the Prime Minister Harold Wilson and

Bobby Moore, who said that 'Alf introduced a club spirit at England level. While he was in charge it was always England United.' Of the 101 players picked during his reign, 92 of them turned up to pay tribute. Malcolm Macdonald was among them:

I loved Alf, I make no bones about it. He was an absolute gentleman and very much a players' manager. At times, I felt as if I wanted to put my arm around Alf and say, 'Do you want a chat? Would you like a hug, just to let you know somebody loves you?' Why I felt like that, I'm not really sure. It was just that he was totally insular and took all the pressure on himself, passing none of it on to his players.

# FOURTEEN

# *St Mary's*

Alf remained in a state of shock for months after his sacking. 'I took a long time to get over it. I was left with a feeling of despair, sadness, and terrific disappointment,' he said later. But he still had to earn his living, for his low pay as England manager meant that he had accumulated no capital, while his £1,200 annual pension was woefully inadequate. Alf later told a family friend, Elaine Coupland, that he even had to fight for that pension: 'He told me that when he was sacked from the manager's job there was a dispute over it and he had to stick up for his rights.' Because of his shyness and his personal dislike of commercialism, he had made no money from personal endorsements, sponsorship, guest appearances or after dinner-speaking. In contrast to his successor Don Revie, Alf felt that there was something distasteful about exploiting his position as England manager for personal gain. The FA Director of Coaching, Allen Wade, who worked at Lancaster Gate for 13 years, estimated that during his reign as manager Alf turned down commercial opportunities worth some £250,000.

Besides, at 54, he was far too young to retire. Football was the only occupation he had known since he left the army at the end of the war and he intended to try to stay in the game.

'I've often said that I would like to return to club football,' he told the *Sunday People* in May 1974:

> I still feel that I have something to offer. I still have the same enthusiasm and regard for the game as I did when I became a professional 31 years ago. It is still the greatest game in the world, perhaps a little cruel at times but, for me and millions of others, it is still the greatest. I feel that I could never be as happy doing anything else but we shall have to wait and see.

There were several offers from abroad, including from Ajax, Athletic Bilbao and even Saudi Arabia, but Alf, typically, was not interested in working with foreign footballers; while he was England manager, he had turned down lucrative offers from Benfica and the Greek Football Federation, which wanted him to coach their national team for £30,000 a year. The continent never attracted him. 'I want to continue to work with English footballers.' The only club in England that tried to hire him in the immediate aftermath of his sacking was Aston Villa, but he was not interested in a step down to the Second Division. Surprisingly, no big First Division club came in for him, club directors being wary of his reputation for autocracy and poor public relations.

It is an irony that Alf's first job after being sacked was in the media. The man notorious for his poor public speaking was hired by ITV to be their analyst for the Home Internationals and the 1974 World Cup in West Germany. Martin Tyler, now one of the most revered figures in TV commentating, was then an assistant on ITV's football programmes:

> It was a great coup for ITV because he did not do much media. What I really remember was his courtesy. He was

unfailingly polite. He was not starry at all. It was a bit like having someone from a different class with us. Even Brian Moore was a little in awe of him. Brian was a gentle, polite man. 'With the greatest respect, Alf, would you mind . . .' he would say. We had heard about Alf's difficult relationship with the press and some of us tended to walk on eggshells, me less so because I was unashamedly a child of 1966. Because I was such a fan, I thought that if he had been nasty to the journalists, it had probably been with good cause. My role was to look after him. I had to make him cups of tea, make sure that his car was parked. We rolled out the red carpet for him and he did not disappoint. I did not find Alf cold. I found that there was a twinkle in his eye. I don't think he was lovable but he was certainly very likeable. The key to him, I think, was his shyness. In my dealings with him, he was great. He was a proper football person. If you wanted to talk football with him, it was never a problem. If you wanted to get into tabloid issues, he just didn't want to know. I could see the qualities that made him such a great manager. I saw something that made me really understand why all the players tried so hard for him. There was a little bit of fear, a lot of respect. On one occasion he was asked to pick an England team against Brian Clough's team for the *On the Ball* programme. Alf was very dismissive about some of Clough's choices, saying 'there's a right couple of wankers in there!' Brian Moore said to me, 'Did he really say wankers?' We had a little chuckle about that. We were like two little kids.

Alf could display his dry humour in this role. During the World Cup finals, he was out in Frankfurt with Hugh Johns, covering a Dutch group game, when suddenly the floodlights failed. Johns, desperate to fill the airtime, asked Alf how long he thought the delay might last. 'I am not an electrician,' was Alf's brief reply. Tommy Docherty, who had managed Scotland in 1971–72, also did some work with Alf in the 1974 World Cup and, despite all the criticism he had given Alf in the past, found him 'very polite. He was very knowledgeable about players and always had interesting views about them. I got on quite well with him then, though he was a shy man. I always found him bashful. If you showed enthusiasm for football, and if he thought you were talking common sense, he had a lot of time for you. But if he felt you were talking rubbish, he'd be rid of you as quickly as possible. He was still very bitter about his sacking then. Quite right. That was a disgrace. It was typical of the amateurs running the professional game.'

Alf's link with ITV did not last long. In April 1975, he lost his position as an analyst. 'ITV bosses consider he has lost touch with modern soccer. On his own admission, most of Sir Alf's soccer watching recently has been confined to a stand seat at Ipswich and an armchair in front of a television set at home,' reported the *Sunday People*. With his taciturnity and clipped voice, Alf was never going to make a long-term success of TV punditry.

Out of soccer for the first time in 31 years, he dabbled a little in business, becoming a director of the Ipswich building firm Sadler & Sons. 'Nice people, and an interest far, far removed from football. Talking about sites and bricks and so on has helped me take a wider view of things,' he explained. Another directorship he took up was at the sports-shoe company Gola, working on foreign promotion. With plenty of spare time, he played golf and badminton, as well as taking more interest in gardening. He also enjoyed spending more time with Vickie – he reckoned that as England manager, he had been away from home around a third of the time. But he could not resist watching football. He and Vickie had season tickets at Ipswich, though Alf also liked to travel round the country. With his usual modesty, he never phoned up clubs asking for a ticket, preferring to go unannounced. Sometimes he bought a seat; if none were available, he stood on the terraces, wearing a bowler hat to games, which he believed acted as a sort of disguise:

> I enjoy watching football this way. Free of responsibility. In the past I didn't go to see matches. I used to go to see players. And because of concentrating on perhaps two or three individuals – their strengths, their weaknesses, charac ters – I would come away not really knowing much about the match itself. That's different now. I see the whole thing and enjoy it.

Towards the end of 1975, he admitted that he was keen to get back into football professionally: 'The longer I have stayed out of it, the more I have missed it. In the past couple of months my toes have started to twitch.' Fortuitously, at this moment, an offer finally turned up from a First Division club, not in management, but in the boardroom. In January 1976, Alf was invited to become a director of Birmingham City and readily accepted. For Alf, it was a chance to return to football in the top flight in a prestigious role. For Birmingham, it was a chance to have one of the biggest names in world football associated with the club. Birmingham City chairman Keith Coombs announced: 'We feel that Sir Alf can help us enormously. I can think of nobody better qualified for a directorship of a First Division club. He is a world-renowned figure in the field of football administration and his experience will be invaluable.' At his first meeting with the press, Alf made a joke about his reputation for being difficult. 'Let's put it this way – I haven't missed you.'

Initially, Alf had no role on the playing side at St Andrew's. That remained in the hands of Willie Bell, who had played alongside Jack Charlton at Leeds. But Bell was presiding over a failing team, one that was perpetually engaged in a relegation fight. The 1977–78 season started disastrously for Bell. After five straight defeats and just one goal, he was sacked. While the club searched for a new boss, Alf was asked to step into the breach on an unpaid basis. He agreed to do so. More than three years after being dumped by England, more than fourteen years after last running a League club, Alf was back in First Division management, though it was not yet on a permanent basis. But even in this temporary role, Alf soon worked his magic, as Birmingham won four of their next five games, their best run in the First Division for four and a half years. Skipper Terry Hibbitt summed up the reason for Alf's immediate success: 'You can put it down to one word, respect. Sir Alf is the sort of person to whom you must respond.' In an interview with the author Dave Bowler, Kevin Dillon, then a 17-year-old, spoke of Alf's immediate impact: 'He had something about him, an aura. He got us all together and the first thing he said was, "Don't call me gaffer or manager, just call me sir," and that broke the ice, really. He was very quietly spoken, but when he said something, you listened.' Dillon also recalled Alf being extremely old-fashioned, especially about money:

He got your trust by being as straight as a die, apart from the contract he tried to offer me. I think he still lived in the 1950s because the wages weren't that good. He got my parents down to go through it all and he was very professional in everything he did. He left a lasting impression that way. I think he thought £10 was a lot of money. I held out, though, and he laughed about it later.

Alf's dislike of the Scots was never far from the surface, according to Jimmy Calderwood, who recalls how, soon after his caretaking appointment, he assembled all the Scottish-born players in the dressing-room. 'Alone with us, Alf said: "Now I know you lot fucking hate me. Well, I have news for you. I fucking hate you lot even more." But you know, I never missed a game for him. He really was a fantastic manager.'

The Birmingham board was so relieved and pleased about the leap in the club's fortunes that in November 1977 Alf was offered the role of consultant manager, with full control of playing affairs. It meant he had to resign from the board, but Alf was only too pleased to do so, especially given the £20,000 salary that went with the post. 'If Birmingham continue to improve and my judgement is right, who knows what we may achieve,' he said. But soon the team started to move in the other direction. Form declined, and the now annual battle against relegation loomed at the start of the new season. The only bright spot was a 3–2 win against Liverpool at Anfield, but even that did not improve Alf's spirits, as Keith Bertschin remembers:

> We got back to the dressing-room and Sir Alf was fuming. He said, 'Well, you did your best to lose that one, didn't you?' What happened was that we went 3–0 up and it was fantastic. The trouble was, suddenly we started thinking we were Liverpool. We started trying to knock the ball around, took our foot off the gas and just like the great team they were, they came right back at us They scored twice late on and in the end we were hanging on desperately. We had won at Anfield but that didn't satisfy Sir Alf. Like all top managers, he was a perfectionist.

In February, Alf became locked in an increasingly bitter three-way dispute with his star player, Trevor Francis, and the board. Fed up with the lack of silverware and fearing that Birmingham's inconsistency was hindering his international progress, Francis was keen to leave the club. Alf wanted to sell him to raise funds for other cash purchases, since Francis was estimated to be worth around £700,000 in 1978, but he resented what he saw as Francis' lack of commitment to the club while he was still on its books. What particularly irked him was Francis' willingness to talk to the press about his determination to leave St Andrew's. Meanwhile, the Birmingham board had grave doubts about the wisdom of selling Francis at all, a decision that would only incur the wrath of already disgruntled fans. The simmering row boiled over at the end of the month. At a board meeting on 20 February, Francis' transfer request had been accepted, as Alf wanted. But at a subsequent meeting three days later, this decision was overturned. Outraged by this volte face, Alf immediately gave fourteen days notice of his resignation as consultant manager. The storm swirling round St Andrew's then intensified as Birmingham lost 4–0 at local rivals Coventry. Terry Hibbitt's mood had utterly changed from his optimism of early in the season. 'Before today I refused to talk about a crisis,' he told the *Birmingham Post*, 'but we are in a crisis now. Something has got to be done and it must be done quickly. Morale is bad and the spirit is low. I have had a bad time in the last three games, but I have not been given any help from anyone. There is no-one helping us and no-one is trying to put things right.' It was a harsh indictment of the Ramsey regime, and worse followed when Trevor Francis launched a personal attack on Alf, claiming to have been shabbily treated. After complaining that Alf had fined him twice for talking to the press in February, he then said Alf had attacked his performances in two crucial derbies against Villa and West Brom. 'He turned round and said that he didn't think I had done much for the club in those matches. I thought it was disgraceful. I was so disgusted that I just walked out of the training ground near Birmingham Airport. I was badly upset. I knew I'd given 100 per cent in both games.'

Alf did not need this sort of pressure. On 8 March at a press conference he confirmed his decision to quit Birmingham, explaining that he had no intention of going back on the board after leaving his managerial post. He described Birmingham's performance against Coventry as 'absolutely disgraceful, the worst I have seen since I joined the club as director two years ago, and I must take part of the blame'. He also took a shot at Francis: 'He's had his say, his wife has had her say – now I'm waiting for the dog.' With that, he was gone. Jim Smith took over at St Andrew's and within twelve months Trevor Francis had become Britain's first £1 million footballer with his move to Nottingham Forest. Having left St Andrew's, Alf said that he would probably 'go back to Ipswich and mope around my garden. As for my further involvement in football, I shall have to wait and see. I shall feel a little lost without it.' After years of financial restraint, Alf was now determined to make some money, to provide some security in old age for himself and Vickie. For the first time, he was even willing to consider offers from abroad. Talk of his taking over as head of the Kuwaiti national team never went further than the rumour stage, but in September 1979 he accepted the post of technical adviser to the Greek club Panathinaikos. Sadly, he lasted barely a year there and was sacked in October 1980 for what the club claimed were his 'failures'. These were said to include his choice of the experienced Ronnie Allen as manager and his inability 'to impose discipline' at the club – not an accusation that had ever been levelled at Alf before. The real reason, however, was the club had just taken on the Austrian coach Helmut Senekowitsch and could not afford both sets of salaries. Alf returned to England, out of management for ever. It was a sad note on which to end a glorious career.

The last decade had been a difficult one for Alf. And now, as he passed into his 60s, he became increasingly bitter about the way he had been treated. Football had proved a fickle mistress. He had given his love to the game and had been coldly betrayed. For a man of great dignity, it was embarrassing for him to be trying to survive on his limited pension of just £25 a week from the FA, eventually supplemented from 1985 by his old age pension of around £70 a week. Rightly, he felt that the winner of the World Cup should not have to endure a financial struggle, especially now that the game was becoming ever wealthier. 'Alf's retirement was one where he had to watch the pennies. But he was a proud Englishman. He didn't want anybody to know that he couldn't afford a new car or new suits. He thought it his own business and nothing to do with anyone else,' said George Cohen. Never a gregarious soul, he retreated further into seclusion with Vickie in his Ipswich home.

Yet the necessity to make money remained, and it was this that compelled him to start working as a columnist on the *Daily Mirror*, with his pieces ghosted by Nigel Clarke, who commanded Alf's respect because he had been a young player with Charlton before his hopes of a professional career were wrecked by injury. Today, Clarke talks with great affection about his ten years working closely with Alf but also with anger at the shameful failure of English football to look after one of its greatest heroes:

The one thing which dominated his later life was that he never had any money. So whenever you said to him, 'Do you want to come and do something for me?', he would reply, 'Oh, well, I don't know.'

'We'll pay you.'

'OK. I'll do that.'

We used to pay him £150 an article. I would meet him at Liverpool Street Station and because of who he was and my regard for him, I was always punctual. He was always a stickler for the old-fashioned discipline so he appreciated that. We would get in a cab and go off to a game. With my notebook, I would sit alongside him. He would give me a run-down on the way a particular player was performing, going into every detail. Sometimes, after just a couple of minutes, he would say, 'Oh no, Lionel' – he always got my name wrong – 'he can't play.' At other times, I would say, after about 15 minutes:

'Well, Alf?'

'Quiet, I'm watching. Just hang on a minute.' I was dealing with a footballing genius. Alf was unfailingly brilliant at spotting people you did not think would make it. He was, for example, years ahead of anyone else in associating Des Walker with England. We had gone to see Forest because everyone was talking about this winger Franz Carr. Yet, as we watched the game, all Alf was telling me about was Des Walker. Alf was watching this player in his own box, even when the ball was at the other end of the field. He said to me:

'This boy will play for England.'

'Come on Alf, he's just been released by Tottenham.'

'Lionel, this boy will play for England.' And he was right, of course. The Lionel thing was quite funny. Alf never could remember my name. I said to him one day, after we had come back from a match:

'It's a not problem, you know, Alf, but my name's not Lionel, it's Nigel. '

'Of course, it's one of those things that afflicts you when you get old.'

'Don't worry.'

'So, you're going to call me tomorrow about the column and we can go over it then?'

'Yes, I'll read it out to you.'

'Thanks for a lovely day, Mike.'

That's what Alf was like, a bit absent-minded about names. I don't think that was anything to do with his Alzheimer's. He was often mixing up people. He was not great at putting names to them.

There was some truth in this. Because of his tunnel vision, Alf could be forgetful. He once spent a day calling Martin Dobson 'Colin', and also picked Rodney Marsh as the penalty taker in one international, overlooking the fact that he had not included Marsh in the team.

Nigel continues:

He was a simple man, who liked during the day to be in the fresh air, tending his garden, and then at night he liked to sit down with a glass of whisky or brandy, and watch television. Beneath that diffidence, aloofness and sometimes even fury, he was a kind man. I'll give you an insight into how kind he was. This was in the mid-1980s. He was asking me about my life and I told him about busting my knee when I was at Charlton and then having to go into journalism. I told him that I had no one to turn to for advice about the big decisions in my early life, because my father was 46 when I was born and he was always ill. So I always had to make my own decisions. 'How sad,' said Alf.

'Well, there was no one I could turn to. My mother was eaten up looking after my father. My brother was away on national service. So I had to sink or swim by my own decisions.'

He said, 'This is terrible. What about now?'

'I still would like a father figure to talk to, to explain things, to ask for advice.'

'I'll be your father. I'll never, ever want you to tell me that you had to come to a decision on your own. Anything you want to ask, any advice you want whatsoever, just someone to talk to, to pour out your heart to, to put an arm around you, I'll do that, I'll come to you, I'll be your father figure.'

I did not know what to say. He said: 'I'll be your father from now on. You haven't got to worry about being alone. Any big decisions, talk to me. Come to me, we'll meet and have dinner.'

It was an extraordinary gesture to make. We celebrated this new closeness with a lunch at the Talbooth in Ipswich, a restaurant he liked. He got monumentally pissed. He said, 'How am I going to get home?'

'I'll have to drive you.'

'NO! I'll drive.'

'Alf, you cannot drive.'

'I will drive.'

And he got into his car, and I drove alongside because he was all over the bloody place. I kind of escorted him home. We finally got there, I don't know how, and I parked at the bottom of his road.

'Are you all right now, Alf?'

'I am perfectly OK. I think I shall go down to the pub and start again.'

'Just go home, Alf, and go to bed.'

Nigel recalls the following incident, which shows how much Alf appreciated public affection beneath his mask of impassivity:

491

I took him to Brighton once to see Mark Lawrenson. There was a debate going on at the time as to whether Lawrenson could play for the English or the Irish. Alf liked him. So when Alf went down to see him, the board at Brighton made a great fuss, gave him a good lunch. Then they asked him if he would do the half-time lottery draw. 'Of course I will. You have been very good hosts.' So, as he walked out onto the pitch at half-time, the announcer said, 'The draw will now be made by Sir Alf Ramsey.' The place absolutely erupted, cheers going right round the ground. He was totally overwhelmed and there was a tear in his eye. He said to me afterwards, 'I never knew I was loved like this.'

But Alf felt far less warm to the FA:

When Alf and I would go to Wembley, the *Mirror* would lay on a nice car for us, which would be waiting outside the *Mirror* building. One time we hit the traffic lights at Holborn tube station. There was an Unwin's off-licence there and Alf coughed a few times loudly.

'Are you all right, Alf?'

'There's an off-licence there.'

'So there is. Driver, just wait for a minute.'

So I went in, got half a bottle of brandy and four plastic cups. And the reason Alf was having a drink was because he had to go to a reception before the game at Wembley and he had to meet some of the ghastly FA people he hated. He wanted a bit of Dutch courage. I once picked him up from one of these receptions and he said, 'Thank you for rescuing me. I don't think I could have stood that for much longer.' He was completely ill at ease in the company of FA people. He just couldn't stand them. He'd just had enough of the FA and all the people connected to it. When we used to go to games, the FA would sometimes send him tickets – and he would sit as far away as possible from a councillor or anyone connected with the FA. I have known him actually exchange his ticket with another spectator so he would be as far away as possible from the FA people in the Royal Box at Wembley. He just loathed them.

It was Alf's *Mirror* column that led Bobby Robson to develop a powerful hostility towards him. Robson was outraged that Alf, who had made loyalty one of the governing principles of his management career, should subject one of his successors in the England job to vitriolic criticism. Robson thought, like other former England managers, Alf should be providing support, not condemnation. 'Neither Walter, Ron, the late Don Revie nor the much lamented Joe Mercer ever tried to take me apart. But Alf Ramsey betrayed that unwritten, unspoken rule by taking my players and myself to task, undermining confidence in the camp and often at crucial times before we set off for European or World Cup finals.' Here is an example of the kind of material Alf wrote about Robson, taken from the *Mirror* in 1989: 'In six years Robson has achieved nothing and now I begin to wonder if he ever will. Tactically I feel he is lacking and the preparation and motivation of his team leave a lot to be desired. Robson seems to spread to his players his doubts, fears and indecision.' The hurt ran deeply for Robson, as he later wrote:

I felt totally betrayed by the man who lived just a few streets away from me and who had managed Ipswich Town and England so successfully. What had I done to deserve such scurrilous attacks? Goodness knows I tried, but even when I offered him a lift back from a Chelsea match, he refused, saying, 'I came by train, and I shall return by train.'

It was almost as if Alf, because of his insecurities, could not bear anyone else to succeed in the job he had once held. He had been the same when Jackie Milburn had taken over at Ipswich, and his feelings about the England management were clouded by his sacking and the sense that less worthy men were being better rewarded that he was. 'I knew I did a good job and then when I saw the men who took over from me and what they were paid, I found that upsetting,' he once said. His antagonism towards Robson was particularly acute because Robson had followed the same pattern of moving from Portman Road into the England job but on far more lucrative terms than Alf's. Nigel Clarke saw the antagonism between Alf and Bobby in operation:

They only lived 300 yards apart in Ipswich, but when they took their dogs for a walk, they would cross to the other side of the road to avoid speaking to each other. I was working as a front-line football writer on the *Mirror* at the time. Robson used to come up to me and say:

'Your mate has done me again.'

'What's the matter?'

'He's accused me of all sorts of things. What's he doing it for? He's only doing it for money, isn't he?'

Bobby felt that Alf's criticisms – which at the time were perfectly valid – were because Alf was getting paid to say them. I said to Alf one day:

'Why don't you meet up with Bob and have a chat?'

'I don't need to pass on anything to him in any shape or form.' Alf felt that Robson was a bit vapid and was too heavily influenced by his England players on selection and tactics.

One issue that particularly rankled with Bobby Robson was Alf's refusal to give him any advice in the run-up to the World

Cup in Mexico in 1986, Robson feeling that Alf's experience of 1970 would have been invaluable. 'The man I could have had serious help from was Sir Alf . . . but we never did discuss Mexico, which I found sad.' Sir Bobby told me that he was mystified by Alf's icy attitude. 'He was a strange fellow. He may have been shy, but he came across as very aloof.' According to the Ipswich journalist Tony Garnett, Alf was partly aggrieved because a meeting had been organised to discuss Mexico, yet Robson did not turn up. 'I arranged the time and the date. I then got a phone call from Alf complaining about Bobby's non-appearance,' says Garnett. 'So Alf felt let down and afterwards would not talk to him.' But Sir Bobby denies this. 'I did try to get an interview with Alf but a date was never fixed. There always seemed to be a problem. Alf kept putting it off. I got to see my predecessor, Ron Greenwood, for a chat about the World Cup and he lived down in Brighton but nothing ever transpired with Alf who was almost my neighbour.'

The problem over the meeting may have arisen over nothing more than a misunderstanding about dates and excessive sensitivity on Alf's part, for Robson says: 'To this day, I've no idea what Alf had against me.' But what was extraordinary about this feud was that it drove Alf to abandon his lifelong antipathy to the Scots and give all the advice he could to Alex Ferguson, the Scottish manager for the 1986 World Cup. As Ferguson later recounted:

I travelled down to Ipswich to talk to Sir Alf Ramsey at his home. His response was tremendous and he could not have been more helpful. He pointed out the difficulties that could arise with unfamiliar food in Mexico and, on his advice, we arranged to take considerable supplies with us. Other valuable hints he passed on were concerned with altitude training and the general handling of players during a World Cup in a foreign country . . . I was glad and grateful to hear him say that we deserved to do well . . .

This is the only recorded instance of Alf ever wishing a Scottish team well.

On a happier note, Alf made a return to England management, though only in fantasy form, when he agreed to have his image used in the strip cartoon Roy of the Rovers in the best-selling boys' magazine *Tiger and Scorcher*. Alf had full copy approval and the child-like nostalgic side of him enjoyed his cartoon role, as former editor Barrie Tomlinson remembers:

In 1982 when Roy of the Rovers was in a coma after being shot, we had to find a new manager, so we asked Alf Ramsey and he said yes. We sent him the script and he loved it, really. He was great fun, lovely to work with. He knew the character and had read stories like that when he was a child. Once I asked him why he hadn't picked Roy in 1966 and he said, 'He was too young at the time, too inexperienced.' He really entered into the spirit of it, so we had a very good relationship, which surprised some people because Alf Ramsey hadn't appeared to be that sort of person.

The cartoon and the column were to be two of Alf's last public roles. By the turn of the decade, he had retreated into full retirement, confining himself mainly to gardening, taking his dachshund for a walk, seeing friends occasionally in Ipswich, and a few rounds of golf at the Rushmere club. 'He was not a great golfer, 20 plus,' says Tony Garnett. 'He was slow round the course but he would not let other players through. I occasionally asked him if he wanted to play but he always refused, saying I would beat him.' Alf's life was totally intertwined with Vickie's, partly because he felt indebted to her: 'I feel I owe my wife a bit of time now. She gave me the licence to do so many things.' Tony Garnett believes that after he finished with football, 'he gave himself up to Vickie'. One of those friends they regularly saw was John Booth, who still runs a caravan park in Suffolk. Today John Booth paints a picture of a gentle, ordinary, existence:

Alf had that reserved public image but I found him very warm. I had a good rapport with him – though I did not like to talk football with him too much for fear of having my head snapped off. He was a very genuine man, never over-the-top but always sincere. He was very comforting when my father died. He came over with Vickie and we all went down to the local church together. He was always immaculate, always with a tie. I never saw him without one. He was such a modest man. He had a train named after him here in Ipswich and it was a nice occasion, but he hated to push any of his achievements down anyone's throat. We shared an interest in gardening. He liked to talk to me about plants and have a look round my garden and the site. He was President of the Fuchsia Society, which named flowers after him and Vickie. He was very good with the visitors to the site, quite happy to chat and have his photograph taken. Sometimes the children of visitors would come over with a ball and he would talk away to them about football. He liked the good things in life: a good Scotch malt – I'd always have that in for him – and good restaurants. He and Vickie were a very close couple; they did everything together. They travelled a lot round the countryside in their Saab; Alf adored that car. He later got a Rover 800 but found it less reliable. He was keen on boxing but football was still his main interest. We'd watch games on Sky a lot. He had not lost his dislike of the press. I remember sitting with him watching an interview with Kenny Dalglish. 'What stupid questions they ask,' he exploded.

For all his fondness for the 1961–62 team, he rarely went to Portman Road, nor did he attend any player reunions. To some in Ipswich, that demonstrated a perverse streak in Alf. Tony Garnett says:

He was a strange fellow. To start with, the club kept a seat reserved for him in the directors' box, which he never used. The club then wrote to him asking him if he could let them know in future when he wanted to come and a seat would be kept for him. Alf took the hump that he had not been given a permanent one and so he would not go. It was fair enough that the club should want to use the seat, given the growing demand from the public. And he did not like reunions. You would have thought he would liked to have seen Jimmy and Andy and Ted. He only had to go down the bloody road.

Ted Phillips, who was perhaps closer to Alf than any other of the 1961–62 side, thinks that Alf's animosity towards Bobby Robson might have been part of the problem:

All the lads kept asking me if I could get Alf to come. So one year I went up to his house and said, 'I've booked you in for the dinner.' And he seemed happy about that. 'I'll come and pick you up.' So on the night I went round to his house, rang the doorbell and Vickie answered. 'Is he ready?' I asked.

'He had to go out,' she replied.

It's very odd. I don't know why he would never come.

Maybe it was because him and Bobby did not get on very well. We have the dinners every year but Alf never came. He never rang me up to say sorry or anything like that. I had gone up all the way for nothing.

One of the tragic reasons that Alf was becoming more reclusive was that, by the early nineties, he was showing the first mild signs of the Alzheimer's which would cast such a terrible blight over the twilight of his life. His own mother Florence had endured the disease for many years and would sometimes be found by neighbours or the police wandering the streets of Dagenham, before she was put into permanent care. Attending a Buckingham Palace garden party with his wife Daphne, George Cohen remembers being struck by the difference in Alf's demeanour from his normal self:

He was being led by the arm by Lady Vickie, and for a little while all seemed well enough when he chatted with the old players. But one by one we noticed that there was something wrong. We noted how carefully he was prompted by Lady Vickie. 'Oh look, Alf,' she would say, 'here is Alan and Leslie,' and 'look Alf, it's George and Daphne'. He was able to take his cues well enough, and talk about football, particularly, with his usual bite but as the afternoon wore on you could see things were not quite right. Later, I told Daphne of my concerns and she was a little surprised, even though her own mother had suffered from the disease. She didn't know Alf so well, had not been exposed so long to the precision of his speech, which at times could be almost painful. At one point he said something to one of the players which was completely wrong. That was the forlorn clincher. We were seeing, beside the lake in the garden of the Palace, the passing of our chief.

Alan Ball believes that the crippling blow of his sacking had a long term effect on Alf's health:

> It broke his heart, it really did. He so loved England. I spoke to him many times afterwards and he told me how much it really, really hurt him. He was never the same man again. I'm sure it contributed to his final illness. Vickie was wonderful to him. At that get-together, we would talk for a few minutes and then he seemed to forget who I was. Immediately Lady Ramsey came in again. 'You always enjoy talking to Alan, don't you?' and he would perk up again. It was terribly sad, and yet very moving at the same time. I loved him to death. He was very, very special in my life.

Friends in Ipswich had also picked up on the change. Ted Phillips played golf with him at Rushmere and could sense that he was slipping:

> Sometimes he would forget where his ball was. He'd be getting ready to hit my ball and I'd say, 'I'm afraid you're in the bushes, Alf, on the other side of the fairway.' Alf insisted one time that he owed me money. It was very sad. We were on the course and he suddenly tried to hand me £100. 'What are you doing, Alf? That's not mine.' I realized then that there was a serious problem.

Tony Garnett recalls an incident at Rushmere, when the conversation turned to Bobby Blackwood, a player Alf had signed from Hearts in the championship-winning season. 'I remember no such player,' said Alf. 'It was then that we began to realize that things were not right.' Alf was entering the long, painful evening of his life. The first public awareness of his decline came in 1993, when he was unable to attend the funeral for Bobby Moore. Fellow ex-manager Malcolm Allison revealed afterwards: 'It's incredibly sad. Sir Alf is not well at all. He has been ill for seven or eight months now. He spent the day at home in Ipswich, although the old Sir Alf would love to have been here.' The disease was insidious rather than aggressive, and he still had periods of lucidity. But a mild stroke during a visit to Cornwall led to further deterioration.

Health problems were compounded by the continuing shortage of money. 'The way the FA treated their 1966 hero was little less than disgraceful,' says Tony Garnett. 'A man who would not have dreamed of taking a cut from commercial deals involving England should have been given the sort of pension to ensure that he lived the rest of his life in considerable comfort.' And the FA's indifference towards Alf's grim retirement did not just revolve around finances. He and Vickie were also deeply angered that he had never received a replica medal for 1966. When the FA finally began talking about making one in 1998, 32 years after the event, Lady Ramsey said wearily: 'It's too late now. Nothing anybody could do would make up for the way he has been treated.' Another perceived snub occurred during the European Championships in England in 1996, the 30th anniversary of the World Cup, win, when the FA approached him to see if he might be involved in one of the ceremonies around the event. According to Nigel Clarke, Alf was willing to take part: 'I promised Alf he could hold on to me, and he said, "As long as you're there, I think I can do it." But the FA seemed to lose interest after Alf had failed to respond to a letter about the ceremony. Well, it was no good just sending him a letter. You had to sit down and explain things to him gently.' The FA spokesman, Alec McGivan, explaining the Association's hesitancy in following up its initial approach, said 'We were led to believe that Alf was unwell.' Alf and Vickie were so hurt that they actually left Britain during the championships, and visited Tanya in America. Lady Ramsey said:

Alf just wanted to get away from it all. He's bitter about things. It's sad but it appears we never treat our heroes very well. Alf is nostalgic about the past. He loves to remember his team and what they achieved. He's the same nice caring man he's always been – a gentle person who deserves more than he has received. It's so sad that those who could have made him a national hero didn't really want to.

On his return from America, his health rapidly worsened, as the Alzheimer's tightened its grip and he developed angina and prostate cancer. On 9 June 1998, he suffered a massive stroke and was taken to Ipswich General Hospital. During his two-month stay there, Vickie was extremely protective of him, wary of the press finding out his true condition, as Ted Phillips recalls:

Vickie was a nice lady, but very private. When Alf was ill, she would not have anyone in the hospital. When I heard – through a friend whose brother was in the same ward – that Alf was in there, I went up to see him. As soon as I arrived, she went bananas. She turned on me, 'Who told you Alf was in here?'

'I got a phone call from a friend.'

She would not let me see him. When I went up again a couple of weeks later, I saw her feeding him. She was very gentle. This time, she let me go to him. I think Alf recognized me.

At the eleventh hour, some of Alf's old antagonists rallied to his side. Bobby Robson, who had learnt of his plight, said he was appalled at the idea of Alf being on a public ward and announced he wanted to assist in paying for private care. I rang the FA and said I'd give £10,000,' says Robson. 'Lady Ramsey said he was getting the best treatment, and she would not accept it.' David Davies of the FA claimed that the Association also offered to help, but again Vickie would have none of it. In August 1998, Alf was transferred from the general hospital to Minsmere House, a specialist unit for geriatric patients. Then in early 1999, he was moved to a nursing home run by the Orbit Housing Association, with Lady Vickie dipping into her own savings to pay the £500 a week bills. Tony Garnett has a heart-rending tale of an incident from the care home: 'One of the nurses looking after him showed him a picture of the 1966 England team: total blank. Then suddenly he pointed to himself and said, "That's Alf Ramsey."'

The end was approaching. Release from mental and physical distress finally came on 28 April 1999. The death certificate cited Alzheimer's and prostate cancer as the fatal causes. A private family service at the Ipswich crematorium on 7 May was followed by the public service at St Mary's Church, Ipswich, at which George Cohen spoke so eloquently and movingly: 'His strength and purpose made it so easy to believe in him. Sad as it is to know that Alf is no longer with us, I feel we are here to celebrate not only the life of a great football manager but also a great Englishman.' The 45-minute service concluded with a rendering of Frank Sinatra's 'My Way'. There are few men for whom Paul Anka's lyrics about cussedness and defiance could be more appropriate. The tributes flooded in. 'A great man and a wonderful manager,' said Gordon Banks. 'He will always be the best,' said Alan Ball. A minute's silence was held on League grounds across the country the following Saturday.

But the shadow of Alf's mistreatment still lingered. In his will, Alf left less than £200,000, two-thirds of which was made up by the value of his Ipswich home, while Vickie's savings had been eaten up by medical bills. She said:

> I just don't know what I will do in the future. But I don't care if I am left with nothing. I still have the memories of that wonderful man and no one can take those away. I could never replace him. We may not have been well off but we had a quality of life. Today football is all about money and how much you can get. But Alf wasn't like that. He loved football and did it for the love of the game. Alf always turned down offers and I don't live in the lap of luxury. I may have to sell up.

Such an eventuality was avoided by Vickie's decision to sell much of Alf's football memorabilia, including his England caps, a replica of the Jules Rimet trophy, and his Tottenham Hotspur medals. In an auction at Christie's in September 2001, the collection fetched £83,000. But the fact that Lady Ramsey felt compelled to auction off such treasures was another indicator of the way he had been forgotten by the football establishment.

Lady Ramsey still lives in the same Ipswich house that she shared with Alf for more than forty years. Anne, the wife of John Elsworthy, recently asked her if she disliked being alone there. Vickie replied: 'Well, it is lonely. But I don't mind. I won't ever leave. I have got my memories.' Especially the memories of that golden afternoon in July 1966, when her shy, stubborn, brilliant husband put England on top of the world.

# Bibliography

Agnew, Paul, *Football Legend: The Authorised Biography of Tom Finney* (Milo Books, 2002)

Allen, Matt, *Jimmy Greaves* (Virgin, 2001)

Allen, Peter, *The Amber Glow* (Mainstream 2000)

Archer, Michael, *History of the World Cup* (Hamlyn, 1978)

Armfield, Jimmy, *The Autobiography* (Headline, 2004)

Ball, Alan, *It's All About A Ball* (W.H.Allen,1978)

Ball, Alan, *Playing Extra Time* (Sidgwick & Jackson, 2004)

Banks, Gordon, *Banks of England* (Arthur Barker, 1980)

Banks, Gordon, *Banksy: My Autobiography* (Michael Joseph, 2002)

Batt, Peter, *Mick Channon: The Authorised Biography* (Highdown, 2004)

Belton, Brian, *Burn Budgie Byrne: Football Inferno* (Breedon Books, 2004)

Bowler, Dave, *Danny Blanchflower: Biography of a Visionary* (Victor Gollancz, 1997)

Bowler, Dave, *Winning Isn't Everything: A Biography of Sir Alf Ramsey* (Victor Gollancz, 1998)

Bowler, Dave, *Three Lions on the Shirt* (Victor Gollancz, 1999)

Bowler, Dave and Reynolds, David, *Ron Reynolds: The Life of a 1950s Footballer* (Orion, 2003)

Bowles, Stan, *The Autobiography* (Orion, 1996)

Bull, David, *Dell Diamond* (Hagiology, 1998)

Bull, David and Jason, Dave, *Full Time at the Dell* (Hagiology, 2001)

Burgess, Ron, *Football My Life* (Souvenir Press, 1953)

Charlton, Bobby, *Forward for England* (Pelham, 1967)

Charlton, Bobby, *This Game of Soccer* (Cassell, 1967)

Charlton, Bobby (with Jones, Ken), *My Most Memorable Matches* (Stanley Paul, 1984)

Charlton, Jack, *The Autobiography* (Partridge Press, 1996)

Cohen, George with Lawton, James, *My Autobiography* (Greenwater, 2003)

Croker, Ted, *The First Voice You Will Hear . . .* (Collins Willow, 1987)

Daniels, Phil, *Moore Than A Legend* (Goal, 1997)

Dawson, Jeff, *Back Home: England and the 1970 World Cup* (Orion, 2001)

Docherty, Tommy, *Call the Doc* (Hamlyn, 1981)

Eastwood, John and Moyse, Tony, *The Men Who Made The Town* (Almedia Books, 1986)

Edworthy, Niall, *The Second Most Important Job in the Country* (Virgin, 1999)

Ferguson, Alex, Sir, *Managing My Life* (Hodder & Stoughton, 1999)

Ferrier, Bob, *Soccer Partnership* (William Heinemann, 1960)

Finn, Ralph, *England: World Champions 1966* (Robert Hale, 1966)

Finn, Ralph, *My Greatest Game* (The Saturn Press, 1951)

Finn, Ralph, *World Cup 1970* (Robert Hale, 1970)

Finney, Tom, *My Autobiography* (Headline, 2003)

Giller, Norman, *Billy Wright: A Hero for All Seasons* (Robson Books, 2002)

Glanville, Brian, *Football Memories* (Virgin, 1999)

Glanville, Brian, *The History of the World Cup* (Times Newspapers, 1973)

Greaves, Jimmy, *Greavsie: The Autobiography* (Time Warner, 2003)

Greaves, Jimmy, *This One's On Me* (Arthur Barker, 1979)

Green, Chris, *The Sack Race: The Story of Football's Gaffers* (Mainstream, 2002)

# Bibliography

Greenwood, Ron, *Yours Sincerely* (Collins Willow, 1984)

Green, Geoffrey, *Soccer: The World Game* (Phoenix House, 1954)

Green, Geoffrey, *Soccer in the Fifties* (Ian Allan, 1974)

Hadgraft, Rob, *Ipswich Town: Champions of England 1961–62* (Desert Island Books, 2002)

Hale, Steve, *Mr Tottenham Hotspur: Bill Nicholson* (Football World, 2005)

Hardaker, Alan, *Hardaker of the League* (Pelham, 1977)

Harris, Norman, *The Charlton Brothers* (Stanley Paul, 1971)

Harris, Ron, *Soccer The Hard Way* (Pelham, 1970)

Hayes, Dean, *England! England! The Complete Who's Who of Players Since 1946* (Sutton, 2004)

Haynes, Johnny, *It's All In The Game* (Arthur Barker, 1962)

Hill, Dave, *England's Glory: 1966 And All That* (Macmillan, 1996)

Hill, Jimmy, *My Autobiography* (Hodder & Stoughton, 1998)

Holley, Duncan and Chalk, Gary, *Saints: A Complete Record, 1885–1987* (Breedon Books, 1987)

Holley, Duncan and Chalk, Gary, *The Alphabet of the Saints* (ACL & Polar, 1992)

Hopcraft, Arthur, *The Football Man* (Collins, 1968)

Holden, Jim, *Stan Cullis* (Breedon Books, 2000)

Hughes, Emlyn, *Crazy Horse* (Arthur Barker, 1980)

Hunter, Norman, *Biting Talk: My Autobiography* (Hodder & Stoughton, 2004)

Hurst, Geoff, *The World Game,* (Stanley Paul, 1967)

Hurst, Geoff, *1966 And All That: My Autobiography* (Headline, 2001)

Hutchinson, Roger, *. . . It Is Now* (Mainstream, 1995)

Jeffs, Peter, *The Golden Age of Football* (Breedon Books, 1991)

Jones, Ken, *Jules Rimet Still Gleaming?* (Virgin, 2003)

Joy, Bernard, *Soccer Tactics* (Phoenix House, 1956)

Keegan, Kevin, *Kevin Keegan* (Arthur Barker, 1977)

Keegan, Kevin, *My Autobiography* (Little Brown & Co., 1997)

Labone, Brian, *Defence at the Top* (Pelham, 1968)

Lawton, Tommy, *My Twenty Years of Soccer* (Heirloom, 1955)

Leatherdale, Clive, *England's Quest for the World Cup* (Desert Island Books, 2002)

Lee, Francis, *Soccer Round the World* (Arthur Barker, 1970)

Lewis, Richard, *England's Eastenders* (Mainstream, 2002)

Liversedge, Stan, *Big Jack: The Life and Times of Jack Charlton* (The Publishing Corporation, 1994)

Liversedge, Stan, *This England Job* (Soccer Books, 1996)

Lofthouse, Nat, *Goals Galore* (Stanley Paul, 1954)

Macdonald, Malcolm with Malam, Colin, *Supermac: My Autobiography* (Highdown, 2003)

Macdonald, Roger and Batty, Eric, *Scientific Soccer in the Seventies* (Pelham, 1971)

McColl, Graham, *England: The Alf Ramsey Years* (Andre Deutch, 1988)

McKinstry, Leo, *Jack and Bobby* (Collins Willow, 2002)

Marquis, Max, *Sir Alf Ramsey: Anatomy of a Football Manager* (Arthur Barker, 1970)

Marsh, Rodney, *Priceless* (Headline, 2001)

Matthews, Stanley, *Football Parade* (Marks & Spencer, 1951)

Matthews, Stanley, *The Way It Was* (Headline, 2000)

Matthews, Tony, *The World Cup Who's Who, 1950–2002* (Britespot, 2002)

Merrick, Gil, *I See It All* (Museum Press, 1954)

Milburn, Jack, *Jackie Milburn: A Man Of Two Halves* (Mainstream, 2003)

Miller, David, *The Boy's of '66: England's Last Glory* (Pavilion, 1986)

Moore, Bobby, *My Soccer Story* (Stanley Paul, 1967)

Moore, Bobby, *England! England!* (Stanley Paul, 1970)

Moore, Brian, *The Final Score* (Hodder & Stoughton, 1999)

Moore, Tina, *Bobby Moore* (Collins Willow, 2005)

Mourant, Andrew and Rollin, Jack, *The Essential History of England* (Headline, 2002)

Moynihan, John, *The Soccer Syndrome* (McGibbon & Kee, 1966)

Mullery, Alan, *In Defence of Spurs* (Stanley Paul, 1969)

# Bibliography

Mullery, Alan, *An Autobiography* (Pelham, 1985)

Nicholson, Bill, *Glory, Glory: My Life With Spurs* (Macmillan, 1984)

Osgood, Peter, *Ossie: King of Stamford Bridge* (Mainstream, 2002)

Palmer, Kevin, *Tottenham Hotspur: Champions of England 1950–51 and 1960–61* (Desert Island Books, 2004)

Pawson, Tony, *The Football Managers* (Methuen, 1973)

Payne, Mike, *England: The Complete Post-War Record* (Breedon Books, 1993)

Peters, Martin, *Goals From Nowhere!* (Stanley Paul, 1969)

Ponting, Ivan and Hale, Steve, *Sir Roger: The Life and Times of Roger Hunt* (Bluecoat Press, 1997)

Powell, Jeff, *Bobby Moore: The Life and Times of a Sporting Legend* (Robson Books, 1993)

Puskas, Ferenc, *Captain of Hungary* (Cassell, 1955)

Ramsey, Alf, *Talking Football* (Stanley Paul, 1952)

Robson, Bobby, *An Englishman Abroad* (Macmillan, 1998)

Rogan, Johnny, *The Football Managers* (Queen Anne Press, 1989)

Rous, Stanley, *Football Worlds* (Faber & Faber, 1978)

Royle, Joe, *My Autobiography* (BBC Books, 2005)

Saffer, David, *The Life and Times of Mick Jones* (Tempus, 2002)

Saffer, David, *The Paul Madeley Story* (Tempus, 2003)

Saffer, David, *Sniffer: The Life and Times of Allan Clarke* (Tempus, 2004)

Shaoul, Mark and Williamson, Tony, *Forever England: A History of the National Side* (Tempus, 2000)

Shepherdson, Harold, *The Magic Sponge* (Pelham, 1968)

Shilton, Peter, *The Autobiography* (Orion, 2004)

Smith, Tommy, *I Did It The Hard Way* (Arthur Barker, 1980)

Soar, Phil, *And The Spurs Go Marching On* (Hamlyn, 1982)

Steen, Rob, *The Mavericks* (Mainstream, 1994)

Stepney, Alex, *Alex Stepney* (Arthur Barker, 1978)

Stiles, Nobby, *Soccer My Battlefield* (Stanley Paul, 1968)

Stiles, Nobby, *After The Ball* (Hodder & Stoughton, 2003)

Thomson, David, *4–2* (Bloomsbury, 1966)

Tyler, Martin, *The Boys of '66* (Hamlyn, 1981)

Venables, Terry, *The Autobiography* (Michael Joseph, 1994)

West, Gordon, *The Championship in My Keeping* (Souvenir Press, 1970)

Wheeler, Kenneth (ed.), *Soccer – the British Way* (Nicholas Kaye, 1963)

Wheeler, Kenneth, *Champions of Soccer* (Pelham, 1969)

Winner, David, *Those Feet* (Orion, 2005)

Wolstenholme, Kenneth, *They Think It's All Over* (Robson, 1996)

Wolstenholme, Kenneth, *50 Sporting Years* (Robson, 1999)

Wright, Billy, *The World's My Football Pitch* (Stanley Paul, 1953)

Wright, Billy, *Football Is My Passport* (Stanley Paul, 1957)

Wright, Billy, *One Hundred Caps and All That* (Robert Hale, 1963)

# Index

# Index

# Index

# Index

# Index

# Index

# Index